LATE-COLONIAL FRENCH CINEMA

Traditions in World Cinema

General Editors
Linda Badley (Middle Tennessee State University)
R. Barton Palmer (Clemson University)

Founding Editor
Steven Jay Schneider (New York University)

Titles in the series include:

Traditions in World Cinema
Linda Badley, R. Barton Palmer and Steven Jay Schneider (eds)

Post-beur Cinema: North African Émigré and Maghrebi-French Filmmaking in France since 2000
Will Higbee

New Taiwanese Cinema in Focus: Moving Within and Beyond the Frame
Flannery Wilson

International Noir
Homer B. Pettey and R. Barton Palmer (eds)

Films on Ice: Cinemas of the Arctic
Scott MacKenzie and Anna Westerståhl Stenport (eds)

Nordic Genre Film: Small Nation Film Cultures in the Global Marketplace
Tommy Gustafsson and Pietari Kääpä (eds)

Contemporary Japanese Cinema Since Hana-Bi
Adam Bingham

Chinese Martial Arts Cinema: The Wuxia Tradition (Second edition)
Stephen Teo

Slow Cinema
Tiago de Luca and Nuno Barradas Jorge

Expressionism in the Cinema
Olaf Brill and Gary D. Rhodes (eds)

French-language Road Cinema: Borders, Diasporas, Migration and 'New Europe'
Michael Gott

Transnational Film Remakes
Iain Robert Smith and Constantine Verevis

Coming-of-Age Cinema in New Zealand
Alistair Fox

New Transnationalisms in Contemporary Latin American Cinemas
Dolores Tierney

Celluloid Singapore: Cinema, Performance and the National
Edna Lim

Short Films from a Small Nation: Danish Informational Cinema 1935–1965
C. Claire Thomson

B-Movie Gothic: International Perspectives
Justin D. Edwards and Johan Höglund (eds)

Francophone Belgian Cinema
Jamie Steele

The New Romanian Cinema
Christina Stojanova (ed) with the participation of Dana Duma

French Blockbusters: Cultural Politics of a Transnational Cinema
Charlie Michael

Nordic Film Cultures and Cinemas of Elsewhere
Anna Westerståhl Stenport and Arne Lunde (eds)

New Realism: Contemporary British Cinema
David Forrest

Contemporary Balkan Cinema: Transnational Exchanges and Global Circuits
Lydia Papadimitriou and Ana Grgić (eds)

Mapping the Rockumentary: Images of Sound and Fury
Gunnar Iversen and Scott MacKenzie (eds)

Images of Apartheid: Filmmaking on the Fringe in the Old South Africa
Calum Waddell

Greek Film Noir
Anna Poupou, Nikitas Fessas, and Maria Chalkou (eds)

Norwegian Nightmares: The Horror Cinema of a Nordic Country
Christer Bakke Andresen

Late-colonial French Cinema: Filming the Algerian War of Independence
Mani Sharpe

Please see our website for a complete list of titles in the series
www.edinburghuniversitypress.com/series/TIWC

LATE-COLONIAL FRENCH CINEMA
Filming the Algerian War of Independence

Mani Sharpe

EDINBURGH
University Press

Edinburgh University Press is one of the leading university presses in the UK.
We publish academic books and journals in our selected subject areas across the
humanities and social sciences, combining cutting-edge scholarship with high editorial
and production values to produce academic works of lasting importance. For more
information visit our website: edinburghuniversitypress.com

© Mani Sharpe, 2023, 2024

Edinburgh University Press Ltd
13 Infirmary Street
Edinburgh EH1 1LT

First published in hardback by Edinburgh University Press 2023

Typeset in 10/12.5 pt Sabon
by IDSUK (DataConnection) Ltd

A CIP record for this book is available from the British Library

ISBN 978 1 4744 1422 7 (hardback)
ISBN 978 1 4744 6202 0 (paperback)
ISBN 978 1 4744 1423 4 (webready PDF)
ISBN 978 1 4744 1424 1 (epub)

The right of Mani Sharpe to be identified as the author of this work has been asserted
in accordance with the Copyright, Designs and Patents Act 1988, and the Copyright
and Related Rights Regulations 2003 (SI No. 2498).

CONTENTS

List of Figures vii
Acknowledgements ix
Traditions in World Cinema xi

    Introduction 1

PART I: SOLDIERS

1. Conscripts and Reservists, Privatisation and Redemption 33
2. Stardom, Atrocity and the Beauty of Violence 56
3. Militarised Masculinity and its Losses 72

PART II: OTHERS

4. Ex-resistants, Conscientious Objectors and the Ethics of Memory 105
5. Female Citizens and Guilt Displacement 133
6. The War as Seen from Algeria by the Settlers 161
7. The War as Spoken by Algerians and the Left 190

CONTENTS

Conclusion 217

Bibliography 224
Filmography 244
Index 249

FIGURES

1.1	Liliane (right) and Juliette (left) perched together in the former's privatised apartment.	40
1.2	Michel (above) and Dédé (below), surrounded by the former's family and guest-neighbours.	41
1.3	A reticent Dédé surrounded by diners.	43
1.4	Frédéric daydreams of his Parisian apartment during his return to the capital.	48
1.5	[Same caption as 1.4 above]	48
1.6	A freelance street photographer (right) takes a photo of Frédéric and Sylvie whilst shopping.	51
1.7	Frédéric and Sylvie cocooned in their home-as-haven.	53
2.1	Gina Lollobrigida on the front cover of *Paris Match*, 293, 6 November 1954. Photo © Paris Match. Reproduced by kind permission.	57
2.2.	Thomas threatens his plot leader.	61
2.3	Raspéguy (right) and Esclavier (left) in *Les Centurions*.	67
3.1	Laurent (left) and Paul (right).	81
3.2	Laurent as abject antihero.	83
3.3	'Not too fast' softly pleads Laurent as he is driven to Fontainebleau by Paul.	88
3.4	Alain ruminates in his clinic room.	92
4.1	Elsa cradles Michel in *La Dénonciation*.	110

FIGURES

4.2	A wounded Michel (left) faces his ambivalent translator (right).	111
4.3	Michel lies on the ground, dying.	116
4.4	Abdelkader Bennehar lies on the ground after being assaulted by the police on 17 October 1961. Photo © Elie Kagan/BDIC.	117
4.5	Cordier (right) confronts Adler (left) in prison.	121
4.6	Cordier standing tall in the courtroom.	130
5.1	The Young Woman waits for her soldier-partner.	140
5.2	Terry (left) avoids the gaze of Gérard (right).	142
5.3	Pierre embraces his partner in a wooded enclave during one of her flashbacks.	148
5.4	A close-up of the Woman's face as Pierre intones: '. . . seventeen dead, twenty-one wounded'.	156
6.1–6.2	A young Jean and his friends cycle through the landscape of the Mitidja.	167
6.3	'Imperial visuality': Jean and his friends run through vineyards.	169
6.4	Jean looks out over Cité Mahieddine, in Algiers.	172
6.5	Jean gazes upon Algiers as a military helicopter traces through the sky.	173
6.6	Boys watch Madeleine as she dances in La Pointe Pescade.	177
6.7	Madeleine dancing against the horizon.	177
6.8	Madeleine and Alain on the motorcycle they use to travel from Algiers to Tipaza.	179
7.1	Image of a survivor-witness being interviewed.	198
7.2	Wide shot of Hamid (back to camera) addressing attendees of a political meeting.	204
7.3	Close-up of a leftist militant.	205
7.4	An example of one of the drawings stitched into the image-track of *J'ai 8 ans*.	206
7.5	Close-up of one of the boys addressing the camera.	214

ACKNOWLEDGEMENTS

This book is the result of numerous collaborations, both professional and personal. In the first instance, I would like to thank the University of Newcastle for funding the PhD out of which this book eventually emerged, and both Guy Austin and Sarah Leahy for bearing with me as I completed my doctorate. Their wisdom, guidance, and generosity was invaluable. In the second instance, I would like to thank Pierre-Louis Patoine, based at Université Sorbonne Nouvelle, for helping me to navigate through the crucial yet challenging early stage of this project, much of which was spent either feverishly photocopying at the Cinémathèque Française, or feverishly writing in Chez Irène et Bernard, on Rue Gauthey, in Paris.

Once I was based at the University of Leeds, various individuals helped edge this book towards completion. Amongst those associated with the French section, I would like to thank Nina Wardleworth, Paul Rowe, Richard Hibbitt, Terry Bradford, Claire Lozier, Kamal Salhi, Margaret Atack, Andy Stafford, Di Holmes, Sarah Waters, Nigel Saint, Isla Paterson, Elizabeth Purdy and Diane Otosaka. Both Max Silverman and Jim House had a formative influence upon this book, providing invaluable advice and support throughout the entire writing process. Jim also provided me with crucial advice on the title.

Another organisation that provided support during the final stages of writing was the Centre for World Cinemas and Digital Cultures, based at the University of Leeds. With this in mind, I must extend thanks to Chris Homewood, Paul Cooke, Thea Pitman, Stephanie Dennison, Vlad Strukov, Rachel Johnson and

Angelos Koutsourakis, who helped to improve an early version of Chapter 5. Both Alan O'Leary (now based at Aarhus University) and Rebecca Jarman proffered priceless feedback on various chapters.

Beyond the University of Leeds, I would like to thank several other individuals, all of whom have helped to bring this book to fruition. Alex Adams offered feedback on Chapters 4 and 6, especially in relation to representations of torture. Nicole Beth Wallenbrock shared her knowledge of parallel cinema with me, as well as providing support when the entire project threatened to unravel. John Trafton helped me to understand the complexities of the Second World War combat film. Both Maria Flood and Hugo Frey read a draft of the Introduction, enabling me to improve it in various ways. Matt Croombs helped me to craft the premise of the book, as did Lia Brozgal – whose knowledge of Jacques Panijel's documentary proved invaluable. Maya Boutaghou, Jennifer Sessions and Anne Donadey provided constructive criticism on a paper that I delivered at the conference, 'Questioning the Archive of Algerian Independence: Towards a Decolonized History' (University of Virginia), in April 2022. Both Irmgard Scharold and Raya Morag helped me to locate academic resources when faced with the logistical challenges of COVID-19, whilst David Forrest shared more practical tips about publishing. Finally, I would like to thank my family, as well as Cheïma and Frank, for their unerring support throughout. Unless otherwise stated, all translations are made by the author.

TRADITIONS IN WORLD CINEMA

General editors: **Linda Badley and R. Barton Palmer**
Founding editor: **Steven Jay Schneider**

Traditions in World Cinema is a series of textbooks and monographs devoted to the analysis of currently popular and previously underexamined or undervalued film movements from around the globe. Also intended for general interest readers, the textbooks in this series offer undergraduate- and graduate-level film students accessible and comprehensive introductions to diverse traditions in world cinema. The monographs open up for advanced academic study more specialised groups of films, including those that require theoretically oriented approaches. Both textbooks and monographs provide thorough examinations of the industrial, cultural and socio-historical conditions of production and reception.

The flagship textbook for the series includes chapters by noted scholars on traditions of acknowledged importance (the French New Wave, German Expressionism), recent and emergent traditions (New Iranian, post-Cinema Novo), and those whose rightful claim to recognition has yet to be established (the Israeli persecution film, global found footage cinema). Other volumes concentrate on individual national, regional or global cinema traditions. As the introductory chapter to each volume makes clear, the films under discussion form a coherent group on the basis of substantive and relatively transparent, if not always obvious, commonalities. These commonalities may be formal, stylistic or thematic, and the groupings may, although they need not, be popularly identified as genres, cycles or movements (Japanese horror, Chinese martial arts cinema, Italian Neorealism). Indeed, in cases in which a group of films is not already commonly identified as a tradition, one purpose of the volume is to establish its claim to importance and make it visible (East Central European Magical Realist cinema, Palestinian cinema).

Textbooks and monographs include:

- An introduction that clarifies the rationale for the grouping of films under examination
- A concise history of the regional, national, or transnational cinema in question
- A summary of previous published work on the tradition
- Contextual analysis of industrial, cultural and socio-historical conditions of production and reception
- Textual analysis of specific and notable films, with clear and judicious application of relevant film theoretical approaches
- Bibliograph(ies)/filmograph(ies).

Monographs may additionally include:

- Discussion of the dynamics of cross-cultural exchange in light of current research and thinking about cultural imperialism and globalisation, as well as issues of regional/national cinema or political/aesthetic movements (such as new waves, postmodernism, or identity politics)
- Interview(s) with key filmmakers working within the tradition.

INTRODUCTION

One of the most famous examples of what I will be calling late-colonial French cinema is Alain Resnais's 1963 *Muriel ou le temps d'un retour/Muriel or the Time of a Return*. An ostensibly mundane tale of middle-class routines, set in Boulogne-sur-Mer, a port-town made of jutting concrete and faded majesty, Resnais's film derives its dark power neither from the pleasures of spectacle nor suspense that subtend the archetypal classical realist narrative, but rather from the jarring interplay that exists between its two central, and highly unconventional, protagonists. One of these is a neurotic ex-soldier named Bernard (Jean-Baptiste Thierée), who has recently returned from Algeria, the geographical site of the war that forms the focus of this book. The other is 'Muriel', a woman whom Bernard initially designates as a friend or potential partner, yet whose body and voice remain entirely un-visualised and un-vocalised within the diegesis. Not only that, but as the plot progresses, the spectator gradually learns – with trepidation, then horror – that 'Muriel' is likely to be little more than a pseudonym, grafted onto the dissolved identity of a female Algerian civilian, tortured and murdered by a group of French soldiers in Algeria, possibly including Bernard.

Considering its subtext of militarised torture, *Muriel ou le temps d'un retour* has frequently been interpreted as a pacifist film, an anti-state film, and an anti-colonial film: pacifist as it focuses on an act of military atrocity rather than an act of military victory; anti-state as it obliquely alludes to the insidious regime of official censorship in place in France at the time (see below); and anti-colonial insofar as it indirectly undermines the ideology of colonialism fuelling the war in which Bernard has fought (Greene 1999: 31–50; O'Brien 2000;

Silverman 2013: 54–60; Flood 2017: 35–56). Focusing on Bernard's antagonistic relationship with former soldier Robert (Philippe Laudenbach), other scholars, however, have proposed a subtly different interpretation of Resnais's modernist conundrum, further complicating our understanding of it. Central to these alternative readings are the ways in which the film seems to gently exonerate Bernard from the military atrocities in which he is initially implicated. In the first instance, this dialectic of implication and exoneration can be glimpsed in a crucial scene[1] that lies at the core of *Muriel ou le temps d'un retour*, and during which Bernard not only provides a verbal account of Muriel's torture, but also 'displaces, delimits, and projects his guilt outwards', onto the body of Robert, who is designated as the ringleader of the operation (Croombs 2013: 17; Gauch 2001: 50; also see Boudjedra 1971: 27). In the second instance, it can be discerned in the vertiginous denouement of the narrative, during which Bernard neither takes full responsibility for the brutal event in which he may or may not have been complicit, nor brings the story of 'Muriel' into the public realm, but instead covertly assassinates Robert, a self-serving gesture that Emma Wilson has diagnosed as a 'redemptive deferral of culpability' (2006: 95). Thus, just as Muriel's death has plunged Bernard into an ethical abyss, permeated with guilt, so too does Robert's death ultimately enable Bernard to ascend out of this abyss, into a realm of absolution. And just as *Muriel ou le temps d'un retour* unfolds as a pacifist plea for peace in Algeria, so too does it end by blurring the specificity of France's collective complicity[2] in the military atrocities to which film obliquely alludes.

As I demonstrate later in this introduction, Alain Resnais was by no means the only French director to chronicle the Algerian War of Independence as it unfolded in colonial Algeria during the late 1950s and early 1960s. Yann Le Masson, Jean Herman, Philippe Durand and Jacques Dupont: these were just some of the other, lesser-known, cineastes who endeavoured to imagine and re-imagine this seismic event, leading to what I will call a 'late-colonial' body of films; one whose significance has – as we will see – largely been overshadowed by a myopic scholarly interest in the 'canonical' works of modern(ist) French cinema. Nor was Resnais the only cultural practitioner to represent the war in such ambivalently pacifist terms: as a locus of military atrocity, a source of ethical ambiguity (given that nobody in the film is ever depicted as incontestably culpable of perpetrating torture), and, perhaps most obliquely, as a political crisis subjected to a process of sublimation, as Bernard acquires salvation from damnation in the death of another, and the film ends with a lingering question: who is ultimately guilty for 'Muriel's' murder? Close examination of the fifteen or so case studies included in the following chapters reveals that the 'redemptive deferral of culpability' that Wilson associates with *Muriel ou le temps d'un retour* actually forms part of a more general trend in late-colonial culture: to represent French society as innocent or absolved of the injustices and atrocities committed in colonial Algeria. Later in this introduction, I will coin the expression 'redemptive pacifism' to designate this phenomenon, but for now, let us first establish the socio-political context of the war around which this book revolves.

The Algerian War of Independence: A Brief History

Fought largely in the north-eastern hinterlands of rural Algeria, but also in urban zones – including the capital, Algiers – and dictated by bouts of guerrilla warfare and counter-insurgency operations, exchanged between armed Algerian nationalists and members of the French army, the Algerian War of Independence (1954–1962),[3] has long been recognised as one of – if not *the* – most contentious conflict in modern French history. The roots of the war can be traced back to 1830, when Algeria was originally colonised by France. Not that this seizing occurred without exertion: even if the coastline regions of Oran and Annaba were swiftly colonised, it took thirty years and hundreds of thousands of colonial officials before the territory of Algeria was 'pacified' by French forces (Sessions 2011). Nor did it lead to a democratic Algerian society, but one instead riven with colonial injustices, injustices that disempowered indigenous Algerians[4] whilst empowering the thousands of European settlers – later marked as *pieds-noirs* – accumulating in the country from Italy, Spain and France. These injustices were territorial, insofar as between the 1830s and the 1930s, approximately 40 per cent of Algerian territory was appropriated by European officials in order to shore up mining and agricultural industries. They were financial, insofar as this sweep towards dispossession stripped many indigenous Algerians of their principal source of income, plunging them into unemployment or destitution. They were social, insofar as colonial racism was a sedimented element of Algerian life; and they were cultural, insofar as colonialism exerted a vampiric force over traditional Algerian art, music and literature, sapping it of its idiosyncrasies, its idioms and its autonomy (Blanchard et al. 2014). Even after Algeria was constitutionally transformed into an integral part of metropolitan France in 1848 – that is to say, into a series of three French provinces, known as *départements* – did an indelible sense of injustice remain, primarily given that this act gradually revealed itself to be little more than a judicial feint, an administrative masquerade, a political patina, choreographed to exalt an equality that was more often than not starkly lacking from the lived reality of indigenous Algerians. As Ferhat Abbas, a pro-independence Algerian politician put it: 'when an Algerian says that he is Arab, French lawyers tell him that he is French. When he demands French rights, the same lawyers tell him that he is Arab' (cited in Stora 2001: 12). Bracketed by a political structure that refused rights and representation to the Algerian majority, a majority that James McDougall has diagnosed as false members of an assimilationist French

Republic (2017: 88), throughout the late 1800s and early 1900s, relations between European settlers and indigenous Algerians thus slowly degraded, as Algerian nationalism slowly grew.

In the history of the Algerian War of Independence, two pivotal events stand out. One of these occurred on 8 May 1945, when the easterly town of Sétif in Algeria was consumed by a cycle of fatalities, perpetrated by: the police, who fired shots at a pro-nationalist rally; indigenous Algerians and European settlers, both of whom caused bloodshed in the days that followed; and the French army, who executed a sequence of reprisals against the Algerian populace, culminating in approximately 6,000 deaths, although this figure is heavily contested (Planche 2006). The other event took place on 1 November 1954, when a series of thirty coordinated assassinations and detonations ripped across rural Algeria, assailing a swathe of police outposts, military bases and industrial facilities. Nine people were killed. Often referred to as *Toussaint Rouge* (Red All-Saints Day), these attacks were accompanied by the publication of a political proclamation thrust into the purview of the public by the recently formed Algerian National Liberation Front (*Front de libération nationale*, henceforth referred to as the FLN), who claimed responsibility for them, thus effectively putting into motion eight years of civil war, between French soldiers and Algerian nationalists ('civil' in the sense that Algeria was constitutionally considered French). Depending on the location, this war took different forms. In rural regions such as the Aurès and Kabylia, paratroopers performing artillery-fuelled manoeuvres clashed against members of the National Liberation Army (*Armée de libération nationale*, ALN), the armed wing of the FLN, who used hit-and-run tactics to target military encampments and colonial infrastructure. In urban regions such as Algiers and Oran, members of the FLN-ALN launched a campaign of bombings and shootings against soldiers and civilian settlers, whilst the French army indulged in indiscriminate roundups, internment and violent interrogations. The war would eventually reach its antagonistic denouement in the year 1962: first with a ceasefire agreement, signed on 18 March as part of the so-called 'Evian Accords', and second, when the President of France, Charles de Gaulle, ceded national sovereignty to Algeria on 5 July, relinquishing power to the FLN.

Nonetheless, to identify 1 November 1954 as the 'start' of the Algerian War of Independence demands a degree of qualification. After all, throughout its duration, the war was officially denied as such by the French Republic, with government officials, including the Socialist Prime Minister Guy Mollet, downplaying the ascendency of armed Algerian nationalism through a myriad of euphemisms: 'operations to maintain order', 'pacification', 'the events'. At the time, this euphemistic vocabulary enabled French colonial officials to circumnavigate laws enshrined in the Geneva Conventions, which did not apply to colonial conflicts or civil ones; later, it would lead historians to diagnose the conflict as 'a war without a name' (Talbott 1981), 'an undeclared war' (Evans 2012) and 'a phoney war' (Stora 2001: 33–41). Yet even as metropolitan politicians were in the process of understating the acceleration of nationalist violence, were they covertly preparing to crush it, in the first instance by legislating the use of conscription in Algeria, and in the second instance, by controversially recalling tens of thousands of 'reservists' who had already completed their military obligations (see Chapter 1 for a fictional depiction of a reservist named Frédéric). These decisions notably cleaved open an immediate difference between the Algerian War of Independence and the Indochina War (1946–54), which did not involve conscript-civilians-in-uniform, but career soldiers, including paratroopers and legionnaires. In March 1956, laws concerning conscription were then bolstered by the Special Powers Act, an equally controversial law which conferred on the French army in Algeria 'extensive and exceptional powers to re-establish order', including supplementing the manpower of conscripts and reservists with security police, gendarmes, legionnaires, paratroopers and Harkis, a group of Algerian auxiliary units who worked with the French army to combat nationalism (Thénault 2012: 68). But re-establish order they did not, and by the end of 1956, the 900,000 troops stationed in Algeria found themselves floundering to halt what looked less like an isolated spate of attacks, and more like a national revolution, spearheaded by the FLN.

However, if we had to identify one pivotal year in the history of the war, then that year would be 1957. It was, after all, the year in which a small number of testimonials published by military personnel returning from service starkly exposed the official policy of 'pacification' as an elaborate facade, cultivated to obscure the excessive military violence that was in reality often indiscriminately directed against the Algerian community. James D. Le Sueur has written eloquently about the significance of 1957 in the continuum of the war, demarcating it as an elemental moment in what he terms 'the turn against silence', in sum, the point at which the unspeakable atrocities being committed in French Algeria were spoken, or rather written, about, notably in a range of pacifist testimonials (2001: 179). These testimonials were threaded through the pages of diverse publications, including the weekly magazine *L'Express*, which printed a section of Jean-Jacques Servan-Schreiber's autobiographical novel *Lieutenant en Algérie/Lieutenant in Algeria* (1957); the liberal Catholic journal, *Esprit*, which circulated an article by a reservist named Robert Bonnaud, entitled 'La Paix des Nementchas/The Peace of the Nementchas' (1957); *Des rappelés témoignent/Mobilised Reservists Bear Witness* (Comité de Résistance Spirituelle 1957), a pamphlet of twenty-four texts, including diary entries, scraps of written testimony and letters, published by the Spiritual Resistance Committee, to which Pierre-Henri Simon's *Contre la torture/Against Torture* (1957) can also be added. Many of these interventions revolved around a metaphorical imaginary of colonial sickness, with allusions to colonial 'cancer' and 'gangrene' proving particularly popular amongst late-colonial commentators. This imaginary can be found in Jean Planchais's 1958 publication *Le Malaise de l'armée/The Sickness of the Army*; Pierre Vidal-Naquet's monograph *La Torture dans la République*, which was translated as *Torture: Cancer of Democracy* (1963); and Agnès Varda's film *Cléo de 5 à 7/Cléo from 5 to 7* (1962), in which the central protagonist's cancer-stricken body operates allegorically for the figurative colonial 'cancer' consuming the nation (Guibbert 1992: 248; Betz 2009: 140; see below). Likewise, in 1959, publishers Les Éditions de Minuit released a collection of testimonies written by Algerian students and professionals tortured in Paris during the war, entitled *La Gangrène/The Gangrene* (Anon. 1959), a collection which apparently inspired the title of a much more recent monograph by Benjamin Stora, subtitled 'Gangrene and Forgetting' (1998). Detainment, summary executions, pillaging and rape: by the time the French army had begun to engage in the Battle of Algiers, a particularly acrimonious period of counterinsurgency that reverberated throughout the capital between September 1956 and October 1957, any chance that European settlers and indigenous Algerians could coexist harmoniously in the 'cancerous' and 'gangrenous' body politic of French Algeria seemed like a fanciful dream.

But amidst this 'sickness', this 'cancer', this 'turn against silence', one question loomed large: torture. Administered in clandestine detention centres such as the infamous Villa Susini, or El Biar, where Henri Alleg, author of *La Question/The Question* (1958),[5] was held, and choreographed by paratroopers and legionnaires, torture sessions usually consisted of two stages. In the first of these, the individual in question would be subjected to a robust bout of verbal questioning, often accompanied by insults and blows, as well as ostensibly arbitrary – yet actually carefully orchestrated – glimpses of other detainees suffering from the aftereffects of torture (Branche 2001: 127–8). If this stage failed to yield the information desired, officials would progress to the second one: torture itself, frequently conducted unexpectedly at night, and which could involve several precise methods. One of these was torture by water, with the victim's mouth being either submerged in a bathtub, or filled with water using a tap, pipe or jerrican. 'Waterboarding is a particularly striking example of clean violence', states Alex Adams, 'it does not leave physical scars, but it causes suffocation, extreme physical pain, and psychological terror' (2016: 23). Another method was conducted through ropes, with the victim being hung from the ceiling, usually by their arms, for a prolonged period of time. A final, more common, method was electrotorture, with a small electric device known as the *gégène*, or magneto, being particularly popular amongst soldiers from 1957 onwards. Composed of a generator capable of producing a high-voltage spark, alongside serrated alligator clips that could be attached to sensitive parts of the body (the penis, breasts, ears, mouth), the *gégène* was a notably less 'clean' form of 'interrogation' than water torture, with skin burns being a recurring complaint amongst victims, alongside rarer cases of heart attacks. Darius Rejali has also pointed out that two types of *gégène* were in fact used by officers – known as *gégèneurs* – during this period: one, a standard model, adapted from machinery used for field telephones, and capable of inducing rapid spasms in the victim; the other, a larger model, nicknamed 'the Wolf', capable of inflicting an all-consuming 'pain that seemed to tear the body in two' (2007: 162). Use of the *gégène* also split opinion. For some, like the paratrooper, Jacques Massu, who famously ordered his officers to bring a *gégène* to his office so that he could experience the effects for himself, the *gégène* was a modern, even civilised piece of equipment, an exemplar of rationality and sense-making, certainly compared to the ostensibly barbaric death-rituals used by Algerian nationalists: disfigurement, throat-slitting, castration (Ross 1995: 108–16). Others framed it as an anomaly utilised exclusively by the Foreign Legion, and hence by non-French men, even if this claim has been robustly contested by historians such as Raphaëlle Branche, who has written what is undoubtedly the most comprehensive work on the subject of torture (2001). Others, for example Henri Alleg, lambasted the *gégène*, and torture more generally, as a practice evoking techniques deployed against French men by the Nazis during the Occupation (1958; Bourdet 1951; Sartre [1957] 2001; see Chapter 4). As the title of Alleg's aforementioned treatise, *The Question*, suggests, many military officers adopted euphemistic terms such as 'questioning', 'aggressive interrogation' (*interrogatoires musclés*) or 'tight interrogation' (*interrogatoires serrés*) to talk about torture, with a clear judicial advantage of these expressions being that none of them denoted violence explicitly (Branche 2001: 60–1). Still others, like the leftist militant Georges-Mathieu Mattéi, brought 'the question' of torture closer to home. In a 1958 article, published in *Esprit*, the author conjured up a disquieting image of an officer who would 'caress the breasts of his wife or girlfriend' in France with the very same hands he had used to objectify bodies tortured in Algeria (818–24). As 'the turn against silence' came to a close in 1958, French Algeria had all but been transformed in the metropolitan imaginary, from a colonial paradise to a cesspit of 'sickness' and atrocity.

Redemptive Pacifism

How were these injustices and atrocities represented culturally – in text, speech and images – as the war was unfolding, and by whom? In order to address this question, a question to which I will return throughout this book, we may productively begin to divide the French colonial population into a series of communities, each of which fostered a different relationship to the war, and all of which will be probed, to varying degrees, in the following chapters. One community that was very much implicated in the decolonisation of Algeria were soldiers, some of whom might have been instrumental in exposing these atrocities to the metropolitan public during the turn against silence, yet many of whom 'did not consider themselves responsible for the situation' as perpetrators, but rather embroiled in it, as victims (Stora 2002). This is an argument pursued by a number of critical thinkers, including Marnia Lazreg, who has coined the expression 'management of consciousness' (2008: 179) to voice reservations about how many conscripts 'refused to assume responsibility for torture' during and after the war. This refusal could be found, for example, in the trial[6] of FLN nationalist Djamila Boupacha (1960–1), during which French military officials consistently endeavoured to absolve Boupacha's torturers from blame – assailing her, assuaging them – or, likewise, in the conscript diaries and confessions that proliferated unbidden into the purview of the public, 'revealing a plasticity of conscience in their authors' (Lazreg 2008: 173). It is an argument proposed by Hugh McDonnell, according to whom the authors of conscript testimonies, published in leftist journals such as *Esprit* or *Les Temps modernes*, 'considered themselves to have arrived pure' in Algeria, that is to say, 'fundamentally innocent', before being 'perverted by the military culture and career officers' (2020: 9). And it is an argument extended to the ambivalent imaginary of late-colonial literature by Emma Kuby (2013) and Philip Dine (1994a). Weighing up the ethics of Gilles Perrault's quasi-autobiographical *Les Parachutistes/Parachutists* (1961), Kuby, for example, concedes that the 'torture and rape of indigenous Algerians might be discussed in excruciating detail in the novel', again displaying an ethos of pacifism ingrained in the turn against silence, yet the ultimate message insinuated therein is that 'young French soldiers are themselves the primary victims of the War' (2013: 143). Dine, meanwhile, shifts his attention to 'Les Étangs de Fontargente/The Fontargente Pools' (1959), a short story of a psychologically distressed veteran by Vladimir Pozner, in which 'rather than the recognition of guilt that is an essential prerequisite for true forgiveness, it is the French nation's collective will to forgetfulness which is evoked' (1994a: 114).

Another community implicated in the war were European settlers. Unlike soldiers, this community was not tied together by a sense of military duty, but by a legacy of territorial occupation, of colonial customs fostered and preserved. Nor were they generally accused of directly perpetrating acts of atrocity, but rather abetting them: first, by supporting the French army, even as it became abundantly clear that the latter had begun to abuse their aforementioned special powers from 1956 onwards; and second, by championing the plight of the Secret Armed Organisation (*Organisation armée secrète*, henceforth referred to as the OAS), a proto-terrorist military organisation formed in 1961 in an ultimately futile attempt at preventing Algeria from achieving independence.[7] Nonetheless, the more we examine the complex cultural history of the settlers, the more we uncover a similar propensity towards self-exculpation as that ingrained within the cultural history of the soldiers. It is for this reason that historian Anne Roche has spoken of the 'strategies of [colonial] denial' adopted by many settlers to 'repress' the 'taboo' elements of the colonial system, that is to say, the legacy of financial, cultural and social injustices elaborated above (1990: 530–1), whilst Naomi Greene suggests that 'the fear and guilt' experienced by this community towards what was essentially 'stolen land', gave rise to a pervasive logic of sublation (negation) and sublimation (idealisation) (1999: 144). With the 'most troubling and "guilty" aspects of French colonialism' fading from the purview of settler narratives (Greene 1999: 135), what emerged instead was a much more serene imaginary of peace and love, reconciliation and innocence, alongside an over-determined obsession with amplifying 'the victimisation of a people who in no way deserved their fate' (Dine 1994a: 151). As Claire Eldridge has perceptively opined (2016), this process of self-victimisation arguably attained its ideological apotheosis in 1962, after 99 per cent of the settlers – approximately 800,000 people – had fled from the nationalist violence consuming French Algeria, seeking refuge in France and beyond, and thus tainting their collective identity with a high degree of pain and pathos (see Chapter 6). Amidst this monumental exodus, many settlers felt, moreover, profoundly abandoned and betrayed by Charles de Gaulle, who they believed to have been in favour of preserving colonialism. This sense of betrayal stemmed partly from a famous speech, delivered by de Gaulle in Algiers in June 1958, and during which he informed a huge crowd of settlers that he had not just understood them ('je vous ai compris'), but that he considered Algeria to 'be composed of only one type of people: the French'. Shortly after this speech, however, de Gaulle performed a political U-turn, putting into motion a series of measures orientated towards Algerian independence.

Still another faction caught up in the late-colonial imbroglio was the French Communist Party, the largest party of the French Left. Like the settlers, members of the Left found themselves seduced into supporting the Special Powers Act in 1956, an act, moreover, decreed by a Socialist Prime Minister, Guy Mollet. Yet, as I demonstrate in Chapter 7, this decision, which effectively rendered the established Left indirectly complicit in the acts of violence perpetrated by the army thereafter, engendered a much more radical yearning for absolution than that expressed by the settlers, prompting some leftists to join the Jeanson Network, a clandestine faction mainly composed of pro-independence French militants, known as *porteurs de valises* – suitcase carriers – who shuttled documentation and funds for the FLN around metropolitan France and beyond (Evans 1997: 4–5). Neither love nor nostalgia but rejuvenation and regeneration thus emerged as the prevailing ideologemes of the radical Left, propelled, as it was, by a yen to achieve political redemption through concrete direct action.

A final community keen to absolve themselves of misdeeds committed in colonial Algeria was metropolitan French society itself. Certainly, this was the opinion of Jean-Paul Sartre, whose majestic essay, '*Vous êtes formidables*/You're

Wonderful', published in the radically leftist *Les Temps modernes* in May 1957, caused a furore amongst intellectuals and the public alike. Toying with the semantic polyvalence of the term 'guilt', which can be used to refer to a judicial status, comparable to criminal responsibility, and a moral feeling, comparable to shame,[8] Sartre begins his essay by suggesting – insisting – that, because the French army was fighting in the name of France, each and every French citizen was personally responsible for, or at least implicated in, the crimes perpetrated against Algerian civilians. 'The fact is that we are ill, very ill, struggling in the midst of a vague nightmare which we can neither flee nor decipher', he laments ([1957] 2001: 64), in turn, iterating the metaphorical imaginary of colonial sickness elaborated above, and gesturing towards the argumentative thrust of a later essay, equally concerned with colonial atrocities, entitled 'Nous sommes tous des assassins/We Are All Murderers' ([1958] 2001). But Sartre does not stop there: he also identifies popular culture as having played a decisive role in enabling the French public to extricate itself from the atrocities being committed in colonial Algeria. Hence the title of the radio programme he examines – entitled 'You're Wonderful' – which offered its listeners 'salvation' from the de-colonial conflict tearing Algeria asunder, 'absolving them' of culpability with tales of everyday generosity (Sartre [1957] 2001: 69, 70). Or *France-Soir*, a daily newspaper which lulled the public into a state of 'false ignorance'; one that, moreover, 'the public had contributed to maintaining' ([1957] 2001: 67, 69, 70). Both drawing from and developing earlier works on phenomenological ontology, for instance *L'Être et le néant/Being and Nothingness* (1943), Sartre calls this collective need for self-evasion and self-expiation 'bad faith' ([1957] 2001: 69, 70). As Storm Heter opines, following Sartre, 'agents in bad faith have a distorted portrait of their moral responsibilities; they have a systematic tendency to place blame in the wrong place' (2006: 70). For Gary Cox, 'a person in bad faith avoids responsibility for his [sic] embodied situation by denying that it is his situation' (2006: 99).

As the war hurtled towards its inexorable climax, neither the soldiers, nor the settlers, nor the established Left, nor metropolitan French society, considered themselves morally guilty of the atrocities being perpetrated in French Algeria. And as Charles de Gaulle signed the aforementioned Evian Accords in March 1962, this moral innocence was complemented by a judicial one, as the president issued the first in a string of amnesties, meaning 'that French administrators and members of the military could not be subject to legal proceedings related to torture, rape, extrajudicial killings and "disappearances"' (Vince 2020: 167). Benjamin Stora, one of the few scholars to conduct a detailed examination of this phenomenon, a phenomenon at once social, cultural, ethical and legal, calls it '*déculpabilisation*', roughly translated as absolution, exculpation or redemption (2004: 108; see also Stora 2002), and which bears certain parallels with Stanley Cohen's concept of 'implicatory denial' as 'a form of self-righteousness that exonerates atrocities and obsessively blames others' (2011: 34, 8–9), or Michael Rothberg's claim that 'forms of implication are difficult to grasp not only because they are complex and shifting, but because they are frequently rendered obscure by forms of psychic and social denial' (2009: 8). 'In France, it was important that any guilt generated in the great divorce', that is to say, the de-linking of France from Algeria, 'was mitigated' (Stora 1998: 20), giving rise to what I would like to call a discourse of 'redemptive pacifism', according to which the war was framed in ontologically negative terms, as a source of pain and atrocity (the 'pacifist' element), whilst France was framed in ethically positive terms, as a country composed of absolved victims and (anti)heroes (the 'redemptive' element). As Françoise Vergès observes, 'the reinvention of France as innocent of colonial crimes was the price society was ready to pay in order to embrace the benefits of modernisation' (2010: 143–4), generating what Maya Boutaghou has termed a cultural trope of 'therapeutic resolution' (2019b: 8), and forecasting what Paul Gilroy has called 'postcolonial melancholia' (2005).[9]

Before we begin to envisage how this discourse of 'redemptive pacifism' translated specifically into the imaginary of French films released during, and immediately after the war, including, as we have seen, Resnais's *Muriel ou le temps d'un retour*, let me clarify that the argument proposed in this book has been implied by certain film scholars before, yet not apropos the same cinematic corpus. In *German Cinema: Terror and Trauma* (2014), Thomas Elsaesser, for one, has spoken eloquently about the strategies of 'guilt management', adopted by German directors in the immediate aftermath of the Second World War (2014: 26–7, 285–305). Examining a range of comedies, melodramas and thrillers produced from the 1940s to the 1960s, for example, *Banditen der Autobahn/Bandits of the Autobahn* (Geza von Cziffra, 1955), and *Der schlaf der gerechten/The Sleep of the Righteous* (Hädrich, 1962), Elsaesser suggests that 'redemption through substitution seems to be the narrative element that works towards cancelling out whatever moral unease or guilt the stories generate', with the result being a range of innocent characters blessed with 'soothed consciences' (2014: 287–8). In the world of French film studies, meanwhile, a similar lexicon has been cultivated to capture the complexity of the films produced in France as the country lurched into liberation. These included: Claude Autant-Lara's *Le Diable au corps/The Devil in the Flesh* (1946), and Julian Duvivier's *Panique/Panic* (1946), both of which not only glossed over, or 'cancelled out', one of the most troubling aspects of the Occupation – collaboration – but 'attested to a need to project the immediate past onto a different set of narratives, removed from the immediate arena of guilt' (Hayward 1993: 129–30). Lynn Higgins concurs, indicating how later films such as *Le Dernier métro/The Last Metro* (Truffaut, 1981) and *Au revoir les enfants/Goodbye, Children* (Malle, 1987), encapsulate 'a ritual of self-accusation and self-forgiveness for [the] national crime [of collaboration]', leading, in turn, to 'a peculiar dynamic of confession, invention and guilt, alongside a desire for absolution and evasion' (1996: 145, 146). Higgins calls this 'a collective gesture of revisionary historiography' (1996: 145).

Shifting time and place, it is a critical interpretation that has been brought to bear upon the ways in which American directors filtered the country's experience of the Vietnam War (1955–75) through a similarly expiatory frame, transforming extra-filmic guilt into filmic innocence, and extra-filmic perpetration into filmic victimhood (it is also worth mentioning here that the Vietnam War shares many parallels with the Algerian War of Independence[10]). Parsing the politics of *The Deer Hunter* (Cimino, 1978), *Rambo: First Blood Part II* (Cosmatos, 1985) and *Full Metal Jacket* (Kubrick, 1987), Linda Dittmar and Gene Michaud have, for instance, concluded that post-Vietnam films frequently 'find something redeeming to say about this war even as they echo the public's myriad and often contradictory misgivings about it' (1991: 7). This is corroborated by Keith Beattie's assertion that 'the pattern of denying guilt, as opposed to widespread confessions of guilt, formed the dominant cultural response to the war in Vietnam' (1998: 41), whilst John Orr has conjectured that many of the American films enumerated above 'tell us that the world can be redeemed from evil' (1993: 30). By the same token, Joseph Sartelle has talked about how American films made during the 1970s and 1980s responded to the Vietnam War – amongst other socio-historical phenomena, including the rise of multiculturalism and feminism – by representing 'the white man as victim' (1996: 522). As Sartelle states: 'white male paranoia movies expressed the white male's sense of resentment and anger in reaction to a perceived loss of privilege; they told us that the normative American white male *felt* like a victim even if the rest of society told him he was the oppressor' (1996: 522–3 [emphasis in original]). Widening the scope of the debate still further, Raya Morag has analysed a trend in contemporary Israeli narrative cinema, glossing how works such as *Beaufort* (Cedar, 2007) and *Lebanon* (Maoz, 2009), transform Israeli soldiers, that is to say, the perpetrators of a spate of atrocities committed against Palestinians during the Second Intifada, into guilt-less, anti-heroic victims. Opines Morag: '[films from this era have a tendency to] re-mythologise the Israeli combat soldier through a process of sacrificial victimization that overshadows the subject position of the perpetrator, and inevitably of the Palestinian victim as well' (2012: 94–5).

Whether studying films about the Second World War, the Vietnam War, or the Second Intifada, what remains implicit in all of these critical interventions – alongside my own – is a symptomatic understanding of cinema as akin to an immense cultural lens, capable of channelling a collective yearning to re-write and re-envisage history, rendering the latter, in turn, less distressing and more palpable, less implicating and more ethically reassuring, for France, at least.

Naomi Greene puts it well: 'if films are sensitive to half-hidden moods, or to unacknowledged desires, they also capture and reflect the ways in which such moods and desires may work to "screen", to soften and repress, the most troubling zones of the national past' (1999: 6). For Frank Wetta, 'the social trauma of a badly conducted war cries out for the comforting fantasy of [cinematic] mythmaking' (1992: 4).

Late-colonial French Cinema

After this brief foray into questions of atrocity and absolution, pacifism and redemption, let us now begin to edge towards what I understand as 'late-colonial French cinema', and why I have chosen this term. In the first instance, I should point out that this book is not about colonial French filmmaking, that is to say, the type of cinematic representation spawned out of the apotheosis of colonial culture in the 1930s, with films such as *Le Grand jeu* (Feyder, 1934), *La Bandera* (Duvivier, 1935), and *Pépé le Moko* (Duvivier, 1937), propagating Orientalist racial-ethnic stereotypes even as they exalted France as a civilizing power in Africa (see Stam and Spence 1983; Sherzer 1996; Ezra 2000). Nor is it about post-colonial French filmmaking, in other words, narratives released definitively after the end of colonialism, such as *Le Crabe-tambour/The Drummer Crab* (Schoendoerffer, 1977), *Outremer/Overseas* (Roüan, 1990), and *Chocolat/Chocolate* (Denis, 1988), infused, as they were, with a much more retrospective, and tangibly nostalgic, re-imagining of France's colonies (see Portuges 1996; Greene 1999; Eades 2006; Scharold 2016a; Boutaghou 2019a; Donadey 2020). Nor still is this book about post-colonial Algerian cinema, a topic that has most comprehensively been studied by Guy Austin (2007a; 2009; 2011; 2012; see also Sharpe 2013; 2015; Flood 2017; Wallenbrock 2020). Rather, I have used the term 'late-colonial' to describe a spate of cinematic narratives that represented the decolonisation of Algeria as it occurred from 1954 to 1962: either from the ideological perspective of French soldiers returning to metropolitan France, or the ideological perspective of French settlers based in French Algeria, or the ideological perspective of the French Left, whose militants – as I show in Chapter 7 – often occupied a liminal space, between territories and communities. Many of the films discussed in this book admittedly appropriate the iconographies of colonial French cinema whilst forecasting the iconographies of post-colonial French cinema, with the Eurocentrism of the former and the nostalgia of the latter being particularly prominent within several of my case studies. But these case studies are also imbued with a constellation of themes – loss, pacifism, emasculation, reconciliation, victimisation and expiation, to name a few – that are very much symptomatic of the de-colonial epoch, leading me, anecdotally, to consider calling my corpus 'de-colonial French cinema', before ultimately abandoning the idea. This decision was taken to avoid any confusion between my case studies and the recent de-colonial turn[11] in the humanities, with the former remaining obliquely tethered to a colonial ideology that the latter unequivocally repudiates.

In its emphasis on temporality, the term 'late-colonial' includes several advantages. First, in terms of my own research, it proved inclusive enough to capture the multiple political perspectives adopted by the films in my corpus, some of which could be described as obliquely pro-colonial, conveying values aligned with the Right, others obliquely anti-colonial, conveying values aligned with the Left, still others which display values more associated with political ambivalence, disengagement, or a complete rejection of politics altogether (it is also worth pointing out here that the terms 'political', 'politically engaged' and 'politicised' are often confusingly used by scholars to implicitly allude to leftist narratives, even if the terms themselves do not designate any political stance per se). In this respect, the lexicon that I deploy in this book is comparable to that used by Mark Betz, Alan O'Leary and Philip Dine, all of whom have commendably defined their corpora with a similar degree of intellectual caution, as consisting of 'films on the Algerian question' (Betz 2009: 103, 107), 'European cinema in its age of modernisation and decolonisation' (Betz 2009: 39), 'end of empire films that deal with the exhaustion of the French and European project' (O'Leary 2019: 27, 73), and 'French cinema of the final stage of the decolonisation of the Maghreb' (Dine 1994b: 24), rather than falling into the trap of categorising the cinematic narratives of this era as either perforce 'political' or perforce 'anti-colonial'. Second, in terms of future research, the term 'late-colonial' is inclusive enough to be used in other contexts, for example, to study cultural narratives produced to imagine and re-imagine the realities of different French territories as they strove for sovereignty (Tunisia, Morocco, Ivory Coast, sub-Saharan Africa, to name a few). Or to analyse narratives that are not cinematic, but literary, photographic or poetic. Or even to interrogate narratives produced by colonial countries other than France, for instance, *Black Narcissus* (Powell and Pressburger, 1947), a British psychological drama film set in the Himalayas and released mere months before India achieved independence from Britain. Finally, as Linda Badley and R. Barton Palmer remind us, if some trends in world cinema are 'self-defining', and others 'self-promoting', then I should stress that designating the films explored in this book as 'late-colonial' is the result of my own critical decision to treat them as a body of work (2006: 2).

Developing these thoughts further, one of the arguments that I make in the following chapters is that late-colonial French cinema should be perceived as a trans-generic body of films, bound up with various formal strategies, narrative conventions, cinematic traditions and tendencies. A distinct tendency with which many of the films discussed in this book could persuasively be allied, for instance, is the French New Wave, or *Nouvelle Vague*. In the most taxonomic readings of this tendency, the French New Wave is taken to encompass five 'Young Turk' directors: François Truffaut, Jean-Luc Godard, Claude Chabrol, Eric Rohmer and Jacques Rivette. Each of these individuals contributed to *Cahiers du cinéma*, an influential cinema journal founded by Doniol-Valcroze, Lo Duca and André Bazin in 1951, before turning their skills towards directing. Each of them was yoked with what was known as the 'Right Bank', insofar as they came from affluent neighbourhoods situated to the right of the River Seine in Paris. And each of them professed their belief in *la politique des auteurs*, an aesthetic credo predicated upon elevating the status of the director to an ideally sovereign artist, or *auteur*, able to wield their camera with the same degree of autonomy as that wielded by the writer over their pen (see Chapter 4). In the late 1960s, Fernando Solanas and Octavio Getino famously deployed the term 'second cinema' to categorise the New Wave, interpreting it simultaneously as an attempt at cleansing or 'decolonising' cinema from the corrupting influence of Hollywoodian 'first cinema', and as a mode of production that was nonetheless vulnerable to being 'institutionalised by neo-colonised or capitalist society' (1970–1: 4).

More supple readings of the New Wave generally maintain the historical scope of this taxonomy – seeing the French New Wave as a tendency that ascended as colonialism receded – even as they reconfigure its criteria.[12] Sometimes, this process of reconfiguration involves populating the New Wave with individuals previously marginalised from it. In lieu of an enshrined pantheon of (male) directors from the Right Bank of the Seine, the history of the New Wave is thus enlarged to include a cluster of slightly older and politically engaged directors from the Left Bank of the Seine, notably Alain Resnais, Agnès Varda and Chris Marker (Temple and Witt 2004: 183). Each of these directors produced at least one film that can hypothetically be considered late-colonial, including the aforementioned *Muriel ou le temps d'un retour*, *La Jetée/The Jetty* (Marker, 1962; mentioned in Chapter 4), and Varda's *Cléo de 5 à 7* (mentioned above and in Chapter 5), although, for reasons elaborated below, none of these films form sustained case studies in this book. Other times, the category of the New Wave is reconfigured towards more general technologies and techniques wielded by directors, including: the Nagra tape recorder, the Caméflex 35mm camera, off-studio filming and modernist formal experimentation, expressed most evidently in camera movement (tracking and panning shots), non-synchronous sound and disjunctive iterations in editing, devised specifically to fracture and fissure the spatio-temporal continuity of classical Hollywood realism. These technologies and techniques can be found in various late-colonial tales explored in this book, including Jacques Rozier's *Adieu Philippine*, Robert Enrico's *La Belle vie*, Doniol-Valcroze's *La Dénonciation*, and Jacques Rivette's *Paris nous appartient*. Louis Malle, director of *Le Feu follet*, meanwhile, has been named as falling 'within and without the New

Wave', 'within' insofar as like New Wave *auteurs*, Malle preferred filming outside of the studio, 'without' as his aesthetic grammar often liberally drew from the mainstream classical tradition (Frey 2004b: 2–11). A similar observation could be made about Jacques Dupont, with the director both indiscriminately drawing and diverging from the iconographic idioms of Jean-Luc Godard's New Wave exemplar, *À bout de souffle/Breathless* (1960), in his curious albeit impetuous psychodrama, *Les Distractions*.

Beyond the New Wave, this book deals with a variety of other cinematic idioms and traditions. In Chapter 2, for instance, I consider the star-studded imaginary of Mark Robson's *Les Centurions*, which projects the war through a deluge of bombastic tropes, pilfered from the Second World War combat film. In Chapters 5 and 7, I filter my ideas through a number of cinematic narratives that have been linked to what is known alternately as 'marginal' (Borde 1962a: 15–17; Guibbert 1992: 247–8) or, more frequently, 'parallel' cinema,[13] with scholars summoning the term 'parallel' as an indication, first, of the perceived anti-colonial or anti-war radicalism of the often short films associated with this trend (frequently shot on 16mm); and second, as an indication of the unofficial ways in which they were funded (privately), distributed (covertly) and screened (clandestinely). These screenings often took place, for example, at union meetings and ciné-clubs, including the Paris-based 'Action', prompting both Jean-Pierre Jeancolas (1979: 160) and Michel Cadé (1997: 49–50) to speak less of a 'parallel cinema' and more of a 'parallel circuit', whilst many scholars have identified René Vautier and Pierre Clément as the most (in)famous proponents of 'parallel' filmmaking.[14] Two 'parallel' films will thus be weighed up in Chapter 5: *Le Retour*, and *Secteur postal 89098*, with both being at least co-directed by ex-soldiers (Yann Le Masson in the former, Philippe Durand in the latter), and both hinging upon a shared thematics of psychic disarray, experienced by military protagonists who drift across the cinematic spaces in question. In Chapter 7, I turn my attention to two 'parallel' documentaries: *Octobre à Paris* and *J'ai 8 ans*, linking them to various trends in documentary practice, including 'the interactive mode' and the voice-of-God tradition. Both of these documentaries could also be linked to a certain category of political cinema, 'consisting of films made by First or Second World people in support of Third World peoples and adhering to the principles of Third Cinema' (Shohat and Stam 1994: 28), or, alternatively as examples of 'the militant image': a term used by Kodwo Eshun and Ros Gray to designate 'any form of image or sound produced in and through film making practices dedicated to the liberation struggles and revolutions of the late twentieth century' (2011: 1). In Chapter 6, I study the politics of what Rebecca Weaver-Hightower and Janne Lahti have termed 'settler cinema' (2020), that is to say, two moving pictures – *Les Oliviers de la justice* and *Au biseau des baisers* – that were not only made by European settlers subsisting in a war-stricken French Algeria, but also thematise the fantasies and anxieties of this very community. As with 'parallel cinema', this is a sub-category of late-colonial filmmaking that has not been extensively treated by scholars working in the domain. Astute readers may notice that this book skirts around what are generally assumed to be the canonical late-colonial films that surfaced during and immediately following the war: Varda's *Cléo de 5 à 7*, Resnais's *Muriel ou le temps d'un retour*, Jean-Luc Godard's *Le Petit soldat/The Little Soldier* (1960/1963), mentioned in Chapters 3, 4 and 5, and Gillo Pontecorvo's *La Bataille d'Alger/The Battle of Algiers* (1966), mentioned in Chapter 7. Given that each of these films has been subjected to sustained academic interpretation by a range of scholars,[15] I have decided to refrain from analysing them as case studies here. Instead, this book is fuelled by a desire to go beyond this canon – to peer behind it, to excavate underneath it – opening up, in turn, an abundant yet unappreciated seam of late-colonial films. These include works by Yann Le Masson, whose sprawling influence on no less than six late-colonial films, listed in Chapter 7, cannot be overestimated. They include works by Jean Herman, director of the remarkable *Actua-tilt* (1961),[16] *Le Chemin de la mauvaise route/The Wrong Path* (1962),[17] and *La Quille/On-Leave* (1963).[18] And they include the oeuvre of Paul Carpita, whose considerable artistry can be seen in late-colonial films such as *La Récréation/Break Time* (1958),[19] *Marseille sans soleil/Marseille Without Sun* (1961),[20] alongside the significantly more complex *Demain L'amour/Love, Tomorrow* (1962).[21] To the omission of canonical films in my corpus can finally be added a string of further omissions, dictated by the unfortunate enduring unavailability of many of the seventy[22] films that could persuasively be defined as 'late-colonial'. I also address this question – the question of accessibility – in the conclusion to the book.

Beyond Censorship

No study of late-colonial French cinema would be complete without a discussion of the censorship commission, which reigned over the French film industry before, during, and after decolonisation, and was informally known as 'Anastasia's Scissors'. As various cultural historians have shown,[23] from 1947 to 1959, censorship was carried out by a team of officials from the National Centre for Cinema and the Moving Image (*Le Centre national du cinéma et de l'image animée*, CNC) and the Ministries of Defence and Information, spearheaded by Louis Terrenoire. It was this team that decided if a film was worthy of a commercial or non-commercial visa, depending on whether it accorded with the generally apolitical, morally conservative,[24] yet also frequently incoherent, criteria of the censors. 'From its inception, the commission did not follow an over-arching template, but evaluated films on a case-by-case basis' (Croombs 2013: 12). For Terrenoire, any film displaying elements of 'ideological propaganda could not be authorised, if only because of the risks involved for public order' (cited in Carta 1962: 172). What actually constituted 'ideological propaganda', was, of course, open to debate, especially as neither the species of explicitly pro-military newsreels parenthetically discussed in Chapter 1 (see Denis 2009), nor the species of explicitly pro-military films discussed in Chapters 2 and 3 (*Les Centurions*, *Les Distractions*), attracted the roving eye of the commission. For films deemed unacceptable, meanwhile, this commission had three methods of restriction at its disposal: prohibition to those under the age of sixteen (from 1959 onwards); cuts and modifications; and, in the most serious cases, temporary or permanent prohibition. In 1959, control of censorship then passed to the Ministry for Cultural Affairs, managed by the intellectual-icon-turned-politician André Malraux, before restrictions placed on directors became even tighter in 1961 with the reformulation of laws associated with pre-censorship, a precautionary system that allowed officials to veto the gestation of a film before shooting had even started (Jeancolas 1979: 26). Arguably the most important change that took place during the 1950s was the introduction of *l'avance sur recettes* (an interest-free advance against box office revenue), granted, or not, after the director had submitted a synopsis to an ad hoc committee (Marie 2003: 53–5). Whilst this incentive has often been credited with catalysing a flurry of *auteur* initiatives, as a form of pre-censorship, it also privileged apolitical projects over political ones.

Different directors responded to, and were affected by, censorship in different ways. Some cineastes, for instance, quickly caved into the whims and the wishes of the state, removing any kind of allusion to the war from their works, and therefore, gently fostering an insidious culture of self-censorship that was effectively self-policing (Stora 2004: 124). Other, more radical filmmakers adopted an entirely different modus operandi, forsaking the official cinema industry for the parallel cinema circuit, and thus, in turn, expanding the aperture of their artistic expression even as they traded in the potential for public exposure (after all, 'parallel' films were never shown in commercial venues). Many directors attempted to 'outsmart the censors' by alluding to the war elliptically, rendering, in turn, 'censorship inoperative for lack of explicit images or lines' (de Baecque 2012: 143). Others were not so savvy, or not so lucky, and were forced to retrospectively 'mutilate' their projects at the behest of the censors. Due to their perceived political subject matter, several of the films examined in the following chapters were prevented from being publicly released until at least the aforementioned Evian Accords of 1962, after which censorship became laxer (see Raymond Lefèvre's 1966 film *Les désaccords d'Évian/The Evian Disagreements* for an anti-state take on this agreement). Such was the case, for instance, with *Adieu Philippine*, filmed in 1960 yet released in 1963 (Chapter 1); *La Belle vie*, filmed in 1962 yet released in 1964 (Chapter 1); Claude Autant-Lara's *Tu ne tueras point*, filmed in 1960 yet released in 1963 (Chapter 4); and *Le Retour*, filmed in 1959 yet released in

1962 (Chapter 5). Others were subjected to acts of prohibition, including *J'ai 8 ans*, filmed in 1961 yet banned until 1971 (Chapter 7); *Octobre à Paris*, filmed in 1962 yet banned until 1973 (Chapter 7); and *Secteur postal 89098*, subjected to a total ban in October 1961, on the pretence that the film 'provocatively and intolerably encouraged military insubordination' (cited in Lefèvre 1997: 43; Chapter 5). In an open discussion with Jean-Luc Godard, René Vautier meanwhile, attested to having been censured not by officials working in France, but rather by the FLN. 'When I showed [*Algérie en flammes*[25] to the FLN] in Cairo, they told me to cut out a sequence in which nationalists are seen crying. I asked them why and they said: "because an Algerian nationalist dies but doesn't cry"'. Vautier refused to mutilate his film and was subsequently imprisoned by the FLN (N'Guyen 2006: 400).

It is important to recognise that the regime of French state censorship elaborated above was not the only reason that late-colonial French films often represented the war using elliptical, muted, or sublimated imagery. Close examination of the cultural landscape reveals that other aesthetic and ideological factors were at work too, even before the censors had decided to release a project to the masses, modify it, defer it, or void it altogether. In two illuminating monographs, both Geneviève Sellier (2008: 137–44) and Antoine de Baecque (2012: 104–28) have, for instance, identified political disengagement as one of the prevailing aesthetic idioms of late-colonial culture, as embedded in the cinematic output of the Right Bank 'Young Turks' as it was in the literary output of the Hussars, a group of disengaged writers whose counterculture I explore in Chapter 3. According to Sellier and de Baecque,[26] this apolitical idiom was particularly apparent in Godard's aforementioned *Le Petit soldat*, arguably banned, as it was, until 1963 by an overzealous censorial team erroneously convinced that the film had taken an unequivocally political stance against the conflict. 'When you see the film', mused Jean de Baroncelli in *Le Monde*, 'you are surprised by the severity of the commission's ruling. The allusions to the Algerian War are in fact discreet, confused, and rarely aggressive' (cited in Sellier 2008: 135). This reading of *Le Petit soldat* is echoed in the work of a variety of scholars, with Matthew Croombs, for example, arguing that 'Godard iterates in anarchic fashion, the political confusion and self-doubt that the war triggered for many French intellectuals' (2013: 18). Benjamin Stora concurs, describing it as '*a first-person narrative* composed of engagement and dis-engagement, right-wing anarchism and leftist politics, the ebb and flow of emotions, and – above all – [a protagonist] that wavers between camps, swaying from the OAS to the FLN' (1998: 249 [emphasis in original]). Godard himself has shed even more light on the matter, describing how the film was based on his own experience of leaving for Switzerland after deserting from the French army, before leaving for France after deserting from the Swiss army. 'My behaviour was anarchic and individualist', he concedes (N'Guyen 2006: 400).

Other late-colonial films were characterised by a similar degree of political ambiguity but for different reasons. Writing for the journal *Combat*, Henry Chapier (1963), for instance, responded to the staggered release of Autant-Lara's *Tu ne tueras point* by chastising it as a film that 'neither deserved the scandal nor the importance that had been thrust upon it by the censors', whilst Lia Brozgal has argued more generally that 'by abolishing an archive', through censorship, for example, the state inadvertently 'creates the conditions for [the archive in question] to become a fetish' (2014: 37). Ivone Margulies (2004) has meanwhile drawn attention to the convoluted politics at play in Edgar Morin and Jean Rouch's leftist experiment in *cinéma vérité*, *Chronique d'un été/Chronicle of a Summer* (1961), with Margulies perceptively commenting that 'the film's turns from inane generality to incomprehensible specificity, from saying everything and then nothing, are due in part to the *self-censored* speech of politicized personages' (2004: 183 [emphasis added by author]). A similar point could also be made about the two leftist parallel documentaries examined in Chapter 7, both of which are pervaded by myriad ideological silences and blind spots, *even after* their directors had managed to bypass the pitfalls of pre-censorship, the lure of self-censorship, and the violent carving up of the filmic image by 'Anastasia's Scissors'.

But perhaps the most telling indication of the 'self-censorship' of which theorists such as Margulies have written can be found not within the diegetic complexities of late-colonial narratives, but beyond them: specifically, in the content of two extra-filmic, or epitextual, interview-surveys, conducted by journalists with industry experts. One of these was published in the weekly news magazine, *L'Express* on 29 September 1960, and was driven by the following questions: 'if censorship didn't exist, would you like to make a film about the Algerian War; and if so, how do you think you would approach this subject?' The responses – proffered by ten renowned directors, including Claude Chabrol, Jacques Doniol-Valcroze, and Pierre Kast – are revealing. Two directors replied 'no' to the question (François Truffaut, René Clair). The rest responded 'yes', yet with screenplay-ideas that essentially reiterated the thematics of the films being produced under censorship. These included: 'the drama of a conscript' (Doniol-Valcroze); 'a narrative illustrating the influence of the War on metropolitan France' (Kast); and 'a tale of deserters destroyed by an unnamed camp' (Chabrol). François Truffaut, ever the iconoclast, justified his negative response by insisting that he 'wouldn't want to add to the current confusion [concerning the war] with a confusing film' (see Daniel 1972: 336–7 and Scharold 2016b: 20). The second, and much more damning, interview-survey in question was published in the weekly film magazine *Film français*, in 1961. This time, the respondents were not only directors, but professionals from different strata of the industry. But the opinions of those interviewed were nonetheless familiar, with Alain Poiré, a producer at Gaumont, insisting that 'censorship wasn't that bad', whilst budding director Edouard Molinaro thought that 'too many people were doing stupid stuff', before calling on the censors to 'slow them down'. Others, like André Cayatte, demanded 'a professional form of censorship' (see Frodon 1995: 145–6). All of which indicated, once again, that the machinations of the censors may have been one catalyst for the depoliticised, politically equivocal, or ideologically soft-focused iconographies of late-colonial cinema, but they were not the only one. As I strive to illustrate throughout this book, there were many other, equally important, reasons for which certain aspects of the war – colonial guilt, in particular – remained both unseen and unspoken.

Methodology, Argument and Structure

Scholarship on late-colonial cinema has passed through various cycles. The earliest attempts at investigating the relationship between French cinema and the war can be found in the leftist and Marxist-inflected film journal *Positif*, which published a plethora of articles on how decolonisation was, or wasn't, being documented by French cineastes at the time (see Borde 1962a; Benayoun 1962; Gozlan 1962). Often these articles pivoted around a polemical attempt at discerning two diametrically opposed camps in the New Wave: one containing the Right Bank Young Turks, affiliated with *Cahiers du cinéma*, who were disparaged for their perceived apolitical formalism (an obsessive concern with film form); the other containing the cineastes of the Left Bank, who were applauded for their perceived political formalism (Higgins 1996: 1–16). As Jim Hillier intimates, '*Cahiers* (as opposed to *Positif*) was very much part of broader political-cultural currents moving steadily to the Right, and which varied between being overtly anti-Left, and simply being silent on political issues such as the Algerian struggle for independence' (1985: 6). It is therefore unsurprising that one of the most political tracts of the era – Yann Le Masson and Olga Baïdar-Poliakoff's 'Manifeste pour un cinéma parallèle/Manifesto for a Parallel Cinema' – would not be written into the pages of *Cahiers*, but those of *Positif* (1962: 18).

During the 1970s, two French authors widened the scope of these early journalistic endeavours into longer scholarly works. The first of these was by Joseph Daniel, whose illuminating yet unappreciated monograph, *Guerre et cinéma: grandes illusions et petits soldats (1895–1971)/War and Cinema: Big Illusions and Small Soldiers (1895–1971)* traced a vastly comprehensive history of how popular, parallel and *auteur* directors had engaged with the war as it was unfolding (1972: 295–395). The second was by Jean-Pierre Jeancolas, whose monograph *Le Cinéma des Français: La Vème République/French Cinema: The Fifth Republic* included two informative chapters on censorship (1979: 27–65) and the politics of late-colonial representation (1979: 103–65), with Jeancolas defining 1956 to 1958 as a historical excursion during which French citizens decided 'to live with a guilty conscience or retreat', and late-colonial French cinema as 'cut off from life, cut off from the present, and cut off from history' (1979: 97). Neither Daniel nor Jeancolas's works were couched in the type of semiotic, psychoanalytic or ideological (neo-Marxist) concepts wielded by many other film scholars during the 1970s, especially those writing in film journals such as *New Left Review*, *Camera Obscura* or *Screen*; nor did they display an engagement with the contemporaneous rise of cultural studies or post-colonial studies; yet both belied a breadth and depth of knowledge and expertise that was clearly the result of extensive and extended archival research. It was only in the 1990s that scholars began to subject the imaginary of late-colonial culture to sustained analysis through the conceptual vocabulary of critical theory. In an important contribution to the field, Philip Dine (1994a), for instance, adopted a quasi-semiotic, neo-Marxist, theoretical paradigm to conceptualise the literature and cinema of Algerian decolonisation, homing in on the ideological workings of 'myth' (3–12), and thus echoing the symptomatic reading of late-colonial domestic culture conducted by Kristin Ross in her seminal work *Fast Cars, Clean Bodies* (1995). Complementing Dine's intervention, Benjamin Stora meanwhile, projected the same culture through a different critical lens (1998; 2004), less aligned with myth and more aligned with what has become one of the most dominant critical paradigms in the humanities, and indeed, in scholarship on late-colonial culture: memory studies. Stora was also instrumental in co-editing an important 1997 collection of essays on the subject,[27] before Naomi Greene released an authoritative monograph, devoted to teasing out the complexities of late-colonial and post-colonial cinema, and which effectively bolted together the two critical concepts held separate by Dine and Stora: 'myth and memory' (1999: 3–13).

More recent scholarship on the subject has tended to fork in divergent directions, depending on whether the scholar in question is affiliated with film studies or French studies. Two theorists who have done much to enrich the debate on late-colonial cinema in the domain of film studies are Matthew Croombs (2010; 2013; 2014; 2017) and Geneviève Sellier (2000; 2008). Both thinkers, like myself, limit the scope of their inquiries to a synchronic snapshot of the epoch: the late 1950s and the early 1960s. Both, likewise, base many of their arguments on theories of political representation initially proposed by the aforementioned critics of *Positif*. But where Croombs follows the 'positive' strand of this journal, critically praising the Left Bank as an inherently political cinema, in much the same way as journalists such as Borde, Benayoun and Gozlan, working in the early 1960s, had done, Sellier trades Croombs's 'positive' interrogation for a 'negative' one, often weaponising the same articles from *Positif* to articulate critical opprobrium for the depoliticising ethos at the core of the Right Bank, and, by extension, *Cahiers du cinéma*.

Glossing this culture, Sellier, for instance, insists that 'Young Turk' directors were often 'more favourable towards "formalist" artistic projects than towards screenplays inscribed in contemporary social and political issues' (2008: 216–17). An at once wider and narrower study of the cinematic landscape of the era has been conducted by Mark Betz in his essential monograph, *Beyond the Subtitle* (2009), in which the author discusses allusions to the political legacy of decolonisation in both Right Bank *and* Left Bank films, before curiously concluding his inquiry by conjecturing that 'a film on the Algerian question' is one that harnesses the mobile female body as an allegory for decolonisation (for example Varda's *Cléo de 5 à 7*, or Jean-Luc Godard's *Vivre sa vie/To Live Her Life* [1962]), even if Betz can only come to this conclusion by ignoring the persistent masculine-centrism of the New Wave, as identified and analysed by Sellier. Ultimately, although I draw from the pioneering collective work of Croombs, Sellier and Betz throughout this book, I also strive to go beyond it: first, by enlarging the scale of my corpus away from the New Wave specifically and towards the trans-generic category of late-colonial filmmaking more generally; and second, by edging the focal point of my analysis away from the politics of cinematic representation and towards more ethically inflected questions regarding guilt and innocence, complicity and absolution, and perpetration and victimhood. As the reader will see, this dual shift – from the New Wave to the late-colonial, and from the political to the ethical – forms the defining feature of my own intervention on the subject.

This book is also in dialogue with two even more recent and equally excellent monographs: Maria Flood's *France, Algeria and the Moving Image* (2017), and Nicole Beth Wallenbrock's *The Franco-Algerian War through a Twenty-First Century Lens* (2020), both of which are rooted more firmly in the domain of French studies, and both of which share various methodological parallels. Unlike my own book, both of these monographs, for instance, interrogate a range of late-colonial and post-colonial films from a diachronic perspective, with Wallenbrock's corpus stretching from 1965 to 2013, and Flood's from 1963 to 2010. Again, unlike this book, both monographs are trans-national studies, with a range of narratives from French directors – for instance *Of Gods and Men/Des hommes et des dieux* (Beauvois, 2010), and *L'Ennemi intime/The Intimate Enemy* (Siri, 2007) – being weighed up against those made by their Algerian counterparts, including *La Nouba des femmes du Mont Chenoua/The Nouba of the Women of Mount Chenoua* (Djebar, 1979), as read by Flood, or, *Cartouches Gauloises/Summer of '62* (Charef, 2007), as read by Wallenbrock. Where both works clearly *do* intersect with my own, however, is in their conceptual scope, with neither scholar deploying one theoretical paradigm to facilitate their analysis, but many. In Wallenbrock's book, we thus find nothing less than a dazzling condensation of critical concepts, such as Jacques Derrida's scission and circumcision, David Harvey's utopian dialectics, Félix Guattari and Gilles Deleuze's de-territorialisation and re-territorialisation, and Thomas Elsaesser's aforementioned 'guilt management'. Flood, meanwhile, looks elsewhere for theoretical inspiration, predicating many of her arguments on Jacques Rancière's notion of dis-identification and Michel Foucault's concept of heterotopia.

Inspired by the work of these thinkers, alongside other important interventions on the subject by Irmgard Scharold (2016a),[28] Maya Boutaghou (2019a),[29] and Anne Donadey (2020),[30] the argumentative compass of this book will thus revolve around one chief question – what is late-colonial French cinema? – with this question, in turn, generating two attendant answers. In the first instance, I will argue that late-colonial cinema represents a formally and thematically important yet unappreciated trend in the continuum of modern French cinema; one that has largely been overshadowed by the insidious effects of state censorship, alongside a narrow scholarly interest in the French New Wave. 'Histories of French cinema', contends Geneviève Sellier, 'all give a privileged place to the New Wave', leading to what the author terms 'a critical doxa' on the subject, more focused on text than context, and on the apoliticism of auteurism than the politics – or, for that matter, ethics – of decolonisation (2008: 2). In the second instance, I will argue that whilst late-colonial French cinema cannot be seen as a coherent cinematic movement, school, or genre of filmmaking – like the Western or musical – it can be seen as a coherent ethical trend, with many of the case studies explored in this book filtering the war through the discourse of 'redemptive pacifism' identified above. In each chapter, I thus use the term 'redemptive pacifism' very specifically: as a means of describing how many late-colonial French films at once seem to emphasise the futility of the conflict through pacifist motifs, whilst representing French communities – notably soldiers, settlers and the Left – as either innocent or absolved of the atrocities committed therein. More details on these arguments and the ethics of 'redemptive pacifism' can be found in the introduction to each chapter, alongside the conclusion.

In terms of trajectory, meanwhile, the seven case-study chapters of this book are organised both thematically and theoretically, with a range of critical approaches and concepts being deployed in each to answer – or at least probe – the central question posed above. In Chapter 1, for example, I read Jacques Rozier's *Adieu Philippine/Goodbye Philippine* (1963) and Robert Enrico's *La Belle vie/The Good Life* (1964), through the theoretical lens of space studies, exploring how both narratives depict military officials returning from Algeria as redeemed or recuperated by the privatised home-as-haven that awaits them. In Chapter 2, I extend these discussions of pacifism and redemption to Alain Cavalier's *L'Insoumis/The Unvanquished* (1964) and Mark Robson's *Les Centurions/Lost Command* (1966), turning my attention to the expiatory power of star bodies and star faces through reference to thinkers working in star studies, and concluding with an interrogation of the intense physicality of the paratroopers that feature in Robson's film. Echoing the concluding thoughts of Chapter 2, Chapter 3, meanwhile, begins with a discussion of paratrooper identity, yet within a different thematic and theoretical context: masculinity and gender studies. Castration, impotence and queerness: such are just some of the themes glossed thereafter, specifically vis-à-vis the alternately virile and victimised military protagonists that people Jacques Dupont's *Les Distractions/Trapped by Fear* (1960) and Louis Malle's *Le Feu follet/The Fire Within* (1963). Both Dupont and Malle's films also draw from the literary counterculture of the aforementioned Hussars, giving rise to a fictional archetype: the quasi-military, politically disengaged, Hussar dandy.

As the subtitle suggests, Part II of this book is less concerned with depictions of French soldiers, and more concerned with how 'other' groups are depicted in late-colonial cinema. Shifting my attention to cinematic codings of memory, and drawing from memory studies, in Chapter 4, I thus examine how Doniol-Valcroze twists his narrative, *La Dénonciation/The Denunciation* (1962), around the curious tale of an ex-Resistant-turned-film producer, before concluding with a reading of Claude Autant-Lara's wildly singular tale of conscientious objection, motivated forgetting and ethical renewal, *Tu ne tueras point/L'Objecteur/Thou Shalt Not Kill* (1963). In Chapter 5, I provisionally invert the terms of my argument, showing how Daniel Goldenberg's *Le Retour/The Return* (1959), Philippe Durand's *Secteur postal 89098/Postal Sector 89098* (1961), and Jacques Rivette's *Paris nous appartient/Paris Belongs to Us* (1961) not only turn around female French civilians – with women waiting for their soldier partners to return from service being a recurring trope therein – but also represent the same women as guilty of a cycle of 'crimes' linked obliquely to the war, a process that I term 'guilt displacement'. Chapter 6, meanwhile, lurches away from films made in metropolitan France by metropolitan directors, and towards two narratives made in French Algeria by European settlers: Jean Pélégri and James Blue's *Les Oliviers de la justice/The Olive Trees of Justice* (1962), and *Au biseau des baisers/Slanted Kisses* (1962), by Guy Gilles and Marc Sator. Deploying the critical paradigm of the gaze, in Chapter 6 I argue that both films re-imagine war-torn Algeria as a hazy idyll, infused with love, reconciliation and innocence. Anchored in documentary studies, Chapter 7 finally attempts to show how both *Octobre à Paris/October in Paris*, by Jacques Panijel (1962) and *J'ai 8 ans/I Am 8 Years Old* (Le Masson, Baïdar-Poliakoff, Vautier, 1961) aspire to grant a voice to Algerians victimised by the colonial French state, even as they function to redeem the reputation of the Left, after the latter had been accused of complicity in colonial atrocities. I should note that each chapter begins with an introduction to the central concepts associated with each critical approach, alongside a summary of how they relate to the discourse of 'redemptive pacifism', elaborated above.

25

Notes

1. This account is famously conjoined with ostensibly archival footage of soldiers performing a series of menial tasks whilst on duty in Algeria, footage that Bernard watches using a projector whilst speaking. For more information see Flood (2017: 47–54).
2. For more details on the question of complicity in relation to the history of decolonisation in Algeria see Debarati Sanyal's illuminating monograph *Memory and Complicity: Migrations of Holocaust Remembrance* (2015; especially pages 9–18). In the introduction, Sanyal, for example, asks: 'how does complicity, rather than affect-based discourses of trauma, shame and melancholy, open a critical engagement with the violence of history?' (2015: 9). I draw liberally from Sanyal's theories in Chapter 4, especially in relation to questions of memory and allegory.
3. It is worth noting that there is a lack of consensus about what to call the war. In 1999, the French National Assembly passed a law officially recognising the events as 'the Algerian War', although this terminology has been criticised for foregrounding the perspective of the French. In Algeria, the war is often called 'the Algerian Revolution', or 'the War of National Liberation'. Drawing from the work of Sylvie Thénault (2012: 14), my own choice of terminology – 'the Algerian War of Independence' – represents an attempt to strike neutral ground between the respective Franco-centrism and Algero-centrism of these different definitions. See Vince (2020: 2) for more details on this debate.
4. A further note on terminology: in this book, I have opted to deploy the term 'indigenous Algerians' to refer to individuals who might have been constitutionally defined as 'French' by the French state, yet, as I show below, were systematically denied privileges accorded to their settler counterparts. Benjamin Stora has addressed the challenges inherent in such linguistic decisions, challenges that stem from the ambiguity of the laws governing French Algeria (1998: 21).
5. *La Question* was – and remains – one of the most important texts to emerge out of the late-colonial crisis. Written in a lucid literary style, *La Question* notably chronicles Alleg's arrest by paratroopers in 1957, after which he was subjected to different forms of torture, including water torture and electrotorture. The book's notoriety also derives from the fact that it was vigorously censored upon publication, before achieving clandestine success in France. By the end of 1958, there were over 162,000 copies in circulation.
6. Boupacha was initially brought to court by the colonial legal system for suspected Algerian militancy, a 'crime' of which she was found guilty. Yet by far the most famous aspect of Boupacha's trial was not the perspective of her prosecutors, but that of her defence, as orchestrated by the French lawyer Gisèle Halimi. As Ryan Kunkle claims, 'Halimi sought to break the usual cycle of trial and execution, which was common for many Algerian nationalists', notably by working with renowned intellectual, Simone de Beauvoir, to bring Boupacha's case to the public sphere (2013: 10). See Surkis (2010) for more details.
7. This campaign was composed of bombings known as *la strounga*, shootings with sub-machine guns, arson with Molotov cocktails and kidnappings. It is also worth pointing out that the OAS was mostly made up of European settlers.

8. This is a distinction that has been discussed by Thomas Elsaesser (2014: 20–2) and, in particular, Paul Ricoeur, in his work, *La Mémoire, l'histoire, l'oubli/Memory, History, Forgetting* (2004: 470–8). In addition to criminal guilt and moral guilt, Ricoeur also explores the phenomenon of what he calls, 'political guilt', a collective form of guilt which recalls the thrust of Sartre's thesis. As Ricoeur states, 'political guilt' 'results from the fact that citizens belong to a political body in the name of which crimes [are often] committed' (2004: 474).
9. Gilroy frames this melancholia as an evasion; it is about avoiding 'the painful obligations to work through the grim details of imperial and colonial history and to transform paralyzing guilt into a more productive shame' (2005: 99).
10. Benjamin Stora has identified at least five similarities between the two wars: neither war was officially declared as such; both involved heavy civilian casualties; both included the perpetration of atrocities, through the use of napalm, for instance; both ended in defeat for a colonial/imperial country (France and America); and both caused profound wounds to be carved in the collective psyche of these countries (2004: 9).
11. 'The decolonial turn' relates to the rise of what some theorists have called decoloniality. As Claire Gallien explains, 'decoloniality is best described as a gesture that denormalizes the normative, problematizes default positions, debunks the aperspectival, destabilizes the structure, [and] rehabilitates epistemic formations that continue to be repressed under coloniality' (2020: 28). It has also been accompanied with calls to decolonise university curricula. For more information on decoloniality, see Mignolo (2007) and Mignolo and Walsh (2018).
12. For more information on the relationship between the French New Wave and decolonisation see Greene (2007), Sellier (2008), de Baecque (2012: 103–57), and Wallenbrock (2020: 21–4).
13. For more information on 'parallel cinema' see Boudjedra (1971: 37–41), Daniel (1972: 342–7), Jeancolas (1979: 155–62), Dine (1994a: 215–32), Gaston-Mathé (1997), Lefèvre (1997), Cadé (1997), Scharold (2016b: 15–18) and Wallenbrock (2020: 19–21). It should also be noted that, whilst the 'parallel' documentaries explored in Chapter 7 were funded, distributed and screened by leftist organisations during the early 1960s, the parallel soldier films discussed in Chapter 5 were not. As such, the former are much more documented by cultural historians than the latter.
14. René Vautier was incarcerated for a year for his anti-colonial documentary *Afrique 50/Africa 50* (1950), whilst Pierre Clément was condemned to 10 years in prison in 1958 after filming colonial atrocities committed in Algeria and Tunisia, before eventually being freed after amnesties signed in 1962. Some 'parallel' films made by Clément include *Réfugiés algériens/Algerian Refugees*, *Sakiet sidi youssef* (both 1958), whilst Vautier's *Algérie en flammes/Algeria is Burning* (1958) is often cited as a seminal intervention in the politics of late-colonial culture. Scholars that have written about Vautier include: Brenez (2004), Croombs (2013: 215–20), Bédjaoui (2014: 62–9), and Wallenbrock (2020: 15–19). For a short yet informative summary of Clément's cinematic oeuvre see Bedjaoui (2014: 69–72).
15. For more information on *Le Petit soldat*, see Dixon (1997), Adams (2016: 108–24), Stora (2004: 135–45), Sellier (2008: 134–9) and Scharold (2016c). For

more information on *Cléo de 5 à 7*, see Flitterman-Lewis (1990), Orpen (2007), Ezra (2010) and Betz (2009: 131–44). For more information on *La Bataille d'Alger* see Tomlinson (2004), Harrison (2007), Flood (2019), alongside Alan O'Leary's monograph on the film (2019). This list is far from exhaustive.

16. By far one of the most complex yet unappreciated late-colonial films discussed in this book, *Actua-tilt* derives its fragmented 'narrative' from the thematics of arcade games, although the term 'narrative' is somewhat misleading, seeing as the film is not based on any kind of causal logic, plot development, or characterisation, but rather on a very loose focus on topics such as stellar exploration, apocalyptic disaster, the commodification of the human body, the shock of modernisation and military warfare. In the first half of the film, the viewer is thus presented with various images of sport- and space-orientated arcade games (with boxing and rockets being two recurring themes), whilst two disembodied narrators – one male, one female – elliptically discuss 'a trip to the moon'. 'None of this will happen', intones the woman, before the man ominously responds, 'it is happening now'. It is not clear what they are referring to. The second part of the film, meanwhile, is even more military-focused, revolving around images of soldiers in the arcade playing light gun games. Wielding a range of plastic weapons, it is at this point in the film that the allusions to the war are at their most evident. It is finally worth noting that the entire film is pervaded by highly rapid and jagged patterns of editing, comparable to the most anxiety-inducing parts of Resnais's *Muriel ou le temps d'un retour*.
17. Focused largely on the existential musings of an eighteen-year-old violent-rocker-outcast, Jean-Claude, and his equally rebellious partner Colette, Herman's documentary notably includes an entire 'chapter' dedicated to 'The Algerian War', in which the couple muse about their predicament, and Jean-Claude confesses to indiscriminately beating Algerians in the street. The project was banned by the censors, yet curiously not for its allusions to military conflict, but for its perceived amorality. For more information, see Herman (1963: 47–9).
18. The film recounts the story of two former soldiers who lose touch with each other after returning from Algeria to Paris. One of them suffers from 'post-service vertigo', recalling Laurent in Jacques Dupont's *Les Distractions/Trapped by Fear* (1960), analysed in Chapter 3.
19. *La Récréation* is a fictional short film in which a teacher recalls his youth whilst thinking about his best friend, killed in action. See Martin (1963a: 63) for more details.
20. In *Marseille sans soleil*, a fictional screenwriter and cinematographer join forces to complete a documentary on Marseilles, after the director of the project is killed during service in Algeria.
21. *Demain L'amour* is the story of a former soldier named Gérard (Jean-Claude Merac) and his partner Madeleine (Corinne Coppier). The film begins with images of Gérard hurtling down a Marseilles country road in a convertible, before violently crashing. As he is transported to hospital, Gérard experiences an extraordinarily complex, and hallucinatory, series of flashbacks, composed of various images. Some of these frame Gérard and Madeleine on a beach. Others are set in a train station when Gérard is called up for service ('when I let go of your hand, I knew that absence would

kill love'). Others depict Gérard scarpering panicked, gun in hand, through rocky terrain, presumably in Algeria. Still others linger on Madeleine as she articulates her intention to end their relationship. Gérard's psychological distress, represented formally through the spatio-temporal fragmentation of the narrative, is thus framed as at once a symptom of the war and the disloyalty of women.

22. For a comprehensive list of these seventy films see Martin (1963a: 60–4, 143–6).
23. For more details on cinematic censorship during the war, see Daniel (1972: 335–9), Jeancolas (1979: 38–40; 2005), Evans (1989), Frodon (1995: 142–9), Lefèvre (1997), Gaston-Mathé (1997), Stora (1998: 38–42; 2004: 111–25), and Denis (2006).
24. Apart from politics, censorship often impinged upon issues of religion and sex, with Jacques Rivette's *La Religieuse/The Nun*, being famously banned in 1966 for its stark anti-Catholicism. For more information see Jeancolas (1979: 27–48).
25. Vautier doesn't explicitly state which of his films was censored, although it is safe to assume that he is talking about *Algérie en flammes*.
26. It is also worth noting that, unlike Sellier, de Baecque goes on to define the work of the 'Young Turks' as 'intrinsically political' (2012: 132), cleaving open what seems like a theoretical contradiction in his otherwise compelling chapter. This contradiction can be seen, for instance, in the author's contention that 'politics was at the core of the New Wave project, that is, the concrete implementation of principles forged in the 1950s through a theory of apolitical cinema' (2012: 132). Or: 'none of the [Young Turks] were directly engaged in making political films, but all conceived of filmmaking politically, that is, as a way to reveal the truth of a present that was, at long last, truly contemporary' (2012: 138). A similar yet more successful attempt at reading the New Wave politically, despite the pervasive political disengagement of its affiliates, can be found in Nancy Virtue's article 'Jacques Demy's *Les Parapluies de Cherbourg*: a national allegory of the French-Algerian war' (2013). Like de Baecque, Virtue begins her argument by stressing the apoliticism of Demy (2013: 129–30), but then goes on to define his film as a political allegory nonetheless. As Virtue insists, 'in order to engage in allegorical interpretation, one need not claim intentionality on the part of the author' (2013: 130).
27. Aligned with the journal *CinémAction*, this edited collection includes a range of essays on the politics of cinematic censorship, European settlers, representations of torture, and images of absence. For more details see Hennebelle et al. (1997).
28. Written in French, Scharold's invaluable edited collection treats a range of filmic representations of the war, including chapters on *Le Petit soldat* and *Muriel ou le temps d'un retour*. It also includes an illuminating section on parallel filmmaking.
29. Examining a range of novels, plays, poetry, documentary films and web-documentaries, Boutaghou's edited collection – composed of a range of chapters written in French – is indispensable reading for scholars interested in cultural representations of the war.
30. Drawing from the work of Henri Rousso (1987) and Benjamin Stora (1998; 2004), Donadey's illuminating book (written in English) is based upon tracing a diachronic history of cinematic representations of the war: from a period of mourning (1962–4), to repression (1964–89), the return of the repressed (1990–8), and difficult anamnesis (1999–present).

PART I

SOLDIERS

I. CONSCRIPTS AND RESERVISTS, PRIVATISATION AND REDEMPTION

It would be no exaggeration to identify the early 1960s – the apex of the war – as a moment in which existing spatial configurations in France, and, in particular, Paris, were not just reconfigured, but positively dismantled, and violently. Whilst American style modernisation was empowering men and women hunting for business opportunities in a country abruptly awash with them, the Minister of Culture, André Malraux, was busy disempowering many Parisians of their right to domestic stability through a campaign of urban renovation known as 'The Law of the Seven Monuments'. According to this legislation, tenants living in *quartiers* such Montparnasse, Belleville and Le Marais did not have the right to appeal when their building was destined for evacuation, destruction or sandblasting (the whitening of facades). Residents forced out of already claustrophobic living spaces were promised temporary housing that frequently never materialised (Feldman 2014: 41–74). The capital, meanwhile, was suddenly inundated with communities from colonised or formally colonised countries – Algeria, Morocco, Tunisia – jostling alongside some of the approximately 1 million European settlers who had felt compelled if not forced into exodus from Algeria in the months preceding and following the attainment of Algerian independence (see Chapter 6 for more details about this community). Writes Bernard Marchand:

> instead of following carefully calculated and accurately executed orders, those responsible for the construction of Paris [in the early 1960s]

progressed in fits and starts, with long periods of negligence separated by outbreaks of fever, in which barriers were suddenly breached. (1993: 290)

One of the most important late-colonial films in this respect was Chris Marker and Pierre Lhomme's documentary, *Le Joli Mai/The Lovely Month of May* (1963), which represented Paris as city fractured into radically different zones: some developed, others undeveloped, some modern, others archaic. Hence the ways in which the documentary juxtaposes scenes of the then-nascent district of la Défense – a conglomeration of corporate enterprises and jutting skyscrapers – against footage shot in a racially marginalised shanty town in Nanterre, positioning the documentary in proximity to other 'shanty town' films such as *Les Enfants des courants d'air/Draft Children* (Luntz, 1959), *L'Amour existe/Love Exists* (Pialat, 1961), *La Poupée/The Doll* (Baratier, 1962), *Nanterre un jour/Nanterre One Day* (Cuau, 1962), and *Octobre à Paris/October in Paris*, by Jacques Panijel (1962; see Chapter 7). Other parts of *Le Joli Mai* are even more orientated towards the wondrous pleasures of the private, domestic realm, with two interviews being crucial in this respect. One of these lingers upon the face of a woman whose application for a state-managed apartment has recently been granted, allowing her to raise her nine children with adequate space and amenities. Another pauses upon the body of a prospective conscript, who wishes for nothing so much as to 'have the pleasure of setting up house' (see Marker 2001; Koide 2019).

Underpinning many of the arguments that I propose within the first chapter of this book is the spatial concept of privatisation, a concept notably elaborated by Henri Lefebvre in his 1961 monograph *Critique de la vie quotidienne II, Fondements d'une sociologie de la quotidienneté/Critique of Everyday Life: Foundations for a Sociology of the Everyday*. A phenomenon at once social and cultural, architectural and urban, individual and collective, according to Lefebvre, privatisation emerges in moments of national strife, for example the widespread urban renewal glossed above, when the domestic realm acquires an inflated, almost metaphysical, importance. No longer is it a space in which an individual simply lives, but a space in which the dweller – or in the case of *Le Joli Mai*, a prospective conscript – can protect themselves from the public domain, alternately perceived as chaotic, threatening, invasive. It is for this reason that Lefebvre diagnoses the privatised home as 'an alibi to escape from failures' ([1961] 2008: 94), whilst Claire Duchen has emphasised how, in the early 1960s, 'the home was placed in opposition to the world outside' (1994: 66), engendering deep changes in policy, urban planning and interior design, alongside collective fantasies of homeownership. Privatisation also led to an exponential growth in household items, consumer durables (televisions, washing machines, fridges) and synthetic materials (aluminium, nylon, Formica, plastiflex), with companies coaxing clients into metamorphosising their home: from a space-to-be-lived-in, into a protective shield of objects and things. Indeed, according to Jean Baudrillard ([1968] 2005: 13–74), the collective longing for late-colonial privatisation proved so all-consuming that it generated a vast, collective culture of privatisation, mediated through the iconographic repertoire of women's magazines (*Marie-Claire*, *Elle* and *Femmes d'aujourd'hui*), architectural magazines (*Maison Française* and *Mobilier et Décoration*), middlebrow literature, newsreels, domestic contests, advertising, department stores (Lévitan and Galeries Barbès) and as I will show, cinema, all of which were predicated on a similar notion of the home as a figurative 'haven' in which 'subjects causing conflict were avoided' (Duchen 1994: 66, 6).

More recent research by Kristin Ross (1995) and Matthew Croombs (2017) has helped to tease out what early work by Baudrillard and Lefebvre often seemed to gesture towards, without rendering explicit: that the central 'failures' neutralised by privatisation were 'failures' specifically and inextricably intertwined with the demise of empire. Croombs, for instance, has eloquently written about how 'the French citizenry was coerced into disavowing the nation's colonial difficulties through a culture saturated with glossy images of plastics, electric appliances, and magazine advertising' (2017: 26), with this culture being both reflected and subverted in the consumerist subtext of Left Bank films such as *La Jetée/The Jetty* (Marker, 1962), *Muriel ou le temps d'un retour/ Muriel or the Time of a Return* (Resnais, 1963; see Britton 1990), and Agnès Varda's *Cléo de 5 à 7/Cléo from 5 to 7* (1962). Studying the domestic imaginary of women's magazines, Ross's argument, in turn, is even more trenchant. For her, the discursive motif of the privatised home that arose in the dawning of privatised culture was nothing but the Janus-face, that is to say, the absolute antithesis, of French Algeria. Thus, where Algeria had been engulfed by a 'dirty war', the modern home would be clean and sterile; where Algeria had been populated by communities politicised by fear, the home would be populated by the apolitical housewife; and where Algeria had been scarred by the perpetration of atrocities, the home would be preserved in a state of 'redemptive hygiene' (1995: 75). In a pivotal part of this hypothesis, Ross elaborates:

> A chain of equivalences is at work here; the prevailing logic runs something like this: if the woman is clean, the family is clean, the nation is clean. If the French woman is dirty, then France is dirty and backward. But France can't be dirty and backward, because that is the role played by the colonies. But there are no more colonies. If Algeria is becoming an independent nation, then France must become a *modern* nation: some distinction between the two must still prevail. France must, so to speak, clean house; reinventing the home is reinventing the nation. And thus, the

new 1950s interior: the home as the basis of the nation's welfare (1995: 78 [emphasis in original]).

Drawing from the theories of privatisation expounded above, this chapter is driven by three aims. Firstly, I will show how Jacques Rozier's *Adieu Philippine/ Goodbye Philippine* (1963) and Robert Enrico's *La Belle vie/The Good Life* (1964) reflect the culture of privatisation that arose during the decolonisation of Algeria. A second aim is to illustrate how both films revolve around an imaginary of 'redemptive hygiene', to requote Ross, enfolding their protagonists in a privatised bubble, composed of household routine, new consumerism, and fundamentally innocent domestic pleasures. A final aim of this chapter is to demonstrate how both narratives hinge upon a recurring figure in late-colonial French cinema, and one that will reappear in the following chapters: the wounded yet exonerated soldier-victim.

ADIEU PHILIPPINE (1963)

To say that expectations surrounding the release of *Adieu Philippine* were immense is an understatement. Perhaps the most important catalyst for this interest was George de Beauregard's decision to produce *Adieu Philippine*, having just financed Godard's *À bout de souffle/Breathless* (1960) to huge success, alongside the fact that a still from the as yet unreleased film graced the front cover of a special issue of *Cahiers du cinéma*, accompanied by a short editorial note calling it 'a startling and convincing example of New Wave filmmaking' (Anon. 1961, inside cover). Yet the development of the project was also beset by a string of setbacks: first due to financial concerns created by Rozier's unorthodox filming style, inherited from his background in television (he often used three or four cameras, allowing shots to run longer than normal in an attempt to capture moments of serendipitous unscripted dialogue), and second, the director's mistaken belief that he could complete filming adequately without a sound engineer, spawning all kinds of issues regarding the synchronisation of speech. As Michel Marie states: 'the sound obtained, recorded under makeshift conditions with a portable tape recorder, was not sufficiently audible, to say nothing of being in sync' (2003: 96). Whilst scholars tend to focus on the impact of these technical mistakes (Zand 1963; Collet 1963; Garson 2009; Neupert 2011), this chapter instead aims to calibrate the late-colonial ethics of the film by analysing how it represents domestic privatised space.

As for the plot, *Adieu Philippine* is a coming-of-age story in which three young protagonists, Liliane (Yveline Céry), Juliette (Stefania Sabatini) and the ambivalent object of their amorous affection, Michel (Jean-Claude Aimini) are forced to reconcile the romantic complications and responsibilities associated with the transition from youth to young adulthood. In the first half of the film, the three lovers spend their days hanging around Paris – a city caught up in the dizzying waves of modernisation engulfing the country more generally – before resolving to embark on an impromptu holiday in Corsica. The brief happiness granted by this trip is, however, cut short at the end of the film, when Michel is forced to leave the island to perform his duty as a conscript.

The home as haven

As Jean Collet points out in a 1963 article, published in *L'Avant-scène du cinéma*, *Adieu Philippine* is a somewhat mercurial film, torn between 'sorrow and innocence' (6), melancholia and euphoria, politicisation and depoliticisation. Melancholic in the sense that, as the spectator quickly uncovers, Michel is an individual destined for what could quite possibly be a swift death as a conscript in Algeria. It is this death, this destiny, that hangs over Michel's head like a sword of Damocles, causing him to ricochet between brio and bitterness. Consider, for example, the ways in which Michel ominously implores Juliette to read his lifeline when they attend a military airshow together at Bourget, shading the art of palmistry with the pathos of tragedy. Or when he impulsively quits his job as a television cable-man so he can experience the pleasures of freedom and unbridled lust at Club Med (a seaside resort in Corsica), before he is called up for military service (addressing a friend, he reasons: 'even if they don't fire me, I want to get away before the army'). Or when he embarks from the waterfront to the war front at the port of Calvi, a scene that, as Antoine De Baecque has illustrated, involves coded allusions to the horror of warfare through the violence of the lyrics[1] stitched into the soundtrack, sung in Corsican (2012: 144). Fleeting though they may be, all of these moments taint the film with a poignancy as emotional as it is pacifist. War is all that Michel can think about.

Contrasting with Michel's world, politicised by decolonisation, however, is Liliane and Juliette's world, depoliticised by modernisation, with both women exhibiting traits of 'innocence, childishness and impertinence' characteristic of the *gamine*, or young girl, a stock character of the New Wave (Vincendeau 2000: 94, 117). From the opening scenes of *Adieu Philippine*, Paris, for Liliane and Juliette, is therefore a hyper-mediatised and infantilised audio-visual playground, fizzing with the pleasures of consumption: objects and things, make-up and hygiene, clothes and commodities. It is a city of leisure through which they saunter – insouciant, irreverent, irresponsible – a city of halcyon youth. All doors open to them, everybody obeys them, nobody criticises them; they are capricious consumers who bend everything and everyone to their will. No matter if the two young women are patently unqualified and brazenly unprofessional, job opportunities in televisual advertising are, somehow, constantly thrown at them, by Michel and others. The result is two scenes swollen with surreal domestic humour: one for a cleaning product named O'Poil 54, the other for fridges, both of which may tip over into farce – thus, in turn, lightly poking fun at the patriarchal values ingrained within contemporaneous discourses of domesticity – yet neither of which displays a radical interrogation of 'the exploitation of women as an image in consumer society' (MacCabe and Mulvey 1989: 50).[2] Writes Geneviève Sellier, 'associated with the society of consumption', women in films such as *Adieu Philippine* 'symbolize its alienating effects by transforming themselves into merchandise for the best price, and thus bear little in common with sexually and socially emancipated media figures like Sagan or Bardot' (2008: 20). Ignorant of the patriarchal foundations of capitalism, or the racialised foundations of colonialism, Liliane and Juliette inhere in a superficial image-world that has everything to do with domestic-consumerist fantasy and very little to do with the Algerian War of Independence, a war they neither understand nor care about.

It is precisely for these reasons that Sellier is critical of *Adieu Philippine*, citing a short yet emotionally stark scene that occurs towards the end of the film – when Michel rebukes Juliette and Liliane for failing to comprehend the gravity of his future, whilst they meander by car through the landscape of Corsica – as both evidence of Rozier's misogynistic yoking of female identity and depoliticisation, and the 'derisive laughter that gives the narrative its dominant tone' (2008: 120). Deduces Sellier: 'for the boy, these are his last pleasures before the war and maybe, before his death; for the girls, it's all part and parcel of their derisive nature as shopgirls' (2008: 120). Equally absorbed by depoliticisation and derision is an earlier scene, set amidst the tastefully furnished walls of an apartment owned by Liliane's parents, and during which Liliane and Juliette blithely contemplate the topic of conscription ('I hate going out with soldiers ... he can't leave ... What can we do?': Liliane). Here, the war is 'de-dramatised' in a number of ways (Bénédict 2001: 85). First, it is notable that this scene does not in any sense express the war visually, either through the type of military photographs that crop up in both Jacques Demy's *Les Parapluies de Cherbourg/The Umbrellas of Cherbourg* (1964; see Chapter 5), and Resnais's aforementioned *Muriel ou le temps d'un retour*, or through the equally visual – yet still more arresting – archival footage of military atrocities to which we are impelled at the start of *La Belle vie* (see below). Instead, by filtering the war through the prism of fictional diegetic dialogue, Rozier presents the spectator with a vastly mediated, and hence distorted, oral account of it: distorted insofar as this account occurs whilst Liliane and Juliette shuttle around the apartment whilst chattering – from bedroom to bedroom and from bedroom to kitchen – constantly preventing us from acquiring epistemological certainty over what is said, and evoking Richard Neupert's reading of *Adieu Philippine* as couched in 'flawed sound-to-image relations' (2011: 36). And distorted insofar as the two *gamines* have neither participated in combat like French soldiers or Algerian nationalists; nor have they intervened in the wider late-colonial debate like intellectuals such as Simone de Beauvoir, but instead thrive in a self-abnegating realm of negatives fueled by two attendant compulsions: a yearning to possess Michel, and a yearning to possess things.

Given that much of this scene consists of images of Liliane and Juliette doing little more than listening to a cha-cha record, one of the many strewn about the former's clean and modestly sized bedroom, its walls conspicuously adorned with pictures of Hollywood movie stars and musicians (Mario Lanza, Elvis Presley, Leny Eversong), here we might forge comparisons between *Adieu Philippine* and the culture of the *copines* (female friends) that proliferated in France during the years of decolonisation; a 'naïve youth culture' founded upon a tripartite focus on female singers (Françoise Hardy, Sylvie Vartan, Sheila), de-sexualised fashion, and pervasive Americophilia (Weiner 2001: 148). In its focus on naivety, this scene also recalls Simone de Beauvoir's notion of 'the Lolita syndrome': a contemporaneous cultural phenomenon predicated upon a similar rendition of French women as neither vamps nor femmes fatales but infantilised 'nymphets' (1962: 10). According to Beauvoir, this phenomenon could be seen most evidently in the culturally constructed body of Brigitte Bardot, although the author's account of the latter is clearly reminiscent of how Rozier imagines female French identity in the scene parsed above: '[Bardot] is without memory, without a past, and thanks to this ignorance, she retains the perfect innocence that is attributed to a mythical childhood' (1962: 18). Anchored to the depoliticised and de-sexualised imaginary of the *gamines*, *copines* and Lolita syndrome, it is therefore unsurprising that almost as soon as Liliane has broached the politics of the war in this scene, Juliette does steer the conversation into unequivocally apolitical territory, crafting an incongruous analogy between military footwear sported by soldiers in Algeria, and high-heeled footwear sported by women in Paris. 'Oh those massive shoes, they're so ugly. Personally, I only like delicate shoes' (Figure 1.1).

But perhaps the most telling – and depoliticising – element of this infantile interaction can be found in neither what is said, nor how it is spoken, nor even who speaks, but rather how it is shot (using a fluid, Jean Renoiresque, cycle of full shots, mid shots, long takes, and tracking shots, all of which convey a high degree of visual exposition about the mise-en-scène), and where it takes place. In the first instance, it is significant that Liliane's apartment is tastefully decorated with precisely the type of consumer durables that were advertised in the culture of privatisation from the period: a cooker, fridge, record player, telephone and hairdryer, all of which frame this space as a technocentric microcosm of hygiene and modernity; one untainted by any trace of France's 'dirty' and 'archaic' past in Algeria. In the second instance, it is worth pointing out the abiding – almost blinding – presence of whiteness that dominates the mise-en-scène of Liliane's dwelling: from the walls to the worktops, from the fridge to the faces of the two friends, who, after all, are both white; even the bedsheets upon which Liliane

Figure 1.1 Liliane (right) and Juliette (left) perched together in the former's privatised apartment.

and Juliette eventually curl up together are bleached white, as are their cotton nightclothes. Racially, sexually, ethically, and intertextually, this whiteness operates on several levels. Racially, it forms an oblique allusion to how France dealt with revelations about its 'dark' colonial past by launching into a collective campaign of whitening, expressed most notably in the aforementioned sandblasting of architectural facades in Paris, which 'ensured the invisibility of alterity' – of racial and ethnic Otherness – 'within the urban fabric of the capital' (Feldman 2014: 74). Sexually, it mirrors the infantile naivety of the two young *gamines*, with Jean Baudrillard defining whiteness as a 'surgical, virginal colour' that was elevated to a similar state of omnipresence in domestic advertisements from the era ([1968] 2005: 33; also see Barthes [1957] 1989a). Ethically, it generates an even more elliptical – yet even more insistent – ambience of purity, with Susan Weiner concluding that 'the complicity between Liliane and Juliette signifies innocence, a world removed from and untouched by wartime, whose most natural context is the childish décor of Liliane's bedroom' (2001: 158, 159). And intertextually, it positions *Adieu Philippine* in relation to Varda's abovementioned *Cléo de 5 à 7*, in which the eponymous white/blonde protagonist of the narrative lives in a similarly achromatic abode; one that Valerie Orpen likens to a Watteau painting (2007: 11). Both Rozier and Varda's films in this respect represent the home as a haven; a superlatively whitened space in which female French citizens shield themselves against the 'dark', 'dirty' and, above all, guilty effects of the war.

Domestic redemption

An alternative example of this motif – through which anxieties related to the war are allayed through depoliticised scenes of privatisation – occurs when Michel returns home to dine with his parents (Maurice Garrel, Arlette Gilbert), their guest-neighbours (Charles Lavialle, Jeanne Perez), and Dédé (Pierre Frag), an old acquaintance who, we learn through snippets of dialogue, has just come back from Algeria, although it is unclear what his role there was (Figure 1.2). Seemingly prosaic, it is a scene whose screenplay has, however, been subjected to sustained critical analysis, including an illuminating yet somewhat reductive article by Michel Marie and Francis Vanoye (1983), who identify, 'between the shots of banal conversation and culinary excess, a number of unspoken, quiet, and silent taboos (the war, the anxiety and resentment of youth, the guilt and impotence of parents)' (1983: 73). 'Resentment' is perhaps a misleading word: certainly neither Michel nor Dédé, the two young adults present here, act in an expressly hostile way towards their hosts. It is only when Michel's parents chastise him for co-buying a car with their finances that he exhibits some kind of ire towards them, however fleeting (he sardonically states that they aren't going to die for having lent him money). So too for what Marie and Vanoye identify as the 'impotence' of Michel's parents, who may be irritated, even exasperated, but certainly do not succumb to the gentle petulance of their child. Indeed, if we had to assign an attribute to Michel's mother and father, it would

Figure 1.2 Michel (above) and Dédé (below), surrounded by the former's family and guest-neighbours.

arguably not be 'impotence' but benevolence. After all, theirs is a household that turns around what appears to be an instinctive, almost quasi-religious credo of giving: giving food, giving advice, giving others space to talk, giving Michel's friend Dédé a space at the table. As with the visions of privatised domesticity propagated in contemporaneous cultural discourses, their world is a world full of good things, offered freely and indiscriminately; it is a world of imaginary plentitude. 'Guilty' they are not.

Likewise, the interior of their detached single-family suburban dwelling, known in France as a *pavillon*, strikes nothing less than a perfect balance between traditional living and modern living, recalling Lefebvre's reading of suburban *pavillons* as symbolically rooted in the notion of splendid, apolitical isolation (1966: 4). Clean, spacious, light and private (in the sense that it is impervious to the voices or gazes of outsiders), as with the apartment in which Liliane lives, almost everything that populates this room appears geared towards enfolding the dweller in a superlative state of comfort: from the old photos perched atop the furniture, to the familiar landscape paintings pinned to the walls, right down to the radio and TV that lie dormant in adjacent corners, ready to lull listeners and viewers into a state of languid stasis in one of the chairs clustered around the dinner table. It from this table that the veritable cornucopia of food arranged for the guests is devoured: pig's head, washed down with lashings of red wine – a drink whose mythosemiotic imagery, according to Roland Barthes, functioned in the collective unconscious 'as an alibi', serving 'to dream and redeem' – evoking, once again, Ross's aforementioned notion of 'redemptive hygiene' (1995: 75; see Sharpe 2017 for more details). And it is around this dinner table, and within this home, this private haven, that the beatific faces of the diners peer at each other, smile at each other, laugh with each other, laugh about each other, conversing convivially and ludically about time present and time past. Apart from Dédé.

Physiognomically, corporeally and vocally, in this scene at least, Dédé is poles apart from his war-bound companion, Michel. So, unlike Michel, who swaggers into his parents' abode with insouciance, reeling off anecdotes and jokes to the other more or less engaged diners, Dédé clasps the hands of his hosts with candor upon arrival, before removing himself, discreetly, from their volley of verbal exchanges. Furthermore, where Michel's vestimentary habits turn around bright light sweaters (when he isn't strolling bare chested along the beaches of Corsica), Dédé opts for the comparatively modest angles of a white shirt and black blazer. Not that the spectator is granted much time to scrutinise his attire. For the majority of the meal, Dédé remains merely a darkened blot that languishes at the bottom of the frame, his back turned to the camera, whilst Michel, positioned at the apex of on-screen space, literally and symbolically dominates his guests. It is only right at the end of this scene that the spectator is granted access to Dédé's tender face, when Michel's father abruptly addresses

Figure 1.3 A reticent Dédé surrounded by diners.

him: 'so what have you got to tell us?'. 'Nothing, nothing, nothing', he replies, as Rozier cuts to a mid-shot of his impassive expression (Figure 1.3).[3]

Much has been made of the significance of Dédé, and what his character reveals, or doesn't, or precisely does because he doesn't, about the war, and about how the war was represented in cinematic narratives of the era. First, in terms of behaviour, Dédé's politeness, gratitude and respectability, as much as the exuberant – vindicating – reception that he is granted by Michel's parents, encourages us to understand him as a morally redeemed individual: as somebody who has been destabilised by a past over which he has endeavoured to gain control and succeeded. Sébastian Bénédict, for one, has talked eloquently about this dining scene, conceiving it as a 'joyous' moment during which 'reality' is eclipsed by 'reverie' (2001: 84), and, in turn, evoking Raya Morag's assertion that 'members of societies that facilitate perpetration by putting soldiers in atrocity-producing situations are not interested in perpetrators acknowledging the traumatic deeds carried out in their name' (2013: 8). Secondly, by casting Dédé as a conspicuously reticent character, Rozier may invite us to acknowledge the omission of his testimony from the film, with Fabrizio Cilento, for instance, talking about how this scene exemplifies 'the impossibility of communicating the experience of the war' (2018: 78–9), but Dédé's quasi-silence, as well as his gently searching gaze, also generates an abiding impression of trauma and victimhood: two attendant conditions carried by a former soldier who 'has been hunted and known fear' (De Baecque 2012: 143). Indeed, according to scholars such as Daniel Zimmerman (1989: 8–9), Bernard Sigg (1989: 18), and Raphaëlle Branche (2005: 16; 2020: 10), conscripts returning from French Algeria in the non-cinematic realm often used silence as a psycho-ethical tactic: to preserve the possibility of being judged innocent of the crimes in which they had become complicit, just as a criminal may reiterate the expression 'no comment' when faced with questions from law enforcement. It is for this reason that Branche has diagnosed the collective silence of the conscripts as a 'pact' (2005: 67), musing upon one particularly telling piece of testimony provided by a soldier named François Richou ('people said that I was silent, but the interrogations, the tortures, the executions, these guilty stories, they can't be told' [cited in Branche 2020: 265]), whilst Sigg deploys a more psychoanalytically inflected lexicon to designate the same phenomenon, talking instead about the dynamics of shame and self-censorship (1989: 19). Clearly driven by a similar desire to preserve his reputation – that is to say, to censor himself, to respect the 'pact' that had been crafted by his fellow veterans – Dédé thus exits this scene as ethically unscathed by the debate that swirls around him. Acting as both an alibi and a carapace, Dédé's silence is his sanctum.

Curiously, for a film whose title obliquely alludes to the departure of conscripts, *Adieu* – goodbye – *Philippine*[4] is much less focused on the two young men who have left or will leave for war (Dédé and Michel, respectively), and much more fixated on the individuals left behind in this exit: young women and members of the older generation. The former, embedded within a world of whiteness and depoliticised to the point of derision, convince themselves that the war is something to be ignored, an abstract event played out on a horizon far removed from the interior island of Liliane's apartment. The latter, meanwhile, help to convince a silent Dédé that the war is something to be forgotten, an awkward, distant, memory that has no place amidst the ethically redeeming animation of a family meal. Nobody in *Adieu Philippine*, it seems, is avowedly guilty or even dimly conscious of the colonial atrocities being committed in French Algeria. Not Michel, not Dédé, not the blissfully naïve Liliane and Juliette; certainly not Michel's family. Instead, Rozier presents the spectator with a world of 'innocence, before rupture, before pain' (Collet 1963: 6), where shimmering stainless-steel worktops and plush settees provide the opportunity for an act of collective expiation from implication in colonial crimes. Just like in Robert Enrico's *La Belle vie*, to which we now turn.

La Belle vie (1964)

In contrast to Jacques Rozier, Robert Enrico quickly proved himself to be a competent and respected director, graduating from the prestigious film school, the Institute for Advanced Cinematographic Studies (*L'Institut des hautes études cinématographiques*, IDHEC), in 1951; completing his military service at the

Armed Forces Cinematographic Service, which produced pro-army media in Algeria from 1956 to 1959; before filming *La Belle vie*, his first full-length film, in the latter half of 1962, with the financial support of an 'advance against earnings' (*avance sur recettes*). However, despite being awarded the enviable Prix Jean-Vigo in 1963, the publication of a long interview with Enrico in *Image et son* (Arnault and Cobast 1964), and a three-page review in *Positif* (Torok 1964), *La Belle vie* was a commercial disaster. One reason for this lack of success was that, unlike Rozier's film, *La Belle vie* was temporarily banned for approaching the war from a less oblique perspective, with the screenplay being notably based on testimonies collected from conscripts. *La Belle vie* was eventually released on January 22, 1964, in mutilated form, although, as with Rozier, Enrico experienced significant problems with distribution. According to Enrico, 'people just stopped talking about it' (Arnault and Cobast 1964: 73). Since the 1960s, *La Belle vie* has acquired a somewhat elusive status in cultural histories of the period. Whilst often evoked in general discussions about decolonisation, cinema and censorship, apart from a short reappraisal of the film by Jean-Paul Fargier (2014), critics rarely dedicate more than a few lines to the film.[5]

Set in July 1961, *La Belle vie* focuses upon the figure of Frédéric (Frédéric de Pasquale), a conscript returning to France after twenty-seven months of military service, and his childhood sweetheart Sylvie (Josée Steiner), a hairdresser, whom Frédéric quickly marries upon his arrival home. The couple embark upon an extravagant honeymoon to Monte Carlo, paid for by Sylvie's older, rich friends, before returning to Paris in order to start their new life as a married couple. However, as the film shows, this period is also marked by a series of personal and political problems, at first linked to Frédéric's inability to adjust to the everyday reality of demobilisation, especially as he is initially unemployed and apparently traumatised by the war; second, as Sylvie quickly becomes pregnant;[6] and last, due to the climate of racialised police surveillance and violence that gripped the capital during the later stages of decolonisation. Eventually, Frédéric manages to earn enough money to buy a new, much larger modernist apartment located on the outskirts of the city. However, as the film ends, the brief period of domestic happiness afforded by this purchase is cut short when Frédéric is suddenly recalled for military service.

Frédéric's domestic dream

Despite being a fictional narrative, *La Belle vie* begins with a montage of archival footage, in which French paratroopers are seen performing military operations in rural and urban French Algeria. According to the credits, these images were generated by *Les Actualités françaises*, one of the five companies responsible for producing newsreels shown in cinemas before film screenings – a curious precursor to televised news – at least until 1969, when the stratospheric rise of television, enabled by privatisation, effectively rendered the service defunct (Desbois 1997: 22–4). Consisting of subtly subversive[7] footage of paras running towards or away from the sound of not-so-distant artillery, these are images that strike an immediate contrast with the elliptical allusions to conflict articulated in many of the fictional films discussed in this book, for example *Adieu Philippine*. In the latter, death is a distant nebula, a cloudy spot in the field of vision, a contingent something that hovers conditionally somewhere, a hazard Dédé might have been exposed to in the past, like Michel might be exposed to in the future. In the former, death is all-consuming, inescapable, a towering threat, which, like other documentary representations of mortality, 'represents the invisible state of nonbeing' (Sobchack 1984: 287). Death is here and death is now.

Luckily, it is a threat from which Frédéric has escaped, geographically and psychically. Geographically, in the sense that, in the very next scene, Frédéric, we learn, has been granted leave, or what is known in French as *la quille*. Tucked away in a suburban train bound for Paris, stretching into the night, far away from Algeria, and far away from death, Frédéric curls himself up into a foetal position in the corner of a carriage, his eyes closed, on the cusp of sleep. Psychically, in the sense that this journey coincides with a formally dazzling dramatisation of a lucid waking dream, experienced by Frédéric, and that will transport him even farther away from the visceral landscape of violence visualised at the start of the film. Discussing the enduring appeal of Freudian psychoanalysis, Vicky Lebeau has succinctly defined the figure of the daydreamer as someone 'who is withdrawn from the world', whilst the phenomenon of the daydream, according to Lebeau, 'involves the creation of a world apart' (2001: 35). Certainly, in *La Belle vie*, Frédéric is prone to the type of daydreams evoked by Lebeau, the first of which begins right here, amidst the corridors of the train. Thus, as the carriages exit from the tenebrous confines of a tunnel, the whiteness of impending bright sky, captured in a dizzyingly rapid tracking shot from atop the front carriage, imperceptibly slides into the whiteness of freshly fallen snow, snow that covers the ground of an immobilised city. It is here that diegetic images of Frédéric's world as he perceives it yield to apperceptive images of Frédéric's world as he imagines it, images which show what might have been or might yet be. With the screen transforming into a projection of Frédéric's mind, over the course of the following few minutes, the spectator is thus presented with a curious glimpse into his psyche, as images of Paris flicker into focus, and Frédéric begins to speak:[8]

> The *quartier*. My *quartier*. How lucky I am to live in Paris. Notre Dame in Paris: Kilometer Zero. I live just next to it. Rue de la Huchette. There, on the left, number 13. It's on the sixth floor, no lift. A little attic

room [*une chambre de bonne*], on the roof, up there, right above Paris. Rue Saint-Séverin, La rue du Chat-qui-Pêche, and others. They're the smallest streets in Paris. The snow here melts slower than anywhere else. My *quartier* is the capital of Paris. Between the river and the mountain [presumably a reference to Montmartre], between Saint Ginette and Luxembourg, and its gardens. Ah . . . It's a kingdom, it's my kingdom. In a few hours I will be down there. I don't believe it.

Temporally, aesthetically and ontologically, Frédéric's fantasy could not be further removed from the painful newsreel footage that bursts into on-screen space during the opening credits of the film. There, soldiers scrambled for cover in a vast, insensate no man's land. Here, people stroll through benevolent streets shimmering with shops, jazz and dancing. There, unknown men were embalmed in the objectivity of newsreels. Here, Frédéric fictionalises his own subjective narrative, providing an example of a more general trend in Enrico's films, which 'often simulate inner life processes that involve abstraction and unfettered movement in time and space' (Simonet and Enrico 1974: 59). There, Algeria was a nightmare, here, Paris is a dream. As Jean Paul Torok perceives, 'in the comfort of his return, Frédéric forgets everything: the patrols, the long nights spent on the peaks of the Aurès Mountains [in Algeria], the ambushes, the fear' (1964: 83). In fact, the more we consider the curious thematics of Frédéric's psychic projections – and, in particular, his insistence on establishing the coordinates of his domestic 'kingdom', which trumps concerns about his partner, for example – the more this scene appears as an individualised expression of the collective fantasies of privatisation analysed by Lefebvre, Ross and others. Ross's assertion that 'privatised space exemplified a flight from violence and history to security and permanence', for example, certainly evokes the lyricism of Frédéric's homo-diegetic soliloquy (1995: 179, 180). In the anticipatory fever of Frédéric's thoughts, home will function as a haven, as it does for Juliette, Liliane and Dédé (Figures 1.4 and 1.5).

It soon becomes clear that there is at least a degree of difference between how Frédéric imagines *la belle vie* of *la quille*, and how he experiences it. In his fantasy, for instance, Frédéric's neighbourhood positively teems with bodies and voices, bearing out a widely held perception that the Latin Quarter had become, in the 1950s, one of the 'most liberal and deliciously shocking *quartiers* in Paris' (Marchand 1993: 294), associated with a new generation of provocative intellectuals (Maurice Blanchot, Jean-Paul Sartre, Georges Bataille), who exchanged their ideas precisely in the type of overground cafes and underground *caves* that wind through the streets of Frédéric's daydreams. Yet, as the couple discover after returning from their honeymoon, this turns out not to be the case. Instead, the Latin Quarter emerges as a *quartier* under siege, contaminated with the very patterns of political violence that Frédéric thinks

Figure 1.4 Frédéric daydreams of his Parisian apartment during his return to the capital.

Figure 1.5 Frédéric daydreams of his Parisian apartment during his return to the capital.

he has left behind in Algeria. In *La Belle vie*, symptoms of the 'gangrenous' (Torok 1964) spread of violence are everywhere in the city's topography: from the police officers that perform stop and searches outside Frédéric's apartment (the couple are frisked, before witnessing an unidentified man subjected to the same treatment), to the returning conscripts that languish in local bars, bored and alone; from the paratrooper that parades on the top of a car through the city, to Frédéric's motorbike, that he finds one morning, charred beyond recognition, presumably by a bomb planted by the proto-fascistic, pro-colonial group the OAS (see Introduction), after he has suffered a prophetic nightmare about explosions in the capital.[9] *La Belle vie* even goes so far as to include archival footage linked to two of the most notorious examples of police violence in French history, conducted on 17 October 1961 and 8 February 1962 (see Chapter 7).[10] In each case, Paris assumes the guise of a quasi-war zone, colonised by the radicalisation of politics generated by decolonisation.

Embodying the 60 per cent of the population who identified as neither of the Right nor of the Left, Frédéric, it is important to stress, is not a man committed to political engagement – be that anti-colonial activism, support for Algerian nationalism, or even anti-war militancy – but rather someone who is unequivocally, and unapologetically, 'apolitical' (Arnault and Cobast 1964: 74). Often this lack of political engagement expresses itself as a perceptual negation. Like Dédé, Frédéric does not want to hear about or talk about what he has experienced in Algeria. On the odd occasion that Sylvie attempts to broach the subject, mutism – the refusal to speak – prevails. Nor does he want to see the colonial-military 'gangrene' that has encroached upon his *quartier*. When the couple first crosses the threshold into Frédéric's domestic 'kingdom', for instance, Enrico intersperses a high angle shot of police officers patrolling the street, with mid, interior shots of Frédéric, who guides Sylvie around his dwelling to her delight, as if it were a hotel, stating, in a tone of voice tinged with false formality, 'on your left, the power sockets, on your right, the kitchen cabinet; the windows look out onto the ocean'. The *quartier* might have been swept up into a maelstrom by patterns of state repression that were, for Algerians at least, so heavy-handed that they verged on terror, but here, perched on an island of domestic space, in their *chambre de bonne*, a space teased once again into splendour by Frédéric's imagination, everything is calm, the couple is safe. They kiss.

Other times, Frédéric's lack of political engagement expresses itself as a territorial retreat: from the public space of the street to the private space of his apartment. One short yet significant example of this behaviour occurs when Frédéric is seen walking alone at a fairground, a scene possibly inspired by Jean Herman's *Actua-tilt* (1961; see Introduction), a film set amidst an amusement arcade cum café, cluttered with visually and sonically jarring games and off duty soldiers, or perhaps Jean-Luc Godard's *Vivre sa vie/To Live Her Life* (1962), which includes a similar scene, blending images of pinball machines, verbal allusions to politics and non-diegetic sounds of machine-gun fire (Betz 2009: 149). As Frédéric plaintively approaches a mock shooting range surrounded by conscripts, Enrico amplifies the diegetic sounds of ammunition generated by the attraction to phantasmagoric dimensions, the result being that we experience the same hallucinatory auditory overload that he experiences, or rather, suffers. Drawn into the subjective undertow of memories repressed yet involuntarily evoked, Frédéric, over-stimulated and over-agitated, is nothing but overcome by this masquerade of violence, which for the conscripts may be artificial, but for him is all too real. So much so that he swiftly returns home, sequestering himself in the soft and silent sanctum of his bedroom, or, more specifically, his bed, just like Juliette and Liliane do in *Adieu Philippine*.

Whether withdrawing into the immateriality of a domestic life dreamt, or the materiality of a domestic dream lived, Frédéric is thus someone whose *modus vivendi*, whose way of life, telegraphs the collective desire to be safe at home that gripped the French nation during the years of decolonisation: he dreams of privatisation privately as the nation did publicly. But, as the narrative progresses, it is also possible to identify a shift in the ways in which Enrico represents Frédéric's relationship to his milieu: from the type of domestic capitulation identified above, in his *chambre de bonne*, to a much more aggressive proclivity towards domestic acquisition. Less and less satisfied with exploiting his domestic 'kingdom' as a sanctuary, Frédéric increasingly demands to touch, grasp, and *possess* it, and all that surrounds it.

'Paris belongs to us'

One of the first things that Frédéric does after having surreptitiously located Sylvie in an underground concert venue in Paris is give her a bejewelled beetle pendant. The gesture might seem altruistic enough were it not for the fact that, as Frédéric explains, the beetle symbolises a loyalty that he, in turn, expects from her. It is also a gesture that belies the ethos of a man who measures his self-worth in the reflection of possessions he has acquired, such as the mechanical equipment that Frédéric wields to capture his clients in his capacity as a professional photographer. Or the photos of women that Frédéric clandestinely consults at various points in the film, some of which form part of a secret photographic archive, housed in the drawers of his desk, others which he pins to the walls of his work-space, creating a rudimentary private gallery. Or the bodies of the multiple women with whom Frédéric indulges in extramarital affairs, shading his initial gift to Sylvie with a dark irony, and supporting the findings of a sociological survey conducted in 1961, which identified one of the defining traits of the New Wave in 'the almost complete sexualisation of male figures' (Bremond et al. 1961: 170). Indeed, out of the four young women who inhabit the film – an unnamed tour guide with whom Frédéric briefly works as a photographer (Lucienne Hamon), his cover-girl lover Kiki (Odile Geoffroy), an old flame named Christiane (Françoise Giret) and, of course, Sylvie – not one escapes his charms. Like Michel in *Adieu Philippine*, Thomas in Alain Cavalier's 1964 *L'Insoumis/The Unvanquished* (Chapter 2), Paul in Jacques Dupont's 1960 *Les Distractions/Trapped by Fear* (Chapter 3), and Pierre in Philippe Durand's 1961 *Secteur postal 89098/Postal Sector 89098* (Chapter 5), Frédéric treats women like suppliant and superficial commodities, either as torsos to be photographed or faces to be caressed, yet rarely as anything other than capricious curios to be acquired and archived by his own, grasping hands.

Acquisition is likewise the subject of a compelling article by Roland-François Lack, who situates the film in relation to a contemporaneous cinematic tendency to promote Paris as 'a continuous spectacle', endowed with 'a commodity culture engineered for consumption', and populated with women eroticised as objects (2010: 135). For Lack, the clearest example of this imagery in *La Belle vie* occurs when the couple indulge in a spending spree on the Champs-Élysées after Frédéric is granted a providential advertising contract, and during which a freelance street photographer, incidentally played by Pierre Frag, who plays Dédé in *Adieu Philippine*, captures an image of the couple as they stroll along the street (Figure 1.6). Fanning himself with a wad of banknotes in a taxi to the centre, Frédéric is suddenly a man endowed with the power to translate

Figure 1.6 A freelance street photographer (right) takes a photo of Frédéric and Sylvie whilst shopping.

labour into financial gain, and financial gain into material possessions. Hence the panoply of presents he buys Sylvie, before seducing her in a changing room (bolstering the impression that she is financially and emotionally dependent on him), but also, more importantly, the vast apartment that they – he – can now afford. When Frédéric declares, in a voice positively ringing with the wonders of capitalism, 'Paris belongs to us' (echoing the title of Rivette's film, *Paris nous appartient*, discussed in Chapter 5), what he really means is Paris, like his wife, belongs to *him*. For all intents and purposes, Sylvie is nothing but a puppet in *La Belle vie*. Like Liliane and Juliette, she understands nothing about Frédéric's military past in Algeria – she too is totally depoliticised – yet accepts his morally bankrupt behaviour with a propensity towards self-abnegation that often resembles a Judeo-Christian ethics of abasement. Leafing through the pages of *Elle* magazine with mute deference, her sole and meagre wish, it seems, is to be part of the privatised fantasy that Frédéric, himself, dreams into reality.

In *La Belle vie*, a circular wheel of consumption is thus set in motion: the more objects, things and spaces Frédéric acquires, the more his ego, damaged in the loss of France's most prized colony, is replenished, rehabilitated and redeemed; and the more Frédéric exercises his subjectivity, recasting himself as a paragon of patriarchy, the more Sylvie is prevented from exercising hers. Much less a political exposé than an exploration of masculine identity, the coda of Enrico's film thus concludes this ontological quest for a state of belonging, through the acquisition of material belongings, when Frédéric eventually decides to erect his 'kingdom' in a low cost *HLM* apartment (*habitation à loyer modéré*), located in one of the high-rise housing blocks, known as *les grands ensembles*, that flourished in France from the mid 1930s until the late 1960s. Examining architectural photographs produced by the state, Raphaële Bertho has identified the early 1960s as a 'rhapsodic', even 'mythical' moment in the history of *les grands ensembles*, insofar as there was widespread consensus, shared amongst urban planners, government officials and urban dwellers alike, that these modernist monoliths, erected according to the aesthetics of statistical architecture and an ethics of *existenzminimum* (subsistence dwelling), could potentially offer a solution to the interminable problem of housing (2014: 3). Such an idealised belief in this visionary project was to some extent justified: in 1964, at least, 90 per cent of people living in an *HLM* in a *grand ensemble* considered themselves to be 'comfortably housed' (Marchand 1993: 286).

It is also a belief that, judging by the final two scenes of *La Belle vie*, the film not only endorses, but positively exalts, generating an undeniable series of parallels between Dédé and Frédéric, both of whom find redemption in the privatised space of the home. In the first of these scenes, the couple host a house-warming party, during which the private rooms of their abode, in a curious scene of transposition, are shown to be capable of generating precisely the verve and vitality that were so sorely lacking from the 'gangrenous' public streets of the Latin Quarter. One partygoer waltzes in brandishing a clarinet, others furnish the couple's apartment with gifts and accoutrements, including a huge photo of Notre Dame, delivered to Frédéric with an affirmation of absolute acquisition: 'now you have *everything*, the apartment and a view over your *quartier* [emphasis added by author]'. Everyone dances, anxieties are allayed, even when the guests stray, as the soiree ends, into the isolated penumbra of the environs. The second scene, by contrast, chronicles the soft and saccharine aftermath of these festivities, when Enrico depicts Sylvie cradled in Frédéric's arms amidst the gossamer folds of their expansive double bed (Figure 1.7). Comfort reigns as Frédéric's benign face assumes the countenance of a man whose (day)dreams of possessing a blissfully privatised interior space, capable of housing the empire of objects he has acquired, have exquisitely come true. Reeling from the loss of France's 'kingdom' in Algeria, Frédéric builds his own.

Or so it seems. Bearing witness, once again, to the aforementioned ambivalence of a film that pulls the spectator in many different directions – at once political, aesthetic and spatial – *La Belle vie* concludes with an event that, on the face of it, appears to subvert the very ideological foundations upon which the narrative is constructed, when Frédéric is recalled for military service the morning after his housewarming party. Above all others, it is this scene that has provoked the most critical discord amongst journalists and scholars, some of whom are convinced that it exposes the consumerist narrative crafted by

Figure 1.7 Frédéric and Sylvie cocooned in their home-as-haven.

the couple as a fragile 'illusion', susceptible to obliteration at any time (Daniel 1972: 348); others who understand it as historically illusory, given that by July 1961, when the film is set, the French state was no longer recalling reservists such as Frédéric (Guibbert 1992: 248); still others, like Jean-Luc Comolli, for whom the ending was 'ideologically illusory' insofar as it 'generated the impression of a politically committed film', when, in reality, it was a 'soft advertisement for images of bourgeois comfort, the tranquillity of the soul, and romantic calm, all of which unfortunately preclude an engagement with politics' (1963: 21). Wary of falling into a facile reading of what is undeniably a complex, and frequently contradictory, narrative, I am more inclined to agree with Comolli on the matter, primarily as, lest we forget, up until this moment, *La Belle vie* features no less than sixty minutes of fictional footage which encourage us to condone 'the needs and advantages of a peaceful consumer society keen to forget the Empire that had just been taken from it' (Eades 2006: 145). Not only that, but it is also in the whiplash ending of *La Belle vie* that the existential tempest consuming Frédéric is at its most pronounced. Neither guilty of perpetrating, nor implicated in abetting, nor even dimly cognisant of any of the atrocities being committed by the army in French Algeria, Frédéric, like Michel and Dédé, is ultimately framed as an innocent victim of a war beyond his control.

Notes

1. De Baecque provides a translation of these lyrics: 'if you fail to put a ring on my finger before leaving for duty, may a shower of bullets burn your brain'.
2. As seen, for example, within Jean-Luc Godard's 1963 *Le Mépris/Contempt*, Simone de Beauvoir's 1966 *Les Belles Images/Pretty Pictures*, and Chantal Akerman's *Saute ma ville/Blow Up My Town* (1968), in which a young housewife (played by Akerman) performs an increasingly disruptive set of domestic duties in her modernised kitchen before annihilating herself with a bomb.
3. Undoubtably the most famous reading of Rozier's film has been performed by Christian Metz, as part of his theory of the Grande Syntagmatique. Forming a 'typology of the diverse ways in which time and space can be ordered through editing within the segments of narrative film' (Stam 2004: 115), Metz's Grande Syntagmatique may have been influential as a methodology in film theory; however, in its aesthetic formalism, inspired by semiology and structural linguistics, it nevertheless tended to drain the films in question of their historical and political relevance (Stam 2004: 117). It is interesting to note in this respect that Metz simply defines the shot from Michel's father to Dédé's non-answer 'as two distinct syntagmas' ([1974] 1991: 155–156), without mentioning anything related to the war.
4. Somewhat convolutedly, the title of Rozier's film appears to have been based upon a 'game' in France, played whenever two almonds are found in the same shell. According to the rules of this game, the person who makes this discovery is obliged

to eat one of the almonds, and give the other to a person of the opposite gender. When the two people in question next meet, a competition then ensues, with the person who first cries 'Bonjour Philippine' being crowned the winner. Liliane and Juliette actually play this game before sleeping in the same bed together, although, of course, Rozier alters the name slightly to reflect Michel's departure. *Philippine* could also be seen as an obscure homophonic reference to Philippeville, a settler town in colonial Algeria, and site of a notorious massacre (see Chapter 6 for more details).
5. See, for example, Daniel (1972: 347–8), Guibbert (1992: 248), Dine (1994a: 222) and Stora (1998: 41; 2004: 177).
6. In a discussion of Philippe de Broca's *Les jeux de l'amour/The Love Game* (1960) and Jean-Luc Godard's *Une Femme est une femme/A Woman is a Woman* (1961), Geneviève Sellier has stated that 'what is never dealt with in these films is the issue of contraception. The problem [plaguing the female protagonists] is having a baby, whereas for the majority of women in France the problem was how to avoid having babies at a time when both contraception and abortion were against the law' (2010: 154). A similar point could be made about *La Belle vie*.
7. By overlaying this footage with a plaintive, non-diegetic piano melody, Enrico shades it with a tone of melancholia that would not have been apparent in its original form.
8. As a tangled knot composed of dream-thoughts, memories and wishes, the temporality of these images is, naturally enough, indeterminate: some depict Paris in the winter, portraying, for example, the ornate majesty of Notre Dame cathedral. Others depict the streets of the city in another, fairer season. Some are nocturnal (including images of a dusky fairground, bars awash with convivial clients). Still others are diurnal, including a slow travelling shot of the facade of a building, located on Rue de la Huchette.
9. During this short scene, sounds of an explosion accompany an extreme wide shot of the nocturnal Parisian skyline, before the camera shifts to a close up of an evidently distraught, sleeping Frédéric. As such, the origins of the explosion remain ambiguous. It is possible that it only exists in Frédéric's dream.
10. I use the expression 'linked to' seeing as this footage actually depicts the aftermath of 'the events' of 17 October. As images of a group of men boarding a plane at Orly surge forth into on-screen space, the voice of a narrator can be heard, stating, soberly that the demonstration has not only led to 11,000 arrests, but also served as the catalyst for sending '1,500 Muslims back to their indigenous country'. See Boudjedra (1971: 39) for more details.

2. STARDOM, ATROCITY AND THE BEAUTY OF VIOLENCE

On 6 November 1954, a curious coupling of text and image appeared on the front cover of *Paris Match*, a weekly news and celebrity magazine published in France (Figure 2.1). On the left: a neatly formatted cover line, informing the reader that 'the wave of terror [had] crossed the Algerian border', in short, elliptically alluding to a spate of attacks perpetrated five days prior by Algerian nationalists in French Algeria against settlers, known as Red All-Saints Day, or *Toussaint Rouge* (see Introduction). On the right: a gently looming photograph of the Italian actress Gina Lollobrigida, whose svelte physique and flawless white complexion temper this announcement with the promise of intimacy. What to make of this puzzling tension between a cluster of words that are themselves misleading[1] and the physiognomy of a cinematic star, whose darkly erotic gaze, orientated towards us, in turn orientates our own gaze away from the trauma of what is written and towards the splendour of what is shown? Should the obscurantism of this cover, that is to say, the ways in which it does not explicitly reveal the 'terror' to which it alludes, be unequivocally attributed to the insidious effects of journalistic (self) censorship, as we might assume, or could we read it another way, aligning it, perhaps, with the ideological processes of 'deformation' and 'distortion' that Roland Barthes would famously explore in his semiological reading of a 1955 *Paris Match* cover, itself featuring a similarly over-determined image of a saluting black soldier ([1957] 1989c: 195)? Even more importantly, what exactly was the relationship between cinematic stardom, de-colonial politics and late-colonial ethics? Such are just some of the questions that I will attempt

Figure 2.1 Gina Lollobrigida on the front cover of Paris Match, 293, 6 November 1954. Photo © Paris Match. Reproduced by kind permission.

to answer in this chapter, turning my attention to two late-colonial narratives, Alain Cavalier's 1964 film noir thriller *L'Insoumis/The Unvanquished* and Mark Robson's combat film *Les Centurions/Lost Command* (1966).

The relationship between politics and stardom is the subject of a voluminous theoretical literature, onto which this chapter aims to build. Many of the concepts that exist within contemporary star studies stem from concepts proposed by the French cultural theorist Edgar Morin, in his pioneering book, *Les Stars/ The Stars*. Published in 1957, the year of the turn against silence, Morin's book is largely concerned with exploring why the multitude of stars aligned with the Golden Age of Hollywood (circa 1920–1950s) had proven to be so appealing to spectators, and how this appeal was generated on-screen. In answer to these questions, Morin significantly identifies one of the central traits of the star in their ability to 'synthesise contradictory qualities', be they physical, sexual, gendered or ethical ([1957] 1984: 40). According to Morin, this process of synthesis was especially evident in two star archetypes – the good-bad-girl and the good-bad-boy – both of which could be seen in myriad films from this epoch. As examples of the former, Morin identifies Brigitte Bardot and Marilyn Monroe as two stars that managed to combine, with explosive results, a series of contradictory values, including innocence and culpability, adulthood and juvenescence, masculinity and femininity ([1957] 1984: 32–42). As examples of the latter, Morin is even more insistent, delineating actors such as William Powell, Wallace Beery and Humphrey Bogart as having embodied a comparable cluster of paradoxical characteristics, including virtue and vice, immanence and transcendence ([1957] 1984: 34). Conjectures Morin, 'the good-bad-boy blends elements of the primitive savage brute with those associated with the virtuous vigilante', leading, in turn, to an outpouring of 'intense erotic energy' ([1957] 1984: 34).

Bolstered by the rise of cultural studies during the 1970s and 1980s, later work extended Morin's concern with spectatorial pleasure to the question of historical context, musing upon how stars act to mirror, or distort, the extra-filmic realities of a country or period. One key scholar in this respect is Richard Dyer, whose book *Stars* ([1979] 1998) proved particularly influential in the domain of star studies. Homing in on the over-determined body of Will Rogers, an American actor aligned with early Westerns, Dyer provocatively suggests that stars perform at least two ideological functions. One of these serves to reinforce social values that are either under threat or in crisis, with this process of reinforcement being evident in how Rogers 'came to embody the American Dream at a point in time when [the Great Depression] had rendered this dream increasingly hard to believe in' ([1979] 1998: 25). Shifting attention to a range of other American actors, including Shirley Temple, Jane Fonda and John Wayne, Dyer then identifies a further ideological function performed by stars such as these, all of which 'concealed and obscured the political issues they embodied' ([1979] 1998: 27). Against the benevolent principles incarnated in the filmic world by characters played by Temple, for instance, Dyer thus juxtaposes the aggressively mercenary principles that proliferated in the extra-filmic world by gangsters such as Al Capone, with the former operating to neutralise, or 'obscure', the impact of latter. In 1930s American cinema, indicates Dyer, 'charity and initiative were the values to be foregrounded, whilst money was ambivalent and repressed' ([1979] 1998: 27). More recently, John Gaffney and Diana Holmes have reiterated Dyer's ideas, insisting that 'a study of stardom can reveal what is becoming and what is being left behind; what is being aspired to and what is being forgotten and denied' (2007: 1).

A different take on the subject was proposed by Ginette Vincendeau in her monumental book *Stars and Stardom in French Cinema* (2000). Both appropriating and extending earlier work on stardom, Vincendeau's book forms an important scholarly intervention for at least two reasons. First, like Dyer but unlike Morin, Vincendeau is keen to look beyond the internal workings of films per se, and towards the extra-filmic workings of history and ideology. Second, unlike both scholars, Vincendeau is – as the title of her book insists – concerned with destabilising the Hollywood-centrism of early star studies, weaving a series of compelling observations about how French stars such as Bourvil or Simone Signoret not only 'embodied the [French] nation', but 'powerfully expressed the contradictions of [French] social change' (2000: 35). Elsewhere, Vincendeau focuses on the totemic star power of Jean Gabin, illustrating how he too incarnated a series of dualities – exceptionality and universality, savagery and delicacy, masculinity and femininity – before reaching the crux of her argument, with astute textual analysis of *La Bandera/Escape from Yesterday* (Duvivier, 1935). Released at the apotheosis of colonial culture in the 1930s and starring Gabin as a member of the Foreign Legion, an organisation likewise depicted in *L'Insoumis*, and, for that matter, *Sergent X./Sergeant X.* (Broderie, 1959), in which a legionnaire is tasked with protecting oil reserves in the Sahara, Vincendeau suggests that *La Bandera* deploys the star 'as a heroic figure': someone who 'restores and redeems the heroism and virility of the [French] military' (2000: 68–9). A comparable argumentative logic also drives Vincendeau and Claude Gauteur's exceptional reading of *La Traversée de Paris/The Trip Across Paris* (Autant-Lara, 1956), as a film that sublimates France's troubling history of collaboration with the Nazis by casting Gabin as an irreverent collaborator oozing with charisma (Vincendeau and Gauteur 2006: 152) (see Chapter 4 for more on Autant-Lara, the Occupation and collaboration).

Two scholars finally worth mentioning in this introduction are Guy Austin and Sarah Leahy, both of whom have extended the debate still further, into the realm of decolonisation. Like Vincendeau, Austin's work is clearly indebted to that undertaken by Morin and Dyer in the late 1950s and late 1970s, projecting their theories through a conceptual lens composed of cultural studies, postcolonial studies and cine-structuralism, a critical approach adopted by theorists such as Thomas Schatz (1981), for whom cinema was a medium geared towards resolving cultural contradictions in symbolic form. 'By means of charisma', writes Austin, 'stars reconcile opposites and thus incarnate idealised solutions to ideological issues' (2003: 2). It is around this claim that Austin weaves many of his case studies, identifying Gérard Depardieu as a star whose arguably 'effeminate' voice functioned to neutralise the aggressive misogyny of his persona, as seen, for example, in Bertrand Blier's 1974 *Les Valseuses/Going Places*, a narrative tellingly released during a particularly volatile period in the gendered politics of France (2003: 80). Elsewhere, Austin ingeniously deploys Kristin Ross's theories of privatisation (see Chapter 1) to conceptualise the star persona of the French actress Catherine Deneuve, whose clean white skin, as displayed within Jacques Demy's late-colonial tale *Les Parapluies de Cherbourg/The Umbrellas of Cherbourg* (1964), Austin links to a collective desire to forget the 'dark' side of colonialism and the 'dirty' war in Algeria (2003: 44–6; see Chapter 5 for more on Demy's film). A strikingly similar argument is crafted by Leahy in her illuminating article 'The matter of myth: Brigitte Bardot, stardom and sex' (2003). Like Austin, Leahy suggests that female film stars such as Bardot were used during decolonisation to erect a politically, ethnically and ethically reassuring vision of a French nation that was, in reality, consumed by political crises, ethnic divisions and thorny questions regarding the ethics of torture. This was crucially even though Bardot had herself adopted an unequivocal stance in the politics of the war, notably by refusing to bow to a campaign of blackmail led by the OAS (see Introduction), by publishing a letter from them demanding that she donate 50,000 NF (new francs) to their campaign in the national news magazine *L'Express*. Neither violence, nor atrocity, nor guilt, but peace and beauty and innocence thus accrued to the culturally constructed star body of Bardot, as France itself lurched, fractured and divided, into the late-colonial epoch. Summarising this process of sublimation, Leahy states:

> Just like the cover of *Paris-Match* described by Barthes, Bardot came to embody a certain unproblematic image of France at this time of decolonisation. Bardot's image unites beauty, prosperity, femininity, fashion and sex appeal; she promotes the idea of a France not in the process of losing her colonies in a very bloody way, but of a country embarking on a sustained period of economic growth and modernisation. (2003: 75)

Drawing from notions of 'synthesis' and 'ideology' associated with Morin and Dyer, theories of late-colonial stardom proposed by Austin and Leahy, alongside Vincendeau's understanding of Gabin's 'redeemed' militarised masculinity, this chapter is split into two sections. In part one, my analysis will thus focus on Alain Cavalier's *L'Insoumis*, illustrating the ways in which Cavalier frames the face of Alain Delon, undoubtedly one of the biggest French film stars of the late-colonial period, as a beautiful object; one that neutralises the paramilitary violence performed by his filmic body. Part two of this chapter then extends these thoughts to Mark Robson's *Les Centurions*, suggesting that a similar tendency towards historical sublimation is at play in Robson's film, specifically in relation to the director's portrayal of paratroopers as visual spectacles to be admired and adored. I ultimately argue that – through their configurations of stardom – neither film represents the French military as guilty of the colonial crimes committed in the extra-filmic world. In both, beauty supersedes violence as France's complicity in atrocities is – to use Dyer's lexicon – 'obscured'.

L'Insoumis (1964)

In terms of setting, *L'Insoumis* takes place largely in Algiers in 1961. In terms of plot, the film chronicles the lead-up to, development of, and fallout from a paramilitary terrorist operation, launched by two legionnaires-turned-OAS-commandos: Thomas Vlassenroot (Alain Delon) and Lieutenant Fraser (Georges Géret).[2] Alongside a settler accomplice named Amério (Robert Castel), the three men, it transpires, plan to kidnap and imprison a leftist lawyer named Dominique Servet (Lea Massari), in order to extract details about her Algerian nationalist clients. Yet no sooner has this conspiracy been hatched than it begins to unravel: first when Thomas is shot by Amério after the former secretly begins to empathise with their prisoner, and then when Thomas feels compelled to imprison lieutenant Fraser, the leader of the operation (Figure 2.2). After the

Figure 2.2 Thomas threatens his plot leader.

chaos of these events, the second part of the film is largely devoted to chronicling the journey undertaken by Thomas as he attempts to return – struggling, wounded, weakened but not defeated – to his native Luxembourg.

Delon, the noir star

Thomas and Lieutenant Fraser sit facing each other. One brandishes a gun; the other, a sharp suit. A light bulb dangles between them, casting harsh shards of light on their faces as they mutter about the pro-colonial plot in preparation. Beyond this circle, the rest of the room is in darkness. As this early scene suggests, and as Cavalier himself later attested (Audé et al. 1981: 15; Père 2017), the influence of film noir on *L'Insoumis* is all-pervasive: from the deep chiaroscuro used here to dramatise the two men concocting their unholy alliance; to Thomas's infatuation with weapons, cars and money; his tragic quest to his family home (a storyline that mirrors John Hudson's classic noir narrative, *The Asphalt Jungle* [1950]); right through to the danger of feminine attachment and entrapment incarnated by Dominique – Thomas's prisoner, lover and indirect executioner, for it is ultimately due to her inability to remain quiet as a hostage that Thomas is shot by his co-conspirator. Crucially, the influence of film noir upon *L'Insoumis* can be glimpsed in Cavalier's depiction of Thomas as a man drawn into an inexorable vortex of violence, from which he is granted little release.

The term 'violence' crops up as much in the reams of scholarship on film noir as it does in the often hagiographic biographies of Delon. Thus, if André Bazin eulogised Humphrey Bogart – *the* star of American film noir, and one of Morin's most lucid examples of the good-bad-boy – as a man for whom 'revolvers become a quasi-intellectual weapon' ([1957] 1985: 99), and Raymond Borde and Étienne Chaumeton observed that noir directors privileged 'rapid, brutal narratives filled with a physical impression of malaise' ([1955] 2002: 142), then Delon's screen identity has been described as 'predatory', 'untamed', even 'cruel' (Hayes 2004: 47; Austin 2003: 55; Vincendeau 2000: 173). In *L'Insoumis*, Thomas's cruelty emerges slowly. Nowhere is it apparent, for example, in the opening scene of the film, during which Thomas – in a spectacular display of altruism – attempts to save a wounded comrade stranded on a rocky precipice in the harsh landscape of the Kabylia Mountains (Algeria) in 1959. It is only once Thomas has deserted from the Legion that his spasmodic outbursts of violence gather pace. Thomas's partner Maria (Viviane Attia), for example, is subjected to a petty yet painful blow to the head when she admits to lying to him, whilst Thomas exhibits an equally disconcerting lack of sympathy after kidnapping Dominique: he calmly quenches his thirst with a crisp beer while she languishes in the stifling heat of the bathroom. Yes, these subtle signs of cruelty are tempered as Thomas gently begins to empathise with the plight of his captive, providing evidence, in short, that he is able to engage with others above and beyond the naked logic of violence. But at the same time, Thomas's empathy is almost immediately exposed as superficial when he shoots and is shot by Amério, an act whose horror is visually expressed in the fragmented montage of objects that follows: a body being dragged away, bullet holes, blood-streaked tiles, shattered glass – glass everywhere. Most spectacularly, Thomas's propensity for inflicting pain is exposed when he propels the head of his betrayed plot leader – Lieutenant Fraser – through a window in a dingy Luxembourgian hotel. In each scene, Cavalier exposes us to an ethics of late-colonial pacifism that hinges upon a thematics of paramilitary violence.

What is interesting about *L'Insoumis* is that Cavalier frames Thomas as an individual with whom the spectator is impelled to identify, despite him lacking even the most basic prerequisites for human subjectivity – feelings, emotions, morality. When assembling the imaginary of popular cinema, it seems, spectatorial identification could be created, quite simply, through a superlative profile. It is a principle that Edgar Morin seemed to grasp instinctively, stating: 'the star is a star because the film's technical system develops and excites a projection-identification, culminating in divinisation precisely when focusing on what man knows to be the most moving thing in the world: a beautiful human face' ([1957] 1984: 148). It is also a principle that French director René Clément took full advantage of in his psychological thriller *Plein Soleil/Purple Noon* (1960), a film whose 'narcissistic display of Delon's face and body' proved so potent that it effectively enabled the actor to subsequently set up Delbeau, the company with which he co-produced *L'Insoumis* (Vincendeau 2000: 173). Indeed, according to Cavalier, the screenplay of *L'Insoumis* was written precisely for Delon, thus granting him an exceptional, and occasionally logistically complex, degree of jurisdiction over his star image, as least for the directors contractually responsible for capturing it (Père 2017).

Delon hardly pioneered the modality of morally ambiguous performance displayed in these early works. As Nick Rees-Roberts and Darren Waldron have pointed out, the star notably drew from the Method as an aesthetic basis for his acting style (2015: 8). Delon's famous silence, for example, not only finds its purest expression in *L'Insoumis*, but also develops the art of 'unverbalised emotion' cultivated in the 1950s by James Dean and Marlon Brando (Naremore 1998: 204). Like these stars, Delon was someone who spoke through the polyphony of the body, oscillating between moments of facial stillness and corporeal kinesis, with the latter being particularly prominent in scenes that precede deeds of brutality in *L'Insoumis*. In an article on the Method, Leo Braudy has argued how Hollywood stars of the 1950s 'acted out the audience's fantasy life, especially interwoven fantasies of impotence and rebellion' (1996: 212). Delon's performance in *L'Insoumis* plainly arose out of a different social climate than that which gave rise to the Method, characterised less by anxieties surrounding the implications of youth culture on American society, and more by anxieties surrounding the implications of colonial atrocity on French society, but the role of the star as a 'cult object that condenses audience fantasies' remained every bit as powerful (Austin 2003: 2).

Likewise, Delon's face has often been described as possessing a mask-like quality: harsh yet majestic, supremely indifferent – a paragon of what Roland Barthes might have termed the degree zero of faciality. Just like a mask, Delon's physiognomy seems to exist in a state of permanent inertia. It is composed of a myriad of micro-movements, devoid of the dynamism normally granted by the gesticulation of the mouth. It is a spectacle often framed as a site of erotic contemplation for the spectator, through close-ups, recalling Noa Steimatsky's understanding of the cinematic face as 'deriving its power not from "what it expresses" but from what it does not give away' (2017: 21). And just like a mask, Delon's platonic profile is a screen, or patina, that conceals. According to Guy Austin, 'behind [Delon's] intimidating beauty [and] expressionless face, there is a hidden sadness that allows the romanticising of [his] image' (2003: 62). Romantic, to be sure, but also aesthetically and ethically reassuring. In *L'Insoumis*, at least, Delon's profile is, even more precisely, a mask that softens the extent of Thomas's complicity in colonial atrocity, with this synthesis of opposing values being artfully albeit indirectly captured in Ginette Vincendeau's description of Delon's paradoxical star image as one underpinned by 'cruel beauty' (2000: 173). Like Morin's figure of the 'good-bad-boy', Thomas is a constellation of star contradictions.

One of the most illuminating pieces of scholarship on Delon's talismanic persona is Steve Neale's 'Masculinity as spectacle', which raises many questions pertinent to this enquiry (1983). Neale begins his argument by illustrating how, in films such as *Le Samouraï/The Samurai* (Melville, 1967), Delon was often tasked with embodying 'images of linguistic and emotional reticence' (1983: 7), an observation that again harks back to the Method. Neale then outlines the ways in which the sexually conservative politics of mainstream cinema essentially prevent 'the male body from existing explicitly as an erotic object' (1983: 8) – as this would risk inducing a state of homoerotic *over*-identification in heterosexual male spectators – but needs to be constantly 'disqualified by images of masculine mutilation and sadism' (1983: 8). Here, Neale moves away from textual analysis of Delon, the star, to explore the oeuvre of Anthony Mann. But, judging from the veritable emporium of swabs, dressings, ointments and strips of hydrophilic gauze which litter *L'Insoumis*, Neale could not have asked for a more persuasive case of his own hypothesis: for every unblemished portrait of Thomas's divine profile, there is an image of his festering gunshot wound. Jean Narboni conceptualised the aesthetics of *L'Insoumis* as 'an aesthetics of pain' (1965: 149), while Cavalier curiously promoted his project as 'the story of a man with a hole in his heart' (Zand 1964). Whilst the French army attempted to preserve the flawless skin of their torture victims in the extra-filmic world, Cavalier subjects Thomas to a gruelling physical ordeal in the filmic world, arguably to compensate for his flawless beauty.

This was not the first time that Cavalier had attempted to grapple with the politics and ethics of decolonisation. In 1962, he had released what is generally considered as one of the most politically engaged cinematic narratives of the late-colonial epoch with Le Combat dans l'île/The Combat on the Island, a formally classical dramatisation of a leftist militant and far-right activist who clash over the heart of a woman. L'Insoumis doesn't exactly replicate the patterns of characterisation seen within Le Combat dans l'île: apart from the elusive references to Dominique's relationship with Algerian nationalists, the modus operandi of leftist militancy dramatised in the latter is curiously absent from the former, for example. And yet, upon reflection, the two narratives appear to share important parallels in the way in which they not only gesture towards – but also temper – the extra-filmic reality of pro-colonial violence, for a society at once captivated and profoundly troubled by the atrocities being conducted in its name. In L'Insoumis, perhaps the most pertinent example of this interplay between violence and beauty, guilt and innocence occurs when Dominique is first dragged into the bathroom of the apartment where she is to be held. Here, bemusement yields to panic as she takes stock of the ominous objects that surround her. A bathtub, a squalid sink, windows boarded up with planks. Ambient horror invades the room: rape, a possibility; torture, a probability; with waterboarding being most likely. For the first time in the film, the pain of Dominique's legal clients threatens to transform into a pain of her own, as Cavalier twists his narrative around the parameters of state censorship. But almost as soon as this oblique reference to colonial inhumanity has been articulated is it subsequently undone: first when Lieutenant Fraser claims that Dominique has 'a warped mind' (thus speciously insinuating that the OAS would never dabble in such practices),[3] and then when the camera cuts to an image of a shirtless Thomas, fraternising with his shirted comrades. Instead of being led to empathise with Dominique, our attention is towed towards Thomas's darkly radiant body. Later, Thomas wakes in the night to discover Dominique pleading, in a voice hoarse with dehydration, for something to drink. Our taciturn anti-hero, by contrast, is well hydrated: immediately before engaging with his bedraggled captive through the keyhole of the bathroom, he pours a bottle of water over his naked torso in a shot saturated with eroticism and noir chiaroscuro. In neither scene is Thomas portrayed as a barbaric right-wing activist, but as a deified object of desire: first, for the spectator, then later for Dominique, who eventually succumbs to his carnal charms.

Despite being hounded by his enraged former lieutenant through the rural hinterlands of France, and despite having to deal with an increasingly painful infected wound, Thomas somehow manages to preserve his deadly charm and fatal composure right up until the elegiac climax of *L'Insoumis*. But now there are neither captives nor accomplices. There is only defeat: a long and unsettling sequence depicts Thomas lurching towards his daughter before collapsing to the ground, the point at which someone 'who doesn't know how to communicate descends into [absolute] silence' (Coureau 1996: 55). It is, by all accounts, an undeniably disconcerting moment in the film. But it is also a moment of sublime pathos, wherein Thomas's crimes, committed under the banner of greed and colonialism – desertion, abduction, assassination – are nothing less than neutralised and sublimated in the gentle arch of his posture, much in the same way as Lollobrigida tempers the allusions to death articulated on the cover of *Paris Match*. Recalling Fabio Poppi and Eduardo Urios-Aparisi's suggestion that 'one of the traditional metaphors established in Western thought is the mapping of physical beauty onto moral goodness' (2018: 306), Thomas's violent tendencies might allude to the naked violence of colonialism, but his perfect profile nevertheless provides the perfect pretext for a society yearning for absolution from complicity in atrocity.

Les Centurions (1966)

A somewhat different take on the war is proposed by Mark Robson, whose 1966 film, *Les Centurions*, recounts the trials and tribulations of a triumvirate of paras, who struggle, firstly, against rural nationalists in the hinterlands of the Aurès Mountains, and then against urban guerrillas in the Battle of Algiers (see Introduction). Produced by Columbia Pictures and filmed by an established Canadian director, who had already made a string of successful films, including *The Bridges at Toko-Ri* (1954), naturally enough, *Les Centurions* reverberates with echoes of American popular culture: from the bombastic images of conflict that evoke the iconography of the Second World War combat film (Basinger 1986), to the vast dusty shots of an 'Algeria' shaded with the spatial iconography of the classic Western (although production actually took place in neither Algeria nor America but Spain), to the star presence of Mexican-American actor Anthony Quinn, who plays the unwieldy Colonel Raspéguy. Raspéguy's brigade, meanwhile, features a motley assortment of French actors, including Maurice Ronet, as a belligerent para named Boisfeuras, and Alain Delon, whose vocation as a sensitive military historian named Esclavier was widely panned by French journalists, primarily as Delon's star persona had already become moored to his body rather than his mind, as we see within *L'Insoumis* (Figure 2.3). That said, *Les Centurions* also shares an important parallel with Cavalier's film in the ways in which it 'erects a reassuring image of France at war', one, moreover, that 'poses no risk to the beliefs of the French public' (Dine 1997: 86). Fascinating yet reassuring for a society yearning for exculpation from colonial atrocities, the war once again emerges as a corporeal spectacle populated by innocent stars.

Figure 2.3 Raspéguy (right) and Esclavier (left) in *Les Centurions*.

Paras as stars, and the ghost of Bigeard

As France heralded the dawn of image culture, mass media and commodity fetishism in the 1950s and 1960s, a new military archetype was born: the paratrooper, or para. Paras only represented 3–5 per cent of the forces on duty in Algeria, but this did not prevent the popular press from elevating paras such as Jacques Massu, Roger Trinquier and Marcel Bigeard to the status of demigods, even though, or perhaps precisely because, these men found themselves increasingly implicated in accusations of atrocity as the war developed. Thus, in July 1957, the year of the turn against silence, *Paris-presse* dedicated a special edition of the review to the paras, their 'stars' (Anon. cited in Talbott 1976: 72), whilst François Nourissier identified paras and celebrities as 'two emblems of the decade' (cited in Perrault 1961: 10). According to Talbott, 'like [Brigitte] Bardot, paras fulfilled escapist fantasies: sex, violence and adventure' (1976: 69–70). And where the archetypal para might have embodied a hyper-virile version of Bardot's androgyny, these two figures shared an important homology in that their images rarely functioned as anything other than physical ciphers, drained of psychological and political depth, and instead 'loaded with sensuality and scandal', 'force and submission', alongside a high 'degree of sexuality for a society evacuated of it'[4] (Nourissier cited in Perrault 1961: 10). Far more corporeal than cerebral, the cultural bodies of Bardot and the paras were, in this respect, all but skin deep: pure lust, pure surface, pure image.

That *Les Centurions* mirrors this aestheticisation of the para body should come as no surprise: the film was, after all, adapted from a pro-military novel written by no less than a paratrooper-turned-journalist, Jean Lartéguy; and Lartéguy had based the central protagonist of his novel – Raspéguy – on Marcel Bigeard, perhaps the most infamous para, known for his 'Rommel style of leadership, jumping with the first wave of paratroopers, and always leading from the front' (Horne 2006: 168). Paratroopers such as Bigeard and Massu were also keen to combine the direct action of guerrilla warfare with the psychological propaganda of pacification, giving rise to a dialectical modality of military strategy labelled 'subversive war', taught, incidentally, at Bigeard's own Jeanne d'Arc specialist officer training school (Thomas 2000: 93). Anchored in this history of military culture, *Les Centurions* is thus a film that constantly foregrounds the visibility of Raspéguy, to the point of excess. In the very first scene, for instance, the spectator is faced with an image of Raspéguy flinging himself over the parapet of a trench during the Battle of Dien Bien Phu (March–May 1954), thus providing dramatic evidence of the virile physical prowess that he will later display, performing an incongruous physical workout in the company of Countess Nathalie de Clairefons (Michèle Morgan), an aristocratic settler he seduces in Bab-El-Oued, before bounding through a gauntlet set up in the Aurès Mountains to weed out weak soldiers from the regiment. Once Raspéguy reaches the barrelling expanse of the battlefield, meanwhile, the extent of this physicality is accentuated still further. Vaults, sprints, lunges and dives: such is the jagged ballet of manoeuvres performed by Raspéguy and his comrades throughout the battle scenes in *Les Centurions*, transforming the war from a political into a purely physical drama – a panoramic orgy of falling torsos – and aligning the narrative with a Hollywood tradition of Second World War combat films, including *Bataan* (Garnett, 1943), *Sands of Iwo Jima* (Dwan, 1949), and Robson's own *Home of the Brave* (1949).

One of the most pervasive criticisms directed against these earlier films was that they subtly transformed the phenomenon of conflict into a pleasurable spectacle. Toby Haggith, for example, has observed that 'the battlefield in feature films involved a composition and artistic quality which was theatrical and intrinsically pleasing' (2002: 344), whereas James Chapman contends that 'even explicitly anti-war films tended to aestheticise the subject' (2008: 80), leading to what has elsewhere been termed 'the pleasure-culture of war' (Dawson 1994: 4). Despite narrating an at least initially unnamed conflict without heroes, without major battles, without glory and without clear victors, but instead 'skirmishes, massacres, and political betrayal' (Multeau 2006: 152), it is precisely this drive towards spectacularisation that subtends the iconography of *Les Centurions*. From the very first scenes, grenades soar over a serrated horizon, fringed either with an expanse of sky or, later, ancient ruins; paras leap from hovering helicopters; a soldier sprints, gun in hand, through no man's land, desperate to save a marooned comrade, and so on. In *L'Insoumis*, the brutality of the pro-colonial OAS may have been translated into a romantic narrative through the beauty of Thomas's face, and the surging affection of his victim. But here it is the militarised violence of the army that is romanticised, erecting a visually pleasing antithesis to the turn against silence. It is significant in this respect that, apart from a brief medium shot of three bloody corpses at the fictional town of Rhalem (a shot apparently inspired by the massacre of nineteen conscripts in the town of Palestro in 1956, who were subjected to various acts of mutilation,[5] likewise evoked in Philippe Vaudoux's 1960 *La Bouche amère/Bitter Aftertaste*[6]), *Les Centurions* features conspicuously few images of raw suffering or death. Instead, as within the archetypal Second World War combat film, combatants either abruptly succumb to their injuries as if they have been struck down with acute narcolepsy, or, more often than not, leap out of the flames of an explosion into an abyss, positioned just outside of the purview of one of the many wide-angle shots used by the director, and embellished with a crackle of pyrotechnics. It is apparently not possible for soldiers or nationalists to die in an abject manner in Robson's narrative, weeping, privately, thinking of their loved ones – longing for them. Death must be anaesthetised or aestheticised, rendered visually pleasurable, like Lollobrigida and Delon. Death, like decolonisation, must be sublimated or, ideally, spectacular.

Spectacular, too, is Quinn, whose exuberant performance split critics, some enthralled by the star's 'proud' and 'imposing' presence (de Baroncelli 1966), others dismayed by the comparatively inconsequential roles that Robson meted out to the rest of the largely French cast, especially Delon. As an actor who had learnt his trade in Hollywood epics such as *The Guns of Navarone* (Thompson, 1961) and *Lawrence of Arabia* (Lean, 1962), Quinn possessed neither the brutal beauty of Delon nor the cerebral vanity of Maurice Ronet, leaving him free from the perceived problems of eroticising a male actor outlined in the previous section. In *Les Centurions*, Quinn's star power emanates from the acrobatic cadence of his voice, the excess of his gestures, his jocular demeanour and, above all, his warm, raspy laugh – an invitation to intimacy severely lacking from Delon's chilly disposition – which instead positions the former in close proximity to one of the biggest stars in American cinema: John Wayne. As Alex Adams has brilliantly shown, the complex nexus of connections between Wayne, Quinn, Raspéguy and Bigeard is also bolstered by the regurgitation, in *Les Centurions*, of many of the spatial tropes associated with the Hollywood Western (2016: 96). So rather than the solitary legionnaire played by Delon in *L'Insoumis*, we get Quinn playing the paratrooper-everyman Raspéguy, with numerous scenes suggesting that the latter is a man feared by some, loved by others, yet respected by all, including his mother, his lover and his native Basque community. The only people who do not respect Raspéguy are his bureaucratic military peers, who accuse him of being a maverick like

Wayne, preferring unusual tactics to established military procedures. Here, it is worth mentioning that Raspéguy's irreverence derives in part from historical fact: no sooner had the war begun than Bigeard earned himself a reputation as an unconventional leader, much to the delight of journalists working for *L'Express*, *Paris-presse* and *France dimanche*. First, there was Bigeard's decision to devise a new para outfit, trimming off the excess material from the shorts in the standard uniform and using it to make a derided cloth cap. Then there was his unusual, though admittedly effective, approach to guerrilla warfare – his belief in cutting off nationalists from the population in order to stem the flow of information and food – compounded by an increasing disrespect for political hierarchy. It was during this time – the late 1950s – that, for right-wing activists, Bigeard became a romanticised hero, whose forced dismissal from the army in 1960 only added to his legacy the pathos of a martyr. But for those on the left, Bigeard's irreverence raised as many questions as it did answers. Questions that orbited anxiously, once again, around the word 'torture'.

As with Cavalier, Robson does not attempt to deny the practice of torture amongst elite military forces based in Algeria. At least two scenes in the film include more or less overt allusions to the torture of Algerian nationalists: first after the tit-for-tat massacre of paras and Algerian civilians that occurs at Rhalem; and second during the Battle of Algiers, when the commandos attempt to crack down on a terrorist cell orchestrated by Doctor Ali Ben Saad (Grégoire Aslan) and Esclavier's improbable combatant girlfriend, Aïcha (Claudia Cardinale), with the latter relationship evoking Jean Wagner's unfinished film *Ce monde banal/This Dull World* (1960).[7] In both of these scenes, Raspéguy is present, yet instead of actively implicating the colonel in torture, Robson preserves Quinn's star charm, framing the systematic atrocities conducted by the army alternately as a deed perpetrated by a cluster of intransigent rebels, or as 'the result of circumstance, a fatal chain of events' (Anon. 1966). 'Do what you need to do', intones Raspéguy, when Esclavier surreptitiously drags Aïcha into a sombre room for 'questioning'. If the act remains shadowy, its intimations are clear: torture is a technique practised beyond the limits of Raspéguy's control and comprehension. Thanks to scholars such as Pierre Vidal-Naquet (2001: 115, 158), Marnia Lazreg (2008: 53–4, 161–2) and Alain Ruscio (2012), we now know that this imagery belies a grim truth. Not only had Bigeard witnessed a female combatant named Louisette Ighilhariz interned in a torture camp near Algiers in 1957, in her own words, 'swimming in a bed full of shit and the blood of dried menses' (cited in Lazreg 2008: 162), but he was also personally involved in the institutionalised torture of suspects during the war, infamously dumping their corpses into the Mediterranean Sea using an ingeniously grim miscellany of cement shoes and body barrels, and thus earning his victims a perverse sobriquet: Bigeard's shrimps. A far cry from the all-American hero portrayed by Quinn/Raspéguy, whose ineffable charm, like Delon/Thomas's face, invites us to read these paramilitary protagonists vicariously, with empathy, with admiration, with adoration. According to John Gaffney and Diana Holmes, during decolonisation, stars 'functioned in part to mask a deeper unarticulated knowledge, almost like a psychically repressed nightmare: the horrors of France's decolonisation process' (2007: 20; see Sharpe 2019a for more details). It is an argument that seems particularly pertinent to the ways in which both *L'Insoumis* and *Les Centurions* seem to 'mask' the guiltiest aspects of the war, transfiguring it from a conflict characterised by absolute violence and an absolute lack of military spectacles, into a spectacular blaze of paramilitary figures – one with a platonic profile, the other a superlative torso – neither directly complicit in the practice of torture, nor truly implicated in the perpetration of colonial atrocities. Much in the same way, in fact, as the sometimes virile, sometimes emasculated, yet always innocent military protagonists analysed in the next chapter of this book.

Notes

1. In its metaphorical imaginary of border crossing, the cover line obliquely suggests that nationalists have traversed the Mediterranean Sea, from colonial Algeria to metropolitan France, in turn, transforming metropolitan French citizens into potential targets of nationalist violence. It is only once the reader delves into the body of the publication that they realise that neither is true.
2. Both Thomas and his lieutenant have also taken part in the Algiers putsch, which occurred in 1961, once it had become clear that de Gaulle viewed the independence of Algeria as inevitable. The aims of the putschists were twofold: to overthrow de Gaulle, and, in so doing, prevent the downfall of French colonial Algeria. The putsch failed merely days after being launched due to organisational weaknesses and a lack of widespread support, in French Algeria as in metropolitan France.
3. Here we might note that the OAS had already been inculpated in various violent acts, including randomly setting an Algerian motorcyclist alight with petrol, and inadvertently blinding André Malraux's four-year-old neighbour in a bomb blast (see Stora 1998: 87–91).
4. Nourissier here seems to be gesturing towards the perceived 'castrating' effects of the war, as analysed in Chapter 3.
5. As Raphaëlle Branche (2010) has detailed, these soldiers were mutilated in several ways, including having their lips, noses and testicles cut off. Their eyes were also gouged out, and their stomachs stuffed with pebbles.
6. Vadoux's long-forgotten film centers on two soldiers, killed after being ambushed in a landscape recalling Algeria.
7. Wagner's film chronicles an equally improbable love story between a French paratrooper and a female FLN militant. As the plot progresses, their relationship disintegrates.

3. MILITARISED MASCULINITY AND ITS LOSSES

In his book *Sex, France, and Arab Men*, historian Todd Shepard states his intention to 'map out important connections between two conversations that have drawn much scholarly attention in recent years, yet which too often ignore each other: histories of empire and histories of sex' (2017: 4). In the introduction to their edited collection, *Gender and French Cinema*, Alex Hughes and James S. Williams articulate a similar injunction, stressing that 'any inventive rethinking of gender and French cinema' should involve an attentiveness to 'vectors of subjective location, such as history, nationality, ethnicity, class, colonialism and post-colonialism' (2001: 8–9). Taking its cue from theorists such as these, this chapter thus aspires to explore the 'often ignored' relationship between the ethics of decolonisation, the politics of cinematic representation and the thematics of masculine identity in two late-colonial narratives: Jacques Dupont's *Les Distractions/Trapped by Fear* (1960), and Louis Malle's psychological drama, *Le Feu follet/The Fire Within* (1963).

Virility and Castration

Since the rise of post-colonial theory in the 1960s and 1970s, an increasing number of scholars, often working within French studies, cultural studies and cultural history, have drawn attention to the relationship between colonisation, colonial culture and patriarchal ideology. According to these theorists, the slow seizing of Algeria by France throughout the 1800s should be seen not only as a military, economic and political process, but also a gendered one; one that involved, and indeed was facilitated through, the insidious victimisation of the female colonised community, alongside the attendant feminisation of colonised territory (see Branche 2001; Lazreg 2008; Brun and Shepard 2016a). As Maria Flood glosses: 'the penetration of the geographical terrain of Algeria by French soldiers was bound up in an imaginary of unveiling, access to the harem, and the literal penetration of women through consensual sex, or rape' (2017: 40).

Less scrutinised yet equally worthy of consideration is the fallout of this history of colonial 'penetration', that is to say, how the protracted withdrawal of soldiers from Algeria during the years of decolonisation may have altered the gendered politics of French culture; how the gendered dynamics of military life may have seeped into metropolitan narratives; how cultural iconographies of gender may have impacted upon the late-colonial debate; and how cinematic images of gendered identities or sexual orientations may have been used to intimate a stance for or against colonialism, the war, or political engagement more generally. One figure that enables us to think through questions such as these is the ideologically over-determined and culturally unstable figure of the paratrooper, or para. In the previous chapter of this book, I interrogated the cultural identity of the paratroopers from the perspective of stardom, parsing how prominent paratroopers such as Colonel Bigeard became stars during the late-colonial crisis, and exploring how Canadian director Mark Robson both drew from and vastly exaggerated the virulent physicality often ascribed to the paratroopers by popular discourses of the period, in the heavily aestheticised, corporeally spectacular imagery of his military blockbuster *Centurions/Lost Command* (1966).

Beyond physicality, a further trope often woven into cultural representations of the paratroopers was excessive virility. Judging from historical accounts of the war, provided by former soldiers, this trope seems to have been rooted in a certain degree of truth. After all, during decolonisation, paratroopers were well known to habitually frequent the many military brothels stationed around rural Algeria (known as BMCs), taking advantage of the fact that these establishments were often exclusively reserved for them and legionnaires alone. Glossing the power dynamics at play within this custom – avowed by some soldiers, disavowed by others – Raphaëlle Branche has, for example, described the practice of soliciting prostitutes in Algeria as 'a collective [act] of initiation', through which a clear 'virile hierarchy' was unequivocally established: paratroopers and members of the Legion at the top, conscripts at the bottom (Branche 2004: 7). No less significant were the symbolic rituals performed by paratroopers after jump-training, a highly ceremonial and unsurprisingly physical rite of passage for any aspiring member of the elite corps, and after which the presiding para-officer would force candidates to kneel, stating 'on your knees girls', before inviting those who had passed to 'stand up [as] men'

(Branche 2004: 4). Due to pageantry such as this, many accounts of paratrooper regiments thus frame them as akin to a clannish cult, tethered to tradition, steeped in history, and seemingly immutable in their attachment to codes and conventions.

But this is not to say that the visual-gendered identity of the paratroopers was entirely impervious to change. Jean-Pierre Bertin-Maghit (2015: 169–78), has, for example, suggested that by the late 1950s, the hypermasculine persona of the paratroopers had been exaggerated to such an extent that it often appeared to generate a breakdown in their gendered identity, edging them away from qualities aligned with heteronormativity, heterosexuality and homosociality, and towards those aligned with an almost queer sensibility, even sensuality. Often, this breakdown of identities occurred in private. The corpus of Bertin-Maghit's monograph, for instance, is composed of a range of amateur military short films, shot very much privately by soldiers stationed in Algeria during the conflict, and many of which are drenched in a conspicuous constellation of paratrooper bodies: 'sculpted bare torsos', 'arms, calves, and spines' (2015: 169–76). Other times, however, the heteronormative stability of the para persona appeared practically to disintegrate in full sight of the public, generating a head-spinning tension between the power of hetero-erotics, as exercised in the colonial custom of soliciting prostitutes, and what could be diagnosed as a quasi-fascistic, quasi-fetishistic infatuation with the homo-erotics of power. Hence the following telling anecdote from the pro-military photographer Marc Flament, as included in Bertin-Maghit's book:

> According to Bigeard, the aesthetic of the military was important, especially within his 3rd Parachute Colonial Regiment. People looked at them. If he wanted his men to be beautiful, the next day they were [. . .]. In the Regiment, many soldiers wore their uniforms as tightly as possible, with some going so far as to completely forgo underwear in the hope that this would preserve the smoothness of their lower attire. Sometimes, the fabric of their trousers would tear as it was so tight. (Flament 1974: 201–3 cited in Bertin-Maghit 2015: 172–3)

To this breakdown in the gendered identity of the paratroopers may also be added a further breakdown, aligned more specifically with the transgression of moral and ethical boundaries. In the Introduction to this book we saw how the late 1950s coincided with the publication of a plethora of pacifist interventions, many of which specifically targeted the institutionalisation of torture by paratroopers in Algeria as the most abhorrent aspect of the war. Moreover, such interventions were also often shaded by the politics of gender and sexuality, drawing attention to the stark fact that perpetrators of torture in Algeria frequently homed in on the sexual organs of their victims, resulting in various instances of vaginal rape, anal rape and the electrocution of the penis or breasts, and giving rise to a 'discourse of sexual deviancy' that both coexisted with, and contributed to, the turn against silence (Kuby 2013; see Introduction for more details about the turn against silence). In two articles published in *L'Express*, for instance, Françoise Giroud chastised the virulent sexual identity of the paratroopers, defining them as 'good boys, gone wrong', whose complicity in often eroticised torture sessions in Algeria led them to 'beat their wives' on their return to France; that is, if they didn't find themselves 'interned in psychiatric hospitals' (1961; 1957). In his 1958 treatise, *La Question/The Question*, Henri Alleg argued that military complexes dedicated to torture in Algeria constituted little more than 'a school in perversion for young French men' (78) – a 'school', that in Alleg's case, was run by the 10th Division of paratroopers under the leadership of General Jacques Massu. In 'Une Victoire/A Victory', Jean-Paul Sartre echoed Alleg's psychosexually inflected account of brutal interrogation, lambasting paratroopers as 'sadists bent over wrecks of human flesh' (1958: 33). In a June 1960 article, published in *Le Monde*, Simone de Beauvoir published a harrowing account of torture sessions conducted in Algeria by French military officials, including paratroopers, against a twenty-two-year-old woman, suspected of nationalist activity, named Djamila Boupacha, who had been raped with a bottle, shocked with electrodes, and beaten to within an inch of her life (see Introduction). Yet, merely five months after the publication of Beauvoir's article, Jacques Dupont would release *Les Distractions*, which, as we will see, arguably features an attempt at *redeeming* the libidinous public image of the paratroopers, whose reputation had been heavily tainted precisely through anti-war interventions such as these.

Militarised virility is not the only gendered posture parsed in the work of the scholars cited above. Oscillating between the cultural identity of the paratroopers and the cultural identity of conscripts, Philip Dine, for instance, brings to light a further sexual trope embedded in certain late-colonial novels: 'neurotic autoeroticism' (2016: 128–32). For Dine, this trope is expressed, for example, in Daniel Zimmerman's 1961 work, *80 exercices en zone interdite/80 Exercises in a Prohibited Area*, during which a conscript, frozen into fear by night-duty in Algeria, succumbs, *in extremis*, to a yearning for compulsive spurts of masturbation; or in Alain Le Carvennec's *La Mémoire chacale/Jackal Memory* (1983), during which an equally anguished soldier develops an obsession with losing his virility, either as a result of literal castration, as infamously executed by Algerian nationalists in the 1956 Massacre of Palestro (see Chapter 2); or through the psychological effects of impotence, a condition that can arise after prolonged exposure to extreme fear (Dine 2016: 130). It is this emphasis on sexual degeneracy, militarised castration, and the potentially impotence-inducing effects of the conflict, that forms the lynchpin of two excellent studies: one by Emma Kuby (2013), the other by Catherine Brun and Todd Shepard (2016b), included as an introduction to their equally essential edited compilation, *Guerre d'Algérie, Le Sexe outragé/The Algerian War: Scandalous Sex(uality)*. But where Dine diagnoses impotence as a symptom of the combat zone, these scholars frame it as a symptom of the torture-chamber, identifying the often sexualised crimes perpetrated within this space as the source of a more generalised 'crisis in the masculinity' of returning ex-soldiers, many of whom were so psychosexually corroded by what they had seen during torture sessions that they were no longer able to engage in intercourse with their metropolitan partners and wives (Kuby 2013: 142–6; Brun and Shepard 2016b: 11, 19–21). As I will show, it is precisely this 'masculinity in crisis' that is conveyed through the figure of Laurent in *Les Distractions*, and Alain in *Le Feu follet*.

Hussar Counter-culture

If the conventions of soldiers stationed in Algeria certainly helped to craft the gendered imaginary of *Les Distractions* and *Le Feu follet*, then an even more metropolitan influence on the two films can be located in the ethos of the Hussars (sometimes spelt 'Hussards' in line with the original French). Originally employed within a military context, to classify a category of cavalryman, the term 'hussar' notably acquired a new significance during the early 1950s: first when aspiring writer, Roger Nimier, foregrounded it in the title of his 1950 work *Le Hussard bleu/The Blue Hussar*, a novel, unsurprisingly, about ten Hussars who form part of the French First Army during its advance into Germany in 1944–5; and then in 1952, when journalist Bernard Frank deployed it in an incendiary article, published in the politically committed, leftist leaning journal *Les Temps modernes*, to describe what he saw as an emerging right-wing trend in French literature. According to Frank, this trend was propelled by three key writers: the aforementioned Nimier, Antoine Blondin and Jacques Laurent. Each of these writers had released at least one novel before the publication of Frank's article, with both their literature and lifestyle admitting a common interest in: the trappings of bourgeois, even aristocratic, high culture and high society; material wealth, generated through a combination of generational pedigree, unbridled nepotism and mercenary careerism, and illustrated most ostentatiously in the acquisition of sports cars; jazz, as played in the nightclub *Le Boeuf sur le Toit*; the power of polemics, with the Hussars proclaiming a particularly provocative interest in recuperating the reputation of collaborationist authors purged after the Second World War (Lucien Rebatet, Céline and Drieu la Rochelle); and, last, 'feminine beauty, the pleasures of seduction', and 'eighteenth-century libertinism' (De Baecque 2012: 110; Hewitt 1995: 291). All of the Hussars were aligned with various right-wing cultural magazines, for example, *Opéra*, *Carrefour*, *La Parisienne* and notably, *Arts*, alongside the publishing house *La Table Ronde*. Crucially, none of them believed in the species of anti-colonial political engagement that had been popularised during the 1950s, primarily in the wake of Sartre's *Qu'est-ce que la littérature?/What is Literature?* (1948), leading Bernard Frank – here, echoing the aforementioned criticism of the paratroopers – to castigate the Hussars, not only for being politically disengaged, apolitical, anti-political, or right-wing, but borderline fascistic. 'As with all fascists', he stated, the Hussars 'despise discussion. They take pleasure in short sentences, a style which they believe they have invented' (1952: 1016).

The relationship between the Hussars, their literature, their journalism, their principles, and the cinematic landscape of the period, is a relationship that has been discussed by a number of scholars.[1] Focusing on the politics of representation, Antoine de Baecque has, for instance, identified at least half a dozen New Wave narratives that appear to turn around the figure of a Hussar dandy, a figure that is 'elegant, decadent, provocative', often right-wing, or at least politically disengaged, and frequently, but not always,[2] masculine (2012: 124). These include: Claude Chabrol's *Les Cousins/The Cousins* (1958), in which a young bourgeois-aristocratic student named Paul (Jean-Claude Brialy) entertains a throng of equally young bourgeois-aristocratic students, through his 'masterful sense of repartee and penchant for crafted phrases' (2012: 124). They include Alain Cavalier's *Le Combat dans l'île/The Combat on the Island* (1962), in which Jean-Louis Trintignant plays Clément, a seductive young man seduced into a spell of fascistic political violence (see Chapter 2). And they include Jean-Luc Godard's *Le Petit Soldat/The Little Soldier* (1960/1963), in which Bruno Forestier (Michel Subor), searches desperately for a political or moral ideal, before morosely slipping into affiliation with a right-wing terrorist organisation (see Chapters 4 and 5). In each of these films, de Baecque finds the tell-tale signs of the Hussar counter-culture.

As Marc Dambre has illustrated, another link between the Hussars and the New Wave could be found in the personal friendships fostered by certain members of both groups, or what might more precisely be called 'non-groups', given that neither had invented the label that had been arbitrarily thrust upon them by journalists (2014: 10). This sense of fraternity was particularly pronounced between Louis Malle and Antoine Blondin, who shared a love for alcoholised sorties and soirees, and Malle and Roger Nimier, with Nimier writing the screenplay for Malle's first film, *Ascenseur pour l'échafaud/Elevator to the Gallows* (1958). 'Together Malle and Nimier would share a passion for rapid cars and trips improvised in the middle of the night', with the latter even going so far as to introduce the former to the notoriously anti-Semitic writer, Céline (Dambre 1989: 463). Not insignificantly, Malle's *Le Feu follet* – the second narrative I discuss below – also formed a relatively faithful cinematic adaptation of an infamous 1931 novel, written by the aforementioned pro-fascist and anti-Semitic novelist, Drieu la Rochelle, whose legacy was subjected to a process of 'protection' and 'revival' by none other than the Hussars (Frey 2004a: 225). Furthermore, in his polemical autobiography, Jacques Dupont gaudily admits to frequently fraternising with members of three right-wing groups whilst filming *Les Distractions*: the OAS (see Introduction), the

Poujadists, who formed part of a highly conservative movement established to shore up the financial interests of provincial traders, and the Hussars (2013: 130).

In this debate, special mention must be made of Geneviève Sellier, whose compelling research has consistently attempted to sharpen into focus two topics often left fuzzy in scholarship on the New Wave: masculinity and politics (2000; 2008: 128–44). As for masculinity, Sellier is unequivocal in her definition of the New Wave as a fundamentally andro-centric (male-centric), even misogynist, tendency in the continuum of French cinema, one that was anchored, sometimes explicitly, sometimes surreptitiously, to a 'masculine singular' perspective (2008). As for politics, Sellier is once again uncompromising, chastising directors such as Jacques Rivette, Louis Malle, Jean-Luc Godard, Alain Cavalier and Jacques Doniol-Valcroze for succumbing to a Hussar-inflected, neo-Romantic, ideology of disengagement during a period that, at least for those on the Sartrean Left, including Bernard Frank, warranted – nay necessitated – a high degree of political engagement and politico-aesthetic clarity (see Chapter 5 for a discussion of how the Hussar counter-culture is expressed in Doniol-Valcroze's 1962 *La Dénonciation/The Denunciation*, specifically in relation to the question of memory). Moreover, it is in the interstices of, and interplay between, these two arguments that Sellier crafts an even more compelling one, conceptualising the apoliticism of the New Wave as, to some extent, symptomatic of the andro-centrism of its imagery. In a discussion of Godard's *Le Petit soldat*, for instance, Sellier argues that the film 'strives to show that the question of political orientation is derisory in relation to the "ontological" question of engagement, insomuch as it alienates the (male) individual' (2000: 479). This hypothesis is echoed in the author's reading of *Le Combat dans l'île*, in which 'objective political categories (left and right) are merged together by a lyrical vision of tragic masculinity' (2008: 141). Finally, in what is undoubtedly the most pertinent case study in her book, Sellier yokes the 'political ambiguity' that pervades Malle/Nimier's aforementioned *Ascenseur pour l'échafaud* to the fact that the antihero of the narrative – a former para turned mercenary secret agent, played by Maurice Ronet, star of *Le Feu follet* – 'only appears to us as beaten down, a loser', reduced to doing battle with the elevator in which he has been farcically trapped during a botched plot to murder his boss (2008: 132).

Drawing from the work of the scholars cited above, this chapter is organised into several parts. In part one, I explore how Jacques Dupont's narrative is divided between two ontologically divergent male protagonists: one, a 'castrated' and victimised lost soldier, crushed by the lingering effects of the war and women; the other, a paratrooper-turned-Hussar, rehabilitated by the modernisation and motorisation of France. In the second part, I extend these discussions to Louis Malle's *Le Feu follet*, illustrating how the film accentuates the subtext of castration that is partly explored in *Les Distractions*, primarily by encouraging the spectator to empathise with a similarly victimised Hussar ex-soldier, rendered both figuratively and literally impotent by the war. In neither film are military protagonists depicted as anything other than absolved of complicity in the type of military atrocities being committed throughout French Algeria in the non-cinematic world.

LES DISTRACTIONS (1960)

Jacques Dupont began his career during the 1950s as a student at the prestigious Paris-based Institute for Advanced Cinematographic Studies (*L'Institut des hautes études cinématographiques*, IDHEC). From these studies followed three moderately successful, if deeply Eurocentric, documentaries – the exotic-ethnographic *Congolaise/Savage Africa* (1950); *Les Routiers du désert/Truckers in the Desert* (1954), a hymn to colonial infrastructure in Algeria; and the pro-military *Crèvecoeur/Heartbreak Ridge* (1955), about French troops enlisted to fight in Korea – before Dupont turned his hand to fiction film, shooting *Les Distractions* over the course of six weeks in Paris in 1960. The same year, the increasingly outspoken and frequently antagonistic director signed an open letter, published in *Le Monde*, *Le Figaro* and *Carrefour*, in which he and 185 other signatories, including the Hussars, Laurent, Nimier and Blondin, publicly lent their support to the army in Algeria, and colonialism more generally. In 1961, Dupont then sharply amplified the stakes at play in his political engagement by offering to work with the then-nascent OAS. As Dupont has revealed, his role in the OAS was twofold: first, to contact high-ranking affiliates of the organisation (including General Faure, one of the instigators of the Algiers Putsch [see Chapter 2]), using a miniscule directory, written on cigarette papers hidden in the soles of his shoes; and second, to facilitate and supervise a series of clandestine meetings between these affiliates, who were driven by the director-turned-activist to a range of strictly confidential rural areas in and around Paris, including Montargis, Orléans, Melun and Rambouillet (Dupont 2013: 127, 133, 141). In 1961, however, Dupont's brief foray into right-wing militancy and popular filmmaking came to an abrupt end, when he was arrested and imprisoned for working for the OAS. Panned by journalists and ignored by scholars since then, *Les Distractions*, with Dupont's legacy, has languished in a critical abyss, undervalued and forgotten. To my knowledge, the only scholar who has dedicated any analysis to the film is Joseph Daniel (1972: 337).

The plot of *Les Distractions* is simple enough. Two paratroopers have returned from French Algeria, respectively scarred and untouched by their experience in the conflict. The first – a reserved young drifter named Laurent Porte (Claude Brasseur, who had actually served in Algeria as a paratrooper) – is quite clearly troubled by his military past: in the opening scene, he is pictured hurtling along the boulevards of Paris in a convertible – stolen, we later learn – before fatally forcing a police motorcyclist off the road. Luckily, all is not lost, as, shortly after, Laurent is granted a surreptitious lifeline from his former paratrooper friend Paul Frapier (Jean-Paul Belmondo; again, a former veteran of the war), who offers to help his neurotic comrade elude capture by the police whilst attempting to juggle his responsibilities as a journalist and photographer for the glossy news magazine *Jours de France*. The remainder of the narrative is thus largely orientated towards chronicling the trials and tribulations of Laurent's act of evasion – played out across the ultra-bourgeois backdrop of central Paris, with the Arc de Triomphe etching a visual motif in various scenes – until he is eventually cornered in a wooden hut located in a rural commune of Paris named Fontainebleau. But, by this point, the sullen veteran has realised that his luck has run dry. The only escape from a lifetime of incarceration: suicide.

Laurent: a lost soldier, castrated

The trope of the 'lost soldier' is woven into many examples of late-colonial French cinema. In Chapter 1, we examined one iteration of this trope in Dédé, the anti-hero of *Adieu Philippine/Goodbye Philippine*, whose taciturn demeanour, I argued, is mirrored in the initial reticence of Frédéric in Enrico's *La Belle vie/The Good Life*, with both figures being designed to elicit empathy in the spectator. In Chapter 2, I developed this point in relation to Thomas in *L'Insoumis/ The Unvanquished*, again examining Cavalier's decision to align veterans with non-speech, alongside the redemptive power of Thomas/Delon's facial beauty. In Dupont's *Les Distractions*, meanwhile, we find a further example of this trope, as incarnated in the wounded character of Laurent. Like Dédé, Frédéric and Thomas, Laurent is a man characterised by various forms of loss, all of which are implicitly linked to the Algerian War of Independence. This loss is professional, in that reinsertion into civilian life has perforce deprived Laurent of his military vocation. It is social, in that armed service seems to have isolated him from the majority of acquaintances and lovers that he may or may not have once frequented; apart from Paul, that is. It is financial, in that he is constantly framed as impoverished, to the point of destitution. It is psychological, in that he often displays a profound lack of confidence in social situations, averting his gaze away from the gazes of others; and it is vocal in that he rarely speaks, and when he does, his voice is flat and monosyllabic. Armand Monjo goes further, diagnosing Dupont's 'lost soldier' as someone who has 'lost his soul' (1960).

But by far the most insidious form of loss with which Laurent is associated is not professional, social, financial or vocal, but sexual, evoking in turn the figure of the 'castrated soldier', as theorised by Dine, Kuby, Brun and Shepard. In *Les Distractions*, this process of 'castration' largely takes place in two domestic spaces that we see in the film: one, a Parisian apartment owned by Paul; the other, a rural habitation, owned by Paul's lover, Dany (Eva Damien), both of which Laurent uses to hide from the police. As for Paul's apartment, many of the film's early scenes, for example, depict Laurent as doing very little within this space, apart, that is, from silently waiting for his friend-turned-host-turned-saviour to return home. Tinkering with trinkets that do not belong to him, loitering awkwardly in rooms that are not his, smoking cigarettes whilst staring blankly at the ceiling, in short, attempting to pass the time but failing, during the twenty-four or so hours that he spends sequestered in solitude in Paul's abode, Laurent is undoubtedly at his most melancholic. Laurent dreads. At one point, the cloistered 'lost soldier' discovers a pistol hidden amidst the clutter of Paul's belongings: aiming it at an image of his pallid face, reflected in a mirror, it is a shot that not only foreshadows the act of self-obliteration that takes place during the film's climax, but also gestures towards a similar fusing of masochism and narcissism as embodied by the suicidal Alain in *Le Feu follet*. As with the archetypal antihero of the Hollywood melodrama, both men express their emotions neither through speech nor gesture but through objects and things. Moreover, when Laurent and Paul are framed together in this domestic setting, the former all but lets himself be dominated by the latter, cleaving open a subtle yet significant series of contrasts between the two men. Paul talks, Laurent doesn't, or does, but mutters. Paul darts around his living quarters with the brio of a man ecstatic (at one point seizing an excessively elongated trumpet, an instrument that, in his own words, he uses 'to annoy people'), while Laurent appears pinned to the spot, maudlin and morose. Tellingly, during one key shot included in this sequence, Paul gently yet forcefully eases Laurent down onto the single sofa bed that lingers in the mise-en-scène, hand-on-shoulder (Figure 3.1), with

Figure 3.1 Laurent (left) and Paul (right).

both act and object once again insisting upon Laurent's implied weakness, his fragility, his frailty: as a paratrooper no longer tasked with protecting France's colonies in dangerous military interventions, but rather reduced to protecting himself in a cocoon of white cotton bed sheets.

Once Laurent decamps to Dany's bolthole, located in Orly, a southern commune in Paris, this emasculation is exacerbated still further. When Paul initially introduces Laurent to Dany as 'a brother from Algeria', for instance, the spectator would be forgiven for expecting at least a modicum of decorum, between two people who know each other (Paul and Dany), and two who do not (Dany and Laurent). In fact, the contrary transpires, as Paul flagrantly and brazenly ushers his 'brother' into an adjacent room, whilst the ardent lovers cavort in private. Similarly, later in the film, Laurent finds himself being incongruously seduced by Dany after voyeuristically peering at a mirror image of her quasi-naked body, recalling, most evidently, the psycho-scopic dynamics of Hitchcock's oeuvre, in which both literally and figuratively maimed men – for example Jeff in *Rear Window* (1954), or Scottie in *Vertigo* (1958) – often stare at sexually liberated female characters through comparable patterns of 'impotent gazing' (Pelko 1992: 114). But what begins with the promise of carnal pleasure terminates in erotic failure: spooked by Dany's revelation that she is aware of his crime, and spooked by Dany's confidence, as a woman unafraid to initiate intercourse, Laurent flees once again into the night, missing the one chance he is given – rather than takes – to prove that 'he is a man'. A comparable instance of sexual ineptitude, suffered again by a former soldier castrated by both late-colonial conflict and unfettered female allure, also occurs at the start of Malle's *Le Feu follet*, discussed below.

At other points, Laurent's ontological condition appears to topple over, from castration to abjection. Leading us into the deepest and most disturbing layers of the late-colonial crisis, one early scene in *Les Distractions*, for example, portrays Laurent carrying a young boy who appears to have fainted to a group of nearby police officers, thus not only generating a moment of narrative tension through the potential for recognition, but also bracketing this 'lost soldier' alongside the de-eroticised rites and rituals of pre-adolescent children. Crucially, this entire sequence takes place in the sunken depths of a blackened back alley in Paris; one located, significantly, below ground level, between two buildings, and behind the neoclassical Haussmannian boulevards to which we are elsewhere exposed. Occupying an interstitial zone filled with dirt, decay and filth, here, Laurent can be seen to instantiate the antithesis of André Malraux's Law of the Seven Monuments, a piece of legislation centered on Paris and orientated towards: the preservation and restoration of official memorials; the razing and rebuilding of districts deemed unsanitary (a lack of cleanliness often implicitly attributed to a high percentage of Algerian inhabitants); and the sandblasting and whitewashing of architectural facades; all of which,

Figure 3.2 Laurent as abject antihero.

according to Hannah Feldman, were engineered to encourage France to forget about the 'dark' colonial past with which Laurent is inextricably intertwined (2014: 48–9; see Chapter 1 for more details). So too for later scenes in the film, during which Laurent is depicted as even more insalubrious, even more diseased and even more abject, anticipating, in turn, the 'prehistoric' and primitive imagery of Claude Chabrol's 1969 horror-thriller *Le Boucher/The Butcher*, which turns around a comparably 'atavistic' veteran of Algeria named Popaul (Austin 1999: 67). After fleeing Dany's embrace for an expanse of wooded wilderness in Milly-la-Forêt, Fontainebleau, we thus watch as Laurent's white trench coat is sullied and stained by pastoral surroundings (trees, hills, a lake in which he washes his face; Figure 3.2), accentuating our impression of an individual less human than animal, less civilised than savage, less of this world than otherworldly, and generating a pervasive sense of malaise in the local community, including one repulsed electronics trader, who flat-out refuses to buy a transistor radio[3] from Laurent – that is, until that latter brandishes the pistol that he has pilfered from Paul's apartment. No shot is more symbolic in this respect than the one that captures a starving Laurent, on his knees, in a farm, gobbling pigswill from a trough.

Coinciding with Laurent's lurch from castrated ex-paratrooper to abject anti-hero is a further metamorphosis, from guilt to innocence. At the start of this case study, I briefly paused upon the 'murder' that Laurent commits in the prelude of *Les Distractions*, after he swerves whilst driving into the path of a policeman-in-pursuit. Drenched in inter- and extra-textuality, it is an image that, for a contemporaneous audience, would invariably have brought to mind the opening sequence of Jean-Luc Godard's *À bout de souffle/Breathless* (1960), in which Michel Poiccard, a petty car thief with a penchant for hotwiring T-Birds and Cadillacs, played by Jean-Paul Belmondo, careers down a barely empty road, impulsively slaying a police officer with a pistol, before escaping into the bucolic environs on foot. Yet where Godard frames Michel's crime as clearly intentional if not impulsive, Dupont frames Laurent's crime as potentially unintentional (perhaps he simply lost control of the vehicle?), opening a certain degree of ambiguity in *Les Distractions* that is gently prised open still further as the narrative develops. Neither Paul nor Dany, for instance, appear convinced of Laurent's guilt – quite the opposite. Nor does Paul challenge Laurent when he attests to his innocence during an automobile excursion together (Laurent: 'it had rained, the road was slippery, I never meant to kill him'. Paul: 'I never doubted you'). Likewise, just as the opening scene of *Les Distractions* appears to mitigate the severity of Laurent's 'crime' even as he is committing it, so too do later scenes in the film appear to amplify the severity of the police force intent on solving it. Jeeps, radios, helicopters, dogs: such are just some of the instruments of detection weaponised by the swarm of CRS officers (Republican Security Companies) tasked with tracking – *hunting down* – Laurent, as he sluggishly flees exhausted through the Forest of Fontainebleau, documented masterfully by Dupont through a cycle of tracking shots, and paired with Richard Cornu's equally suspenseful orchestral-militaristic score. A logic of ironic superfluity is woven into this manhunt, pivoting, as it does, between a team of policemen so laden with artillery that they come to resemble paratroopers – instinctive, inexorable, ruthless – and a former paratrooper who appears to have retained next to nothing from his military para-past: no athleticism, no acumen, no stamina. Nobody can help Laurent, he has nowhere to go. At one point, Paul, who has incongruously been tasked with bringing the stand-off to a peaceful conclusion, turns to the superintendent in charge of the operation: 'all of this, for one man? It's disgusting.'

Stripped of his virility by the after-effects of war, sexually humiliated by his male acquaintances and female non-lovers, before being hounded into suicidal submission by the state for a 'crime' he possibly did not commit, in sum, which was probably just a tragic accident, it is at this point in the film that Laurent once again begins to look curiously like Dédé, the 'lost soldier' from Rozier's *Adieu Philippine*, whose wounded fragility I argued in Chapter 1, gently encourages the spectator to forget about the army's complicity in atrocities in Algeria. Both the 'dining scene' in Rozier's film and the 'manhunt scene' in Dupont's film, in this respect, can effectively be seen to pivot around a similar process of sublimation, transforming soldiers into expiated victims with which we are encouraged to sympathise.

Paul: a paratrooper-turned-Hussar

There is also another way in which Dupont's narrative can be said to sublimate the politico-ethical dynamics of the war. But here, the act of sublimation in question is not performed through the transformation of a paratrooper into a castrated and innocent victim of excessive state violence – as is the case with Laurent – but rather through the transformation of a paratrooper into a dapper Hussar named Paul. Traces of this transformation can be identified in various aspects of Paul's persona. Professionally, for example, the simple fact that Paul works as a reporter-photographer for a glitzy, and highly successful, cultural magazine – *Jours de France* – is, of course, significant, insofar as it evokes Blondin, Nimier and Laurent's journalistic aspirations, as pursued in a range of similar publications: *Opéra, Carrefour, La Parisienne, Arts*. Socially, likewise, Paul is someone who clearly embodies the spirit of insolence and insouciance so dear to the Hussars, practically to the point of perfection. Often, this insolence is expressed in an excess of proximity, with Paul brazenly talking at, or talking over, people who clearly do not want to talk (Laurent); platonically touching and erotically caressing people who want neither to be touched nor caressed (Laurent; the carousel of lovers that Paul frequents throughout the film); or even physically attacking individuals who dare to challenge him, as is the case with a fellow barfly, who makes the 'mistake' of chastising Paul for reneging on an anticipated financial deal. Other times, Paul's insolence is expressed in a lack of proximity, with the ex-paratrooper abruptly absenting himself from situations in which he should, from a moral perspective, arguably be present. Such is the case, for example, when Laurent is left alone in Paul's apartment almost immediately after the two men have been reacquainted (Laurent: 'listen Paul, I need to tell you . . . Paul: 'not now, I am in a hurry'); or when Paul's on-and-off, too-tender girlfriend Véra, played by Alexandra Stewart (who also features in Malle's *Le Feu follet*) is stranded in an unfamiliar bar – Café Curieux – crammed with predatory male clients. Seldom does Paul speak in anything other than a Hussar-inflected stream of 'questionable syllogisms and glib provocations' (De Baecque 2012: 121), more often than not fuelled by a potent Hussar cocktail of martinis, whisky and bourgeois soirees, including one held on the rooftop of *Jours de France*, when Paul, ever the socialite, mingles with an elite constellation of stars and star-makers, playboys and cover-girls, journalists and cinephiles (including Claude Chabrol, whose film *Les Cousins* was punctuated with Hussar motifs). Even Paul's attire, composed, as it is, of a snappy combination of single-breasted jackets and tapered trousers, bespeaks a certain Hussar dandyism. Shabby he is not.

One of the most important aspects of *Les Distractions* is the Austin-Healey 100/4 sports car that Paul uses to career around the capital. It is a visual motif that betrays a certain self-reflexivity woven into the film: both Belmondo and

Dupont, after all, were avid car lovers, with the latter using the fees advanced by the producers of *Les Distractions* to buy a spacious Buick convertible, which he then put to use as a kind of clandestine mobile meeting room for members of the OAS (Dupont 2013: 127). It is also a visual motif that once more positions Paul in extra-textual proximity to the Hussars. In her seminal work, *Fast Cars, Clean Bodies*, Kristin Ross, has, for instance, identified Roger Nimier as an ardent aficionado of automobiles, with this obsession being expressed in: the Aston Martin DB4 that Nimier famously drove (a gift from his publisher, Gaston Gallimard); Nimier's interest in the Paris Motor Show, an event that he frequently reviewed in the pages of *Elle* and *Arts*; the inconspicuous auto-centrism of Nimier's forays into screenwriting, with Malle/Nimier's aforementioned *Ascenseur pour l'échafaud* tellingly turning around a tale of two juvenescent outcasts who steal a Mercedes from a former paratrooper; a thematic likewise echoed in Jean Valère's car-infatuated *Les Grandes personnes/Time Out for Love* (1961), itself an adaptation of Nimier's novel *Histoire d'un amour/Love Story* (1953); before Nimier would himself eventually be annihilated by the very fetish-object he adored, through a devastating car crash, in September 1962 (Ross 1995: 26, 40–2, 202). Just behind Paul's derisive rictus can therefore be glimpsed the shadow of Nimier's steely gaze, and just behind Paul's glimmering Austin-Healey can be glimpsed the shadow of Nimier's Aston Martin, once sublimely contoured and envied, later grotesquely mangled and pitied.

Just as Paul's Austin-Healey marks him out as an apostle of the Hussars, so too does it confer upon him a distinctive aura of authority. With this in mind, the simple fact that Paul possesses his convertible is in the first instance significant, notably as it separates him from the 92 per cent of the French population who could not afford to buy a car, let alone a convertible, in the early 1960s (especially members of the rural working-class), with Paul's purchasing power presumably being a perk of his professional vocation as a reporter-photographer, a role clearly 'created out of the reified instrumental relations of bourgeois market society' (Ross 1995: 160). It also distinguishes Paul from Laurent, with the latter being more aligned with the 'degraded forms of automotive being, of Heideggerian *dasein* [existence]' that John Orr associates with cinematic images of 'renting, stealing and borrowing', all of which are performed by Belmondo as Michel in Godard's *À bout de souffle* (1993: 130). In this respect, Paul bears more than a passing similarity to the figure of Frédéric in *La Belle vie*, whose metamorphosis – from unemployed loner to affluent homeowner – I discussed in Chapter 1. Both films essentially chart the ontological recuperation of former soldiers through images of consumerist acquisition.

To this sign of Paul's financial superiority can also be added a further indication of his social superiority, expressed more specifically in how Paul parades his prized car-possession in front of the same whitewashed architectural facades behind which Laurent lurks, many of which are located in the most affluent *quartiers* of Paris: Saint-Germain-des-Prés, Montparnasse, and, especially, the Champs-Élysées.[4] Neatly incarnating both the needs of a modernised post-war workforce demanding mobility, and the impulses of a commodified generation consuming commodities, in this 'society of the spectacle', to cite Guy Debord (1967), Paul is nothing less than spectacular. He is also addicted to speed. When Paul and Laurent flee to Dany's abode in Orly, for example (stopping off in the Forest of Fontainebleau), the two former paratroopers are pictured hurtling along the motorway through a frenetic carousel of nine different shots: one that frames the two men from the seats located behind them (known as a 'French over'); two that are placed on a car mount, capturing the men through the windshield from the perspective of the bonnet; one that exposes us to a sublimely panoramic vision of Paris-as-horizon (neatly harnessing the mobility of the car to pander to spectatorial visual pleasure); and one that is little more than a vertiginous close-up of a tyre in motion; with all of these shots effectively marking the scene as a radical departure from the Hollywood studio tradition of filming talking heads against a process screen. The overall feeling is one of transcendental perception, a too-fast-to-think mentality, or what Jean Baudrillard, writing in 1968, called 'mechanical euphoria', 'grounded in the miracle of motion' ([1968] 2005: 66; see Chapter 6 for a further discussion of 'panoramic gazing').

There is also a gendered edge to this automotive imaginary. During the 1950s, France witnessed the emergence of a recurring cultural idiom that compared the mechanical curvature of automobiles to the corporeal curvature of women, and the act of driving to the act of sexual intercourse. It was this idiom that Roland Barthes addressed in his compelling essay, '*La nouvelle Citroën*/The New Citroën', released as part of his compilation *Mythologies*, and in which Barthes mused upon, firstly, the over-determined semantics of Citroën's new automotive model – the DS, or 'déesse', translated into English as 'the Goddess' – and secondly, the semiological valence of automotive exhibitions (for example the Paris Motor Show), at which the cars on show were fetishistically 'explored with an intense, amorous studiousness', their 'bodywork touched, the upholstery palpated, the doors caressed, and the cushions fondled' by a range of prospective (male) clients ([1957] 1989d: 142). It was also an analogy woven into many film noirs – a cycle of films from which the French New Wave famously drew – including *They Live by Night* (Ray, 1948), and *The Lady from Shanghai* (Welles, 1947), with both noir narratives insisting upon the perversely erotic-aphrodisiac appeal of driving, as a 'speeding prelude to lust, dance, danger and romance' (Orr 1993: 130). And it is an idiom stitched into *Les Distractions*, during which Paul often weaponises his Austin-Healey to entice and enthral the harem of young women that unconditionally dote upon him, including: Arabelle (an aspiring cover-girl played by Sylva Koscina); Dany (the femme fatale that Laurent fails to sleep with in Orly, after Paul has successfully done so); and, above all, Véra, Paul's long-suffering inamorata, and with whom Paul is seen during one key driving-date scene, which blends automotive pleasure with visual pleasure, and visual pleasure with virile pleasure. The scene in question depicts the two lovers driving by various landmarks in Paris, including the Arc de Triomphe, Opéra, and Place de la Concorde, before finally retiring to a hotel located in the affluent 17th arrondissement, on Avenue Mac-Mahon. Entirely devoid of close-ups or dialogue, the function of this automotive date appears twofold: first, to grant the spectator a visual tour of the capital, temporarily transforming the film into a kind of cine-tourism; and, second, to further bolster our understanding of driving as an erotically charged activity, akin to foreplay. A further crucial moment in this respect occurs during Paul and Laurent's aforementioned motorway excursion to Fontainebleau, when the latter gently requests that the former drive 'not too fast' (Figure 3.3). The implication here being that reckless driving is a test of masculinity, a test, moreover, passed by virile men like Paul, and failed by emasculated men like Laurent.

Virility is, of course, a trait that I touched upon in the introduction of this chapter, drawing attention to the significance of colonial brothels in Algeria (often exclusively reserved for paratroopers and legionnaires), alongside the highly gendered military rituals performed by established and aspiring paratroopers alike. Representing a curious blend of colonial, military and cinematic influences, *Les Distractions* can, meanwhile, be said to both regurgitate and

Figure 3.3 'Not too fast' softly pleads Laurent as he is driven to Fontainebleau by Paul.

reconfigure the cultural archetype of the virile paratrooper: regurgitate insofar as Paul is someone blessed with a superlative surfeit of machismo, effortlessly enchanting almost all of the female protagonists he encounters in the capital; and reconfigure insofar as Dupont's film is absolutely not set in Algeria (as is the case in Mark Robson's *Les Centurions/Lost Command*, for instance [see Chapter 2]); but rather in the most sought-after *quartiers* of Paris. Nor is the target of Paul's virility Algerian prostitutes, but rather French cover-girls. All of which seems symptomatic of an attempt at sublimating the perceived sexual potency of the paratroopers, rendering them, in turn, less militarised and more metropolitan, less threatening and more familiar; in short, more like the irreverent Hussars to whom Paul is implicitly compared.

Still more compelling are certain moments in Dupont's narrative that appear to go beyond this process of sublimation, suggesting not only that paratroopers can be virile and charming, but also that this virility could justifiably be violent, and that this violence is – and should be – accepted in French society. A scene that functions in precisely this manner is the one that takes place approximately halfway into the film, when Paul almost strikes Véra after she gently caresses his hand in a local bar, a threat to which she subsequently responds neither with disgust nor disapprobation but by further intensifying the tone of her romantic soliloquies. Later in *Les Distractions*, Véra will likewise plead with Paul to 'get angry with her' after she has attempted to commit suicide due to the anguish of unrequited love, with both scenes depicting Paul's doleful lover as driven by a masochistic yearning to be punished by his libertine passions. Another pivotal moment in this respect occurs immediately after the bar scene identified above, when Paul pays a drunken visit to Véra's colleague and fellow model, Arabelle. Not that Arabelle appears pleased by the timing of Paul's charm offensive (he arrives at three in the morning), nor by his increasingly impertinent behaviour: she brusquely serves him a scotch ('without ice, never with ice' he emphasises insouciantly), before firmly demanding he leave the premises, quickly and quietly. But as is so often the case in Dupont's narrative, these pleas appear to fall on Paul's deaf ears. Instead, in what is undeniably the most damning evidence of Dupont's misogynistic conception of women, as 'dirty objects and orifices', 'undressed if possible' (Durand 1961: 91), Arabelle eventually succumbs to Paul's violent act of 'seduction' (he forces her body down onto the sofa whilst she protests – in other words, by no means consents to his advances), before she later playfully dismisses the episode as behaviour characteristic of a 'Hussar'.

What lingers once again in the ideological-historical backdrop of these scenes is, of course, the litany of atrocities being executed by high-ranking military officials stationed in French Algeria. Thus, where paratroopers were busy amplifying their virility to such an extent that it had arguably come to resemble a quasi-fascistic will-to-power, weaponised against colonised populations through prostitution, via the character of Paul, Dupont re-imagines this virility in softer and more sublimated terms, as a quality associated with charm, automobiles and cocktail parties.[5] And where the same paratroopers were orchestrating often eroticised torture sessions against suspected (male) and female nationalists, some of whom were raped or subjected to instances of sexualised violence (for instance, Djamila Boupacha), Dupont re-imagines a world in which precisely this type of violence is not just tacitly condoned by French citizens, but willingly encouraged by the very women it affects.

Queerness

Paul and Laurent's relationship does not only revolve around a common interest in heterosexual and heteronormative sexual liaisons. At various points in the film, the two ex-paratroopers also share moments of homosocial intimacy, far away from the morass of emotionally sapping female lovers that swarm around the streets of Paris, and which, at points, seem to edge the men into homoerotic territory. Signs of this queer subtext are littered throughout the film. When the caretaker of Paul's apartment block notices that he has brought a young man home with him, for example, Paul's response is, in the first instance, both obscurantist and revealing: 'he is a suffering friend/lover', blurts the ruffled Hussar, with his use of the term 'copain' preserving the ambiguity of their relationship (in French, 'copain' is often paired with 'petit', with the resulting collocation 'petit copain' meaning boyfriend); and his use of the term 'suffering', once again underlining Laurent's status in the film, as a man 'castrated'. Later, when Paul lends Laurent a set of clothes to maintain his friend's anonymity, the latter seems at least initially hesitant to undress in front of the former, until Paul insists: 'what are you waiting for?', with the following scene, that is to say, the one that is cut out of the narrative, presumably chronicling Paul's reaction to Laurent's semi-naked body. Later still, when Paul attempts to provide Véra with a 'rationale' for his behaviour – his supreme indifference, his Hussar egotism, his proclivity towards misogyny – once again, his words assume a homoerotic hue. 'I had a male friend' Paul intones ('un copain'), as the couple lie in bed together: 'a real one'. Once again, the camera then cuts, thus gesturing towards something unsaid, something unspoken, something unseen.

To identify a covert homoerotic subtext in a film narrative I have previously interpreted as rampantly heterosexual, might, at first glance, appear odd, even unjustified. Yet, on closer inspection, the two forms of gendered representation are perhaps not as divergent as they might at first seem. In her illuminating book on stars and stardom in French cinema, Ginette Vincendeau, has for instance, indicated that, in the 1960s, Belmondo's 'hyper-masculine macho image' was often put to use in the company of other male protagonists, 'with women acting as heterosexual tokens' (2000: 163). Equally significant is the fact that during this period Belmondo was frequently cast in buddy movies

(*Classe tous risques/Consider All Risks* [Sautet, 1960]; *Un singe en hiver/A Monkey in Winter* [Verneuil, 1962]), a genre of filmmaking that has alternately been diagnosed as 'implicitly homosexual' and 'covertly homoerotic' (Austin 2008: 79; Tasker 1993: 45), and with which *Les Distractions* may persuasively be aligned, with the 'buddies' here being Paul and Laurent. Analysing a range of classical Hollywood narratives, including *Singin' in the Rain* (Kelly and Donen, 1952) and *Gentlemen Prefer Blondes* (Hawks, 1953), Alexander Doty has likewise insisted that 'basically heterocentrist texts can contain queer elements', before clarifying: 'the queer often operates in the nonqueer, as the nonqueer does in the queer' (1993: 3). But undoubtedly the most pertinent scholar in this case is Jean-Pierre Bertin-Maghit, whose aforementioned study of amateur military films presents us with the possibility to craft an even more precise hypothesis: that *Les Distractions* forms a warped mirror-image of the often queer rites and rituals performed by paratroopers stationed in Algeria. A more recent film that functions both similarly and differently to *Les Distractions* is *Beau travail/Good Work* (Denis, 1999), which depicts a community of legionnaires permeated with repressed homosexual desires. Unlike Dupont's work, however, *Beau travail* constantly foregrounds this repression to the point of excess, emphasising it with a modernist sensibility largely lacking from *Les Distractions*.[6]

What is even more compelling about *Les Distractions* is that this queer subtext sometimes seems to expedite the process of ontological recuperation that I have previously associated with Paul. Two scenes in particular illustrate this point. One of these takes place when Paul and Laurent flee to a secluded bucolic enclave located in the Forest of Fontainebleau, whilst the latter evades the police. From the wine that they share, to Richard Cornu's whimsical orchestral score, to the series of highly physical military manoeuvres that they perform on the ground, evoking the paratrooper tradition of 'jump training': everything about the scene, right down to its setting, far away from the emasculated claustrophobia of the domestic realm, conveys an atmosphere of homosocial-erotic intimacy. Crucially, unlike the sense of maimed masculinity that elsewhere emanates from the body of Laurent, here, Dupont's lost soldier appears cured of 'castration', nostalgically reminiscing about his military past with Paul, the man who restores his masculine ego. The other scene occurs at the climax of the narrative, when Laurent is cornered in a cabin, located, symbolically, amidst the same expanse of woodland in Fontainebleau. Sensing the jaws of the police closing around Laurent, Paul once again harnesses the power of his magnetic charm, incredibly persuading the officers present to purchase a small batch of wine and bread for him and his marooned and soon-to-be-doomed comrade, on the pretext that this will encourage Laurent to surrender. But surrender he doesn't. And what emerges instead is a vastly lyrical, deeply elegiac, and similarly homosocial-erotic cycle of shots, during which Paul and Laurent huddle together in the hut: a late-colonial 'last supper' before the latter, undefeated, turns the gun – *Paul's* gun – on himself, choosing self-destruction over capitulation. Not incidentally, it is also an act performed by a similarly 'castrated' veteran of the war in Louis Malle's sober magnum opus, *Le Feu follet*.

LE FEU FOLLET (1963)

Inspired by an acrimonious novel published in 1931 by the anti-Semitic and pro-Nazi novelist Drieu la Rochelle, Louis Malle's understandably controversial fifth feature-length film, *Le Feu follet*, recounts the final forty-eight hours of Alain Leroy (Maurice Ronet), a down-and-out former playboy and military officer voluntarily detained in a Versailles sanatorium for alcohol addiction, acute depression and suicidal ideation. Naturally enough, Alain's life is marked by a state of disarray: in the opening scene, the spectator is forced to witness his infidelity – committed with a friend of his estranged wife, Dorothy – before he spends the rest of the day ruminating unhealthily about mortality in the claustrophobic miasma of his clinic room (Figure 3.4). It is in this room that the spectator is introduced to a mirror upon which Alain has ominously scrawled

Figure 3.4 Alain ruminates in his clinic room.

a cryptic memento: 'the 23 July'. As the spectator will learn, this memento corresponds to the date of his anticipated demise.

The remainder of the film is thus devoted to chronicling Alain's last day on earth as he visits a carousel of old acquaintances in Paris. These encompass: a middle-aged Egyptologist, Dubourg (Bernard Noël); a charismatic art enthusiast (Jeanne Moreau), whose charm is only tainted by her opium-addled poet-friends; two brothers involved in the campaign of pro-colonial violence orchestrated by the OAS (played by Romain Bouteille and François Gragnon); and a clique of aristocratic acquaintances that Alain meets at a dinner party. Yet, as with almost all the encounters that dictate the ambience of Alain's last day, this party only serves to emphasise his isolation from a world that he consistently designates both meaningless and riddled with 'mediocrity'. His suicide at the end of the film – performed on 23 July, as planned – thus forms the logical response to this lack of meaning. It also signals the final stage of an episodic descent into a state of psychosexual impotence and political disengagement.

Impotence

Le Feu follet might not feature any images of Algeria, any images of soldiers in uniform, or even anyone remotely interested in talking about conflict, but it is a film permeated with a welter of oblique allusions to the war. The Luger pistol, for instance, that Alain cradles in his hands throughout the narrative (owned, in real-life, by Malle, himself a veteran), was a weapon of choice for the army in Algeria (Grant 2018: 4). So too for Alain's alcoholism, which reminds us of the alcoholic tendencies of soldiers stationed in the colonies, many of whom drank excessively to counter 'boredom and solitude' (Branche 2003: 411). Alain's depression could persuasively be regarded as an elliptical indication of post-traumatic stress disorder, again from which many ex-conscripts suffered.[7] Likewise his suicide, which was an act performed by an admittedly small number of veterans, irrevocably scarred by the naked colonial violence to which they had been exposed, and in which they had perhaps been rendered complicit (see Bernard-Aubert's romantic drama *Les lâches vivent d'espoir/My Baby is Black!* [1960] for a comparable scene of attempted suicide, yet performed by a prospective rather than returning conscript).

At the beginning of this chapter, I outlined the ways in which soldiers returning from Algeria were often associated with a loss of virility, a crisis in masculinity, catalysed alternately through the potentially impotence-inducing effects of fear in battle, sexualised rituals of torture, or, for that matter, the emasculating experience of romantic betrayal (see Chapter 5 for more details about betrayal). In the opening scene of *Le Feu follet*, Malle gestures towards a similar crisis in masculinity when ex-soldier Alain fails to sexually please his American lover, Lydia (Léna Skerla), during intercourse. 'I hate myself', claims

Alain, before Lydia unconvincingly insists that she feels 'satisfied'. Her hollow eyes, however, belie the hollowness of her words: there is nothing sensual about this sterile and static encounter of pallid waxy bodies. In existing scholarship on the film, Alain's implied impotence – to which later scenes, discussed below, even more explicitly gesture – has been conceptualised in a number of ways. René Fugler, for example, parses 'the erosion of vital energy' that takes place throughout *Le Feu follet*, marking Alain as someone who embodies 'the drying up of desire, the paralysis of willpower' (1964). In the words of Robert Benayoun, 'at the heart of Alain's desire lies pain' (1963: 7). Claude Mauriac associates Alain with 'virility under threat' (1963). Nathan Southern and Jacques Weissgerber are even more precise in their analysis, defining Alain's *mâle-être* as deriving from 'doubts about his ability to give Lydia orgasms' (2006: 82). However, what none of these scholars do is go beyond framing Alain's condition in vaguely psychological, vaguely existential or vaguely metaphysical terms, refusing, in short, to consider how the aetiology – that is to say, the root cause – of Alain's psychosexual predicament may be anchored in the late-colonial politics and ethics of the era. Alain might not talk about the war, but his body speaks where he is silent.

Le Feu follet is far more explicit when it comes to how Alain's libidinous inadequacies have impacted upon his life. The effects of Alain's impotence can be discerned, for example, in his relationship with alcohol, which, in addition to obliquely evoking military service, also acts as a coping mechanism, prompting the relapsing alcoholic to confess to Dubourg that he 'drinks because [he] make[s] love badly'. Signs of sexual dysfunction can also be seen in Alain's relationship with women, who function either as fetishised yet distant objects of adulation (as with the photographs of female stars affixed to his bedroom mirror – Marilyn Monroe, etcetera); or mollycoddling surrogate mothers. Both Dorothy and Lydia, for instance, act in a manner that is both caring and castrating: the more they assert their financial autonomy over Alain – respectively paying for his treatment and writing him a cheque for an invented debt – the less the latter asserts his. 'In more than one sense, Alain is a "kept man" – not only living under strict rules at the clinic, but also in relation to his estranged wife' (Saddington 2010: 82). Likewise, the remnants of Alain's impotence can be identified in his lack of artistic motivation, with various scenes suggesting that the recovering addict has attempted to keep a diary of his rehabilitation, thus potentially erecting a surrogate facade of credibility that would compensate for the shame of being 'castrated' – by war and by women – before any hopes of this endeavour coming to fruition are thwarted when Alain abruptly crushes his notes in a haze of disenchantment. Finally, Alain's impotence can be glimpsed in the protracted lurch that he performs towards political disengagement. In the narrative, this political inertia is woven into two early scenes that take place before Alain's trip to Paris: first, when he responds to his doctor's inquiries about his military past as an officer in Algeria with indifference (stating 'it's irrelevant'); and second, when he brusquely refuses to engage in conversation about the war with a fellow barfly (he almost knocks over his glass in irritation). But whilst these early scenes largely mitigate Alain's desire to disengage from political matters by placing him in dialogue with two individuals apparently disconnected from politics, Alain's later contact with activists for whom political action is paramount brings the extent of this disengagement into sharp relief, as a malaise inextricably intertwined with his quest for virility.

A prime example of this lurch – from psychosexual impotence to political disengagement – occurs in a scene that does not appear in Drieu's novel, when the increasingly disillusioned ex-officer decides to visit Jérome and François Minville, two former military comrades turned OAS members at the chic Café de Flore. Despite being surrounded by people, the brothers do not attempt to hide the extent of their activism. They have no qualms, for example, about divulging the details of a recent spell in prison for what could have hypothetically been an extremely violent act of pro-colonial terrorism, given that the modus operandi of the OAS often involved plastic bombs concealed around the premises of left-wing intellectuals, including Sartre. Nor do they seem perturbed about revealing their desire to continue on this path until the job is done. 'We are stubborn', hyperbolises François, whilst Alain unsuccessfully attempts to convince them of their naivety. But it's too late: they have already left, without paying the bill. End of conversation.

When asked to explain his reasons for interposing this scene into an otherwise largely faithful adaptation of Drieu's original novel, Malle framed his decision as a question of narrative logic, stating that he wanted to 'increase the number of ideological positions with which Alain disagrees, thus providing an even more watertight rationale for taking his own life' (Martin 1963b). But does Alain's encounter with the OAS really offer the acrimonious clash between ideologies that Malle seems to imply? One part of the sequence that suggests otherwise is the series of panning shots that immediately follows the departure of the Minville brothers, when Alain pauses to reflect on the café terrace after being subjected to their condescending diatribe. For any 'politically engaged' member of 1960s French society, this would have been the moment to take action against the OAS, especially as two of its members had just brazenly revealed their future plans for chaos. But instead, Alain tumbles back into a state of profound sexual anxiety: illustrated first in his self-effacing reaction to the alluring gaze of a female client, who rocks back and forward on her chair in a seductive manner before losing interest, and then towards an unidentified male client, with whom he shares a moment of confused intimacy in the toilets of the café (the two men gaze at each other intensely via a mirror on the wall). If the sequence could be applauded for offering an important if cloaked queer counterpoint to the pervasive heteronormativity, even homophobia, of post-war French society[8] – aligning *Le Feu Follet* with the discreet homo-eroticism of Claude Chabrol's *Le Beau Serge/Handsome Serge* (1958), the vaguely gender-bending aesthetics of Jean-Luc Godard's *À bout de souffle* (1960), the mildly transgender iconography of François Truffaut's *Jules et Jim/Jules and Jim* (1962), the fluid sexuality of Marcel Carné's *Les Tricheurs/ Young Sinners* (1958), and the disavowed queerness of *Les Distractions* – it could equally be criticised for abruptly shifting the focus of the narrative, away from the radicalisation of politics generated in the decolonisation of Algeria (for more details on queerness in the New Wave see Asibong 2012). Recalling Geneviève Sellier's definition of *Ascenseur pour l'échafaud* as a film that 'occults politics under the cover of individual tragedy' (2008: 133), in this key scene, the value of political activism against the OAS disappears behind a smokescreen of phallic anxiety, of 'individual tragedy', of castration, as Alain is held captive by his flailing desire.

A Hussar, castrated

Perhaps unsurprisingly – given the aforementioned subtext of political disengagement woven into *Le Feu follet* – a number of commentators have compared the film to the work of the Hussars. Hugo Frey, for instance, has described how 'political engagement is ignored' in the film, in favour of 'psychological pity', catalysed through Alain's status as 'a tragic, romantic, elegant anti-hero' (2004a: 228). Antoine de Baecque goes further, framing *Le Feu follet* as the cinematic equivalent of Nimier's aforementioned work, *Le Hussard bleu* (2012: 128), and Alain as

> endowed with several of the requisite attributes of the Hussar dandy: he, too, likes guns, women, death, literature, and he, too, lives in a time warp where the present pales by comparison with a past in which Alain 'used to command'. (2012: 126)

Yet, if Alain undeniably incarnates the turn away from political militancy that characterised the work of the Hussars, and exists within the same ultra-bourgeois-aristocratic milieu that they did, the dynamics of this analogy must also be treated with caution: first because the scene elaborated above appears to undermine the legitimacy of the reactionary Right by depicting the OAS as exaggerated comic caricatures of political activism; and second, as *Le Feu follet* is conspicuously devoid of the libertinism that subtends the archetypal Hussar text. In relation to this libertinism, Jacques Laurent's *Caroline Chérie* (1947), for example, revels in the debauchery and sexual transgression of a sixteen-year-old adolescent caught up in the French Revolution, whilst Nimier's *Le Hussar bleu* focuses on the carnal escapades of a military cavalryman. In fact, Alain shares more similarities with 'the dandy-like *minet* [darling] of the affluent bourgeoisie, of whom we find a cinematic expression in the intellectual heroes of art cinema such as Jean-Pierre Léaud and Marcello Mastroianni' (Vincendeau 2000: 161). This fragility appears to have been lost on Antoine Blondin who – in an act of dazzling journalistic misinterpretation – completely subverted the sexual politics of Malle's narrative by describing it as 'oozing with virility' (1963: 7). It is anything but that.

Alain's encounter with OAS activism is not the only example of how Malle elevates the question of wounded male sexuality above political concerns, represented subsequently as derisory, even though it does form an exemplary instance of this phenomenon. It also occurs during the aristocratic dinner party hosted by Cyrille (Jacques Sereys), when Alain – by this point intoxicated by his first sip of alcohol in months – tumbles into the presence of Marc Brancion (Tony Taffin). Imposing, eminent and portentous, in Drieu's novel, Brancion is framed as a rich and virile entrepreneur whose colonial exploits in Asia have brought him extraordinary wealth (he is alternately described as possessing 'the face of a hero', and as 'a force of nature'). Malle maintains Brancion's sexual potency, his unyielding gaze and wanderlust (at one point, the latter vigorously demonstrates his knowledge of Oriental erotica to an entranced throng of female guests), whilst granting him an important if very much ambiguous political edge. Whilst Alain rests before dinner, Cyrille describes Brancion as a 'controversial intellectual', whereas a further clue to the latter's political persuasion emerges when he responds with disgust to an anecdote revealing Alain's lack of respect for the Tomb of the Unknown Soldier (a historical war monument located in Paris), thus perhaps elliptically suggesting that Brancion is an advocate for the army in Algeria, or at least harbours certain pro-military sympathies. Crucially, like the Minville brothers, Brancion's dedication to action rather than inaction induces what turns out to be the definitive crisis in Alain's short life, a life carved in two by the taste of cold flesh and burning nostalgia and private malady and days and days of sickly reverie. To put it bluntly: 'psychosexual collapse' (Frey 2004b: 26) As the party reaches its melodramatic denouement, Alain thus abruptly addresses Brancion in a groundswell of inebriated emotion:

> just so you know, I'm a man, but I've never had money or women. Yet I'm very active. The thing is, I can't reach out with my hands . . . I can't touch things . . . and when I touch things . . . I feel nothing.

Immediately after, the agonised swain complains of being 'unable to desire the women at the party'.

Recalling the gendered politics of Drieu's novel,[9] Alain's soliloquy strikes an unsettling balance, between humanist empathy and narcissistic egocentrism.

Empathetic in the sense that it is delivered with an unexpected touch of pathos that once again raises the possibility of a submerged subtext of quasi-queer, quasi-masochistic, quasi-misogynistic impotence, expressed in Alain's increasingly homoerotic attempts at salvaging the loss of his own virility by taking vicarious pleasure in the virility of others. And egocentric in that it continues to coil the narrative around the lynchpin of ontology – of what it means to be 'a man', or what happens when one is no longer 'a man' – rather than fostering the political debate that briefly threatens to engulf the dinner party. So much so, in fact, that the two chief questions generated in this scene – why Brancion has come to be known as a controversial intellectual, and what his political position actually is – remain curiously unresolved as Alain exits the property. On one side, a virile political activist, on the other, an emasculated apolitical dandy.

Self-death

Not incidentally, it is also at Cyrille's dinner party that Alain's destiny begins to sharpen into focus. 'We fade away fast', he insinuates, before the final stage of the film provides an agonisingly stark depiction of Alain's protracted self-eradication, executed with a single Luger shot to the heart (see front cover of book). Set amidst the antiquated majesty of Alain's clinic room, and composed of a series of long takes, whose dilated duration and unwavering stasis mirror 'the decrease in psychomotor activity characteristic of depression' (Kristeva 1989: 10), this scene is equally notable insofar as it evokes various European literary trends from the 1700s, 1800s and early 1900s, all of which romanticised self-death as an act of 'aesthetic self-assertion and social and metaphysical transcendence' (Livak 2000: 247). Leonid Livak, for instance, has identified traces of this tendency in the Romanticism of the eighteenth century, as embodied in Goethe's anti-hero Werther; in the nineteenth-century proto-Surrealist and Symbolist legacies of Lautréamont and Rimbaud, who 'incarnated a [quasi-suicidal] ideal of social and existential evasion' (2000: 246); in the work of inter-war Surrealists, such as Louis Aragon and Antonin Artaud, for whom 'suicide was a way of 'transcending everyday life' (2000: 250); and in the radical Dadaism of poet, Jacques Rigaut, whose meticulously planned death at the age of thirty in 1929 was hailed by many avant-garde intellectuals as the epitome of 'artistic "sincerity"' (2000: 253). Rigaut, in particular, is an important point of reference here, if only because Drieu la Rochelle's original novel formed an elegiac, quasi-biographic mediation on Rigaut's passing (the aforementioned anecdote about the Tomb of the Unknown Soldier is often attributed to him). It was also followed by Drieu's own suicide in 1945, as the author became aware of the mortal judicial implications of being a pro-Nazi collaborator in a post-Nazi world. To say that *Le Feu follet* is haunted by multiple legacies of death is therefore not an exaggeration: behind Alain's demise lies Drieu's suicide, and behind Drieu's suicide lies Rigaut's demise. Even Malle himself has confessed to sporadically questioning the worth of life, aligning him too with these doomed figures (Martin 1963b).

As for the psychological logic that drives Alain's decision, scholars seem conflicted. In what is undoubtedly the most lucid reading of this scene, John Saddington has, for instance, insisted that Alain's suicide lacks 'any clear explanatory structure', aligning his death-drive with what, in the nineteenth century, was sometimes described as 'obscure melancholia' (2010: 92), and again recalling the Dadaist-Surrealists of the inter-war years, for whom suicide had to be unmotivated to be of artistic value. 'One could not die "for a reason"' (Livak 2000: 252). Robert Benayoun sees it another way, identifying Alain's suicide as a gesture that may *seem* unmotivated, yet actually performs a powerful psychosexual function: to 'restore his desire' (1963: 7). It is a reading supported by Drieu's novel, which exalts Alain's self-death 'as proof that [he] really is a man' (1959: 172). Thus, where impotence has left Alain unable to control the bodies of the women that sap his vitality, suicide enables him to take full control over his own body, albeit by nihilistically eliminating the life from it. And where impotence has engendered a combination of pity and indifference in the female figures that nurture Alain (certainly compared to the masculine gravitas of Brancion), suicide will force these figures into a state of mourning and pathos, guilt and responsibility (see Chapter 5 for more details about women and guilt). In the final shot of *Le Feu follet*, Alain's suicide note – superimposed as an inter-title over an image of his lifeless face – is even more explicit, condensing the masochistic-misogynistic-narcissistic subtext of psychosocial castration that subtends the entire narrative. Addressing an anonymous, although presumably female, protagonist (Dorothy?), this note reads: 'I am killing myself because you didn't love me, because I didn't love you. I am killing myself because our ties were loose, to tighten them. I am going to leave an indelible stain on you.'

Lastly, to a gender-inflected reading of this scene, we may also add a more politically and ethically orientated one. In Geneviève Sellier's aforementioned monograph, the author describes how Godard's *Le Petit soldat* 'recounts the tragic story of a man who tries in vain to free himself from the trap of political allegiance to become himself' (2008: 136). Extending this thesis to the denouement of Malle's film, we might say that *Le Feu follet* turns around a man who attempts to free himself from the trap of political allegiance by *destroying* himself. In *Le Feu follet*, suicide is thus Alain's calling card, his lyrical destiny, a Romantic gesture that provides a simultaneous solution to the 'problem' of impotence and the 'problem' of politics, as embodied and exacerbated by the action of the Minville brothers and Brancion. Beyond history, beyond militancy, beyond the emasculating sequelae inflicted upon Alain's body, by women, by war and by the virility of others, in the sublime succour of suicide,

Alain is innocent and free, a victimised and vindicated veteran, like Laurent in *Les Distractions*. In the next chapter of this book, we will find a strikingly similar fusing of political disengagement and self-victimisation in Jacques Doniol-Valcroze's 1962 film, *La Dénonciation*, which, not incidentally, features none other than Maurice Ronet as an apolitical and absolved Hussar dandy.

Notes

1. See, for example, Pascal Ory (1985), Hugo Frey (2004a; 2004b), Philippe D'Hugues (2006), Paul Renard (2010), Antoine de Baecque (2012), Marc Dambre (2014), and Geneviève Sellier (2000; 2008).
2. It is worth noting that Françoise Sagan's ethos of 'Saganism' has often been defined as a female equivalent to the andro-centric counter-culture of the Hussars, associated, as it was, with 'sports cars, bottles of scotch, short-lived love affairs, etc' (Truffaut cited in Marie 2003: 101). Susan Weiner identifies one cinematic instance of this 'Saganism' in Mic, the female antihero of Marcel Carné's *Les Tricheurs/Young Sinners* (1958), and who lives a life replete with 'easy money, wild parties, jazz, Jaguars, and free love in Saint-Germain-des-Prés' (2001: 165). Another is Juliette, as played by Bridgitte Bardot in *Et Dieu . . . créa la femme/And God Created Woman* (Vadim, 1956). For more details see De Baecque (1998: 127), Marie (2003: 98–103), and Weiner (2001: 163–9).
3. An over-determined object, this radio is important for a least two reasons. First, insofar as Laurent steals it from a car – an act that once again defines him as estranged from the world of modernisation and motorisation of which Paul is the embodiment; and second, as it evokes the lived reality of the war, albeit obliquely. As Susan Weiner reveals: 'the transistor radio's portability and price made it the ideal going-away present many parents offered sons called to serve in Algeria – a gift that was, furthermore, recommended by military hierarchy as a way for the young soldier to fill his empty hours, and was available for purchase through the army magazine *Bled*' (2001: 144).
4. Both *La Belle vie* and *Les Distractions* feature an almost obsessive focus on the Champs-Élysées and the Arc de Triomphe, in particular. In Enrico's film, Frédéric takes Sylvie to the Champs-Élysées when he receives a providential photography contract; in Dupont's film, Paul takes Véra to the Champs-Élysées in order to court her. Once they have managed to dream their consumerist fantasies into reality, both Frédéric and Paul also articulate an expression included in the title of a further film examined in this book: 'Paris nous appartient [Paris belongs to us]' (see Chapter 1 and Chapter 5).
5. Philip Dine crafts a similar argument about Robson's *Les Centurions*, exploring how the images of paratrooper virility woven into the film simultaneously exalt the reputation of the French army whilst undermining the claims of anti-military intellectuals (2016: 124).
6. For more details see Hayward (2001), Beugnet and Sillers (2001) and Cooper (2001).
7. While post-traumatic stress disorder was only formally recognised as a legitimate medical condition in 1980, some estimates suggest that as many as 250,000–300,000

veterans from the Algerian War of Independence may suffer from the condition (Inrep 2011: 43–7).
8. As Richard Dyer states, 'the postwar period was markedly homophobic. The anti-gay legislation introduced under Vichy in 1942 was maintained, and the Paris police began cracking down on homosexuality from 1949 on; anti-gay laws were to be strengthened under Charles de Gaulle' (2000: 128).
9. According to Allen Thiher, in Drieu's novel, 'women are both the object desired and the source of emasculation that destroys desire. In reaction to this constant castration, Alain gives in to fantasies in which he seems to seek self-humiliation' (1973: 38).

PART II

OTHERS

4. EX-RESISTANTS, CONSCIENTIOUS OBJECTORS AND THE ETHICS OF MEMORY

'We live by forgetting our metamorphoses.' This obtuse epigraph – included as an extradiegetic insert at the beginning of Jacques Doniol-Valcroze's *La Dénonciation/The Denunciation* (1962), although plucked from a poem published by Paul Eluard in 1946 – is a fitting precursor to the dialectic of remembering and forgetting that I associate with the two case studies of this chapter: Doniol-Valcroze's film and Claude Autant-Lara's *Tu ne tueras point/L'Objecteur/ Thou Shalt Not Kill* (1963).[1] For if both works were released at the end of the Algerian War of Independence, and if they both expose us, disquietingly, to some of the most violent crimes committed during the Occupation of France (1940–4), crimes encroaching on the unthinkable, yet mediated in the films through thought, then they both erect what is ultimately a reassuring, even idealised, vision of the late-colonial present, in which French citizens shed the guilt of the war in order to embrace, vindicated and virtuous, the bliss of the future. Peace is paramount, the two films proclaim, as their protagonists waver and falter, between states of pathological anamnesis and redemptive amnesia.

This chapter will essentially aim to straddle two critical trends in memory studies, one of which is anchored in notions of disclosure, justice and remembering, the other, in notions of denial, injustice and forgetting. As for the former, recent discussions regarding the poetics and aesthetics of memory (Rothberg 2009; Silverman 2013) have done much to draw attention to the significance of a figurative trope used by many French and francophone thinkers working in the 1950s and early 1960s. At once spatial and temporal, this trope was premised upon the pervasively held belief that the atrocities being perpetrated by the French army in French Algeria during the late 1950s and early 1960s, for example torture, were justifiably comparable to the atrocities that had been perpetrated during the rise of National Socialism in the 1930s and early 1940s by various German organisations. These included: the Wehrmacht (a coupling of the German army, air force and navy); the Schutzstaffel, or SS (a paramilitary group consisting of hard-line supporters of Nazism); and the Gestapo (the secret police). As Jean-Paul Sartre pithily put it: 'colonialism over there [in Algeria], fascism over here [in France]: one and the same thing' ([1962] 2001: 73). Charlotte Delbo, Frantz Fanon, Albert Memmi and Aimé Césaire were just some of the intellectuals convinced of the import of this transhistorical trope, with Philip Dine going so far as to call it 'inescapable' (1995). Judging from the cinematic landscape of the era, it also seeped into many late-colonial films. In *Muriel ou le temps d'un retour/Muriel or the Time of a Return* (1963), for example, Alain Resnais chronicles the vicissitudes of a mother struggling to placate the mercurial behaviour of her son – a former conscript in Algeria, acquainted with a member of the right-wing terrorist organisation, the OAS (see Introduction) – amidst the exhausted ruins of a town which endured sustained bombing during the Second World War. In *La Belle vie/The Good Life* (Enrico, 1964), Frédéric drifts listlessly into a local cinema, where he – and we – are exposed to documentary footage of Nazi demonstrations, atrocities and the vilification of Jews during the Occupation, before a disembodied voice drives the point home: 'do you really want this to happen again?' (see Chapter 1). In the reverse-ethnographic documentary *Chronique d'un été/Chronicle of A Summer* (1961), Edgar Morin and Jean Rouch place footage of a discussion in which one of the participants reveals that she is a survivor of the concentration camps, directly after a discussion about race and the war. In Henri Colpi's *Une aussi longue absence/A Very Long Absence* (1961), an amnestic drifter appears in Puteaux, a Parisian commune, prompting the owner of the local *bistrot* to question whether he is her long-lost husband, rounded up sixteen years earlier by German soldiers, whilst another character muses elliptically about the effects of the war upon the French psyche. In *Octobre à Paris/October in Paris* (1962), Jacques Panijel overlays stark archival footage taken at a police massacre committed at Charonne metro station on the 8 February 1962 with the universalising epigram: 'everyone is a Jew, everyone is an Arab' (see Chapter 7). In each of these scenes, memories collide as the past and present are condensed into a figurative constellation of meanings and messages.

The 'inescapable' presence of this trope in 1950s and early 1960s French culture has been corroborated by various cultural theorists; however, its value remains subject to discussion. Both Michael Rothberg and Max Silverman have, for instance, done much to promote a politicised understanding of this trope, coining the terms 'multidirectional memory' (Rothberg 2009) and 'palimpsestic memory' (Silverman 2013) to refer to its structure, and imbuing it with three central powers. The first of these is the power to disclose certain truths about decolonisation and the Holocaust, with Silverman reading several narratives in which 'the present is shown to be shadowed or haunted by a past which is not immediately visible but is progressively *brought into view*' (2013: 3 [emphasis added by author]). A second power relates to the potential for generating empathy for, and transversal solidarity between, the communities often represented in this complex layering of spatio-temporal planes (for instance the Jews and Algerians to which Panijel above refers), with Rothberg defining his notion of multidirectional memory as 'the grounds on which people construct and act upon visions of justice' (2009: 19). This brings us to a third power attributed to this particular staging of memory: the power to prevent amnesia, that is to say, to encourage the readers of a text, or the spectators of a film, to remember the severity of past crimes to avoid making them, or condoning them, in the present. During the Algerian War of Independence, 'many observers understood the French state's widespread use of extrajudicial violence as a reawakening of the past', states Rothberg, before intimating how this process of 'reawakening' manifests itself in *Chronique d'un été* (2009: 175–98). Silverman concurs, pointing out the myriad ways in which so-called Left Bank directors such as Alain Resnais (*Muriel ou le temps d'un retour*) and Chris Marker (*La Jetée/The Jetty* [1962]) assembled their films upon an often dystopian, 'concentrationary universe', 'relating the Nazi camps to the broader history of human subjection in the modern world', including 'the barbarity of colonialism' (2013: 14). Elsewhere, Silverman goes further, aligning multidirectional configurations of memory with 'a reappraisal of the human in the wake of extreme terror' (2013: 4).

Other theorists appear less convinced of the political, ethical or representational merit of this hybrid imaginary. In a thought-provoking yet somewhat contradictory chapter,[2] Philip Dine, for instance, has examined the same turn towards spatio-temporal collision as that analysed by Silverman and Rothberg, but comes to a radically different conclusion: that correspondences drawn between epochs by French artists actively functioned to 'hide' the Algerian War of Independence from the purview of the public, 'denying' it visibility, and, in turn, encouraging French citizens to forget about decolonisation, even as it was occurring (1995: 269–70). Benjamin Stora has similarly claimed that, during the 1960s, 'the conflictual and anguish-laden memory of the Occupation momentarily covered up the significance of the Algerian War', leading to the spread of 'amnesia' (1998: 226). Echoing the focus of this chapter, and indeed, this book, Stora moreover posits that 'forgetting the "events" of the War helped French citizens to absolve themselves of crimes committed during it' (1998: 8). Likewise for Alex Adams, whose brilliant analysis of Jean-Luc Godard's *Le Petit soldat/The Little Soldier* (1960/1963) illustrates how the film might craft a 'multidirectional' or 'palimpsestic' nexus of allusions to wars past and present, but in so doing, surreptitiously skews the ethical stakes in the war by privileging the victimhood of a disengaged, even anarchic, member of a right-wing terrorist organisation named Thomas (Bruno Subor). 'The film's focus on French suffering and its insistence on using old narratives to explain new political phenomena', insists Adams, 'results in the occulting of aspects of the war – such as the nature of Algerian anticolonialism and the Muslim experience of suffering under colonial rule – without which it is impossible to explain' (2016: 116). As we will see, this argument is one that could also be made in relation to Doniol-Valcroze's *La Dénonciation*, equally consumed, as it is, not just with 'French suffering', but also the suffering of a politically disengaged Hussar dandy (see Chapter 4 for more on the Hussars).

Not all theorists have felt it necessary to take sides in this critical debate. In an incredibly lucid monograph, Debarati Sanyal, for instance, has made a claim for reading the transhistorical metaphorical imaginary deployed by many French cultural practitioners during the post-Second World War epoch as a double edged sword: capable, on the one hand, of teasing into visibility acts of violence rendered invisible by state censorship, 'producing solidarities and affiliations across historical and ethnocultural lines', and, on the other hand, of 'driving us to dangerous intersections', where 'divisions are deepened', 'certain histories are occluded', 'difference is eclipsed into sameness' and 'identification leads to appropriation or disavowal' (2015: 2, 18). Thus, according to Sanyal, even as Albert Camus's *La Peste/The Plague* (1947) weaves an allegorical tale about the limitations of French colonialism in French Algeria, so too does it 'perpetrate an aesthetic extermination of Algerians' in the country, chiefly by removing them from the novel (2015: 100 [see Chapter 6 for more details about Camus and the absence of Algerians in settler cinema]). And even as Alain Resnais's *Nuit et brouillard/Night and Fog* (1956) crafts a powerful exhortation to remember the litany of atrocities committed under the banner of Nazi ideology, so too has the director been 'accused of symbolic collaboration with genocide in his failure to convey the specifically Jewish nature of the Final Solution' (Sanyal 2015: 100). Elsewhere, Sanyal pertinently frames Resnais's documentary as one that 'seems to perpetuate a depoliticising vision of culpability', as France's collective complicity in the Holocaust is obliquely obscured (2015: 103).

Extending Sanyal's brilliantly nuanced conception of post-Holocaust culture to that of late-colonialism, yet also drawing from the theories of Rothberg, Silverman, Adams and others aligned with memory studies, this chapter will thus be organised into four sections, all of which relate back to the discourse of 'redemptive pacifism' identified in the Introduction of this book. In the first section, I question the political merit of the flashbacks that feature in *La Dénonciation*, illustrating how they operate in a 'multidirectional' or 'palimpsestic' fashion to reveal troubling truths suppressed by the French state, both after the Occupation and during decolonisation. In the second section, I invert the terms of this reading, interpreting the same flashbacks as part of a more general tendency in late-colonial culture to represent French citizens as innocent victims of state abuse, and interrogating the subtext of motivated forgetting, political disengagement and ethical redemption that subtends *La Dénonciation* more generally. The third section shifts towards a discussion of *Tu ne tueras point*, arguing that the film displays a strikingly similar instance of 'multidirectional' memory, again mediated through the parameters of a flashback, however, this time experienced by a guilt-ridden German soldier-priest. The fourth section will then conclude with some final thoughts on Autant-Lara's representation of redemptive amnesia and conscientious objection, as an act performed by a French citizen blissfully shorn of implication in military atrocities.

La Dénonciation (1962)

Jacques Doniol-Valcroze was a man whose personal history was marked as much by artistic creativity as it was by political contradiction. Thus, not only was he a self-proclaimed 'leftist libertine' (Sellier 2000: 483), who had previously fought as a Resistant with the 2nd Armoured Division during the Occupation, before participating in the September 1960 Manifesto of the 121 (*Manifeste des 121*), an open letter to the government justifying acts of military disobedience (see Chapter 7), but he was also the co-founder and editor of *Cahiers du cinéma*, a journal whose Young Turk critics, including Truffaut, Rivette, Godard and Chabrol, positively embraced a combination of Hussar apoliticism and right-wing provocation, as a tonic to what they perceived as the moralising didacticism of left-wing intellectuals, such as Sartre. As Antoine de Baecque glosses, 'in the virulent polemics of the time, *Cahiers* was called a "fascist publication", and the films themselves were charged with a spirit of "right-wing anarchism"' (2012: 104). Mirroring these contradictions, *La Dénonciation* thus begins when the left-wing film producer Michel Jussieu (Maurice Ronet) accidently stumbles across the body of an individual hidden in a dimly lit Parisian stripclub (Playboy), on 26 October 1961, before being himself beaten into unconsciousness by initially unidentified men. It is around this initial discovery that the hermeneutics of the narrative henceforth revolve: first, through the revelation that the body belongs to a former paratrooper and member of the OAS, murdered as a result of divisions within the group, second, through Michel's attempts at piecing together a coherent narrative of the crime scene (obscured through the symptoms of quasi-amnesia), and third, through the involuntary resurgence of a series of repressed memories, formed during Michel's participation in the Resistance, and which lead him ultimately to an easeful death.

The burden of anamnesis

In a compelling book, Maureen Turim (1989) has analysed how the narrative device of the flashback was deployed in 1940s film noir, parsing how noir narratives, such as *Double Indemnity* (Wilder, 1944) and *Citizen Kane* (Welles, 1941), 'portray their own versions of how memories are stored, how they are repressed, and how they return from the repressed' (1989: 19; also see Atack 2006: 163). In the noir-inspired landscape of *La Dénonciation*, meanwhile, a strikingly similar instance of this 'return of the repressed' occurs when Michel and his wife Elsa (Françoise Brion) retreat to bed after a boozy sortie (Figure 4.1). They languorously confer about the police chief, Malterer (Sacha Pitoëff), with whom Michel, according to Elsa, is 'collaborating', before the mood of the scene abruptly falters, recalling Jean Dréville's late-colonial noir melodrama *Les Suspects/The Suspects* (1957).[3] Shrill stringed music, coupled with a premonitory non-diegetic voice-over provided by Laurent Terzieff, who plays the central protagonist of *Tu ne tueras point*, invades the soundtrack. A phone rings – nobody speaks. A close-up of Michel's fearful face looms sharply into vision. It is then, and only then, once the spectator has been made aware that something is happening, or has happened, or will happen, or could happen, that Michel is abruptly plucked from

Figure 4.1 Elsa cradles Michel in *La Dénonciation*.

the domestic haven of the present in order to be dropped, brusquely, into the miasmatic confines of a windowless building, in the past. Time forks violently.

A piercing scream. A light switched off. A body being dragged down a sterile corridor. Such is the confused slideshow of images that shudders, vividly, through the flashback that follows, when a palpably more youthful yet decidedly more bruised Michel is hauled before two unidentified men in a dingy office. Suddenly, insignia sewn into the attire of one of the men – 'SS' – as well as the poster of Hitler that adorns an adjacent wall, spell out the contours of a historical period – the Occupation – inflecting Michel's limp body, naked from the waist upwards, with the indicia of fascistic violence. Due to his participation in the Resistance, he has, we glean, been tortured by the SS: pulverised, dehumanised, but not defeated. Indeed, almost as soon as Michel has vigorously refused to provide details of his Resistance network, he is handed a psychological lifeline from the translator present in the room (Jean-Claude Darnal), who discreetly informs him that his superior has already solicited all of the information he ostensibly requires from former bouts of interrogation (Figure 4.2). 'The colonel knows everything', the translator intones. To which Michel naturally replies by relinquishing, through gritted teeth, everything *he* knows about his Resistance network: dates, times, places; nothing is spared. Except Michel's life.

Figure 4.2 A wounded Michel (left) faces his ambivalent translator (right).

As formally conventional as this flashback might be, it also displays a startlingly unconventional concern with the vicissitudes of French history. After all, it was precisely the type of questions generated in this scene – whether acts of denunciation or collaboration were ever justified, and if so, under what circumstances – that went not only unposed but also unanswered for almost twenty years in French culture: from the mid 1940s to the mid 1960s. Instead, as Naomi Greene has glossed, during this period, collective 'memories of the Vichy past were governed, in France, by a pervasive climate of bad faith, of amnesia and repression', of lies and alibis, 'of self-serving half-truths' (1999: 37, 46), all of which were engineered, with the tacit acquiescence of the people, to help soften, assuage and displace the guilt generated by the most troubling aspects of this troubling era. Some of these half-truths were dreamt up by the then president, Charles de Gaulle, whose towering 'post-war rhetoric of victory' (Higgins 1996: 185), steeped in hagiography, martyrology, bombastic metaphors and rhetorical devices, as much as insistent, over-determined allusions to the approximately 77,000 Resistants who had died weapon in hand, or after withstanding torture (for example Jean Moulin), recuperated France from a state of wounded shame to pristine pride. Others were proffered by directors working in the state endorsed cinema industry, for example, Louis Daquin, in his *Patrie/Homeland* (1946), René Clément, in his *La Bataille du rail/The Battle of the Rails* (1946), Christian Maudet (aka Christian-Jaque), in his *Babette s'en va-t-en guerre/Babette Goes to War* (1959), and François Villiers, in his *La Verte moisson/Green Harvest* (1959), all of which mythologised the French Resistance still further. As Susan Hayward muses,

> during the post-war years [many aspects of the Occupation] were too unpleasant or unmentionable to be screened. [France's] humiliation and guilt did not make for easy speculation. Small wonder then that the industry followed the general trend at that time of indirect denial. (1993: 147)

By 1959, the sheer popularity of this denial had attained such a state of ubiquity that Doniol-Valcroze himself, writing in *France Observateur*, could castigate it, poetically, as 'the opium of the people' (cited in Jeancolas 1979: 106).

Exposing us to the effects of this 'opium', this 'denial', during a flashback that appears later in *La Dénonciation*, the spectator thus learns of how Michel managed to preserve 'not only his life, but also his honour', principally by withholding details of his act of denunciation from his friends and acquaintances, just as de Gaulle and the directors listed above withheld the most shameful aspects of the history of Occupation from an acquiescent French society. Even when summoned to the post-war trial of the translator present during his torture a neurasthenic Michel continues to deceive those around him. The difference here is that the ethos that Michel incarnates no longer impinges on questions of honour, but mortality, and his decision not to reveal the aforementioned benevolence of the translator, for fear that this revelation could taint his own prestigious legacy, effectively amounts to an act of murder. Retreating into mute silence, into political quietism, into a bittersweet state of bad faith, Michel indirectly kills the very man who indirectly saved him.

The only person that Michel is unable to deceive is, apparently, himself, or rather, his mind. Indeed, the more we compare the psychological subtext of *La Dénonciation* with the wider cinematic and political impulses that crafted the culture of the era, the more we realise that the film is little more than an elaborate psycho-political allegory; one notably through which Michel's futile attempt at interring the private guilt of his act of denunciation personifies the pervasive public climate of bad faith that shaped public memories of Vichy after the Liberation. When, in the paralytic white heat of anamnesis, Michel experiences the return of personal memories repressed in the folds of his subjective unconscious, what he is really experiencing, then, is the return of supra-personal memories repressed in the folds of the nation's collective unconscious. Leading the spectator gently yet disquietingly into what Marc Ferro has called the hidden 'psycho-socio-historical zones' of the national imaginary (1988: 82–3), Michel involuntarily recalls what France had wilfully forgotten.

Torture: becoming a victim

Just as *La Dénonciation* discloses certain truths disavowed in the past, so too does it disclose certain truths disavowed in the present. As with several other films discussed in this book, Doniol-Valcroze's narrative can, first of all, be seen to chronicle what many left-wing intellectuals writing in the late 1950s and early 1960s metaphorised as the 'gangrenous seeping' (Kuby 2013: 138) of pro-colonial violence, from the tactics of 'pacification' adopted by soldiers in Algeria (especially during the Battle of Algiers), to the tactics of intimidation adopted by the OAS in France. In Enrico's *La Belle vie/The Good Life* (1964), Frédéric's motorbike is split asunder by an explosion in Paris, presumably an act of the OAS (Chapter 1). In Alain Cavalier's *L'Insoumis/The Unvanquished* (1964), Thomas is unwillingly absorbed into an OAS kidnapping, which almost culminates in torture (Chapter 2). In Jacques Rivette's *Paris nous appartient/ Paris Belongs to Us* (1961), the 'fascistic' modus operandi of the French army is perversely rewired into the body of a femme fatale (Chapter 5). But in Doniol-Valcroze's film, the OAS, composed again of former paras, inhabits an even more hard-boiled world of havoc. Daggers, pistols, a stool transformed into an object of hurting: so perilous is the array of weapons clenched by the malefactors of the OAS that often their principles appear not so much guided by a political credo than a bastardised take on the *omertà* of the Mafia.

Weapons capable of puncturing Michel's etiolated skin are not necessarily weapons capable of puncturing his moral conscience, however. Nor are they capable of altering his volition. The only person who *is* able to do this, it seems, is the police chief Malterer, whose name, uttered, as we have seen, alongside the trigger word 'collaboration', sets in motion a darkly vertiginous chain of audio-visual correspondences that bloom in the private space of Michel's mind, as much as in the public space of the cinematic screen: past, present, Nazis, police. This metaphorical chain is only woven once – in the transition to the aforementioned flashback of torture – but this is apparently all that Doniol-Valcroze needed to gesture towards a further stark truth about late-colonial French society: that the 'gangrene' or 'cancer' of political violence that had infected returning soldiers and the OAS was also a 'gangrene' that had infected the French state. In Chapter 7, I talk much more about this process, explaining how it led, first to the institutionalisation of torture as a method of dehumanising suspected Algerian nationalists living in the capital, and second, to the night of brutal repression that took place on the 17 October 1961, when the then Prefect of Police, Maurice Papon, encouraged his officers to deploy extreme violence against a demonstration composed of Algerian protesters. For now, let us conclude that if Malterer triggers Michel into recalling his own memories of torture during the Occupation, it is curiously not because the police chief subjects him to violence in the diegesis, but rather because Michel's unconscious mind functions as a kind of extra-diegetic seismograph, registering and telegraphing the state-endorsed torture being weaponised by Malterer's equivalent in the non-cinematic world: Papon.

There is a substantial body of scholarship that conceives of torture as an over-determined visual idiom, coterminous with metaphor and allegory,[4] and deployed as such by artists during decolonisation to coax into clarity the bodies and voices of Algerians not only tortured by the state, but also visibly erased by the state's censorial regime. In an important chapter on late-colonial French cinema, Raphaëlle Branche has, for instance, described how, by comparing the Algerian War of Independence to the Second World War, French directors working during the 1960s 'attempted to expose the truth' of the former through allusions to the latter, before concluding: 'and it was almost always [through the visual trope of] torture that these comparisons were made' (1997: 60). Similarly, in his monograph, *Multidirectional Memory*, Michael Rothberg homes in on a corpus of metropolitan late-colonial texts which 'juxtaposed the German occupation and Genocide of World War II with the practices of torture [. . .] deployed by the French state to maintain its most prized colonial possession' (2009: 134). Both Branche and Rothberg raise the question of whether Michel's flashback should be read as evidence of a trans-historical allegory of victimisation; one through which the pain experienced by Algerians subjected to violent interrogation in Paris and Algeria can be glimpsed between the lines, or rather lacerations, carved in Michel's body by the SS.[5]

Be that as it may, it is also possible to read Michel's flashback from a radically different perspective altogether. In an illuminating chapter, Emily Tomlinson has, for instance, examined the ethics of pain and memory in films such as Marker's *La Jetée* and Godard's *Le Petit soldat*. For Tomlinson, films like these might feature scenes of torture allegorically linked to the perpetration of colonial atrocities, but they also crucially tend to frame French citizens as the innocent victims – rather than guilty perpetrators – of such atrocities (2001: 52). Hence the ways in which Marker's *La Jetée* turns around a French man interrogated by fascistic German scientists in a concentrationary dystopia, whilst *Le Petit soldat* infamously exposes us to images of a disengaged member of the Right being waterboarded and electrocuted by Algerian members of the FLN. Such a hypothesis, echoed equally in Benjamin Stora's declaration that 'to avoid guilt, the end of the War coincided with a process of [Franco-centric self] victimisation' (2002), or Tzvetan Todorov's claim, articulated in a discussion of the Occupation of France by the Nazis, that 'obsessing over the past allows us [French citizens] to turn our back on the present', especially if this obsession involves the commemoration of victims (1992: 54), raises a number of thorny questions regarding our interpretation of *La Dénonciation*, recalling the discussions of appropriation through identification (Sanyal) and occulted suffering (Adams) explored in the introduction to this chapter. Thus, rather than conceiving of Michel's flashbacks of torture as an allegorical gesture *towards* the suffering of Algerians subjected to colonial violence, it is also possible to understand these flashbacks as an example of the cultural trend elaborated above: to divert attention *away* from the suffering of Algerians, through a focus on French victimhood. Indeed, we have already seen this process of victimisation at play within *Adieu Philippine/Goodbye Philippine* (1963), via the figure of Dédé (Chapter 1), in *La Belle vie/The Good Life* (1964), via the figure of Frédéric (Chapter 1), and in *Les Distractions/Trapped by Fear* (1960), via the figure of Laurent (Chapter 3). Although they have not been tortured like Michel, all of these Franco-centric characters are clearly designed to elicit sympathy in the spectator, framed, as they are, as wounded and traumatised victims of colonial violence.

Coinciding with Michel's ethical shift, from privileged producer of films to agonised victim of torture, is a further ethnic transformation, from Eurocentric Self to racialised Other. As Michael O'Riley has claimed, 'imperialism is characterized by territorialist encroachment, a cultural drive to occupy the position of the Other' (2010: 2), whilst Mark Osteen has made a similar point about film noir, stating that in the archetypal noir imaginary, white protagonists are often '"noired" – made into surrogate African Americans' – notably by depicting them as marginalised, persecuted and fragile, as within *The Man I Love* (Walsh, 1947) (Osteen 2013: 155). Parsing the politics of what he calls 'the racial unconscious' of film noir, Julian Murphet has crafted a comparable argument, asserting 'that the most significant achievement of *film noir* was to have invented a new kind of character, *a new white man*, whose existential gravity, misogyny and cynicism cohered into a new and arresting paradigm of American identity', a paradigm 'from which African-Americans were excluded and to which the French intellectuals of the period were inordinately attracted' (1998: 24 [emphasis in original]). In the noir inflected landscape of *La Dénonciation*, meanwhile, a comparable 'drive to occupy the position of the Other', to cite O'Riley, can be glimpsed most evidently in the two campaigns of harassment to which Michel is exposed in the narrative present, a present from which – as in many New Wave films – both African Americans and Algerians are entirely absent.[6] One of these is concocted by the OAS, an organisation that submits Michel to what is essentially a depoliticised and de-racialised version of the persecution and 'hate' often meted out to Algerian nationalists in the non-fictional world (Thénault 2008: 988). The other, less brutal but more affecting, is engineered by Malterer, who aggravates the paramilitary aggression displayed by the OAS, but inverts it: not stalking Michel out into the public space of the city, but luring him back into the private space of an office; ensnaring him, entrapping him, monitoring him, again significantly through precisely the kind of panoptic administrative surveillance weaponised by Papon against Algerians in the extra-cinematic realm. For example, when Malterer asks his assistant if 'their suspects [including Michel] are on file', the latter replies: 'of course, everyone is on file', in turn, universalising a regime of bureaucratic oppression that was, in reality, specifically skewed towards controlling the Algerian community in Paris. Even Michel's untimely death could be linked to the deaths of Algerians in the capital, with the final shot of the film exhibiting an uncanny resemblance to a famous photograph of an Algerian man named Abdelkader Bennehar, killed during an infamous massacre committed by the French police on 17 October 1961 (Figures 4.3 and 4.4; see Chapter 7 for more details about this massacre). In each of these shots and scenes,

Figure 4.3 Michel lies on the ground, dying.

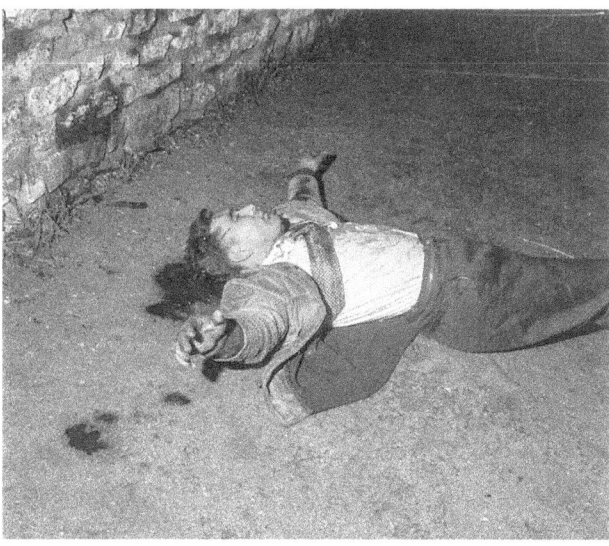

Figure 4.4 Abdelkader Bennehar lies on the ground after being assaulted by the police on October 17, 1961. Photo © Elie Kagan/BDIC.

La Dénonciation arguably represents Michel as a 'surrogate' for the absent Algerian Other, in turn, conferring upon the former the status of the latter as the primary casualty of the war.

From amnesia to absolution

Interrogating the vexed ethics of victimisation in the film also raises further ethical questions, relating back to Tomlinson's observations regarding memory, and Doniol-Vacroze's decision to frame Michel as an individual suffering from the symptoms of amnesia, in much the same way as Autant-Lara turns *Tu ne tueras point* around a man with 'no-memory' (see below). In a stimulating monograph on popular memory and oral history, Martin Evans has stressed how direct experience of Resistance during the 1940s often fostered a belief in 'truth, justice, and decisive action' in the late 1950s (1997: 41), leading many ex-Resistants to join radically militant leftist organisations such as the Jeanson Network (see Introduction and Chapter 7), or *les barbouzes*, an armed group of leftist counter-insurgents, whose aim was to block the rise of the OAS through force. In *La Dénonciation*, meanwhile, this belief in 'truth and justice' is personified by Malet (Raymond Gérôme), Michel's former Resistance leader and confidant, whose piercing eyes and chiselled intonation, as much as his proclivity for axioms, adages, aphorisms and dictums ('the only freedom that counts is the freedom to jeopardise your own freedom') belie the academicism of a man for whom political principles are clearly paramount.

Possessing neither the unwieldy gravitas nor the unwavering conviction of Malet, Michel, by contrast, appears to have more or less forgotten, or at least forsaken, the anti-fascist values that he once espoused as a Resistant. In scene after scene, we thus watch as he positively squanders his opportunities to inculpate members of the OAS, crushing the jigsaw puzzle letters they send him in frustration, swallowing rather than sharing the knowledge he gleans of their pyramidal cell structure, before eventually retreating into the same shell of political quietism, the same cocoon of bad faith that he displays in the post-Liberation period. We have, of course, seen this before: when Michel, referring to the salvo of harassment launched against him by the OAS, intones morosely, that 'none of this concerns me', he sounds a lot like the debonair dandy of *Le Feu follet* – Alain – played again by Maurice Ronet. Or when the narrator proclaims that 'Michel understood that the time to make choices had passed', he practically regurgitates what Bruno (Michel Subor) affirms at the start of Godard's *Le Petit soldat*: 'for me, the time for action is past . . . I'm older now . . . The time for reflection begins.' In different ways, each of these films romanticise political disengagement and right-wing anarchism by subtly encouraging the spectator to enter into an empathetic relationship with a Hussar antihero, for whom militant progressivism, especially against the reactionary Right, matters little.

Indeed, the more *La Dénonciation* develops, the more Michel appears as a protagonist divided: split between a desire to assume responsibility for his actions in the past and a desire to forget his leftist responsibilities in the present, feeling neither impelled to combat the OAS nor guilty if his actions allow them to continue their campaign of terror. This blurring of political affinities is particularly evident towards the end of the narrative, when Michel's unwillingness to answer Malterer's interrogatory questions with anything but insouciance enables the OAS to exist in a temporary state of legal impunity. 'To give in is to give in to everything', conjectures Michel, after refusing to 'give in' to Malterer's congenially elaborated demands. But behind Michel's words lies an awkward truth: by refusing to assist Malterer, he indirectly abets the OAS, causing an incensed Raymond Borde to castigate *La Dénonciation* as an ideologically schizophrenic film, out of tune with the radicalisation of politics animating French society. 'It reminds me of the kind of middle-class vomit [*vomissure petite-bourgeoise*] spewed by Camus', he demurred, 'of those indulgent doubts engineered to legitimise a lack of decision-making' (1962b: 48). Articulating an equal degree of opprobrium, Marcel Martin belaboured Michel's 'silence as tantamount to complicity with the OAS' (1962).

Nowhere is this flickering of a guilt at once avowed and disavowed more apparent than in the characteristically oblique final scene of *La Dénonciation*, when Michel recklessly gravitates towards an associate of the OAS, who subsequently pumps no less than six shots from a pistol into his spine. Immanent justice? Certainly, this is how Marcel Martin (1962) perceived Michel's demise, focusing on the brief flashback that occurs just before these shots are fired, when the face of the translator that Michel had condemned to death returns to merge with the face of the OAS affiliate, in short, suggesting that Michel allows himself to be slain by the one he had slain. Nonetheless, even as the physiognomy of Michel's OAS adversary assumes the physiognomy of another, Michel's motivations seem to equivocate between one logic and another. Reading the film 'as a long search for self, which also leads, in the purest Romantic tradition, to death', Geneviève Sellier (2000: 485), for instance, understands this scene as the point at which Michel both redeems himself for his complicity with the OAS and definitively absolves himself of guilt, recalling, most evidently, the poetic deaths of Thomas and Alain in *L'Insoumis* and *Le Feu follet* (see Chapters 2 and 3). No longer hunted down by his antagonistic adversaries, it is thus within the whiplash denouement of *La Dénonciation* that Michel appears to decisively forget about his past as an anti-fascist Resistant, forget about the castrating domestic routine of his wife, forget about the didactic political logorrhoea of the left-wing Malet and the judicial injunctions of Malterer, in short, forget about everything apart from what suddenly emerges as his divine aspiration: to exist in a state of guilt-free amnesia, as a victimised Hussar, for eternity. And, as we will see, it is precisely this merging of motivated forgetting with ethical absolution that drives Claude Autant-Lara's wildly singular film, *Tu ne tueras point*.

Tu ne tueras point (1963)

Inspired by the details of a double trial that took place in 1949, Claude Autant-Lara began developing *Tu ne tueras point* with scriptwriters Jean Aurenche and Pierre Bost in 1950, five years after the end of the Second World War, and four years before the unofficial start of the Algerian War of Independence. The project immediately stalled. Due to its controversial subject matter, few French producers showed anything more than a passing interest in it, forcing Autant-Lara to seek, and eventually acquire, foreign investment from producers based in Italy, Liechtenstein and Yugoslavia, during the 1950s. What followed was ten years of instability for Autant-Lara, marked, on the one hand, by the success of *La Traversée de Paris/The Trip Across Paris* (1956), and *En cas de malheur/Love Is My Profession* (1958), and, on the other hand, by a devastating campaign of critical denigration, spearheaded by François Truffaut, who famously pigeonholed Autant-Lara as part of *le cinéma de papa* (daddy's cinema) in his 1954 article 'Une certaine tendance du cinéma français'. According to journalists such as Marcel Ranchal and Paul-Louis Thirard, Autant-Lara was 'the number one enemy of the New Wave' (1963; 1961). Amidst this furore, filming for *Tu ne tueras point* eventually began in 1960. Shot in Belgrade, in extremely challenging conditions, the process was marred by a plethora of financial and logistical problems; Jean-Pierre Bleys points out, for example, that Autant-Lara had to send at least two engineers home as they were too drunk to work (2018: 475). It is perhaps unsurprising, therefore, that, despite being screened around Europe, in Italy, Belgium, England and France (clandestinely in 1962, publicly in 1963), and despite generating a huge amount of press, both positive and negative, *Tu ne tueras point* has not fared well in the continuum of French cinema, certainly compared to narratives associated with the New Wave pantheon. It remains, to this day, a spectral film, largely unavailable and largely unknown, in France and elsewhere.

The narrative itself is a tale of two at least initially unacquainted members of the Church: one who is wracked with a guilty conscience for obeying military orders, and one who is blessed with a clear conscience for disobeying military orders. In the first stage of *Tu ne tueras point*, the spectator is thus introduced to a German priest and former member of the Wehrmacht, named Adler (played by Horst Frank, and based on the authentic figure of Aloïs Bauer), who is arrested in 1949 by Allied forces. His crime: killing a French Resistant at a factory in the suburbs of Paris (Puteaux), during the chaotic Liberation of France in August 1944. Whilst awaiting his sentence in a military prison, Adler meets a young French draftee called Jean-François Cordier (played by Laurent Terzieff and based on the authentic figure of Jean-Bernard Moreau), who refuses to comply with the demands of military officials when summoned to a local barracks, identifying himself as a conscientious objector due to his Catholicism (Figure 4.5). Little by little, Autant-Lara prises open the ethical fissure instantiated by these two protagonists, until the film reaches its climax, when the two men are summoned to appear at the same military courthouse: *Cherche-Midi*, in Paris. Whilst Adler is acquitted of his crime, Cordier is sentenced to two years imprisonment – infinitely renewable – for military insubordination.

Adler: guilty memories of war

Conceived in 1950 yet filmed in 1960, *Tu ne tueras point* might have been an unusually laborious project to execute, but it was also a project that both echoed and partook in what was nothing less than a seismic shift in how French directors remembered, misremembered and memorialised the country's former occupiers, Germany. As Joseph Daniel has illustrated, before 1955, French war films tended to denigrate German national identity through the recurring figure of the sadistic German military official.[7] Frequently, this official was a member of the SS or Gestapo, who was more often than not clearly marked

Figure 4.5 Cordier (right) confronts Adler (left) in prison.

as a threatening Other through the contours of their face and body: chiselled features, piercing eyes (often ringed by circular glasses), mechanical gestures, coupled with a mechanical acquiescence towards the values of National Socialism (1972: 215–19, 311–19 [see the aforementioned torture scene in *La Dénonciation* for an exemplary instance of this trope]). It was only after 1955 that these stereotypes began to subside, yielding to more nuanced representations of Germans as neither 'perverse enemies' nor 'barbarous automatons', but rather individuals endowed with subjective identities and personal histories, for example those that populated films such as *La Chatte/The Cat* (Decoin, 1959), and *Léon Morin, prêtre/Léon Morin, Priest* (Melville, 1961). By the late 1950s, some directors had even gone so far as to trade in scenes of Franco-German fraternity between soldiers, before Alain Resnais dismantled a final taboo in his 1959 work, *Hiroshima mon amour/Hiroshima, My Love*, depicting a transnational romance between a French woman and a German soldier during Occupation.

Released amidst this period of radical change, it is therefore perhaps unsurprising that Autant-Lara fissures the German protagonists that populate his film along a profoundly dualistic fault line: as either callous or humane. Many of the traits linked to the pre-1955 tendency towards Germanophobia can be glimpsed, for example, in the character of Stein (Vladeta Dragutinovic), an unwieldy, hard-faced sergeant, whose contribution to the screenplay never really amounts to anything more than spitting guttural interjections ('ach! och!') and incongruous injunctions ('a man like me will always give orders to a man like you') at the bemused faces of those that surround him. Yet, as with Decoin, Melville and Resnais, to this malevolent embodiment of German Otherness, Autant-Lara also adds a comparatively benevolent, that is to say, ethically complex, counterpoint, in the figure of Adler.

Evidence of this dualism can be seen in one of the earliest scenes in the film, when Stein first notifies Adler that the Allied military government is investigating their involvement in the aforementioned killing of a Resistant. The scene begins placidly enough, with an image of Stein leaping off a train onto the fringes of a bucolic football pitch in Mayen, Germany, circa 1948. Over the next few seconds, the camera follows Stein as he paces towards a set of goalposts, a newspaper bearing details of the investigation clutched in hand. Next, a tracking shot, as the spectator is rapidly towed towards the animated spine of an as yet unidentified goalkeeper, readying himself to parry away shots by the opposing team. This, we learn, is Adler.

That Adler and Stein have met before is not initially apparent in this scene, entirely lacking as it is in the signs of recollection that frequently accompany acts of recognition. Indeed, judging from the fact that Adler glances twice at Stein without engaging with him, before the latter barks, frustrated, 'don't you recognise me?', Stein is not just someone that Adler has tried, consciously or unconsciously, and partially successfully, to forget in the past, distracting himself through hobbies such as football, and integrating himself into a supportive community of acquaintances composed, as we will learn, of fellow members of the Church, but also someone that he flatly attempts to repudiate in the present. 'I don't have time for this', bemoans Adler, turning not towards, but away from Stein, in other words, turning his back, literally and figuratively, on a past from which he has apparently attempted to flee, and hence displaying the same 'will not to know, the refuge of blindness, the tactics of semi-passive, semi-active forgetfulness' that Paul Ricoeur associates with the post-Second World War German psyche (2004: 467). Only when Stein, the harbinger of bad news, brusquely circumnavigates the parameters of the goalposts, wrenching Adler out of the flow of the match, and thus, in turn, abruptly detuning the playful melody of his existence, does the latter acknowledge Stein's presence in the here and the now. And only when Stein violently thrusts the incriminating newspaper into the hands of Adler ('don't you understand? They are calling it murder!'), does the latter acknowledge the gravity of their predicament. Recalling the aforementioned collaboration conversation in *La Dénonciation*, it is the point at which a stream of disavowed memories suddenly contaminates the fragile purity of Adler's conscience, although only later in the film will these memories be visualised on-screen.

Much of the subsequent impetus of Autant-Lara's film derives from an ambiguity as to whether Adler is guilty or innocent of the crimes to which Stein elliptically alludes in this scene, and how this guilt, or innocence, is determined. Shortly after this interaction, for instance, Adler retreats back into the shell of his diocese, submitting himself to the authority of the Father of the Church, who induces him – *impels* him – to surrender to the French authorities, as 'he has not done anything wrong'. 'Right from the first few minutes of the film, the Church therefore removes the problem of responsibility' from Adler's situation (Bertin-Maghit and Marty 2001: 141), accurately forecasting the ways in which the law will subsequently treat him with clemency and charity, as a fundamentally honest, morally upstanding individual who just happened to become embroiled in a limit-situation outside of his control. Acquitted by the avatars of Catholicism and the jurors of the court, publicly at least, Adler bathes in an aura of innocence.

Privately, however, it is an entirely different story. In 1947, the existentialist philosopher Karl Jaspers published a controversial yet influential treatise, entitled *The Question of German Guilt*, in which he raised the question of whether, in addition to being deemed criminally responsible for crimes committed during the Second World War, those who had participated in war crimes felt morally culpable for their actions. Certainly, if we take Adler's behaviour in *Tu ne tueras point* as a psychosocial barometer for the era, the answer appears to be yes – and emphatically. In scene after scene, we thus watch as his psyche positively splinters under the weight of what Jaspers calls 'the jurisdiction of the conscience and the soul' (2000: 25–6). Often this process of 'splintering' assumes the guise of a slow tremor that creeps across Adler's face: from a gentle lowering of his eyelids, to the anguished arching of an eyebrow, to a bead of hot sweat that streams down his cheek, before said cheek is cusped by a hand raised in shame, and said hand becomes two hands, which cradle a defeated head. Other times, it alters Adler's voice, diminishing it to a tremulous quaver or amplifying it to a distressing howl – his mouth, in both cases, upended into a grimace. Still other times, it seizes control of Adler's motor-sensory capacities completely, forcing him to violently genuflect, during one early scene, in the presence of his Father. Contrite and contorted, Adler is moral guilt embodied.

But by far the most potent scene of moral guilt occurs in what turns out to be the first and last flashback in the film, when the spectator is led both beyond the present-tense temporality of the narrative, into the hidden folds of the past, and behind the mask-like patina of Adler's Aryan physiognomy, into the mental landscape of his mind. Triggered during Mass in the prison chapel, a religious ceremony orientated towards moral but not legal confession, the flashback in question exposes the spectator to a visual representation of what happened in August 1944, when – as we will learn – Stein mercilessly ordered Adler to execute one of three Resistants caught by the Wehrmacht in an occupied factory near Paris. As within many of the scenes set in the present, much of the power of this lurch towards interiority-anteriority derives from

Autant-Lara's deft ability to harness 'the mythical aura of the cinematic face' (Steimatsky 2017: 1). The closer Adler unwillingly creeps towards the moment he must execute his captive, the more his gentle head thus wavers and trembles, perspiration flowing freely; and the more his soon-to-be-victim, an equally soft-skinned Resistant named Herclos (Zoran Milosavljevic), edges towards *his* fate, the more he in turn appears sucked into the vacuum of Adler's tormented and profoundly guilty gaze. Groping for words that cruelly elude him, Herclos falls instead into catatonic silence.

Equally silent is the journey performed by Adler and Herclos, after the former is ordered to lead the latter underground: from the disordered yet fundamentally intelligible office spaces that sprawl across the factory, populated by a familiar carousel of stereotyped German soldiers, to a phantasmagoric concrete vault that lies directly below it, until the anguished priest finally summons up the courage to kill. Set in a nightmarish zone of primal fears, at once overdetermined and indeterminate, beyond the frontier of morality and beyond the frontier of mortality, it is also at this point that the ontological stability of the images that unfold onscreen begins to disintegrate, suggesting that the two men have left the terrain of history for that of the psyche. This process of disintegration can be glimpsed, for example, in the gloom that pervades the penumbra of the vault, generating the impression of a perceptually hazy universe, less anchored in the scopic clarity of sight – of seeing in the present – and more in the metaphysical obscurity of recollection. So too for the series of slow horizontal tracking shots that Autant-Lara uses to frame Adler's face as he drifts listlessly through a warren of forbidding corridors, shots that, as in the films of Alain Resnais, can be said to hypostatise mental displacements performed by the mind in time, during the process of remembering, through acts of physical displacement, performed by the body, in space (Greene 1999: 32–3). Even the topological descent performed by Adler and his prisoner, as they penetrate, inexorably spiralling, deeper and deeper into the substrata of the factory, until they reach a dank cellar where the latter will perish at the hands of the former, could hypothetically be linked to the ways in which Adler has himself been drawn into the undertow of buried memories by Stein. Especially, that is, if we take into consideration Gaston Bachelard's Jung-inspired phenomenological diagnosis of cellars as psychic representations of the unconscious (2014: 38–43), or the tendency, reiterated in a long history of philosophical, religious and cultural discourses, to associate unredeemed guilt with vertical depth (Ricoeur 2004: 45). In *La Dénonciation*, for instance, the narrator describes Michel's 'shame' as 'a secret' he has attempted to 'bury in the deepest depths of his being', before his 'collaboration' with Malterer causes it 'resurface'. In *Tu ne tueras pas*, meanwhile, Stein may talk about how 'he has fallen into a hole', but Adler goes further, descending into what essentially constitutes a spatialised manifestation of his own mental hell. Like the mythical figure of Lazarus, Adler is someone who has 'experienced death before returning to the land of the living' (Silverman 2015: 5).

But there is yet another dimension to the meanings and messages that reverberate discreetly through the metaphorical architecture of these 'multidirectional' memories of violence. Structured by a constellation of disquieting images of a past that Adler has tried to forget, this flashback seems to communicate, elliptically yet undeniably, with an extrajudicial tactic, deployed clandestinely during the 1950s and early 1960s by the French army in Algeria, to eliminate suspected nationalists. Known as 'la corvée de bois' – loosely translated as 'wood duty' – this tactic usually involved leading the suspect, or group of suspects, to a secluded area, under the pretence that they would be required to collect wood for a fire, or – even more perversely – be set free. As the suspect or suspects began to disperse into the wilderness, the soldier in charge would unleash a hail of bullets (usually with a 12.7 calibre machine gun, like that wielded by Adler); the deaths would be explained away by what served for many years as an almost watertight alibi: the suspect(s) had tried to flee (Branche 2001: 72–6). The following testimony was originally included in a letter by a young soldier in Algeria, published in 1958; it bears more than a few parallels with the shape of Adler's recollections in *Tu ne tueras point*.

> One day, the lieutenant came up to me and said: 'I don't like little girls. Get ready, the next one is for you.' A few days later, we had eight prisoners that needed to be killed after being tortured. He called me over, and, in front of my friends, said: 'this one is yours little girl. Go ahead!' I went over to the guy: he looked at me. I can still see his eyes watching me. It made me feel sick. I fired. My friends killed the others. (Cited in Vidal-Naquet 1972: 137–8)

Discussing the ethics of the New Wave and the New Novel, Lynn Higgins has perceptively opined: 'looking back' to the period of the Occupation 'remains a dangerous enterprise fraught with the risk of contamination by guilty secrets', especially when this act of 'looking back' is performed through the narrative device of the flashback, and especially when this flashback revolves around what Higgins calls, paraphrasing Freud and the psycho-historian Robert Lifton, 'a primal scene of ultimate horror' (1996: 147). Higgins's observation primarily concerns a spate of historical melodramas released during the 1970s and 1980s, notably Truffaut's 1981 *Le Dernier métro/The Last Metro*. Nevertheless, as our reading of Adler's guilty memories of war has revealed, these attempts at 'looking back' not only occurred much earlier in the continuum of French film history than Higgins suggests – the early 1960s, to be precise – but also, in the case of *Tu ne tueras point* at least, seemed to function according to a process of 'displacement' or 'substitution', through which the filmic body of a German priest comes to be associated with the extra-filmic atrocities perpetrated by French soldiers in Algeria. We will return to this question of 'guilt displacement' in the next chapter of this book, specifically with regards to images of French female civilians. For now, let us turn our attention to the transcendental French hero of *Tu ne tueras point*, Jean-François Cordier.

Cordier: forgetting and expiation

Just as the Second World War etched a deep moral wound in the collective German psyche, so too did it etch a deep moral wound in the collective French psyche. The fact that France had allowed itself to drift, as if sleepwalking, from tacitly accepting ostensibly paltry acts of financial collaboration with the Nazis (including those infamously committed by Autant-Lara himself),[8] to endorsing cultural events that propagated anti-Semitic stereotypes (for instance the infamous 'France and the Jew' exhibition, held between 1941 and 1942, at the Berlitz cinema on 'Les Grands Boulevards'), before administrative officials such as Maurice Papon adopted an expressly instrumental role in the deportation of around 76,000 Jews (a third of whom were French citizens, 4,000 of them children), arguably infected the nation with what has often been diagnosed as a 'historical disease, contagion' or 'neurosis': collective memories of guilt (Higgins 1996: 146; Rousso 1987).

Not that this psychosocial 'disease' was expressed in cinematic narratives produced in the post-Liberation era, *La Dénonciation* notwithstanding. Instead, French directors working during the late 1940s and 1950s invited spectators to take pleasure in films that respectively amplified and avoided the most grandiose and guilty aspects of France's past, a process of historical revision that, in turn, helped 'appease the conscience' of French citizens, 'restoring their self-esteem' (Hoffmann 1991: vii). Sometimes this process of national regeneration through selective forgetting was enabled through a retreat into the vestiges of a distant era, for example the so-called golden age of the belle époque (especially films set in the years before the First World War). Many of Autant-Lara's earlier works, for instance, display this nostalgia (see Tony Williams's aptly named article, 'Escape from an oppressive present' [2018], for more details). Other times, it was performed by exalting the legacy of Resistance under Occupation, as within the aforementioned spate of war films produced by directors such as Daquin, Clément or Calef. In *Tu ne tueras point*, meanwhile, Autant-Lara crafts what is an undeniably atypical, yet no less potent, further example of this cultural trend towards 'recuperation' (Jeancolas 1979: 106), extolling France's future – its shift into the post-Second World War period, as much as into the years of decolonisation – through the allegorical body of a conscientious objector, namely Cordier.

As with Adler, Cordier's entrance into the narrative coincides with a scene of jarring mis-recognition between two men: one harbours memories of a shared past, one does not, or pretends not to, feigning amnesia. In the case of Cordier, this interaction takes place when he is hailed by an individual introducing himself as Mimì in a Parisian café, immediately before the former refuses to comply with his military obligations at a local barracks. 'Don't you recognise me?', splutters Mimì, regurgitating verbatim the brusque words that Stein throws at Adler at the start of the film. 'No' replies Cordier, before softly conceding. Yes, the two men do know each other, or have known each other. But in exactly what capacity – when, where and how? All remains unclear.

What is interesting about this scene is that the psychological interplay it depicts – between an individual struck down by a lack of memory (Cordier) and an individual who tacitly accepts this lack, rather than probing it (Mimì) – seems to extend, in a less explicit but more insidious form, to the ways in which Cordier then engages with other protagonists in the film. The carousel of military officials that Cordier encounters, for instance, possess no personal memories of him, and besides, are only concerned with one thing: squeezing the perceived petulance out of this young man, first through stiff, combative debates that rarely touch on anything other than metaphysical questions of morality and theology ('so you could say that your conscience is forbidding you to serve your country?' 'no ... It doesn't forbid me to serve it, but to go to war'), or, when these attempts at proselytisation fail, the reified, naked logic of the law, and so on. No less superficial are the terse conversations that Cordier has with Adler, both before and after the latter has been plunged into the aforementioned flashback, an ordeal to which Cordier is crucially at no point subjected. Indeed, unlike Adler, who has apparently resigned himself to an existence lived in thrall to the dark sway of associative memory (as Michel has in *La Dénonciation*), Cordier, by contrast, seems more or less impervious to mnemonic triggers: no person, no word, no situation, nothing seems able to edge his psyche into a state of recall, raising vast questions about his past life that remain fundamentally unanswered: what was Cordier's role in the Second World War? Was he a collaborator, like the translator in *La Dénonciation*, or a Resistant, like Herclos in *Tu ne tueras pas*? Did he witness any atrocities? Is Catholicism the *only* catalyst for his act of conscientious objection? Only once does the embattled pacifist display any degree of recollection in *Tu ne tueras point*, when his mother visits him in prison. Straining to remember the name of a restaurant from years gone by, it is here that Cordier experiences a tender yet brief moment of nostalgia, before making a telling admission. 'I have no memory', he laments.

Unsurprisingly, Autant-Lara's portrayal of a conscientious objector with 'no memory' prompted a certain degree of pushback from critics and journalists. Many saw in Cordier less a psychologically realised protagonist in the classical realist tradition, than a one-dimensional spokesman for the ethics of pacifism;[9] the cinematic equivalent of a politico-ethical thesis, embodied on-screen.

Writing in the left-leaning newspaper *Combat*, Henry Chapier was particularly dismissive of *Tu ne tueras point*, defining it in 1961 as suffused with 'didactic dialogues, hollow arguments, proliferating cliches, and moral repulsion'. In 1963, Chapier followed this up with a similarly damning review, criticising the film as being akin to a 'demagogue' who 'assaults the spectator'. But if Chapier's reservations admit a certain truth regarding Cordier's lack of characterological depth, then it is also true that the director's decision to turn a large part of the narrative around a French citizen immune from the tide of traumatic recollections that plague Adler also performs a powerful ideological function: to appease France's aforementioned desire to avoid the most troubling zones of the Occupation. Indeed, to examine the psychological interplay between Cordier and his past is arguably to examine the psychosocial interplay between France and its past: the less Cordier remembers about his own personal life, the less France, in turn, appears infected by the 'disease' of moral guilt that had ravaged the collective psyche of its citizens. 'It doesn't take much to make the [French] public feel better about themselves', demurred Chapier, wryly, about the film (1963).

I have written elsewhere (2019b) about the fascinating providence of Autant-Lara's decision to steer his narrative towards the trials and tribulations of a young French man – Cordier – who decides to become a conscientious objector in 1949, one year before the director began working on the project himself. One reason that this visual trope proved so timely was that, during the 1950s, conscientious objection became a belief system, amongst others, used by approximately 450 anti-war militants, to justify their resistance to the conflict in French Algeria. Susan Weiner puts the figure even lower, claiming that 'only about a hundred young men refused to fight in Algeria, unlike the ten thousand Americans who refused to fight in the Vietnam War' (2001: 155). These included: Jean Le Meur, whose role in Algeria as a second lieutenant not only exposed him to torture, but formed the basis of a famous article published in *Esprit* in 1959; the anarcho-pacifist Louis Lecoin, who began a campaign to legalise his beliefs in 1958, emerging victorious in 1963, and who was photographed next to a promotional poster for *Tu ne tueras point* at a 1962 screening in Belgium; and perhaps most importantly, the cluster of intellectuals, academics and artists, including Laurent Terzieff and Doniol-Valcroze, who signed the Manifesto of the 121 (see above), the aims of which included legalising conscientious objection. So fortuitous was Autant-Lara's decision to explore the ethics of pacifism, four years *before* the unofficial start of the war, that when the film was finally released in France in the early 1960s, certain journalists identified Cordier's values as further evidence, beyond the polysemic layering of meanings in Adler's flashback, that the film should be viewed as what Ismail Xavier has called an 'unconscious' allegory for the conflict in Algeria, that is to say, an allegory that 'cannot be seen either as an intrinsic property of the text, or as the product of a [director's] intention' (2004: 341). As Georges Sadoul mused in his review of *Tu ne tueras point*: 'a film, or, more generally, a work of art, gains its meaning from how it relates (consciously or not), to an era and its concerns. If these concerns change, so do the meanings of the film' (1962a). Michel Capdenac was even more emphatic, framing the problem that Cordier faces as a problem faced by 'every Frenchman' living in a 'period of shame and rupture' (1963).

Even so, it is important to recognise that Cordier's decisions and predicament are very different to those taken and experienced by the vast majority of soldiers during the 1950s, dovetailing with Tramor Quemeneur's observation that many pacifist narratives 'tended to focus on "exceptional cases"' of resistance, for example Le Meur or Lecoin (2011: 60), or Benjamin Stora's assertion that 'French cinema contributed to a mythological reconstruction of the refusal of colonial war' (2014: 99; also see Scharold 2016b: 21). As someone who has extricated himself from the theatre of conflict, Cordier has therefore not seen, not heard, not participated in, and thus not at all been rendered complicit within the military atrocities to which many soldiers had been exposed in Algeria, leading to a subtext of expiation that once again links the film to the discourse of 'redemptive pacifism' outlined in the introduction to this book. In one of the most telling scenes in *Tu ne tueras point*, for example, Cordier is inspected by a military physician (Mica Orlovic), who attempts to persuade his sanguine patient to be falsely diagnosed as mentally unstable, enabling the latter to be discreetly discharged into civilian life and the former to be spared scandal.[10] As it turns out, Cordier flatly refuses, and the medical examiner has no choice but to imprison him, not despite, but precisely because of the exemplary clarity of his cognitive faculties and the unwavering conviction of his beliefs. 'For me,' laments the doctor, 'you are mentally healthy, but it would be good for everyone if you were crazy.' 'So I will let you decide: mentally healthy or crazy?' 'Mentally healthy' asserts Cordier, thus precipitating his impending imprisonment for the non-crime of conscientious objection – 'non-crime' insofar as *Tu ne tueras point* consistently insists that the French legal system is guilty of unjustifiably punishing a fundamentally innocent young man.

Jean-Pierre Bertin-Maghit and Alain Marty, meanwhile, have identified Cordier's unwieldy posture as an overcharged site of meaning, drawing attention to the ways in which he rarely lowers himself in the presence of his military adversaries, as Adler guiltily does, but rather brazens out the film in a state of virtuous verticality, telegraphing the immovability of his pacifist values through the immovability of his sinewy body, and evoking Paul Ricoeur's understanding of 'the spirit of forgiveness' as being expressed through 'great height', in contradistinction to 'the abyss of guilt' into which Adler descends (2004: 483). For Bertin-Maghit and Marty, this marriage of posture and

Figure 4.6 Cordier standing tall in the courtroom.

power, of corporeality and morality, of pacifism and redemption, is particularly evident when Cordier first encounters the captain of the army barracks, in which he is due to be drafted, with the latter docilely sitting, 'dominated', where the former proudly stands, 'dominating' (2001: 141). More telling yet is the climatic courtroom scene, during which Cordier displays an even more astute degree of intellectual clarity, defending his ethos standing upright, whilst the members of the military jury meting out 'justice' are depicted sitting down, consumed by farce and unprofessionalism (Figure 4.6). It is also at this point that Cordier's absolution – emphatically proclaimed by the identificatory mechanisms of the film, yet emphatically denied by the judicial outcome of the trial – begins to approximate the ethical tenor embodied by the myriad soldiers already glossed in this book: Dédé, Michel, Frédéric, Thomas, Raspéguy, Laurent and Paul. But where the innocence of these militarised protagonists is at least partly diluted by the fact that they have participated in, or are participating in, or will participate in the war, the conviction of Cordier's total anti-militarism elevates his innocence to a quasi-metaphysical realm of absolutes.

Notes

1. Autant-Lara changed the name of his project due to political pressures placed on French producers, from *L'Objecteur* to *Tu ne tueras point*.
2. Dine might begin his chapter by stressing the aforementioned mechanisms of 'denial' in late-colonial works of fiction and film, yet the majority of his analysis actually appears to suggest the opposite: that texts by Jean-Paul Sartre and Alain Resnais, for example, were instrumental in disclosing information about the war to the public thorough the rhetorical figure of transnational allegory.

3. *Les Suspects* recounts the trials and tribulations of Commissaire Perrache (Charles Vanel), the head of the French intelligence service, who aspires to crush the FLN in the same way as Malterer (see below) aspires to crush the OAS.
4. Discussing the allegorical value of a film raises a number of complex questions about the legibility of the meanings conveyed, the intentionality of the author, the comprehension of the spectator and the historical context in which the film in question was developed, filmed and screened. Debarati Sanyal has described how, for example, 'both the commodity object and the object of allegorical representation are hollowed out ciphers that are unmoored from the context and injected with meaning, yet that meaning is arbitrary and infinitely substitutable' (2015: 161). For further information see Chambers (2010), Virtue (2013), Xavier (2004), and, in particular, Sanyal (2015: 114–23, 149–81).
5. During an interview with *Libération*, Doniol-Valcroze elliptically stated that 'the shots of interrogation and torture committed by the Gestapo [*sic* – the attire of the soldier suggests he is a member of the SS] repeatedly appear in the context of 1961' (Fabre 1961).
6. This process of erasing the Algerian population from narratives ostensibly about the war has been discussed before, primarily by Benjamin Stora (2004: 202–4), and Guy Austin (2007a: 182–5). Austin's claim that French directors often 'depicted Algeria [as a space] from which Algerians were themselves absent' (2007a: 185), could, for example, be applied to the ways in which directors such as Doniol-Valcroze depicted France – and, in particular, Paris – as a space from which Algerians were absent, when, as Jacques Panijel's documentary *Octobre à Paris* forcefully shows, this was far from the case (see Chapter 7). See Chapter 6 for a further discussion of how this process of ethnic erasure functions in *Au biseau des baisers/Slanted Kisses* (Gilles and Sator, 1962). Caroline Eades has also talked about the racial/ethnic dynamics of the French New Wave, suggesting that it represented decolonisation as a 'white masquerade' (2006: 222).
7. Jean-Pierre Melville's *Le silence de la mer/The Silence of the Sea* (1949) is a clear exception here, featuring, as it does, a compassionate German soldier who does not pledge allegiance to Nazism.
8. The fact that Autant-Lara collaborated with the Nazis is beyond doubt; however, to what extent remains unclear. Sylvie Lindeperg (2014: 354–68) has, for instance, outlined a disagreement that took place between Autant-Lara and a Jewish producer named Pierre Braunberger, who produced *La Dénonciation*. According to Braunberger, Autant-Lara was not only an anti-Semite, but had actually been elected as a representative for the Commissariat-General for Jewish Affairs, an administrative body set up by the collaborationist Vichy government to put into motion anti-Jewish legislation. Hugo Frey has also written an illuminating chapter on the persistence of anti-Semitism in French cinema, including details of Autant-Lara's admiration for Céline, alongside his later political affiliations with the extreme right-wing party, the Front National (2014: 157–88).
9. It is worth pointing out that the politics of pacifism that underpin the narrative are extremely ambiguous. On one hand, in relation to the history of the Algerian War, they may be seen to mirror the political values of the Left, and, in particular,

the leftist slogan of Peace in Algeria (see Chapter 7). On the other hand, in relation to the history of the Second World War, they may be seen to mirror the political values of defeatism and Collaboration, values which were increasingly viewed as 'perverse' in the post-Liberation years (Ingman 1995: 209).

10. This scene recalls certain scenes in Marcel Carné's *Les Tricheurs/Young Sinners* (1958), in which Laurent Terzieff plays Alain, a nihilistic Hussar rebel whose abdomen and pectorals are often displayed – eroticised – for the spectator. *Les Tricheurs* has also been read as an obliquely late-colonial narrative by Susan Weiner (2001: 163–9).

5. FEMALE CITIZENS AND GUILT DISPLACEMENT

So far, this book has explored a range of late-colonial films, many of which revolve around male soldiers leaving for, returning from, or fighting in Algeria. Traces of this masculine and military-centric logic can be found in the two conscripts that feature in Jacques Rozier's 1963 *Adieu Philippine/ Goodbye Philippine* (Dédé and Michel); the reservist that features in Robert Enrico's 1964 *La Belle vie/The Good Life* (Frédéric); the physically flawless legionnaire that features in Alain Cavalier's 1964 *L'Insoumis/The Unvanquished* (Thomas); the supremely athletic paratroopers that feature in both Mark Robson's 1966 *Les Centurions/Lost Command* and Jacques Dupont's 1960 *Les Distractions/Trapped by Fear* (Raspéguy, Laurent, Paul); whilst Claude Autant-Lara edges the debate into more ethically ambiguous territory by turning his narrative around a conscientious objector named Cordier. Nonetheless, as this chapter will show, male soldiers are not the only characters that draw us into the universe of late-colonial cinema. In films such as *Le Retour/The Return* (Goldenberg, 1959), *Paris nous appartient/ Paris Belongs to Us* (Rivette, 1961) and *Secteur postal 89098/Postal Sector 89098* (Durand, 1961), it is less male identity than female identity that is at stake. Even more specifically, this chapter will argue that these films share a common parallel insofar as they represent female French citizens as guilty of a range of 'crimes' linked elliptically to the Algerian War of Independence.

French Women and the War

Exploring the relationship between French women and the Algerian War of Independence generates a number of challenges. One immediate challenge concerns the inherent ambiguity of the term 'French women', if only in the sense that it does not, in and of itself, distinguish between female citizens living in mainland France and female settlers living in colonial Algeria (a territory which was constitutionally part of France, making them technically French). In the interest of clarity, let me stress that this chapter will be restricted to images of the former, whilst cinematic representations of the latter are at least parenthetically discussed in Chapters 2 and 6.[1] Another challenge inherent in this inquiry relates to a paucity of historical research. Compared to the abundance of studies that have examined how Algerian women were victimised by colonisation, and how they fought against it (Khanna 2008; MacMaster 2009; Vince 2015), as well as how French female settlers were caught up in the late-colonial crisis, especially when forced to flee Algeria in the exodus of 1962 (Hubbell 2015; Eldridge 2016), the question of how *metropolitan* French women felt about the war is seldom probed by historians. Neither Alistair Horne (2006) nor Benjamin Stora (1998; 2004), for instance, devote any analysis to this topic, preferring instead to assemble a macro-chronology of major political events catalysed by male soldiers, male politicians and male intellectuals. Nor, more surprisingly, is it a topic explored in seminal accounts of how women's rights and women's lives changed in post-Second World War France, with both Claire Duchen (1994: 59) and Claire Laubier (2005: 46) framing decolonisation as a generalised crisis for the nation, rather than a localised crisis for French women. Lastly, to these two challenges, one lexical, one academic, we can add a third, one related specifically to the question of research justification. After all, unlike female Algerian nationalists committed to violently combatting the French army and settlers in Algeria – as depicted in Pontecorvo's *La Bataille d'Alger/The Battle of Algiers* (1966), and René Vautier's *Algérie en flames/Algeria is Burning* (1958) – metropolitan French women did not partake in any armed military operations against the 'enemy', even if they were legally able to join the French army in Algeria as nurses.[2] Nor were they faced with the type of existential and ethical dilemmas that had arisen during the Occupation of France, a period in which all French citizens, irrespective of their gender, were constantly forced into making often life-or-death decisions, between collaborating with the Nazis or defying them. Nor, apart from a few rare yet important exceptions,[3] did French women politically militate against the war or colonialism, generally succumbing instead to the same depoliticised state of mind that had seized the rest of the population, known in France, as '*immobilisme*' or do-nothingness (Weiner 2001: 142). All of which leads us to a rather vexed question: why study the relationship between the late-colonial crisis and French women, when this relationship seems to have been tenuous, at best?

To answer this question, we need to recalibrate our understanding of military conflict. Margaret Higonnet has written that 'war must be understood as a *gendering* activity, one that ritually marks the gender of all members of society, whether or not they are combatants' (1987: 4 [emphasis in original]). Higonnet draws this argument from an analysis of the first two world wars, yet the same principle clearly applies to the Algerian predicament. Just because French women might have been relegated to a position of generalised non-participation in the war clearly does not mean that they remained emotionally indifferent to it, or unaffected by it. Sisters of brothers, mothers of sons, female friends of soldiers, female lovers of soldiers, not to mention wives: the trauma undoubtedly experienced by many French women, faced not only with the prolonged absence of a loved one from the rites and routines of everyday life, but death itself, the death of a loved one, should not be overlooked, as is often the case in the event-orientated macro-histories of the war assembled by Stora and Horne, and so on. One work that has proved illuminating in this regard is a remarkable yet little-known monograph entitled *L'amour en guerre: Sur les traces d'une correspondance pendant la guerre d'Algérie/Love in War: Tracing the Contours of a Correspondence During the Algerian War* (Deshayes and Pohn-Weidinger 2017), in which the authors effectively conduct a micro-historical examination of seventy-nine epistles (letters), sent between 1959 and 1962 by a conscript stationed in Algeria ('Bernard') and his female partner ('Aimée'); both are anonymised in the publication through pseudonyms. As the authors point out, 'even if it has been depicted in numerous books' the Algerian War of Independence 'has rarely been narrated from the point of view of loved ones', left behind when soldiers departed for Algeria (2017: 25). Written by one such 'loved one', 'Aimée's' letters thus offer a devastatingly stark glimpse into how young French women dealt with the personal and private challenges posed by military conflict. Here is a fragment of one of many included in *Love in War*:

> Could it be that to love means to wait, to endlessly wait?
> I therefore love because I wait, and I will continue to wait!
> Maybe truly
> My heart is languid, indefinitely languid
> My body is nothing more than a huge wound. I am suffering,
> Suffering from not having seen you for two long days. ('Aimée' cited in Deshayes and Pohn-Weidinger 2017: 15)

As we will see, the epistolary medium (letter-writing) explored with such rigor and sensitivity by Deshayes and Pohn-Weidinger is also a medium woven into the audio-visual strategies deployed within at least two of the three films discussed in this chapter: Goldenberg's *Le Retour* and Durard's *Secteur postal 89098*. Yet, where the authors of *Love in War* represent 'Aimée's' correspondence with a palpable degree of sensitivity,[4] gently drawing readers into her world, providing us with intimate knowledge of her everyday life and contributing to an understanding of French women as emotional victims of the late-colonial predicament, the same cannot be said of either Goldenberg or Durand's narratives. Instead, in these films, the female partners of male soldiers are re-imagined in unequivocally negative terms: as scheming and duplicitous perpetrators of (emotional) violence.

War, Women and French Cinema

As a range of scholars have shown, one of the most compelling aspects of military conflict is that it often gives rise to a process of displacement through which the guilt experienced by male soldiers overcome by opposing armies, or engaged in acts of military atrocity in the non-cinematic world, finds itself reformulated and redirected onto the bodies of civilian women in the cinematic world, generating, in turn, an antagonistic ambience of feminine, rather than masculine, culpability. Frequently, this is an argument developed in relation to cultural narratives produced in the aftermath of the First and Second World Wars, especially within 'defeated' countries such as Germany, Japan, Italy and France. In her illuminating monograph *The Cinema of Things*, Elizabeth Ezra, for example, pinpoints Louis Feuillade's silent serial film *Les Vampires/The Vampires* (1915–16) as one such narrative, eloquently interpreting the central female figure of the intrigue – the totemic Irma Vep, played by Musidora – as a figure of 'exaggerated culpability': someone who functions less as a protagonist endowed with psychological impulses, and more as a complex condensation of the 'guilt of survivors, of [French] men who did not fight in the [First World War], or those who did fight and lived to tell about it' (2018: 109). It is an argument echoed by Geneviève Sellier and Noël Burch (2000), Susan Hayward (2005: 90–1), Sarah Leahy (2007) and Susan Weiner (2001: 107–38), all of whom have explored how post-Liberation French cinema worked through the guilt of the Occupation, first by shifting it from the collective realm of war and politics to the realm of individualised sexuality and emotions; second by grafting this revised, sexual guilt onto the bodies of female protagonists, often depicted as consumed by irrepressible libidinous urges or disloyal to their betrayed soldier-husbands; and third by punishing these women accordingly, specifically by subjecting them to instances of 'justified' diegetic violence, as within Marc Allégret's 1949 *Manèges/Merry-Go-Round* (Leahy and Hayward 2000: 85–6). In her chapter 'Gender Panic' (2007), for instance, Leahy identifies *la garce* – the bitch – as a figure that crystallises this dynamic of displacement, supporting her theories through astute textual analysis of *Panique/Panic* (Duvivier, 1946) and *Quai des Orfèvres/Quay of the Goldsmiths* (Clouzot, 1947). Writes Leahy:

> in the misogynistic climate of the Liberation, narratives such as these laid the blame [for France's military defeat] squarely at the women's feet: *the garce* is duplicitous, adulterous, and guilty, or both *fatale* and victim, leading her man to his death through the pursuit of her own desire. (2007: 106)

Examining the imaginary of what they term 'noir realism', an amalgamation of poetic realism and film noir, Burch and Sellier concur, diagnosing the *garce* as 'a beautiful and deceptive young woman who acts as a scapegoat for the national community, with this process being all the more effective insofar as it is largely invisible' (2014: 249). This argument is mirrored in that pursued by Weiner, who identifies *Avant le déluge/Before the Deluge* (Cayatte, 1954) and *Le Repôs du guerrier/Love on a Pillow* (Vadim, 1962) as two films which 'imagined a way to repudiate and excise national shame by putting the sexualised young female' – designated as an *enfant terrible* by Weiner – 'on trial as the sign of all that was wrong, unnatural, and impure in postwar France' (2001: 138). Dilating the scope of our inquiry, Raya Morag has talked eloquently about how *Z32* (2008) – an Israeli documentary directed by Avi Mograbi – features non-fictional footage of an Israeli soldier who 'transfers his guilt to his girlfriend' through what Morag alternately calls 'repeated narrativization' and 'guilt transference' (2012: 107). Last but not least, it is a hypothesis most famously developed in relation to the figure of the femme fatale of 1940s American film noir, a cycle of films from which Rivette's *Paris nous appartient* most conspicuously draws. In the introduction to the edited collection *Women in Film Noir*, Ann Kaplan thus links the gendered politics of film noir to the post-Second World War period, in which

> the depressed peace-time economy brought an end to myths central to the American Dream and caused widespread disillusionment among veterans. There were also sudden fluctuations in the numbers of women entering (during the war) and then leaving (post-war) the job market. Thus the film noir *expresses* alienation, locates its cause squarely in the excesses of female sexuality ('natural' consequences of women's independence), and punishes that excess in order to re-place it within the patriarchal order. (1998: 17 [emphasis in original])

To my knowledge, only two scholars have attempted to extend this argument to the iconographies of French late-colonial filmmaking. One of these is Adam

Lowenstein, who reads Georges Franju's proto-horror nightmare *Les Yeux sans visage/Eyes Without a Face* (1960), as a complex gendered-political allegory, exploring how the film 'displaces the [militarised] masculine violence of [the Algerian War of Independence] onto a network of violence exchanged between [civilian] women' (1998: 50). As Lowenstein contends, this 'network' is largely made up of two female protagonists. One of these is Christiane (Edith Scob), the victim of a harrowing automobile accident, whose scarred face, burnt beyond recognition, has compelled her to wear a prosthetic plastic mask, enabling her to hide her emotions and thus deceive others. The other is a disturbed nurse named Louise (Alida Valli), who appears gripped by a perversely sadistic-altruistic yearning to procure a new face for Christine, namely by prising it from one of the unsuspecting skin-graft candidates that she lures into the eerie Gothic mansion-cum-operating theatre that forms the setting of the diegesis. Indeed, it is amidst the mise-en-scène of this mansion that the most infamous scene in *Les Yeux sans visage* occurs, when Louise helps to surgically remove the facial skin from an unwilling 'patient', crucially, in an operation that mirrors the ways in which soldiers stationed in French Algeria burnt the faces of their victims during electrotorture (Loweinstein 1998: 50–1; 2005: 43–4, 50–2).

Beyond Lowenstein, the other scholar who has proved particularly pertinent in the development of this chapter is Mark Betz, who has crafted an elaborate argument about representations of female mobility in New Wave narratives such as Agnès Varda's *Cléo de 5 à 7/Cléo from 5 to 7* (1962),[5] Jean-Luc Godard's *Vivre sa vie/To Live Her Life* (1962), Louis Malle's *Ascenseur pour l'échafaud/Elevator to the Gallows* (1958), and Roger Vadim's *Et Dieu . . . créa la femme/And God Created Woman* (1956), exploring how these films (excluding Varda's) yoke together anxiety-inducing images of late-colonial politics with anxiety-inducing images of female sexual guilt (2009: 93–177). In Godard's work, for example, Betz uncovers elliptical allusions to the OAS (see Introduction), blended with stark scenes of prostitution, a vocation pursued by a disenchanted *flâneuse* played by Anna Karina. According to Betz, these scenes 'function to *displace* onto modern femininity all that [Godard] finds questionable about contemporary commodity, media and political culture' (2009: 151 [emphasis added by author]). In Malle's film, Betz locates a similar analogy, one expressed in the predicament that transpires between a former paratrooper and his femme fatale lover, played by Jeanne Moreau, 'who seduces the hero into his criminal actions and fate' (2009: 155; also see Sellier 2008: 131–3; and Chapter 3). For Betz, in both films, sexually guilty women are associated with the 'dark' side of France's colonial empire.

Taking up the themes outlined in this introduction, this chapter is structured into three sections. In the first, I briefly outline the plot of *Le Retour*, pausing to consider the subtext of emotional duplicity that subtends the film, with particular emphasis on how Goldenberg frames the female face. I then consider how this subtext is likewise threaded into the narrative of *Paris nous appartient*, specifically in relation to a profoundly mysterious, sexually promiscuous and quasi-fascistic femme fatale named Terry. In the last section I show how this tendency towards representing female French citizens as the source of an all-pervasive anxiety reaches its apotheosis in *Secteur postal 89098*, an often referenced yet seldom analysed film, dedicated to chronicling the breakdown of love between an absent soldier and his pining partner. Ultimately, I suggest that each of these late-colonial films exemplifies the dynamics of gendered 'guilt displacement' elaborated above, 'symbolising women as national scapegoats, and bearing the wartime sins of the nation out into the wilderness of moral opprobrium' (Hipkins and Plain 2007: 19).

LE RETOUR (1959)

Filmed in 1959, *Le Retour* is a short film directed by Daniel Goldenberg, in collaboration with the ex-paratrooper, Yann le Masson (see Chapter 7), who was responsible for cinematography, alongside Georges Barsky. According to the credits, the screenplay was based on an obscure short story by the French-Greek author Gisèle Prassinos, whose alignment with Surrealism may account for the somewhat oneiric ambience that pervades *Le Retour*, in which the rites and rituals of everyday life are defamailiarised so as to render them strange and otherworldly. At the point of writing, no scholarship – whether journalistic or academic – exists on *Le Retour*, undoubtedly due to the fact that the film has, for many years, remained essentially unavailable to the public. The only way to see *Le Retour* is by consulting on-site archives at *Le Forum des images*, in Paris.

The plot is a simple cycle, composed of three acts. In the first, we are introduced to a young unnamed woman (played by Lucie Arnold, henceforth referred to as 'the Young Woman'), who lingers within a crowd of people assembled at the Gare de Lyon train station in Paris, waiting for her unnamed soldier-partner (played by Jean-Claude Rolland, henceforth referred to as 'the Soldier') to return from Algeria, via Marseilles. What emerges in this first act is the centrality of the Young Woman's face – close-ups of which are juxtaposed against long shots of crowds – to the intrigue. What also emerges is the silence of the Young Woman, entirely stripped, as she is, of synchronised speech, performed, for example, as dialogue with the individuals that surround her. Point-of-view shots chronicling her silent perception of the station thus bleed into silent close-ups of apperception, as the Young Woman seems to indulge in various moments of prospective and retrospective introspection, with the resulting combination of this dialectic suggesting anticipation, trepidation, even suspense (Figure 5.1). It is at this point, whilst the Young Woman paces

Figure 5.1 The Young Woman waits for her soldier-partner.

back and forth amidst the hustle and bustle of the station, that we hear a disembodied masculine voice, overlaid on top of images of her countenance.

> I know you are at the train station. I am looking for your face. You will perhaps be unable to recognise me as I have been away for so long. My train arrives in a few minutes. Yes, I have changed. I have demobilised. You should smile, with that smile I love. Yes, I always touch my eyebrow whilst thinking.

Has the Soldier 'changed', as this monologue suggests? If so, how? What did the Soldier look like before being conscripted into the army? What does he look like now? Perhaps he has lost a limb in warfare or been facially scarred by combat? It is against the backdrop of such questions that the second act of *Le Retour* begins, when the Soldier slowly descends from a train that arrives on the platform where the Young Woman awaits. Amidst jubilant images of young couples embracing, kissing, smiling at each other, reuniting with each other, the narrative then performs two key peripeteia (turning points). One of these relates to the body of the Soldier, which, whilst clearly weighed down by the effects of fatigue, even exhaustion, has evidently neither been maimed nor disfigured by warfare, at least. The other relates to the behaviour of the Young Woman, who, against all expectations, suddenly seems overcome by an inexplicable yearning to avoid their encounter – inexplicable as her soldier-lover has not been physically altered as expected – hiding from him within the folds of crowds that surround her, until he leaves the station in tears.

In the third and final act of *Le Retour*, we are then exposed to even more puzzling images of the Young Woman and the Soldier meandering through the environs of the train station, before the former eventually decides to visit the latter in his meagre studio apartment, essentially breaking into it whilst her exhausted soldier-partner sleeps. Once again, this gesture is framed as inexplicable: after all, if the Young Woman, for whatever reason, didn't deem it appropriate for the two lovers to meet at the station, then what drives her to abruptly reverse this decision by inviting herself unannounced into his abode? Equally inexplicable is the highly disturbing final shot of *Le Retour*, which essentially depicts what earlier scenes deferred: a silent corporeal embrace between the Young Woman and the Soldier, with the latter remaining blissfully oblivious as to the ambivalence of the former. Fifty-eight seconds long, and composed of a slow-tracking shot that starts by framing the couple standing next to the Soldier's bed, before creeping gently towards the Young Woman's now tear-soaked face, her gaze disconcertingly aimed directly at the camera in a fourth-wall break, it is, above all, in this shot that the ideological process of 'guilt displacement', as elaborated in the introduction, can be seen to operate. For what this shot does, elliptically yet unmistakably, is suggest that French women are capable of hiding their feelings, their intentions, their emotions behind a mask-like facade of fake-tears; in short, that they are deceptive, duplicitous and opaque, and should not be trusted. To the feminised 'crime' of emotional manipulation, chronicled at the train station, *Le Retour* thus adds the feminised 'crime' of emotional duplicity, with both 'crimes' targeting the innocent and wounded Soldier, who, let us not forget, was precisely the type of figure who had tumbled into a state of complicity in colonial atrocities perpetrated in the non-cinematic world. Doubly damned, the Young Woman exits *Le Retour* as guilt incarnate.

Paris nous appartient (1961)

A similar process of guilt displacement can be found in Jacques Rivette's *Paris nous appartient*, which revolves around the perspective of Anne Goupil (Betty Schneider), a young student who has just moved from Châteauroux to Paris in the summer of 1957. Despite being set at the height of the Algerian War of Independence, *Paris nous appartient* begins by repressing the visibility of this crisis through an ostensibly anodyne image of Anne revising in her tiny apartment, before her brother Pierre (François Maistre) invites her to a party hosted by a famous painter. It is at this party that Rivette introduces us to the warren of elusive intellectuals and exiles that reappear sporadically throughout

LATE-COLONIAL FRENCH CINEMA

Figure 5.2 Terry (left) avoids the gaze of Gérard (right).

the film, including; Philip (Daniel Crohem), an American journalist who has moved to France in order to escape the demagogic ultra-nationalism of Senator McCarthy; Gérard Lenz (Giani Esposito), a sensitive and brooding theatre director in the process of producing a version of Shakespeare's Jacobean play, *Pericles, Prince of Tyre*; and Terry Yordan (Françoise Prévost), a contemptuous femme fatale who is maligned by many of the disconsolate down-and-outs that Anne meets during her search for 'truth' (Figure 5.2). The remainder of the film thus chronicles Anne's first few months in the capital – her studies in literature, her newfound love for theatre, her attempts at negotiating the pitfalls of patriarchal desire. What she actually discovers is the existence of a mysterious fascistic organisation implicitly gendered as female.

The feminisation of fascism

Paris nous appartient begins with an unusual sense of finality and political tension. An enigmatic Spanish composer known as Juan has recently committed suicide in Paris after resisting then fleeing Francisco Franco's fascist regime (1936–75), leading a number of guests at Bernard's party to compare him to García Lorca, a Spanish playwright assassinated by Franco's nationalist militia in 1936. Others compare Juan to Vladimir Mayakovsky, a Russian poet, whose suicide was largely read as a Stalinist murder conspiracy, whilst a reserved Spanish 'anarchist' performs a melancholic dirge on a guitar previously owned by his late friend. If Mary Wiles has described Juan as a 'Sartrean antihero' and 'republican warrior' (2012: 13, 14), it is undoubtedly because the dour and dithyrambic ambience of Bernard's party at least initially implies that the former has sacrificed his life for a revolutionary cause.

As with the ideological debate that swirls amongst Bernard's guests, Juan's privileged status a political martyr is short-lived. When Anne flees the claustrophobic confines of Bernard's apartment in boredom, she suddenly stumbles upon a dramatic altercation between Philip, who has been asked to leave the premises after drinking himself into a stupor, and Terry, who has just arrived at the party. Suddenly, Philip flies into an inebriated rage, slapping Terry in front of her new partner Gérard and accusing her of Juan's murder in a gesture drenched in sexual jealousy. 'You killed him' (Philip) . . . 'I had nothing to do with it' (Terry). In what turns out to be a precursor for the patterns of victimhood, persecution and displacement that characterise the remainder of the film, the allusions to radical politics articulated at Bernard's soirée abruptly disappear behind Philip's attempt at placing the blame for Juan's death squarely on the shoulders of his ex-lover, Terry.

Paris nous appartient has been defined by Michel Marie (2003), Émile Breton (2016) and Mary Wiles (2012) as an allegory for the fear of colonial fascism that arose largely in response to the use of torture by the French army in Algeria, but also due to the similarly heavy-handed methods of control mobilised by the French police to suppress Algerian nationalism in Paris. As we have seen, the logic of this interpretation depends partly on the backdrop of political exile that frames the lives of Juan and Philip, and partly on a string of opaque allusions to a fascistic 'organisation' that has apparently already gently seduced a number of Bernard's guests, including Pierre, Terry and de Georges, a shady economist played by Jean-Marie Robain. Hence Michel Marie's definition of *Paris nous appartient* as 'a remarkable account of the intellectual mood at the end of the Fourth Republic', which was dissolved partly in response to a putsch orchestrated by army officials, 'with its military and political plots surrounding the Algerian War' (2003: 84). Mary Wiles sees it another way:

> It could be that the film's commemorative allusion to the Spanish Civil War, appearing not long after France's defeat in Indochina and at the height of the Algerian conflict, is reinvented in and for the historical moment, *displacing the contemporaneous crises to an "elsewhere"*. Indeed, the artist's inability to represent the crisis in communication and the cascade of whispered innuendos at the soirée could testify to the intense censorship that the Algerian conflict provoked and that was in full force at the time the film was made. (2012: 15 [emphasis added by author])

Wiles's interpretation is clearly persuasive. Yet what remains unexplored, or at least implicit, in this interpretation are the ways in which these allegorical allusions to colonial fascism are often predicated upon an ontological dichotomy: between man as the innocent victim of violence, and woman as the guilty perpetrator of violence, with the latter forming the italicised 'elsewhere' of Wiles's quotation. Catalysed by the scene discussed above, this process of displacement occurs again and again in the film, including when Philip apostrophises about an opaque fraternity of 'un-nameable leaders', menacing the world and menacing Gérard, before almost immediately pleading with Anne to 'beware of Terry'. Or when Juan's ex-lover frames Juan's death as a political 'plot', before describing it as the inevitable outcome of his relationship with Terry, who, in her own words, 'led him astray'. Or when Philip, Terry and Anne discover Gérard's limp and lifeless body splayed poetically on his bed. Suicide? Political assassination? Or murder committed *in vacuo* by a jealous femme fatale? Once again, the film's logic of deadly ritual is at least initially framed in an ideological cast: 'maybe they can push their victims to suicide . . .', muses Philip, his use of the plural pronoun 'they' suggesting multiplicity, shared complicity, the machinations of an organisation, before Rivette gently edges the parameters of the conspiracy from the realm of politics to that of gender. 'It's all my fault', states Terry, flatly, her face, a picture of sexual guilt.

Woman as mystery

When Terry does not pose a threat, she is imbued with mystery, generating a number of scenes that share various parallels with those that we find in *Le Retour*. Mystery: Terry's ossified profile and tendency towards reticence, both of which stand in contrast to Philip's frequently sweaty brow and Gérard's softer, more quizzical countenance. Mystery: Terry's opaque sunglasses, that she wears whilst voyeuristically watching Anne perform a recital of *Pericles*. Mystery: the deep chiaroscuro of Terry's apartment, or what might be considered a contemporary equivalent to the deathly crypts that populated classic Gothic narratives before reappearing under the guise of 'cheap dives [and] shadowy doorways' (Place 1989: 41) in 1940s film noir, and again in the 'one-removed but transparently related language of doors, gates, portals, channels and inner rooms' that crops up throughout the classic horror film (Clover 2015: 48, 101). Finally, Terry's mystery is evident in her implied promiscuity. At no point in the film, for example, does she ever provide an adequate reason for leaving Philip, Juan and Gérard, but rather appears beset by an insatiable although unexplained desire for sexual conquest, for the pleasures of the flesh.

Rivette's representation of Terry as a locus of mystery can be read in several ways. From the perspective of intertextuality, for instance, *Paris nous appartient* clearly evokes the gendered politics of American film noirs such as *Double Indemnity* (Wilder, 1944) and *Murder My Sweet* (Dmytryk, 1944), in which 'the seductive power attributed to [femmes fatales] exemplifies [a] disparity between seeming and being, the visible and the knowable' (Doane 1991: 46). Hence Claude-Jean Philippe's diagnosis of Terry as somebody who 'seems to possess dangerous secrets' (1966), whilst Almut Steinlein goes further, describing her as 'privy to a secret that she alone understands' (2007: 216). Understanding is, however, different from recounting. It is also different from revealing. And it is drastically different from taking action. Whilst initially confined to the politics of gender, the implications of Terry's mysterious behaviour upon the narrative gradually begin to germinate – from episodic spurts of incongruous reticence to full-blown incomprehensible monologues – until it eventually begins to trespass, in certain shots, upon the kingdom of politics. In one particular scene that takes place towards the end of the narrative, Anne arrives at Terry's apartment in a desperately futile attempt at determining Gérard's location after he threatens to commit suicide. Suddenly, the surface of Rivette's Paris gives way to a distinctly oneiric topography, composed of tight murky corridors, a claustrophobic communal area, shrouded in darkness by a curtain pulled tight over the window, and a hidden chamber to which Philip secretly retreats, whilst Terry begins to apprehensively auto-narrate her own history of exile from McCarthy's America, providing a compelling if not enigmatic antithesis to Philip's own campaign of virile slander. But if the spectator is expecting a revelation to level the deceptive logic of the diegesis, they will be disappointed: just as Terry's apartment oozes an ambience of feminine mystery, her monologue remains profoundly mysterious. At no point in the scene does she, for example, directly discuss the impact of McCarthy's neo-fascistic witch-hunt upon American politics, and how this has led, in the film at least, to the emergence of a fascistic faction operating in Paris, but rather retreats into a highly evasive commentary regarding 'the greatest conspiracy that has ever existed'. When Anne enquires to whom Terry is referring, her response is unremittingly opaque: 'the same ones'. A similar pattern of political mystification reoccurs in the climatic final sequence of the narrative, when several characters incongruously find themselves holed up in an isolated keeper's lodge in Ermenonville, located in the north of Paris, although, as Roland-François Lack points out, Philip describes the action as taking place in Antony, located in the south of Paris (2010: 143). It is at this point that Terry shoots Pierre after she falsely suspects he is guilty of Gérard's death, before once again erupting into a highly convoluted monologue concerning 'money, policing, political parties . . . all the faces of fascism'.

In criticism on the film, scholars have defined the political ambiguity that subtends *Paris nous appartient* in a number of ways: as an aesthetic vestige of Bazin's ideology of obscurity (Gozlan 1962); as a phenomenological commentary on the 'infernal logic of secrecy' (Morrey and Smith 2015: 24); as a throwback to Balzac's nineteenth-century brand of literary realism (Breton 2016); and, perhaps more persuasively, as a symptom of the regime of censorship in operation in France during the 1950s and 1960s (Wiles 2012). What fewer thinkers have considered is the possibility – explored above – that this ambiguity is at least partly a symptom of Rivette's representation of a femme fatale, Terry, who is obliquely analogised with a fascistic 'secret' that she 'alone understands'. Only Almut Steinlein has broached this hypothesis, albeit in a way that does not distinguish between genders, by claiming that 'the testimonies articulated by the different characters cloud the plot instead of explaining it' (2007: 219). Rather than ascending through exposition to a moment of resolution, *Paris nous appartient* therefore descends, through dialogue, into modernist equivocacy, generating along the way a towering myriad of mysteries: some linked to gender, others linked to politics, some linked to France, others linked to Spain and America, yet all tied in some fashion to the body of Terry, the archetypal femme fatale, spider-woman, man-eater. In the next section of this chapter, we will see how this trope of woman-as-mystery re-emerges in *Secteur postal 89098*, which, like Rivette's film, arguably displaces the guilt for the crimes perpetrated by French soldiers in the extra-filmic world onto the bodies of the metropolitan female citizens that inhabit the filmic world. For now, let us simply state that both works turn around psychologically elusive and sexually guilty seductive sirens, whose aesthetically pleasing yet ultimately unreadable mask-like faces function as much to generate fascination in their awe-struck partners as they do a mood of sinking, sickly, dread.

Secteur postal 89098 (1961)

Filmed over the course of four weekends in 1959 by Philippe Durand, a former soldier turned director, author and lecturer in film,[6] who had not only lost a leg in Algeria in 1956, but also been forced to spend a year convalescing in a military hospital upon his return to France, *Secteur postal 89098* (subjected to a total ban by the censors in October 1961), is unequivocally one of the most deeply affective yet critically neglected late-colonial films to feature in this book. Like *Le Retour*, it is also a film that is often bracketed somewhat superficially under the rubric of 'parallel cinema' seeing as it was made with Durand's own finances, alongside the financial support of his acquaintances (Arnault 1970: 32).

The narrative itself focuses largely, and somewhat unusually, on the figure of an unnamed young woman (played by Nathalie Pasco, listed as 'Her/She' in the screenplay, and henceforth referred to as 'the Woman'), who does little more than meander melancholically around Paris and its environs (including the 1st, 7th, 16th and 18th arrondissements), thinking about and waiting for her soldier-boyfriend Pierre (Claude Debord) to return from Algeria, and travelling to and from her workplace (an office located in the 7th arrondissement), all the while dreaming about becoming a model. Set largely in the streets of the capital, and totally devoid of scenes of combat, that is to say, of soldiers frozen into a state of fear or belligerence by the late-colonial crisis, to look at the image-track of *Secteur postal 89098* is thus to be exposed to a series of episodic urban perambulations that appear sometimes prosaic, sometimes poetic, often temporally disorientating, but seldom psychologically traumatic and never explicitly physically violent. Raymond Borde, for example, compares the image-track to 'photos taken during a family outing on a Sunday' (1962a: 16). It is only once we attune our critical and perceptual faculties to the repertoire of modernist formal strategies weaponised by Durand – notably his decision to completely replace all synchronised sounds, including speech, with a series of what might be termed, following Michel Chion (1994: 73), unvisualised monologues, unvisualised in that they are never articulated by a mouth that we see – that we realise how aesthetically ambitious, politically singular and thematically disturbing *Secteur postal 89098* really is. We will return to the question of the voice in the final section of this analysis, for now, all the reader needs to know is that the provenance of the speech woven into the soundtrack is often extremely ambiguous.

Two faces: one absent, one eroticised

In the second shot of *Secteur postal 89098*, a face – the Woman's face – held in abeyance at a three-quarter angle, in close-up, presents itself to us. A pair of refined eyebrows arch above two ochre eyes, ringed with under-eye skin, cast into shadow. A curve of full lips, pursed in non-speech, lie perpendicular to a stretch of hazelnut brown hair, which edges, in turn, down the right-hand margin of the screen. A vast envelope of porcelain skin, unscathed by the ravages of age, illness or epidermal functions (perspiration, twitching, blotchiness), constitutes a central facial column of sorts, evoking the pale composure of Audrey Hepburn. Unembellished by excessive make-up, this skin is preserved in a state of unsullied purity, of exquisite chastity, of limpid beauty. Tentatively, a female voice rings out in the soundtrack, apparently alluding to the name of a man who had once stood upon the unoccupied bucolic pathway, visualised in the opening shot of the film, yet now absent from it: 'Pierre'.

Subtly subverting the cinematic convention of the shot-reverse-shot by conjugating the face of a woman with a space in which a face *is not* rather than *is*, together these two shots form a deceptively beguiling, and subtly disorientating, start to the film. They also gesture towards one of the main themes of *Secteur postal 89098*: absence, or to be more precise, Pierre's absence from Paris, having been shipped off to Algeria before the narrative is launched into orbit. True, in the very next scene – as within certain other parts of the film – the spectator is disarmed by idealised images of Pierre and the Woman, frolicking amorously in back-streets, parks and woodlands located in and around the commune, Chaumont-en-Vexin, suggesting that the central temporality of the narrative perhaps chronicles his return (Figure 5.3). But, actually, close examination of

Figure 5.3 Pierre embraces his partner in a wooded enclave during one of her flashbacks.

these scenes, which are sometimes, although not always, bracketed by close-ups of the Woman, as she closes her eyes, apparently indulging in a moment of recall, alongside the commentary with which they are paired,[7] reveals that they are most likely composed of distant flashbacks that emanate from her psyche, leading us to a somewhat startling conclusion: that not once in the present-tense of the story does Pierre feature as an embodied image.

The subtext of absence is a subtext that pervades many late-colonial films.[8] Most of the time, these films are populated with soldiers who endeavour to reintegrate themselves into a society from which they have been absent, for example, Frédéric in *La Belle vie*, Bernard in Resnais's *Muriel ou le temps d'un retour/Muriel, or The Time of Return* (1963), Antoine in Varda's *Cléo de 5 à 7*, Gérard in Paul Carpita's *Demain L'amour/Love, Tomorrow* (1962; see Introduction), the soldier protagonist of Guy Chalon's *58 2/B* (1959),[9] alongside the wounded veteran of Goldenberg's *Le Retour*. Other times, the protagonist in question endeavours to live in a society from which they will soon be absent, for example, Michel in Rozier's *Adieu Philippine*, and the prospective soldier of Ado Kyrou's *Parfois le Dimanche/Sometimes on Sunday* (1959).[10] Less common are late-colonial works that are dedicated to exploring the emotional fallout of military duty as the individual in question is performing it, as within *Secteur postal 89098*. In his monograph *Guerre et cinéma/War and Cinema*, Joseph Daniel identifies one such film, classifying Jacques Demy's famously saccharine musical, *Les Parapluies de Cherbourg/The Umbrellas of Cherbourg* (1964),[11] as a narrative that is largely, if not exclusively, devoted to chronicling how the departure of a young soldier-mechanic named Guy (Nino Castelnuovo) 'has deformed the memories' of his girlfriend Geneviève (Catherine Deneuve), 'eroding their love', and catapulting her, somewhat guiltily, into a relationship with another man (1972: 348). Despite being draped in an aesthetically pleasing haze of Eastman colours and operatic dialogues, at the core of Demy's psychodrama thus lies a subtly misogynistic message: that no matter how amorous or ardent soldiers in Algeria might be, the devotion of their partners cannot be guaranteed, and betrayal is not just to be expected, but practically inevitable. In his compelling book *Stars in Modern French Film*, Guy Austin goes further, conjecturing that the control Geneviève willingly surrenders in her body, through infidelity, is recuperated and channelled into the lineaments of her face, as the latter, slowly but surely, morphs, from a landscape redolent with emotions, with affect, with feelings, to one positively devoid of them: a de-personalised, de-subjectified 'white mask' (2003: 42). It is a motif to which we will shortly return.

Like Geneviève in *Les Parapluies de Cherbourg*, the Woman in Durand's film is someone who presents herself, at least initially, as devoted to her absent partner, Pierre. Apart from the aforementioned close-up that opens the narrative, numerous early scenes depict her alone, strolling plaintively through the capital, pensive and contemplative, drained of volition, thinking about him and reminiscing about their past together. Often, these images are conjoined with monologues that support such a reading, painting a picture of the Woman as a lover bereft, sullen and sedate, pining for her soulmate, without whom she cannot – will not – survive. It is only once the Woman has taken time to reflect upon how lacking in excitement her life is in Paris, and how long Pierre has been in Algeria ('one hundred and four Sundays without you', she intones at one point), does the anesthetised innocence of her porcelain face suddenly begin to crack, in a scene that is as elliptical as it is disturbing.

The scene in question begins when the Woman is captured perambulating at Montmartre, a topographic vantage point offering unimpeded views over Paris. As we gaze at her profile, she gazes at the horizon, smoking a cigarette. Calm reigns. It is at this point that diegetic footage of the Woman's face yields to a rapid montage of twenty-one, non-diegetic visual inserts, some of which consist of still images, transposed, for example, from advertising material used to promote the release of popular films, few of which last more than two seconds, and many of which feature young white female film stars, in various stages of undress. Two shots in this montage, for instance, are taken from promotional photographs, alternating between Brigitte Bardot, a *brisé* fan in hand, on the set of *La Femme et le Pantin/The Devil is a Woman* (Duvivier, 1959), and Romy Schneider, peering salaciously into a mirror in *Die Halbzarte/Eva* (Thiele, 1959). Others are plucked from promotional posters used to advertise the release of Luis Saslavsky's 1959 film *Ce corps tant désiré/Way of the Wicked*, and Alessandro Blasetti's 1959 documentary, *Nuits d'Europe/European Nights*. In the former, the spectator discovers the legs of a scantily clad Belinda Lee – the star of Saslavsky's erotically charged drama, whereas the latter visualises the fetishised heads of three cabaret dancers, bedecked in feathers. Still other shots represent nothing more than a fragment of an unidentified female body: two eyes, looming, like orbs; a knee sheathed seductively into a stocking, and so on.[12]

Ricocheting frantically between the bodies of these women, none of whom have previously appeared in the narrative or will reappear in the narrative, or even have any direct relevance to the narrative, other than the fact that they have attained the status of cover-girl stardom to which the Woman discreetly aspires, it is no exaggeration to describe this as a supremely disconcerting moment in the film. Part of the reason that this scene is *so* disconcerting, I think, is because it illustrates, even exemplifies, the radical potential of film form to alter the meaning of film content, echoing, in turn, Durand's own compelling and comprehensive historical-theoretical research on Soviet Montage, as elaborated in his book *Moteur! Coupez!/Motor! Cut!* (1988: 261–319). Durand's use of editing during this scene, for example, not only clearly evokes the parameters of high velocity, machine-gun cutting at play in many of Sergei Eisenstein's films, including *Stachka/Strike* (1925), *Bronenosets Potyomkin/Battleship Potemkin* (1925) and *Oktyabr': Desyat' dney kotorye potryasli mir/October: Ten Days That Shook the World* (1927), but also pleats the bodies of the aforementioned female stars – the content of the shots – into a grotesque slide-show of heads and limbs that flicker spasmodically in and out of on-screen space. To this use of excessive editing, we may add a similarly excessive use of framing, with Durand's frenzied combination of close-ups, extreme close-ups, wide shots and long shots, again approximating the scale and proportion-orientated formalism of Eisenstein's films, where one witnesses perceptual leaps, 'from face to body, and from body to other detail, to the setting, and the image as a whole' – all of which is symptomatic of an 'eccentric-ecstatic' focus on 'corporeality' (Steimatsky 2017: 47). Aggressively funnelled through Durand's Soviet-inspired montage, the female film stars that feature within this 'scene' are instead reduced to nothing more than a vulgar agglomeration of over-sexualised and under-represented body parts.

But perhaps the most discordant – and most confounding – aspect of this montage can be found neither in the literal cuts that Durand carves in the filmic image through editing, nor in the representational cuts that he carves in the female star-body through framing, both of which are symptomatic of a modernist emphasis on bodily fragmentation (Coates 2012: 24), but rather in the connections cultivated through these cuts, and, more specifically, the ways in which the camera returns insistently to the face of the Woman, three times, as the montage develops. To be sure, at no point in this scene does Durand assemble any kind of explicit or specific analogy between *their* bodies and *her* visage, both of which seem to jostle for visibility, whilst the screen splinters into quasi-abstraction. Rather, the overarching logic of this scene seems to be governed by a more supple, associative logic, evoking Lev Kuleshov's famous experiments in Soviet Montage, conducted in the 1910s and 1920s, and during which the impassive face of Ivan Mosjoukine was intercut with three different images – a bowl of soup, a girl dead in a coffin and a woman lying seductively on a sofa – in turn, assembling the illusion that Mosjoukine was experiencing three different emotions: hunger, sorrow and lust (this illusion is often referred to as 'the Kuleshov effect').[13] Lodged syntagmatically in-between the non-diegetic female star bodies that frame her, as Mosjoukine was lodged syntagmatically in-between the non-diegetic objects that framed him, the face of the Woman thus exits this scene irrevocably and indelibly altered. No longer pristine or pure, through the power of montage, the lineaments of her visage seem to darken, accruing the burden of the 'grotesque' shots of female sexuality that surround her, and therefore ultimately intimating that just beneath the glossy weave of the Woman's blank face lurks a mind aroused by an aberrant maelstrom of erotic desires.[14] For the first time in the film, the Woman is depicted as sexually guilty.

Sexual guilt and emotional duplicity

In the opening remarks of this chapter, I listed a number of post-war films in which women are framed as duplicitous: from the post-Occupation noir duplicity that pervades *Panique* and *Quai des Orfèvres*, to the late-colonial duplicity that pervades *Les Yeux sans visage*, *Paris nous appartient* and *Le Retour*. Like these narratives, *Secteur postal 89098* too envisions the female face as an elusive territory that expressly does not divulge the thoughts, feelings, fantasies of its owner. But where directors such as Duvivier, Franju and Rivette generally stage this duplicity through synchronised dialogue, performed between two protagonists – a woman who lies, and a man who doesn't – Durand adopts a subtly different approach, cleaving open a comparable epistemological crisis within a single protagonist, the Woman, who appears, curiously, to lie to herself. Two facial close-ups in particular illustrate this point, both of which occur when the Woman is alone. During the first of these – a nocturnal shot, set again at Montmartre – we are invited to contemplate the Woman's becalmed face, positioned at a three-quarter angle, as a unvisualised voice rings out, ostensibly tracing the train of her thoughts: 'Pierre, you should know that you need to come back, that I am waiting for you.' There is just one problem: the Woman articulates this internal monologue almost immediately after she has been seen entwined in a romantic embrace with an unidentified male character (henceforth referred to as the 'Other Man', played by Claude Hainaut); in short, when her patience has already expired and her loyalty has already snapped, following an implied struggle with illicit carnal cravings. Even more startling is a further shot that occurs not long after this one, when the Woman is likewise captured abruptly in close-up, her lips now curled into a delicate smile. Yet even as Durand represents the Woman's face as open and innocent, so too does he juxtapose it against a further troubling monologue that again appears to flow out her mind. 'How can you think that the passing of time won't affect our love?' the Woman barks, bitterly – as her face beams, blissfully – before insisting: 'How can you think that things are going in the same direction as the desires of the heart?'

In different ways, shots such as these are clearly designed to worry rather than reassure the spectator, forcing us to radically question not only the authenticity of the information that the Woman transmits through the quivering cadence of her words, but also the authenticity of the emotions that she telegraphs through the surface of her now mask-like face. Throughout much of the psychologically jarring and temporally hazy second half of *Secteur postal 89098*, uncertainties about the Woman thus abound, evoking notably the work of Jean-Luc Godard, in which 'female sexuality and femininity are associated with secrets, with something that lies "darkly" behind the mask' (Mulvey 1996: 46), a trope seen, for example, in the director's late-colonial tale of gendered conspiracy, *Le Petit soldat/The Little Soldier* (Godard 1960/1963).[15] Why does the Woman promise to remain devoted to Pierre ('nobody will ever make me smile like you'), if this promise is emphatically broken almost as soon as it has been made? Why does the Woman constantly mutter Pierre's name when in the presence of the Other Man?[16] Does she engage in sexual activity with the Other Man as one particularly elliptical scene, set in woodland, ostensibly suggests, or is this a flashback of a moment of erstwhile intimacy with Pierre?[17] The only thing that we can be sure of (or can we?) during all of these scenes is that the Woman has guiltily entered into a relationship with a new lover who is not Pierre – compensating for the loss of love engendered in his absence through lust – before naively convincing herself, consciously or unconsciously, that some kind of future with her beloved former partner is still not only possible, but positively probable. And that, due to her increasingly mercurial behaviour, which often teeters so close to the precipice of the illogical that it seems potentially pathological, the Woman is not to be trusted. Especially as she herself is apparently incapable of separating truth from illusion.

Epistles and atrocity

At the start of this section, I alluded briefly to the audio-visual virtuosity of *Secteur postal 89098*, pointing towards, without elaborating upon, Durand's decision to erase all traces of synchronised sound (and therefore all traces of synchronised dialogue), from his film, which instead features a series of incredibly rich, yet obscure, unvisualised monologues, performed by the Woman and Pierre (see Chapter 7 for more about the politics of the voice). Sometimes, these monologues seem to be instances of what David Bordwell and Kristin Thompson call 'internal diegetic sound' (2017: 291), that is to say, when a director combines a shot of an unspeaking face with an instance of non-localised speech, in order to generate the impression that the character in question is thinking the words we hear. We have already examined two examples of this phenomenon, first in the close-up of the Woman that surges forth into on-screen space in the first few seconds of the film, whilst a female voice – presumably echoing the Woman's thoughts – softly pleads 'Pierre', and second in the aforementioned shots of the Woman 'deceiving herself'. Frequently, however, this interpretation does not seem to hold water, and the monologues we hear instead appear to be exercises in the kind of non-diegetic 'voice-over dialogues' woven into Alain Resnais's 1959 film, *Hiroshima mon amour* (Martin 2013: 270), before we realise that Durand's film is, astonishingly, even more singular, and even more unconventional than this, and the words spoken in the soundtrack actually correspond to a series of written *letters*, exchanged between Pierre from Algeria and the Woman from Paris. Hence the title of the film, *Postal Sector 89098*.[18]

At once paralleling and re-configuring the conventions of what have been called 'epistolary films' (Rascaroli 2017: 143–63) and 'film-letters' (Naficy 2001: 101–32), close examination of the soundtrack of *Secteur postal 89098* reveals that it features approximately fifteen verbalised epistolary correspondences: seven from the Woman, six from Pierre, although, in contrast to the vast majority of 'film-letters', at no point do we see the characters actually engaged in writing. Sometimes, these correspondences form but a tiny, de-contextualised, single word or single sentence fragment of a much longer epistle to which we are neither visually nor orally exposed ('Pierre'; 'A Sunday without you'; 'one hundred and thirty-five Sundays without you'). It is during these moments that the boundary between verbalised thoughts and verbalised words becomes blurred (especially when the monologue in question is matched with a close-up), preventing the spectator from coming to any clear conclusion as to the source of the speech heard, and positioning the film in proximity to similar modernist experiments in epistolary filmmaking, conducted, for example, by Chris Marker, in his 1957 *Lettre de Sibérie/Letter from Siberia* (see Naficy 2001: 146–51). Other times, the sheer length of the monologues (many of which are over twenty-five lines long in the screenplay, lasting between two and three minutes in the film, and bridging several shots), suggests that they represent an entire letter, transposed in its totality, from pen to voice, from page to speech.

In his book *Algeria: France's Undeclared War*, Martin Evans has talked about the stream of letters sent by conscripts and reservists engaged in combat in Algeria to partners and family members in France (2012: 169–70). Sometimes testimonial, often personal and occasionally harrowing, it was effectively through these letters, these epistles, that the metropolitan public first privately learnt of the atrocities being committed during the war, before a small group of anti-colonial publishers, flouting the parameters of official censorship, began to make them available, publicly. Hence, the publication of *De La pacification à la répression/From Pacification to Repression* (1957), a compilation of letters written by a Christian soldier named Jean Muller, fatally wounded during service; *Des Rappelés témoignent/Mobilised Reservists Bear Witness* (Anon. 1957), a pamphlet of twenty-four texts, comprising letters, diary entries and written testimonies; to which the publication of two more recent collections can be added. One of these is the aforementioned *Love in War*, the other, a painfully lyrical assemblage of epistles, originally written by André Segura, killed in combat in 1959 (Lefeuvre et al. 2004). 'Written to loved ones during long bouts of lassitude and boredom', rarely did these letters 'hold back', parses Evans, but rather 'confided, in detail, the horror of the War' (2012: 169).[19]

Drenched in a similar tenor of 'horror', and often paired with baroque, non-diegetic chords, played by a lute (the only music we hear in the film), much of Pierre's correspondence sounds like a verbalised version of these written epistles. At one point in the film, for instance, he recalls 'finding three squadron leaders naked and mutilated', in what could plausibly be interpreted as an allusion to the infamous massacre of Palestro (see Chapter 2 for more details on how Mark Robson represents this event in *Les Centurions*). At another, Pierre remembers hearing 'jackals howling in the distance' when he was on night duty, before adding: 'armed guards must have been beating them to shut them up'. Reimagining Algerians tortured by the army as jackals struck into submission, the latter anecdote, in particular, is a brief yet especially disquieting moment of metaphor that regurgitates, almost verbatim, certain lines from *Des rappelés témoignent* ('yesterday, I thought I heard jackals, but as it continued [. . .] I realised it was a child being tortured' [cited in Chapeu 2004: 94–5]). It also evokes Jean-Paul Sartre's 1960 play, *Les Séquestrés d'Altona/The Condemned of Altona*, in which both 'the victims and the perpetrators [of torture] become insect, vermin, cockroach, or crab' (Sanyal 2010: 61), or Stanislas Hutin's description of electrotorture as producing screams that sound 'like a pig whose throat has been cut' (cited in Branche 2001: 59). In each case, decolonisation is envisioned as a nauseating and nightmarish, dehumanised dystopia, littered with pestilence. Still more intriguing is the fact that Pierre does not once implicate himself in the perpetration of these atrocities, the vast majority of which he associates with unnamed others: 'men fighting over water'; 'armed guards'; 'a colonel in Constantine', who complains farcically about 'being too hot'. Nor are they generally articulated when Pierre occupies our field of vision – he is, after all, only visible as a flickering figment of his lover's memory in the first half of the film, and almost completely absent, as an embodied image, from the second half of it – but when our gaze is instead tellingly towed towards the fetishised physiognomy of the Woman.

I have already outlined the ways in which Durand's narrative frames the Woman as guilty of precisely the two crimes imputed to the Young Woman in Goldenberg's *Le Retour*: betrayal and duplicity. Yet, like Georges Franju's representation of a young woman consumed by a desire to procure a new face for another through torture (*Les Yeux sans visage*), and like Jacques Rivette's representation of a quasi-fascistic femme fatale who may or may not be responsible for the deaths of several men in Paris, *Secteur postal 89098* does more than that: it also elliptically intimates that the Woman is somehow guilty of complicity in the perpetration of colonial atrocities committed in French Algeria. In *Secteur postal 89098*, perhaps the most disquieting instance of this displacement of guilt occurs just after the eleventh minute of the film. It consists of nothing more than a single thirteen-second long close-up of the Woman as she leans back against a tree, gently rocking her head from side to side whilst languidly blinking, as if tumbling in and out of the recesses of her psyche. In and of itself, there is nothing in this facial image to suggest anything other than a pleasurable moment of apperception, contemplation or perhaps erotic reverie, especially as the forest is the site of a previous sexual encounter. Still, when it comes to what we hear rather than what we view, disturbing emotions abruptly write themselves into the lineaments of her features, evoking Michel Chion's notion of screen speech,[20] when a protagonist located off-screen or in non-diegetic space (as within Durand's film) orally addresses a protagonist on-screen, with our visual perception of the latter being subsequently altered by the auditory properties of the former (2009: 360, 362). 'Last night, three soldiers didn't come back. In one month, seventeen dead, twenty-one wounded', gravely intones an unseen Pierre, as the Woman's visage offers itself to us. The effect is stark, brutal, abhorrent. Impossible to spirit away the epistolary allusions to 'the dead and wounded' that seem to coarsen the mineral-white surface of the Woman's skin, metamorphosing the gentle horizontal swaying of her head into a nightmarish expression of psychic distress, and transforming the fluttering of her eyelids into what now appears to be an agonised attempt at shielding her vision, and therefore her memory, from the scenes of atrocity that she, rather than he, seems to have seen (Figure 5.4). A similar but even more brutal instance of this 'screen speech' occurs just over half-way into the film, when the Woman is pictured languidly strolling alongside the Seine.[21] Composed of almost two minutes of tightly cropped tracking shots depicting nothing other than the Woman's profile – her sleek brown hair aesthetically framed against the tonalities of bleached white clouds, suspended, in turn, in a gently overcast sky – one could hardly ask for a better example of the fetishisation of the female face that characterises many of the peripatetic shots in *Secteur postal 89098*. But the calmer the image-track, the starker the soundtrack, with Pierre practically

Figure 5.4 A close-up of the Woman's face as Pierre intones: '... seventeen dead, twenty-one wounded'.

assaulting the Woman's image with a litany of harrowing anecdotes about the war, for example, when he nostalgically rhapsodises about a 'soldier-friend who used to be a beekeeper', before clarifying: 'his coffin was send to Lille'; or when he recalls his squadron 'dragging wounded fellaghas [Algerian nationalists] to a mountainous ridge' after engaging in combat. Over and over Pierre delivers such revelations, with the cumulative effect of this audio-visual montage being that the Woman's radiant skin seems once again burdened by his colonial guilt, a guilt at once articulated and distorted, shared and displaced: from Pierre's invisible body to the Woman's visible face. In this respect, *Secteur postal 89098* not only chronicles the trials and tribulations of a soldier who 'confides the horror of the War' to his partner through a range of spoken epistles, to re-quote Martin Evans, but crucially goes further, 'transforming the beauty of the female face into a site of testimony to the horrors of violence' (McNeill 2010: 121).[22] As the source of deeply felt dread, a plethora of anxieties, a nexus of conspiracies and multiple layers of guilt, the Woman is horror itself.

Notes

1. I am referring specifically to the Countess Nathalie de Clairefons, who features in *Les Centurions*, Maria, who features in *L'Insoumis*, and Madeleine, who features in Guy Gilles and Marc Sator's *Au biseau des baisers/Slanted Kisses* (1962), all of whom are female French settlers.

2. As Élodie Jauneau points out, French women have technically been able to join the French army since 1938, a right enshrined in the Paul-Boncour Law. In Algeria at least, women's role in the conflict was restricted to providing medical care as mobile medico-social workers and flight nurses, or as part of the specialised administrative sections civil-military programme. The latter was set up in an attempt to win over the hearts and minds of indigenous Algerians, principally by providing them with educative, medical and agricultural support. Jauneau estimates that there were 6,000 female nurses in Algeria by the end of the War (2012: 1, 9).
3. Two high-profile female intellectuals who did write about the war were Simone de Beauvoir, whose autobiographical *La Force des choses: II/Force of Circumstance: II* included a chapter dedicated to the politics of decolonisation ([1963] 2014: 223–38), and the historian Madeleine Rebérioux (1964). Martin Evans has also drawn attention to a number of women involved in the Jeanson Network, which I mention in the Introduction (2012: 276–7, 279–80; 1997: 57–66).
4. The authors display a notable degree of restraint when dealing with the revelation – expressed euphemistically through the lines of their corpus – that 'Aimée' has died during childbirth, whilst 'Bernard' remains stranded in Algeria (2017: 253–90).
5. One of the most theorised late-colonial French films, *Cléo de 5 à 7* tells the tale of a neurotic star singer in Paris, named Cléo, who is diagnosed with a mysterious, invisible illness. Much has been written about the dichotomous structure of *Cléo de 5 à 7*, split, as it is, between early scenes in which Cléo narcissistically panders to the collective gaze of other men and later scenes in which she appears to repudiate this gaze (see Flitterman-Lewis 1990). It is also worth noting that *Cléo de 5 à 7* features one of the most softened and sublimated cinematic images of the French army in the character of Antoine (Antoine Bourseiller), an incredibly gentle soldier that Cléo providentially meets at the Parc Montsouris. I provide a brief list of scholarship on Varda's film in the Introduction.
6. During his lifetime (1932–2007), Durand directed more than fifty films (captured mainly on 35mm and 16mm), wrote four incredibly illuminating academic textbooks on film theory (including one published by the internationally renowned, Éditions du Cerf), and taught film at *l'Institut Lumière* in Lyon and at Les Beaux-Arts de Quimper. Despite this prodigious output, Durand was, and remains, an almost entirely unknown figure in the world of academia. The only scholars who have written about *Secteur postal 89098* at any length are Raymond Borde, who provides a brief summary of the film in his famous article 'le Cinéma marginal et la guerre d'Algérie', published in *Positif* (1962a: 16), Raymond Lefèvre, who discusses how it was banned by the censors (1997: 42–3), Joseph Daniel, who identifies Durand as a member of the 'Jean Vigo group', and defines *Secteur postal 89098* as an instance of 'parallel cinema' (1972: 338), and, in particular, François Chevassu (1962), who not only proffers a description of each and every shot woven into the film, but also analyses its themes and formal innovation.
7. One of the reasons that these flashbacks are so ambiguous is because they are not framed by the constellation of visual, aural and verbal cues that traditionally mark

shifts in time in the classical Hollywood narrative (see Chapter 4 for more information on memory and flashbacks). Instead, the spectator is forced to join the dots between the temporality of the Woman's monologues ('our bridge from long ago'; 'I used to like your mouth on my stomach, the sun used to warm my skin'), and the content of the shots (the Woman and Pierre standing next to a bridge; images of Pierre kissing her bathed in sunlight). Often the relationship between these two elements is, however, tenuous.

8. On representations of military 'absence' in late-colonial cinema, see Cadé (1997: 53–6), Martin (1963a: 147), and Daniel (1972: 347–8). Durand himself identifies 'absence' as 'responsible for the slow erosion that eats away at the love [that features in his film], diluting it and eroding it' (cited in Cadé 1997: 55).
9. Produced by the 'Jean-Vigo Group', Chalon's film turns around a soldier haunted by his memories of military service in Algeria.
10. Kyrou's Surrealist-inspired short film tells the tale of a young couple whose love is jeopardised by the looming threat of conscription.
11. Demy's film has been subjected to sustained analysis since its release. Rodney Hill describes the war as both 'a structuring absence' 'and a major plot point' in *Les Parapluies de Cherbourg*, primarily as the 'middle section of the film unfolds in response to Guy's "absence"' (2008: 37). Undoubtedly the most thorough piece of research on Demy's 'allegorical' representation of the war has been written by Nancy Virtue (2013).
12. As with many of the other scenes that I discuss here, this montage of shots is actually even more formally complex than this. For example, immediately before this montage takes place, the Woman makes an elliptical spoken reference to feeling 'ashamed' about 'reading promises in the newspapers', which at once appears to predict the promotional material that follows, whilst emphasising her status as 'sexually guilty'. This montage also includes a close-up of the Woman that will later re-emerge when she is first seen with the Other Man (see below), again scrambling conventional notions of causality, in favour of a more episodic, even hallucinatory, temporality. Moments such as these encourage an understanding of the film as an example of modernist art cinema, on a par with Alain Resnais's much better known, and acclaimed, *Muriel ou le temps d'un retour*.
13. As many scholars have pointed out, Kuleshov's experiment also generated two further illusions: first, that Mosjoukine was looking at the objects in question, and second, that the emotions detailed above were being acted out through barely perceptible tremors in the landscape of his face. For more information on the Kuleshov effect, see Mikhail Yampolsky and Larry Joseph (1994), Steimatsky (2017: 153–63) and Coates (2012: 16–17).
14. Close examination of these images reveals a certain gendered-thematic inconsistency in Durand's imaginary. If, as I suggest, these images are intended to represent a visualisation of the Woman's (heterosexual) erotic urges, then a much more logical motif would be the *eroticised male body*. That Durand decides against this, consciously or not, is surely evidence of the heteronormative conventions that governed 1960s French cinema. For more information about the politics of gender, see Chapter 2 and Chapter 3.

15. In *Le Petit soldat*, this emphasis on 'secrets' is perhaps most apparent during an incongruously impromptu photography session between Bruno (Michel Subor) and Véronica (Anna Karina), with the former musing philosophically: 'when you photograph a face you photograph the soul that is behind it', whilst the latter is seized in an aesthetically pleasing close-up. What Bruno fails to grasp, however, is that the face that he sees before him is a face that precisely does not reflect the mind – or 'soul' – that lies behind it. And what Bruno instead captures with his camera is a photo of a facial mask: one belonging to an individual who both betrays and deceives him.
16. The first time this occurs is when the spectator is introduced to the Other Man, fostering a sense of perceptual confusion. In other words, even as our gaze dimly registers the arrival of a new character in the diegesis, our ears are encouraged to falsely believe that this is Pierre.
17. The two-shot scene in question takes place in a bucolic landscape, much like the one visualised in the idealised memories that flow in and out of the first half of the film. We watch as an individual that vaguely resembles Pierre clambers down a precipice with the Woman; however, as both are framed from behind, we cannot be sure that it is indeed him. The next shot – of limbs on a grassy embankment, presumably entwined in sex – could therefore hypothetically depict either Pierre and the Woman, or the Other Man and the Woman.
18. Postal sectors formed the crux of a system that enabled civilians to send letters from France to their soldier-partners in Algeria. For example, a letter might be addressed to 'Sargent Loupin, SP 69421'.
19. For more information on letter writing during the war see Lemalet (1992), Stora (1998: 54–5), D. Le Sueur (2001: 156–9) and Eveno (2005).
20. Chion pertinently notes that 'screen speech' often appears at its most devastating – and arguably most misogynistic – when the disembodied voice in question is male and aggressive, and the embodied protagonist in question is a *guilty, duplicitous* and *beautiful* young woman. For example, in Juan Antonio Bardem's film *Death of a Cyclist* (1955), which dedicates 'a large share of the shots to showing the exquisite Lucia Bosé in frontal close-ups, whilst she hears remarks that invariably echo her secret' (she is complicit in an unintentional murder) (2009: 363). Or during a famous scene in Hitchcock's *North by Northwest* (1959), in which the central female protagonist, a femme fatale named Eve, must remain as facially composed as possible, whilst a male character, talking from over her shoulder, violently accuses her of infidelity, as she is framed in close-up.
21. According to François Chevassu, the buildings that we see in the background of this scene are abattoirs – an observation that, if true, would support an understanding of the Woman as someone literally and figuratively framed by death (1962: 27). Likewise, whether Pierre actually survives his ordeal in Algeria is a question *Secteur postal 89098* leaves unresolved. This ambiguity is most apparent in the final few minutes of the film, when the camera tracks slowly through the streets of Paris, before finally arriving at the gates of the Val-de-Grâce military hospital. If this climax certainly *suggests* that Pierre has returned, wounded, from Algeria to Paris, the fact that he does not feature as an embodied image in any of these tracking shots prevents us from confirming this hypothesis unequivocally.

22. McNeill makes this argument in the context of Jean-Luc Godard's *Histoire(s) du cinéma/Histories of Cinema* (1989–99), and Chris Marker's *Level Five* (1996), neither of which can persuasively be defined as late-colonial French films. In their chapter, 'Year Zero: Faciality', Gilles Deleuze and Felix Guattari describe representations of the face in equally negative terms, although their argument is much more orientated towards questions of ontology, epistemology and Western capitalism than my own. '*The face, what a horror.* It is naturally a lunar landscape, with its pores, planes, matts, bright colors, whiteness, and holes: there is no need for a close-up to make it inhuman; it is naturally a close-up, and naturally inhuman, a monstrous hood' (1987: 190 [emphasis in original]).

6. THE WAR AS SEEN FROM ALGERIA BY THE SETTLERS

Taking a further step away from narratives that turn around military personnel (Chapters 1–3), Resistants-turned-OAS abettors (Chapter 4), conscientious objectors (Chapter 4) or female civilians (Chapter 5), this chapter focuses instead on two late-colonial films that draw poignancy from the concerns and desires of European settlers: *Les Oliviers de la justice/The Olive Trees of Justice* (1962), by Jean Pélégri and James Blue, and *Au biseau des baisers/Slanted Kisses* (1962), by Guy Gilles and Marc Sator. Forged after the conquest of Algeria in 1830, the settlers (later labelled *les pieds-noirs*), were a socially and religiously diverse community, whose geographical bastion extended largely throughout the northern coastal towns: Oran, Bône, Philippeville, Algiers (which features in both films), and the rural vistas of the Mitidja, as featured in *Les Oliviers de la justice*. Out of a total population of 10 million, just under a million were settlers, yet, irrespective of their origins, they possessed enormous privileges systematically denied to indigenous Algerians, including: economic privileges fostered by the expropriation of land, often exploited to produce wine, even though it was anathema to the largely Muslim population; educational privileges; legal privileges (the right to vote); and French citizenship, which was extended to those originating from Italy and Spain. In 1961, Frantz Fanon famously attested to how these privileges had manifested themselves in the 'brightly lit streets of the settler's town: well-fed, easy-going; its belly always full of good things' ([1961] 1963: 39).

Privileges so ingrained in the fabric of everyday colonial life that they seemed natural and immutable were, unsurprisingly, privileges that turned the settlers into what was increasingly considered a legitimate target of nationalist violence during decolonisation, giving rise to a series of atrocities of escalating ferocity. In 1945, armed men associated with the Algerian nationalist politician Messali Hadj killed approximately a hundred European settlers in the north-eastern town of Sétif, after having been prevented from unfurling banners during a pro-independence demonstration, catalysing, in turn, a vertiginous torrent of retributive attacks against indigenous Algerians, perpetrated by settler vigilantes and the French army. In 1955, two FLN leaders residing in Constantine launched a policy of total war on all colonial inhabitants (military and civil), leading to what is now known as the Philippeville Massacre, during which seventy-one European settlers were slaughtered. In September 1956, three *mujahida* (female freedom fighters) – Zohra Drif, Djamila Bouhired and Samia Lakhdari – famously planted a series of bombs in cafes located around the settler neighbourhoods of Algiers, fatally wounding three European civilians. In July 1962, approximately a thousand settlers were killed when a wave of Algerians indiscriminately attacked the European community of Oran (Horne 2006: 23–8, 118–22, 185–7, 533).

Emboldened by privilege, imperilled by violence, consumed by anxieties about what their so-called country would become: such were the conflicting factors that coalesced in the slippery identity of the settlers, whose history continues to split academics, divided as to whether to paint them as politically regressive reactionaries, in that they frequently endorsed patterns of violence inflicted upon Algerian citizens by the army and the OAS (see Introduction); or sacrificial lambs-turned-refugees, in that they were treated with indifference if not derision by metropolitan communities. This was especially the case after the mass exodus of 1962, when 99 per cent of the settlers – around 800,000 individuals – arrived in France by boat, seeking asylum from the violence sprawling through French Algeria (Barclay et al. 2018; Hubbell 2015). It was also this nexus of contradictions that catalysed an incredibly prescient study by a young Pierre Nora, entitled *Les Français d'Algérie/The French of Algeria* ([1961] 2012). Summoning a similar psycho-historical methodology to that used years later by cultural historians such as Henri Rousso (1987; Rousso and Conan 1992) and Benjamin Stora (1998; 2004), Nora's thesis was predicated upon the persuasively argued belief that the settlers had, consciously or not, systematically denied, disavowed and 'scotomised' the most traumatic and guilty aspects of their history through the fantasmatic imaginary of their culture ([1961] 2012: 207). Neither belligerence nor violence but peace and reconciliation thus emerged as the overarching moods of their literary and, as we will see, cinematic narratives. And neither guilt nor shame but innocence and absolution were the values embodied by the protagonists of these narratives, linking back to the discourse of 'redemptive pacifism' elaborated in the introduction to this book. It is a hypothesis corroborated by Claire Eldridge, who has commented that 'although regarded by many as at best complicit in, and at worst the perpetrators of, a system of colonial domination, the *pieds-noirs* view themselves as innocent casualties of a destructive and erroneous historical force: de-colonisation' (2010: 123). Naomi Greene has come to a similar conclusion regarding Brigitte Roüan's *Outremer/Overseas* (1990), eloquently illustrating how the film at once charts the vicissitudes of decolonisation through a tale of three settler sisters living in French Algeria, and 'softens the most brutal and guilt-ridden realities' of this process by couching it in 'an atemporal world of primal moments, infused with love and passion, longing and desire' (1999: 146–7). Finally, it is a hypothesis supported by the two films probed in this chapter, each of which deploys the perceptual idiom of gazing to craft an image of the settlers as 'innocent casualties of de-colonisation'.

The Late-colonial Gaze

The gaze has been a recurring concern for thinkers associated with critical theory, post-colonial theory and film theory, yet depending on the methodology cultivated, and the socio-historical context in question, it has been conceptualised in different ways. In the 1940s and 1950s, during the rise of Negritude and the emergence of anti-colonial nationalism throughout France's increasingly fragile empire, intellectuals such as Jean-Paul Sartre and Frantz Fanon harnessed theoretical trends in psychoanalysis, phenomenology and existentialism, to diagnose and lambast what both saw as a deeply entrenched hierarchy, at once ethnic and ocular: between 'the white man' who 'enjoyed the privilege of seeing without being seen' (Sartre [1948] 1964/1965: 13), and the black man, who existed as the object of this gaze: 'dislocated, distorted and imprisoned' by it (Fanon [1952] 2008: 85, 86). Fanon's famous phenomenological account of being hailed by a white child, who cries out "'Look, a Negro!"' in his presence ([1952] 2008: 84), is, in particular, often cited as a seminal point in critical race theory, if only as it seemed to predict, with incredible clairvoyance, many of the debates about the power of the look that would take place much later: first in the rise of cultural studies, post-colonial studies and psychoanalytically inflected film theories, for example apparatus theory, during the 1960s, 1970s and 1980s, and then again in the so-called visual turn in the 1990s.

Beyond works by Sartre and Fanon, another early intervention in these debates was Alain Robbe-Grillet's 1957 novel *La Jalousie/Jealousy*, which turns around the psycho-sexual-racial micro-drama of a newly wed couple who travel from France to what is presumably the Ivory Coast – granted independence from French colonial rule in 1960 – on their honeymoon (the setting of their excursion is not explicitly clear). Not that this trip accrues any scenes of ardent romance, as one might expect. Instead, the novel is largely dedicated to documenting, in minute detail, a pattern of obsessive-compulsive behaviour exhibited by the husband, who appears devoured by an unexplained impulse: to peer from the domestic space of the couple's rented villa, through the slatted blinds of a 'jalousie window', onto the surrounding banana plantation. So complex was the darkly metaphorical imaginary at work in *La Jalousie* that it prompted Jacques Leenhardt to devote an entire monograph to it (1973), spawning, in turn, two key arguments, both of which have proven crucial to the elaboration of my own. In the first instance, Leenhardt argues that late-colonial cultures often respond to the threat of nationalism by both intensifying and sublimating the power of 'the white gaze' as theorised by Sartre, before secondly suggesting that this process of intensification gives rise to a visual iconography of 'morbid geometrism', based on a pathological yearning for 'symmetry, planning and logic' (1973: 55). As Leenhardt glosses: 'faced with the possible twilight of colonialism, morbid geometrism performs a very clear ideological function. It is the sign of a Cartesian [colonial power] trying to [visually] control a [colonised] reality that no longer submits, but rebels' (1973: 55).

It is only relatively recently that theorists have begun to grapple with the visual power relations at play in cinema, and the ethnic power relations at play in the colony. For example, in a compelling article entitled 'Imaging terra incognita: the disciplinary gaze of empire' (1991), Ella Shohat argues convincingly that contemporary Hollywood remains shackled to a neo-colonial imaginary, inherited from the iconography of colonial films made in France, England and America during the 1920s and 1930s, and subtended by two attendant concerns: landscape and looking. Examining films such as *The Sheik* (Melford, 1921), *Bird of Paradise* (Vidor, 1932), *The Mummy* (Freund, 1932), and *Pépé le Moko* (Duvivier, 1937), Shohat suggests that 'technological inventions [in the world of cinema] mapped the globe as a neatly organised space of knowledge' (1991: 67). Elsewhere, in a chapter co-written with Robert Stam, her theories appear to edge even closer to those originally proposed by Sartre and Leenhardt. 'The colonist trains on the colonised a look of desire, of appropriation, of surveillance. He overlooks, surveys, oversees, without being looked at, surveyed, or overseen' (2014: 285).

As with her brilliant monograph *Unthinking Eurocentrism*, co-authored with Stam (1994), Shohat's article is an undeniably important contribution to debates surrounding ethnicity and visuality, although it should be noted that the decolonisation of Algeria is not the central concern of her thesis, but a minor one. In order to address *this* event, and the cinematic iconographies that it engendered, we must look towards the work of two further thinkers. One of these is Guy Austin, who has queried the configurations of embodied and disembodied gazing woven into Gillo Pontecorvo's late-colonial opus, *La Bataille d'Alger/The Battle of Algiers* (1966), performed respectively by the paratrooper protagonists and the cinematic apparatus. 'The spatial relation between high and low' writes Austin, 'clearly expresses the power relations of colonisers and colonised', before pointing to how Pontecorvo mobilises the visual motif 'of redemptive [white] light' to convey the rise of the FLN as a 'higher, quasi-imperial power' (2012: 38, 40). The other thinker who has helped craft the argument of this chapter is Nicholas Mirzoeff, whose seminal book *The Right to Look* (2011) explores the dynamics of 'imperial visuality', characterised by 'panoramic height' and surveillance (2011: 15–17, 22). Even if Mirzoeff's book is more concerned with the *longue durée* of colonialism than this chapter, musing eloquently about the forms of looking that governed plantation slavery in the Americas from the 1600s to the 1800s, it has nevertheless proved crucial in enabling me to conceptualise the curious interplay of gazes – at once disembodied and embodied – that flicker in and out of focus in both of my case studies.

Divided into two sections, this chapter will therefore unfold as follows. In the first section, I consider the dynamics of looking that underpin *Les Oliviers de la justice*, drawing attention to the visual trope of *flânerie* (strolling), depictions of military visuality, alongside the film's subtext of colonial reconciliation. Extending these ideas to the love-struck imaginary of *Au biseau des baisers*, in the second section, I show how Gilles and Sator's film revolves around two types of gaze – one amorous, one panoramic – before concluding with some thoughts on the allegorical value of light and darkness. In neither *Les Oliviers de la justice* nor *Au biseau des baisers*, I ultimately argue, are settlers represented as perpetrators of colonial atrocity, but rather as innocent victims of the late-colonial epoch.

LES OLIVIERS DE LA JUSTICE (1962)

Les Oliviers de la justice was originally conceived as a tripartite adaptation project between the French producer Georges Derocles, who owned a production company in Algeria (*Les Studios Africa*); the American director James Blue, who had shot a range of short films in collaboration with Derocles's company after having moved to Algiers; and Jean Pélégri, a settler novelist who had released his first work, *Les Oliviers de la justice*, to great acclaim, in 1959. Together, the three men set about translating Pélégri's novel from page to screen. Recruiting a number of indigenous Algerian actors and operators, Pélégri granted himself a polymorphous role in the project, contributing to the adaptation as co-screenwriter, co-director (alongside Blue) and actor (he plays one of the main roles in the film). Filming took place in Algiers and the Mitidja, a rural plain stretching along the outskirts of northern Algeria, at the height of the war, in September 1961. As Jean Narboni (2004) and Marc Sator (Lequeret 2004) later revealed, Blue often used two cameras in order to reduce the amount of time spent *in extremis* in what Narboni cites as 'dangerous zones' (2004: 26); a reinforced Renault to protect the directors from attacks, especially after threats made by the FLN and OAS,[1] alongside a spate of urban protests that had taken place in Algiers on the 11 December 1960;[2] whilst the project was given the false title of *Vendanges* (Harvest) in order to further stave off potentially hostile factions from interrogating the intent of the directorial team. The narrative itself documents forty-eight hours in the life of Jean (played by an authentic settler named Pierre Prothon), a gentle young man who travels from France to Bab-el-Oued in Algiers to comfort, and eventually bury, his moribund father, Michel (Jean Pélégri), who, we learn, was the owner and manager of a wine estate located in the Mitidja, during the 1920s. What initially appears as an anecdotal narrative of family tragedy, slowly, however, reveals itself to be a complex political allegory, in which Jean comes to embody a 'civilised', 'modern' and 'innocent' alternative to the hard-line colonial ethos incarnated by Michel.

Landscape and looking

At the beginning of this chapter, I outlined the dynamics of three comparable colonial gazes: 'the white gaze', as conceptualised by Sartre, fictionalised by Robbe-Grillet, and analysed by Leenhardt; the 'disciplinary gaze of empire', as understood by Shohat; and 'imperial visuality', as glossed by Mirzoeff. In different ways, all of these gazes relate to the visual imaginary of *Les Oliviers de la justice*, at least partly indebted, as it is, to the ruling precepts of colonial visual culture. The influence of this culture is particularly apparent during the myriad of flashbacks embedded within the film, many of which fuse together two types of gaze: one embodied, wielded by Jean and aligned with the human faculty of seeing, one disembodied, wielded by the directors and aligned with the cinematic process of filming. Both gazes are orientated towards the colonised landscape that surrounds them, and both effectively emanate from Jean's mind, visualised during acts of recollection (see Chapter 4 for more details about memory). In one key flashback comprising a cycle of seven tracking and panning shots, for example, the spectator watches as a young Jean cycles through the environs of his father's estate in the Mitidja, hailing a string of Algerian employees, and thus establishing a simple formula: the more colonised territory that Jean covers by bike, the more of it he sees, and the more colonised territory the camera covers through movement, the more of it we see (Figures 6.1 and 6.2). Intertextually, this flashback plays with the formal innovations of the French director Jean Renoir, whose works *La Grande Illusion/The Grand Illusion* (1937) and *La Règle du jeu/The Rules of the Game* (1939) hinged upon a strikingly similar combination of camera motion and character motion. Ideologically, it can be said to perform a powerful sublimation of colonial history: first, by filtering this history through the subjective perspective of a blissfully innocent child, entirely removed from the litany of colonial injustices in which his father Michel is partly complicit,[3] and second, by portraying the Algerian workers on the estate as neither antagonistic nor politicised but mute and acquiescent. Underpinned by a disavowed yen for total visibility and inter-ethnic harmony, it is in the form

Figure 6.1 A young Jean and his friends cycle through the landscape of the Mitidja.

Figure 6.2 A young Jean and his friends cycle through the landscape of the Mitidja.

and content of this flashback that we first begin to glimpse the ideological contours of late-colonial settler cinema.

Other flashbacks in *Les Oliviers de la justice* are even more orientated towards the landscape of the Mitidja, with the lens of the camera adopting a perspectival position entirely unmoored from Jean's embodied perception of the world. One brief 'scene' that functions in this fashion occurs approximately a quarter of the way into the film, when the spectator is presented with four shots of the family's wine estate, including: a slow zoom in shot of a dozing Algerian farmer, a slow panning shot of habitations owned by the workers and, crucially, two extreme wide-angled, zoom out shots, both of which invite us to contemplate the expansive scale of the family's vines, framed alternately by the immense horizon and a mountainous backdrop. Entirely evacuated of images of Jean as an embodied protagonist, it is during moments such as these that the continuity of the narrative breaks down, and what we are instead faced with is an agricultural panorama, arranged purely for the visual pleasure of the spectator. It is also worth pointing out that this panorama invokes one of the formative myths of colonial ideology: that the Mitidja was an Edenic idyll, characterised by a pioneering culture of colonial cultivation. During the early 1970s, this myth would notably be regurgitated by the settler author Gabriel Conesa, for whom the Mitidja was 'a fertile land where [settlers] could bury their past, and sow the sorrows of their hunger and courage' (1970: 9–10). A still more panoramic flashback occurs later in *Les Oliviers de la justice*, when Jean and his young and sprightly companions don various pieces of colonial attire in a juvenescent imitation of colonial labour. Thematically, this flashback invokes James Blue's earlier short film *Amal* (1960), in which a pre-adolescent settler boy makes an impulsive trip to a fertile agricultural paradise, situated 'just over the hill' from his own, agriculturally impoverished village.[4] Formally, it includes what is undoubtedly the most condensed instance of 'imperial visuality' in the entire film, when Blue and Pélégri cut to an extremely wide, low-to-high vertical panning shot of the children running collectively through the vineyards (Figure 6.3), with the compositional symmetry of the vines evoking Leenhardt's concept of 'morbid geometrism', or, looking further, the harmonious aesthetics and 'expansionist' ideology of the Hollywood Western (Dyer 1997: 36). Captured as if from an all-seeing pyramid, it is likewise at this point in the scene that the disembodied God's-eye view of the camera is joined with an excerpt of disembodied voice-of-God commentary, articulated by an adult Jean. Exercising his transcendental knowledge of the landscape that sprawls out before us, he intones:

> People always told me about the shrubs and swamps that were there before the farm, where jackals and hyenas prowled, and people died of malaria. It was [my father] that toiled the land, purifying it, and planting trees and vines. It was his work.

Figure 6.3 'Imperial visuality': Jean and his friends run through vineyards.

Deeply implicated in the politics of 'panoramic perspectivism' that Mirzoeff associates with 'imperial visuality', alongside Shohat's notion of 'landscape and looking', shots like these clearly perform an ideological function, evoking the figurative imaginary of Robbe-Grillet's *La Jalousie*, in which 'the husband's *imperium* [power] over the plantation aligns him with visual mastery and regressive colonial ideology' (Leenhardt 1973: 52 [emphasis in original]). However, where Robbe-Grillet's prose can only obliquely gesture towards this 'visual mastery' through non-pictorial literary motifs, the mechanical eye of Pélégri and Blue's camera enables us, as spectators, to see it, to survey it and to vicariously experience it. And where *La Jalousie* subtly undermines colonialism by representing the husband's 'visual mastery' as compulsive and pathological, *Les Oliviers de la justice* subtly upholds colonialism by representing Jean's 'visual mastery' as fundamentally infantile and innocent.

Urban seeing

Just as Jean is constantly depicted as travelling through – and looking upon – the rural landscape of the Mitidja in the narrative past, so too is he constantly depicted as travelling through – and looking upon – the urban landscape of Algiers in the narrative present. And just as scenes set in the past draw from a polyvalent pool of cinematic traditions – colonial cinema, Jean Renoir's 'mobile frame', and the Hollywood Western – so too do scenes set in the present draw from a similarly polyvalent range of cinematic trends, including European art cinema and both observational and poetic documentary. Infused with the sense of 'mobility that characterises the Western settler colonial film' (Flood 2020: 180), much of *Les Oliviers de la justice* thus offers up images of Jean doing little more than gently ambling through the settler zone of Bab-el-Oued where his family lives in an apartment (rented in the extra-filmic world by Blue himself). This visual trope appears during four key moments: first, in the opening prelude, when Jean meanders back to his parents' abode after shopping for necessities; second, when he visits a local market, purchasing a batch of fish from a trader, before stumbling across a bomb defusal operation, performed by French soldiers;[5] third, when he ascends the slopes of Cité Mahieddine to visit a former acquaintance (see below); and finally, when he drifts into a café after Michel has died, making use of the telephone to call a relative. In each of these excursions, the directors use a variety of techniques reminiscent of the French New Wave and Italian neorealism, including location filming, natural light and ambient sounds, alongside the type of urban peregrinations that we find in Agnès Varda's *Cléo de 5 à 7/Cléo from 5 to 7* (1962) and Vittorio De Sica's, *Ladri di biciclette/Bicycle Thieves* (1948). As with the mobile protagonists that roam and rove through films such as these, Jean could here be defined as a *flâneur*,[6] that is to say, an individual who exposes us to changes in the modern metropolis through the simple act of seeing and strolling. Interrogating the politics and poetics of the female equivalent of the *flâneur* – the *flâneuse* – Mark Betz has argued that many films aligned with early 1960s European art cinema foreground 'wandering women', 'whose circulation in and around the changing faces of the city [. . .], may be read as symptoms of broader European anxieties concerning colonial war, de-colonisation, and modernisation' (2009: 38). Even if Betz draws an argument from his case studies that is radically different from my own,[7] much of the imagery that illuminates the present tense of *Les Oliviers de la justice* clearly chimes with Betz's contention that the figure of the *flâneur* 'embodies the loss of Empire' (2009: 39), with this 'loss' being represented allegorically, through the aleatory, alienated and aimless peregrinations performed both by the protagonists that populate Betz's corpus and by Jean in *Les Oliviers de la justice*. As France lost its grip on Algeria, Jean loses his way in Algiers.

As for the mise-en-scène of Jean's journeys, several of them take place against the Boulevard de l'Impératrice, a bay-side promenade located in the settler *quartier* of Bab-el-Oued, and composed of an architectural network of facades and arcades, vaults and arches, roads and avenues. As Hannah Feldman has pointed out, the Boulevard de l'Impératrice was originally designed (in 1860–6) to 'symbolically transform Algiers from the military camp it had been, to a city of free exchange, a city of pleasantness [*une ville de plaisance*]' (2014: 57), gracing many postcards produced during the colonial epoch, alongside the visual vocabulary of films such as *Pépé le Moko* and *La Bataille d'Alger* (O'Leary 2019: 23–36). That Jean is drawn to look upon the smooth surface of this colonial complex is therefore unsurprising: after all, it was originally conceived as a site from which the settlers, in particular, could see and be seen. Not only that, but the Boulevard de l'Impératrice is also the site of another type of gaze that Blue and Pélégri project onto Algiers, although one that is less tethered to the *flânerie* of European art cinema. Several of the shots included in the film, for example, form little more than non-fictional footage of anonymous non-actors, many of whom simply stroll down the avenues of the Boulevard, or otherwise rest languidly on the balustrades separating it from the sea. Captured from within the confines of a travelling car, the unadulterated voyeurism of such footage alludes to at least two trends in documentary filmmaking.[8] One of these is observational documentary, a mode of filmmaking popularised in America during the early 1960s with works such as *Primary* (Drew, 1960), and in which documentarians 'aspired to invisibility', 'playing the role of uninvolved bystander' (Barnouw 1993: 254). The other is the type of poetic documentaries crafted in the 1920s by the Soviet filmmaker Dziga Vertov. In *Chelovek s kino-apparatom/ Man with a Movie Camera* (1929), for example, Vertov wielded his camera on the streets of Moscow in a strikingly similar way to how Blue and Pélégri would later wield theirs in Algiers. Both *Man with a Movie Camera* and *Les Oliviers de la justice* harness the power of the 'disembodied, all-seeing lens', or what Vertov called *kino-eye/cine-eye*, to capture the modern world 'as if discovered for the first time' (Elsaesser and Hagener 2015: 97).

Coinciding with this emphasis on looking at the architecture of Algiers whilst moving horizontally within it, is an emphasis on looking down at Algiers whilst situated vertically above it. Twice in *Les Oliviers de la justice* is a French military helicopter pictured at the port of the capital, forming a narratively disorientating yet historically accurate indication of how such machinery had been used by the French army in the non-cinematic world, especially during the Battle of Algiers (see Introduction). 'Information taken from above by helicopters helped paratroopers such as Marcel Bigeard to build up a picture of the FLN's command structure', states Martin Evans (2012: 205), whilst Nicholas Mirzoeff has diagnosed aerial photographs as the embodiment of 'military-industrial visuality' (2011: 39). Paul Virilio is more poetic, glossing how military 'sight machines', such as helicopters, aeroplanes and drones, have approximated the eye of an 'all-seeing Divinity [. . .] allowing everything to be seen and known, at every moment and in every place' (1999: 4). For astute viewers, Blue and Pélégri's emphasis on the 'military-industrial visuality' of the French army may recall Pontecorvo's *La Bataille d'Alger*, a film in which helicopters, suspended above Algiers, form the nexus of a metaphorical chain of associations, including: 'elevation, illumination, and the imperial eagle' (Austin

2012: 39). Nonetheless, it is important to note that where Pontecorvo forces us to 'see and hear the helicopters from within the Casbah', that is to say, from within a part of Algiers traditionally inhabited by indigenous Algerians, and whose labyrinthine warren of streets was used by the FLN during the war (Shohat and Stam 1994: 252), the helicopters that we see in Les Oliviers de la justice are invariably perceived from the point of view of Jean and the Eurocentric settler-colonial world he inhabits. A prime example of this conflation of settler-colonial perspective and military-colonial perspective occurs when Jean peers out of the window of his family's apartment, glimpsing a helicopter in the sky. After an eye-line match cut, we too are led to look upon this military machine as it hovers against the horizon; yet the scene concludes with neither an escalation of aggression nor a descent into anxiety but with a close-up of Jean's placid and impassive face. A similar yet still more striking moment takes place when Jean scales the heights of Cité Mahieddine,[9] a shantytown located on a plateau in central Algiers (Figure 6.4). At one point in this ascent, we watch as Jean peers out over the landscape of the capital, looking down onto it, as it, in turn, sprawls out before us, in an extreme wide shot (Figure 6.5). Summoning up the iconography of a famous scene in *Pépé le Moko*, when the perspective of the eponymous protagonist corresponds to that later 'granted to the French [army] by altitude (high buildings, helicopters)' (O'Leary 2019: 26) in *Les Oliviers*

Figure 6.4 Jean looks out over Cité Mahieddine, in Algiers.

THE WAR AS SEEN FROM ALGERIA BY THE SETTLERS

Figure 6.5 Jean gazes upon Algiers as a military helicopter traces through the sky.

de la justice, it is an image criss-crossed by three panoptic gazes. One of these is settler-human, aligned with Jean. Another is cinematic-mechanical, aligned with the camera. A third is military-industrial, aligned with the helicopter. And all three of these gazes operate together, in this shot at least, to generate an impression of absolute colonial vision, and absolute colonial power.

Visions of reconciliation

In an illuminating article, Claire Eldridge has spoken eloquently about how, during the post-colonial period, the settlers 'attempted to redeem themselves from the taint of the perpetrator label', 'rehabilitating their collective image' through various political tactics, including an ideology of reconciliation orientated towards peace (2010: 128, 133). Reconciliation was also the touchstone for many of the policies put in place by the French state after 1945, including elevating Arabic to an official language alongside French, granting Algerian women the vote and creating an elected assembly in Algeria that could, on paper, hold the power to change laws in metropolitan France (for more on reconciliation see Dine 1994a: 64–88; 146–77 and D. Le Sueur 2001: 17–98). It was legislative changes such as these that gave settlers such as Pélégri, Blue, Gilles and Sator hope that a fraternal colonial Algeria was possible, despite the bloodshed of the past.

Epitomising this bid for 'redemption', 'rehabilitation' and 'reconciliation', many of the later scenes in *Les Oliviers de la justice* thus seem to perform less a narrative function than an ideological one, providing evidence of Jean's compassion for indigenous Algerians, and thus implicitly framing him as a fundamentally benevolent individual. This is especially true of the scenes in which Jean's propensity towards wandering brings him into direct contact with the Algerian populace, for instance when he momentarily fraternises with a trader at a local market, or when he shares a warm beverage with a childhood friend named Idir, in a moment sparkling with candour and conviviality. As someone who desires to see and to be seen desirably, here, Jean leans less towards anxiously gazing upon the world of indigenous Algerians and more towards deferentially permeating the world of indigenous Algerians – speaking to them, consorting with them – as anonymous bodies in a crowd become personalised faces of an encounter.

Drawing attention to the visibility of faces in *Les Oliviers de la justice* also presents us with the chance to delve, momentarily, into still another influence on the film: the work of the post-war French *auteur* Robert Bresson.[10] Generally acclaimed as the pioneer of an idiosyncratic formal style, defined alternately as 'spiritual' (Sontag 2009: 177–95) or 'transcendental' (Schrader 2018), Bresson was the director of a number of a critically acclaimed works realised during the 1950s, including: *Journal d'un curé de campagne*/*Diary of a Country Priest* (1951), *Un condamné à mort s'est échappé*/*A Man Escaped* (1956) and *Pickpocket* (1959), in which Jean Pélégri played a central role as a police inspector. Bresson was also, crucially, a director whose narratives inaugurated a radically novel method of framing the human face, imagining it neither as an arena of vocal articulation, nor as a landscape of physiognomic expression, as within classical Hollywood cinema, but rather as a silent mask, from which no words, no feelings, no affect, nothing, ideally, was generated. Anchored in reticence, a rhetorical technique based upon eclipsing speech with silence, as Noa Steimatsky has suggested, Bresson's cinematic aesthetic 'was at once subtle, oblique, and devastating: it could cast an ordinary glance to the limits', posing important questions about exteriority and interiority, self and other, and 'the ethics of encounter' (2017: 228).

It is precisely this 'ethics of encounter' that is foregrounded when Jean enters the home of his former babysitter, Fatima (Fatima Moktari), approximately thirty minutes into the film. Suddenly, the scopic grammar of the film changes, with shaky exterior mid-shots yielding to a perfect circle of Bressonian close-ups, whilst Jean's deferent, earnest gaze is now positively mirrored in that of his benign and benevolent host. Sutured together through a cycle of shot-reverse shots, the two individuals coexist – unified, reconciled – in a state of mute intimacy. An intimacy so absolute that it verges on the epiphanic is an intimacy, unsurprisingly, that Jean longs to establish with as many people as possible, including his childhood friend Boralfa. In one of the most Bressonian scenes in the film,[11] Boralfa thus bears witness to his experience of colonial discrimination, whilst Jean gazes on, his face a picture of understanding and empathy. Approximately six minutes long, this scene is significant insofar as it features non-fictional footage of Boralfa the actor talking to Pélégri the director, who had asked the former to simply recount his own experiences of living under colonial rule. When Boralfa refers to 'Mr Jean', he is thus referring to Jean Pélégri, not the fictional Jean of the film (Meurice 1962: 59). Incarnating the values of what Albert Memmi termed 'the leftist coloniser', crucially, Jean here presents himself as someone who aspires to be a European settler in a 'colonised country ruled not by the army, but rather the divine right of love,[12] renewed confidence, and the fraternity of peoples' (2003: 84).

A similar yet even more impassioned 'fraternal' exchange takes place at Michel's funeral, when Jean searches in the congregation for someone who can help him make sense of the political tempest that has consumed the region. The camera pauses in a close-up of Boralfa's face. As within the work of Bresson, infinitesimal physiognomic movements acquire monumental dimensions, as Jean first glances at Boralfa then joins him, with both men indulging in a profound moment of unspoken comprehension, of 'righteous gazing' (Frodon 2004). So profound, in fact, that it causes Jean to abruptly abandon his plans of returning to France, even if, in the non-cinematic world, it was precisely during this period that the settlers were being forced to *leave* Algeria, notably after being accused of complicity in precisely the type of injustices and atrocities that *Les Oliviers de la justice* almost completely elides. As I will now show, a strikingly similar transformation of history into myth, atrocity into love, and culpability into absolution also takes place in *Au biseau des baisers* – again through the silent language of looking.

AU BISEAU DES BAISERS (1962)

Au biseau des baisers was filmed on 35mm in Algeria during the summer of 1959 by two young settlers: Guy Gilles and Marc Sator.[13] Before launching the project, Gilles had completed an art degree at Les Beaux-Arts (studying painting, drawing and interior design), worked as a journalist for *L'Echo d'Alger*, and begun his military service in an administrative department in Algiers. The film was shot over the course of two months, every Saturday and Sunday, as Gilles was only available then. Sator, meanwhile, had studied physics, providing the perfect scientific counterpoint to Gilles's artistic disposition. The duo also benefitted from the talent of James Blue, who acted as co-cinematographer on the project, which was screened in a limited number of cinemas in Paris in October 1962. According to two journalistic reviews of the film, written in 1962 and 1964, *Au biseau des baisers* was included as a prologue to the Italian feature length film *Maciste contre le fantôme/ Maciste Against the Ghost* (Gentilomo and Corbucci, 1961). It is also worth mentioning that just a year after filming *Au biseau des baisers*, Gilles would leave Algiers for Paris, armed with a suitcase, a painting of his mother and dreams of infiltrating the New Wave in the hope of finding fame. That he did not manage to integrate this scene can be attributed to a number of factors.[14]

Like *Les Oliviers de la justice*, the plot of *Au biseau des baisers* is, on the surface, incredibly simple. Two young lovers (played by Alain Gual and Madeleine Serra, a professional dancer at Algiers Opera, who had also worked in television), decide to make the short trip from La Madrague in Algiers (where Gilles had lived as a child; famously eulogised in a song by Brigitte Bardot, released in 1962[15]), to Tipaza, a port town located in the north of the country, on a Sunday afternoon. Not that the couple have any concrete plans: indeed, once they reach their destination, they appear to do very little, spending their time meandering through streets and jetties shimmering with sunlight, before retreating to the coastline after romantic doubts begin to seep into their increasingly anxious verbal exchanges. And it is here, on a maudlin shore, that the film concludes, whilst the sun slowly but surely sets. It is a melancholic ending to a narrative that, like *Les Oliviers de la justice*, constructs the illusion of a country filled with love and innocence rather than atrocity and guilt.

The amorous gaze

Au biseau des baisers, first scene. A cluster of unidentified teenage boys sporting swimwear, and etched with the corporeal indicia of preadolescent lust, linger insouciantly on a sun-drenched jetty, framed by the vast sea and horizon, scrutinising something located in off-screen space. As the camera slowly pans, this something – or rather someone – is revealed to be the contours of a young woman, whose gentle gestures bespeak the language of ballet: arabesques, pirouette, en pointe; whilst her abbreviated attire – a black leotard – provides an opaque indication of her soon-to-be-revealed identity as a European settler named Madeleine (Figures 6.6 and 6.7). Curiously impervious to the presence of her audience, the dancer edges towards the camera across the jetty whilst the boys gaze on: their eyes transfixed, their bodies languorous. In this oneiric dreamscape devoid of exposition – which, according to Gilles, was filmed by him and him alone – the woman offers herself as an object, or spectacle, to be looked at, to be desired, to be loved. This scene also arguably chimes with a wider tendency amongst artists associated with the New Novel to assemble protagonists within a geometric landscape like chess pieces (see, for example, certain scenes in Alain Robbe-Grillet's *Le Voyeur/The Voyeur* [1955], *L'Année dernière à Marienbad/Last Year in Marienbad* [Resnais, 1961], for which Robbe-Grillet wrote the screenplay, or Marguerite Duras's

Figure 6.6 Boys watch Madeleine as she dances in La Pointe Pescade.

Figure 6.7 Madeleine dancing against the horizon.

Moderato Cantabile [1958]). According to Gilles, Duras loved *Au biseau des baisers* so much that she asked him to be the cinematographer for her own project; he declined.

Although assembled using highly unconventional strategies of framing equally inflected by Gilles's studies in painting,[16] the theme of preadolescent gazing that motivates this scene, and, as we have seen, the flashbacks of *Les Oliviers de la justice*, was by no means ground-breaking. During the 1940s, a generation of Italian directors had already filmed a number of works in which the horror of Nazi rule was registered precisely through the traumatised eyes of young witnesses, caught up in what Elizabeth Alsop has termed 'choral gazing' (2014: 35) (see for example Rossellini's *Germania anno zero/Germany, Year Zero* [1948]), whilst, in the 1950s, François Truffaut famously stripped this trope of its political element by instead exposing his young protagonists to visual scenes of abuse, love and transgression (Lebeau 2008: 69–85). Truffaut's short 1957 film, *Les Mistons/The Mischief Makers*, in particular, turns around a group of preadolescent boys that hunt down alternately voyeuristic and fetishistic glimpses of their amorous obsession – a young woman named Bernadette – in much the same way as the boys that feature at the start of *Au biseau des baisers* appear so captivated by the object of their look that they are plunged into a state of libidinal paralysis. The difference, of course, is that, unlike Truffaut's films, which were generally set in affluent *quartiers* in Paris during periods of non-conflict, this scene, and indeed the remainder of *Au biseau des baisers*, was filmed in French Algeria, a region that, by this point, had already been irrevocably riven by five long years of political violence.

That this violence is neither visualised explicitly nor echoed discreetly in this scene is symptomatic of a number of factors. Firstly, whereas *Les Oliviers de la justice* is at least partly set in the heavily militarised streets of Bab-el-Oued (a district which formed the epicentre of attacks perpetrated by the FLN and OAS), the concrete jetty featured in the opening shots of *Au biseau des baisers* was located in La Pointe Pescade, a comparatively isolated, and therefore becalmed, north-westerly coastal town, whose economy, at least until 1962, depended almost exclusively upon colonial tourism, hospitality and entertainment. Cleansed of the tensions that tugged at the seams of communities living in zones such as Bab-el-Oued, it is thus unsurprising that the landscape appears to have been enshrined as a paradisiac frieze, frozen in time and space. But there are other aesthetic factors, too. Consider, for a moment, the sense of utter stillness that irradiates from the bodies of the boys, assembled in such a way as to mirror the geometric architecture of the jetty, and reminiscent of many of Gilles's later films, which often revolved around the simple idiom of 'an encounter, between the seen and the seer, between a skin and a light' (Uzal 2014: 69). Or the measured gait of the dancer, whose arms trace perfect circles in a sky devoid of imperfection. Or the slow, wide pan that Gilles conjures up to capture this curiously serendipitous encounter, between an unidentified *they* who stare placidly, and an unidentified *she* who undulates gently. The scene might only be a few seconds long, but these seconds were apparently all that Gilles needed to begin to transform French Algeria from a notorious arena of settler fear and injustice, into a dreamlike realm of soft and hazy preadolescent lust.

Unlike Truffaut, Gilles and Sator do not dedicate the remainder of their film to exploring the libidinous impulses of *pre*adolescent gazing, as such. Just as the setting abruptly shifts after this opening scene – from a serene jetty to an urban road – so too is the group of early-teen boys that feature therein swiftly yet definitively usurped by two late-teen lovers: Alain and Madeleine (Figure 6.8), who have spent the last few weekends together, courting each other. Alain, we learn, is an accounting assistant graced with sad eyes and a propensity towards charmingly awkward conversation. 'You talk like a book', he tells his interlocutor at a market in Algiers, before elaborating, 'which is pretty stupid as I have never heard a book speak'. Madeleine, meanwhile, is, naturally enough, a ballet student, who reveals that the dreamlike scene that features at the start of the film was precisely that – a dream – *her* dream;

Figure 6.8 Madeleine and Alain on the motorcycle they use to travel from Algiers to Tipaza.

undoubtedly the most striking aspect of Madeleine's look is the distinctive black beehive that she sports precariously atop her head. Neither protagonist is endowed with much depth, whether psychological, intellectual, or political. Both, however, are part of the settler community, and display the tell-tale signs of adolescent (rather than adult) love.[17]

As cultural critics such as Philip Dine (1994a: 79–82) and Lucienne Martini (1997: 21) have perceived, love was an ideologeme that featured within many narratives produced during the war by settler authors. Sometimes the love in question was directed towards the geographical territory of Algeria, giving rise to heavily lyrical passages eulogising the vanishing beauty of the horizon, the august light of dusk and dawn, and the diaphanous folds of the Mediterranean Sea (see novels by Marie Cardinal and Anne Lanta). Other times, the love expressed was a love directed towards the colonised community, although it is important to note that these emotions rarely evolved beyond the level of platonic tenderness without being shaded by psychosexual pathology or racial transgression. Hence the titles of settler novels such as *Nous nous aimerons demain/We Will Love Each Other Tomorrow* (Stil 1957), or Jean Brune's *Cette haine qui ressemble à l'amour/This Hate That Looks Like Love* (1961). In Albert Camus's *Noces à Tipasa/Nuptials at Tipasa* – which, as we will see, forms an important intertext in the film – the author waxes lyrically yet nebulously about 'loving an entire race, born from the sun and the sea' ([1937] 1959: 21). Still other times, settler authors managed to neatly thread together both types of love into narratives permeated with emotional attachments at once territorial and social. By interspersing past images of colonial farmland with present images of inter-ethnic reconciliation, *Les Oliviers de la justice*, for example, does just that.

A curious outlier in this corpus, *Au biseau des baisers* both indulges in and reconfigures this trend towards framing Algeria as a site of amorous encounter. As in the work of Cardinal, Stil, Brune, Lanta and Camus, the architecture of emotions that subtends *Au biseau des baisers* appears driven by a similar belief in love as a haven, or antidote, to the trauma of war, with Lanta, for instance, stating 'above and beyond the sadness of wars, I want to tell a story of love' (1999: 11–12). In *Au biseau des baisers*, Alain and Madeleine may thus be tender, contemplative, intimate, or elegiac, but they are never outraged, nor terrified, nor even mildly irritated; traumatised they are not. Only once does Madeleine allude to the conflict, the better to forget it: 'it's when everything is beautiful that we are at our ugliest. Wars shouldn't exist', she intones sedately, as the couple gaze amorously at each other. Apart from a cluster of lyrics that feature on the soundtrack,[18] it is the first and last time anyone alludes to the political crisis driving the country to the point of breakdown. Here and throughout, the pleasure of looking is equated with the pleasure of loving, and the pleasure of loving is equated with the pleasure of forgetting.[19]

What distinguishes *Au biseau des baisers* from many of the narratives produced by the settler authors cited above is the extent to which the two juvenescent protagonists direct their love inwards, towards each other, rather than outwards, towards the colonised communities that surround them. This quasi-colonial tendency to evacuate Algeria of its inhabitants, transforming it into nothing but an empty landscape, has been theorised before. Indeed, as early as 1961 Pierre Nora had already begun chastising European settlers for 'denying the existence of Arabs' ([1961] 2012: 116), whilst David Carroll has argued that the settler imaginary expresses a yen to 'live in a world inhabited exclusively by French *pieds-noirs*, whereas in reality, they lived in a French colony in which the overwhelming majority of inhabitants were Arab or Berber' (2007: 22). It is also a cultural phenomenon analysed by scholars working with the medium of cinema. Guy Austin, for one, has shown how late-colonial films such as Jacques Demy's *Les Parapluies de Cherbourg* (1964) represented Algeria as a 'tabula rasa' (blank slate), suggesting that there was 'nothing to see in Algeria' (2007a: 182–185), whilst Maria Flood has deployed the notion of 'terra nullius' (nobody's land) to identify a neo-colonial imaginary at play in Xavier Beauvois's 2010 *Des hommes et des dieux*/*Of Gods and Men* (2017: 121). Rebecca Weaver-Hightower and Janne Lahti have spoken more broadly about how 'global settler cinema' turns around 'stories of empty lands, settler civilizations, righteousness, othering and elimination' (2020: 4). Forming an early filmic instance of this tendency towards 'eliminating' the indigenous populace of Algiers from on-screen space, shunning them from sight, many of the shots used in *Au biseau des baisers* (which was originally intended to be a silent film, driven by gesture rather than dialogue) thus reiterate a remarkably myopic exchange of glances, to the point of solipsism: Alain looks at Madeleine, Madeleine looks at Alain; they smile, embrace. No one else speaks, sees, or is seen, erecting a vision of Algeria as an ontological *huis clos*, beyond history and beyond time. Infatuated with each other, consumed by each other, Alain and Madeleine see nobody but each other. Their love is, in a word, blind.

Panoramic gazes

There is another species of late-colonial gaze that exists in *Au biseau des baisers*. But it is not an amorous gaze directed inwards, towards the eyes of a significant other, or the body of an apotheosised dancer, but rather a panoramic gaze, directed outwards, towards the empty – in other words, radically depopulated – landscape of Algeria. Echoing the excursions performed by Jean, the late-colonial *flâneur* of *Les Oliviers de la justice*, yet elongating these excursions to quasi-epic proportions, many of the shots in *Au biseau des baisers* thus resemble little more than an extended travelogue, facilitated by various gaits of locomotion – walking, running, swimming – punctuated intermittently by the frenetic speed of a motorbike, and propelled by a wanderlust ostensibly driven less by a destination than it is by a sense: sight. It is for this reason that the trip that Alain and Madeleine make in the film cannot be defined as sightseeing as such, given that no sites are seen. Instead, the couple are inexorably drawn to landscapes which enable aspirations of total or absolute vision; landscapes not impeded by the animation of crowds, even less by the in-animation of monuments, but instead characterised by nothing but total immersion in immensity, in infinity, in soft flatness: roads, beaches, the sky and the sea.

A significant intertext in *Au biseau des baisers* is a short novella published by Albert Camus in 1937, entitled *Noces à Tipasa*. Madeleine directly quotes from it at one point in the film, stating (in French): 'in the spring, Tipasa is inhabited by gods, and the gods speak in the sun, the scent of absinthe leaves, the silver armour of the sea, and the raw blue sky'. Although *Au biseau des baisers* begins in Algiers, whereas *Noces* does not,[20] both works are set largely in Tipaza (that Camus spells Tipasa, in line with conventions established during the Roman Empire). Both works turn around the same attempt at plunging the reader, or spectator, into a quasi-spiritual, quasi-mystical terrain, associated with lyrical beauty and sensual excess. And, most importantly, both works feature couples who perform rites propelled not so much by a desire to *do*, but rather by a Zen-like desire to simply *be* and to *see*, 'allowing for no space or distance between the perceiver and the perceived' (Brown 2004: 33). Allusions to what James Brown has theorised as 'cosmic seeing' (2004: 60), thus pepper Camus's novella, as when one of the protagonists extols, 'to see, and to see on this earth, how can one forget this rule?' ([1937] 1959: 15), before rhapsodising about eating fresh fruit: 'my teeth wrapped around the peach, I listen to my blood pumping up to my ears, I look with all of my eyes' ([1937] 1959: 17). That the object of this gaze is rarely delineated apparently matters little in *Noces*, which, not incidentally, features no indigenous Algerians. All that is important is that a settler is exercising their power of sight.

It is precisely this propensity towards 'looking with all eyes' that structures one of the most important scenes in *Au biseau des baisers*, when Alain and Madeleine hurtle down the roads leading from Algiers to Tipaza by motorbike. Composed of a sweeping salvo of three rapid-fire panning shots and five tracking shots (three of which are taken from the perspective of the couple), from a narrative point of view, this scene achieves very little. From an ideological point of view, however, it is highly significant, insofar as it once again evokes the cluster of concepts elaborated at the start of this chapter: from Sartre's 'white gaze' to Shohat's 'disciplinary gaze of empire', to Mirzoeff's 'imperial visuality'. It also recalls Michel Foucault's notion of 'panoptic gazing', 'when one sees everything without ever being seen' ([1975] 1995: 202), John Urry's concept of 'the tourist gaze' (1990),[21] or what Kristin Ross has conceptualised as 'panoramic perception', that is to say, the logistics of perception that prevail 'when the viewer no longer belongs to the same space as the perceived object', as within a train or car (1995: 3). Perched atop their motorbike, not only are the lovers able to leapfrog between Algiers and Tipaza with absolute ease, but they are equally capable of seizing glimpses of unwitting members of the populace with absolute impunity, providing the spectator with furtive snapshots of a family languishing beside the road, a young boy with a shopping bag, three stocky men in white vests, and a woman in the *haïk* (a white outer garment often worn by Arabs in Algeria), none of whom, judging from their startled expressions, had been consulted by Gilles and Sator before filming, and none of whom are granted more than a few milliseconds to gaze curiously back at the camera, before being usurped by the serenity of the skyline. At once accelerated and expansive, unfettered and unregulated, totalising and telescopic, it is here, more than any other scene, that the late-colonial gaze possessed by the couple betrays their absolute power – their imperium – as Europeans, bringing to mind Sartre's observation that 'for three thousand years, the white man was only a look' ([1948] 1964/1965: 13).

Complementing these patterns of embodied panoramic gazing, performed by Alain and Madeleine, are patterns of disembodied panoramic gazing, performed by the camera. Consider, for instance, the two extreme long shots that immediately follow Madeleine's dream scene, both of which are captured from the dizzying height of towering buildings. In the first, the camera peers down on Alain as he traces through traffic on his motorbike in the Darse de l'Amirauté in Algiers, before panning upwards to a cloudless sky. Immediately afterwards, the camera pans down from the sky to pause on the distant contours of a square, framed by the Casbah. Neither of these shots is taken from the perspective of a protagonist, yet both present the viewer with a quasi-cartographic, panoramic vision of the capital.

Seeing requires presence; it often requires power. To gaze from a space, the gazer frequently needs to have been able to gain access to that space, by freedom of movement, force, negotiation or, quite simply, by taking advantage of the insidious authority commanded by settlers living in a colonised society. Whether Gilles and Sator were threatened by the FLN or OAS for filming in Algiers, as Blue and Pélégri were during filming for *Les Oliviers de la justice*, is unknown. What is certain is that these shots form stubborn proof that two European directors have seen Algiers from an architectural apex unoccupied by resistance, whether pro- or anti-colonial, and that this act of seeing has been captured by the mechanical eye of their camera.

Likewise, just as these shots form an ontological expression of power, so too do they hark back to visual cultures that legitimised colonial power. In his enlightening book *Empire of Landscape* (2009), John Zarobell has analysed the ideological impulses that gave rise to Jean-Charles Langois's *Panorama of Algiers* (1833), an immense *panorama rotunda* (circular room), in which the viewer was invited to peer through darkness at a series of fifty-metre high paintings of the colonised city, illuminated by gas lights and windows. For Zarobell, the most important aspect of this panorama was not what it represented, but how it represented, specifically, by inviting the spectator to cast their gaze over the architecture of the newly acquired capital from a transcendental perspective, like that pioneered by Renaissance painters during the 1400s and 1500s, 'allowing, in turn, the fantastical acquisition of colonial territory by Parisian viewers' (2009: 12). Although separated from Langois's installation by over a hundred years, it is precisely this visual idiom of Algiers-as-landscape, seized from a vantage point at once panoramic and perspectival, that emerged in late-colonial settler films such as *Les Oliviers de la justice* and *Au biseau des baisers*, once again suturing the viewer into a spectatorial position 'in which their centrality is unquestioned and their power is unlimited' (Zarobell 2009: 6). It is also a style of framing that Blue and Pélégri deploy when the couple reach Tipaza. Although here, the vertical (pan)oramas deployed in early shots of Algiers are generally replaced by the type of horizontal (pan)oramas often used during Jean's flashbacks in *Les Oliviers de la justice*, the vantage point in question is usually a dune or a jetty rather than an architectural edifice, and the field of vision is rarely populated by anything other than the two lovers cruising down an empty road on their motorbike, or sifting through vegetation scattered across the coastline. Many of these later panning shots echo a tendency within settler culture to abstract and romanticise Algeria, projecting it through a soft-focus lens composed of what Safaa Fathy and Jacques Derrida have exalted as 'places known and dreamed of: deserts, oceans, marine spaces; dry lands, coasts and beaches' (2000: 23), and resonating with Camus's vision of Tipaza as a mystical idyll, where the 'sea sucks with the sound of kissing' ([1937] 1959: 12). They are also assembled in such a way that Algeria emerges as a compositionally harmonious landscape, filled with little more than a geometrically aligned matrix of straight lines and coloured shapes, all of which evokes Leenhardt's aforementioned notion of 'morbid geometrism' as a late-colonial phenomenon characterised by an obsessive craving for 'symmetry, planning and logic'. To the seduction of flora, the directors thus add the pleasure of order, as, once again, the country is dragged, via the embodied and disembodied mechanisms of late-colonial gazing, from a state of colonial injustice and guilt into the realm of visual spectacle and innocence.

Light and darkness

For a film that implicitly frames the act of looking as an act of empowerment, it is perhaps unsurprising that light – unstained white sunlight – is everywhere in at least the first half of *Au biseau des baisers*, smothering the landscape with an oily glaze, and draping the lovers, like many other protagonists in

Gilles's films, at least, in 'a solar eroticism' (Lépingle 2014a: 227). Only once do Alain and Madeleine enter into the penumbra of an architectural structure – a semi-covered building entwined with fishing pools – before continuing their pilgrimage through a world of shimmering white streets, beaches, jetties, roads, promenades, esplanades and promontories, bracketed in Algiers (whose sobriquet 'The White' stems from the non-colour of its architecture) by similarly speckless buildings. Theirs is a life lived in high contrast. So bright are certain shots in the narrative that objects start to lose their contours, their ontological status as things-in-themselves: the peak of a white hut bleeds into the white brilliance of the sky, so too do the blond locks of a local singer; horizons disappear in-between the bright tonalities of clouds and waves. As we know from Mathieu Macheret, shots like these align *Au biseau des baisers* with Impressionist cinema, insofar as they 'contain time in light, allowing it to float freely within the cinematic frame and beyond it' (2008). The overarching brightness of the film also contributes to a vision of Algeria as an Edenic, almost prehistoric idyll (it is never bright to the point of blindness, as within Camus's 1942 work *L'Étranger/The Stranger*,[22] for example), all the while allowing the configurations of amorous and panoramic gazing that dominate the film to exist and subsist.

That is, until the end of *Au biseau des baisers*, when Alain and Madeleine descend into a sandy bay adjacent to a cluster of famous Roman ruins[23] in Tipaza (to which Camus alludes in his novella), before gazing out onto the very expanse of water used to transport thousands of settlers to France during the exodus of 1962. For the first time in the film, the white glow of previous scenes yields to an abiding impression of darkness, expressed through: the ochre and iron rock formations that creep along the coast, dominating on-screen space; the long shadows that begin to cling to the feet of the lovers as they trail towards the sea, stretching out on the sand; the murky still pool into which they momentarily peer, reflecting eyes that now seem unable to look at each other, and, above all, the crepuscular sun, glowing red and golden. No longer a swirl of pale whites, colour is here contrapuntal and divided. It is also the point at which the couple's relationship appears, unexpectedly, untenable. Madeleine, for one, finds herself unable to ignore the impermanence of affective ties. In a soliloquy as sober as it is melancholic, she laments: 'I can't believe in love like you do. If I know love will die, then it's already dead. The sun is going down, we need to end this.'

The decline of the day, the decline of affection: that Madeleine's words spin an analogy between the sun and love is clear enough. Less clear, however, are the contours of a further analogy, woven deep within the visual and verbal thickets of this scene, between emotions and empire. Madeleine's thinly veiled suggestion that she needs to separate from Alain, for instance, can be read as a thickly veiled suggestion that Algeria is in the process of separating from

France, particularly as the iconography of the sun was frequently used by a range of metropolitan and settler artists during decolonisation to allegorically allude to the rise and demise of colonial rule. Robbe-Grillet's aforementioned *La Jalousie*, for example, summons the trope of the night 'to symbolize the dusk of white men' (Leenhardt 1973: 72), whilst Gilles's first project – a similarly tragic tale of adolescents haunted by a feeling of fatality in Algeria – was tellingly named *Soleil éteint*/*Setting Sun* (1958). Deeply implicated in this solar imaginary, the final scene of *Au biseau des baisers* can thus be regarded as an attempt at both chronicling and sublimating the decolonisation of Algeria, transforming it from a political revolution punctuated by settler massacres to one contained within the softened realm of diurnal/nocturnal activity and juvenescent love.

But there is still another image included in this scene that further complicates our apprehension of it. Barely a few seconds long, and profoundly elliptical, the image in question occurs as the couple discuss their relationship in the failing light of the evening. Suddenly, the camera cuts abruptly to an unidentified young man brandishing a rifle, somewhere on a sandy shoreline, perhaps with the two lovers, perhaps not, while his weaponry, if not his casual attire, belies his status as a soldier. He aims, lingers and fires, before the third shot in this triptych captures his target: the sun, bleeding into the mountainous range located across the bay: Mount Chenoua.[24] In a later interview (Lequeret 2004), Marc Sator revealed that these shots were inspired by a similar scene in Fritz Lang's *Le Tombeau hindou*/*The Indian Tomb* (1959); they also mirror the opening sequence of Godard's *À bout de souffle*/*Breathless* (1960), when Michel fires brazenly at the sky from his automobile. What Sator doesn't elaborate on are the metaphorical implications of this over-determined image, which, if pushed to its logical conclusion, opaquely implies that the figurative light of colonial ideology is being extinguished by the very people tasked with upholding it: the army. Shaded with pathos rather than tainted with guilt – in short, blissfully ignorant of their role in the crisis enveloping the country – Alain and Madeleine thus ultimately exit the narrative ethically unscathed by the weapon of violence that inculpates the soldier. As darkness consumes the lovers, they remain innocent victims of the events that swirl around them.

Notes

1. It is somewhat ironic that the OAS threatened the directors, given that, as we will see, the film clearly supports the idea of French Algeria.
2. These protests were not only led by pro-colonial *ultras*, who clashed with armed gendarmes and anti-riot units amidst the Haussmannian architecture of La Rue Michelet, but also by thousands of Algerians, who poured out of the racially excluded shantytowns into the colonial settler *quartiers*, demanding the right to the

city. See the famous coda of Gillo Pontecorvo's 1966 film *La Bataille d'Alger* for an incredibly realistic, if decontextualised, depiction of these protests. Alan O'Leary talks about both film and event in Chapter 2 of his *The Battle of Algiers* (2019: 27–30).
3. One scene depicts Michel threatening an Algerian man with a large stick, after the latter expresses an interest in working on the farm. Another chronicles Michel's decision to desecrate a string of burial shrines (marabouts) in the interest of his own vineyards.
4. Woven into this narrative is a subtle educative subtext which at once provides the spectator with simple techniques to optimise soil quality whilst at the same time justifying the expropriation of land by colonial farmers. Unsurprisingly, the film was financed by the Forestry Commission in Algeria, an organisation inextricably linked to the colonial apparatus.
5. It is worth pointing out that, unbeknownst to onlookers, this bomb was fake, planted by soldiers performing for the camera. As Jean-Michel Meurice (1962) illustrates, this blurring of fiction and non-fiction is characteristic of the film more generally.
6. See Silverman (1999: 67–9) for more detail on the cultural history of the *flâneur*, especially in relation to the history of nineteenth-century modernism.
7. Betz's claim that the defining figure of late-colonial French cinema is a female *flâneuse* is not supported by the variety of films that I analyse in this book, many of which feature male soldiers (see Chapters 1–4 for more details). At the risk of conjecture, Betz may have derived this argument from Valerie Orpen's claim that 'the late 1950s and early 1960s seemed to be a time in which female characters were an excellent means of conveying a general post-war societal malaise' (2007: 60).
8. These shots form a precursor to *La Bataille d'Alger*, in which passers-by, walking through Algiers, are filmed apparently without consent (see O'Leary 2019: 86 for more details). They also gesture towards Blue's later interest in documentary rather than fiction. In both *Who Killed the Fourth Ward?* (1978) and *The Invisible City* (1979), Blue used a range of innovative formal strategies to chronicle the housing crisis in Houston, America. See Lunenfeld's article on Blue's 'complex documentary' practice (1994) for more details.
9. This ascent also features a cycle of non-fictional shots in which Algerians return the gaze of the camera with palpable hostility. For Philip Dine, these shots are both logistically daring and 'mystifying', namely as nowhere in this scene do the directors explain the presumably anti-colonial impetus behind this hostility (1997: 83). For more on the return of the gaze phenomenon in colonial cinema see Amad (2013).
10. These parallels – between the work of Bresson and *Les Oliviers de la justice* – were identified by a number of journalists writing at the time of the film's release, including an anonymous author writing for *Le Nouveau Candide* (Anon. 1962a), and Georges Sadoul, writing for *Les Lettres françaises* (1962b). In an interview published in *Cahiers du cinéma*, Marc Sator also reminisced about how James Blue discovered Bresson in a *ciné-club* set up in Algiers (Lequeret 2004: 25).
11. This scene is reminiscent of a famous moment in *Journal d'un curé de campagne/ The Diary of a Country Priest*, during which two looming heads gaze at each other

in the half-light of a confessional. See Bazin (1951: 14) and Steimatsky (2017: 232–3), for details.

12. In the film, Jean states that his father had lived 'a story of love and hate'. Many journalists have also made references to these terms, including an article that featured in *Paris Presse*, entitled '*Les Oliviers de la justice*: a hymn of love to a native land' (Aubriant 1962). See below for more on the late-colonial ethics of 'love'.

13. Even less analysed than Guy Gilles or James Blue, Marc Sator remains a largely unknown figure in the history of French cinema. Unlike Gilles, he continued to live in Algeria until 1967, teaching classes on cinema at the National Centre for Cinema, and even managing to shoot his own full-length film, *L'Été algérien/Algerian Summer* (1964). Incidentally, Sator's mother (Marie Decaître) plays the role of Jean's mother in *Les Oliviers de la justice* (Lequeret 2004).

14. Gaël Lépingle (2014b: 21–2, 24–8), for example, cites three possible reasons for Gilles's marginalisation from the New Wave: first, in the director's idealistic, almost utopian, vision of the world (in contrast to the emphasis on modern alienation that characterised many New Wave narratives); second, in Gilles's overt homosexuality (in contrast to the heteronormative values generally espoused by the New Wave); and third, in Gilles's artisanal and marginal modus operandi, which often included working without authorisation or the right to distribution (which contrasted with the mercenary degree of careerism displayed by directors such as Godard and Truffaut). For Lépingle, all of these factors contributed to Gilles's status in the early 1960s Parisian film scene, 'as a crazed amateur' (2014b: 24).

15. Written by Jean-Max Rivière – who also curiously composed the soundtrack for *Au biseau des baisers* – the song, named 'La Madrague', was one of Bardot's most popular. Like Gilles and Sator's film, the lyrics are founded upon erasing the indigenous population from sight. The first line, in this respect, is telling: 'on the abandoned beach'.

16. Although Gilles's favourite painters were Modigliani, Chagall and Soutine, this scene bears many similarities with the formal and thematic conventions of Renaissance painting and the European nude, exemplified, for example, in Botticelli's *The Birth of Venus* (1480s).

17. Upon reflection, Gilles and Sator's decision to focus on adolescents rather than adults appears to serve at least two politico-ideological functions. First, insofar as it helps authorise an image of Algeria as little more than a glorified settler playground (given that adolescence is frequently associated with freedom); and second, insofar as it encourages us to view the settlers as a community largely devoid of culpability for, and cognisance of, the perpetration of colonial injustices. In both cases, the power of adolescence, as a transitional age marked by liberty, irresponsibility and naivety, is harnessed to erect an idealised settler vision of decolonisation.

18. The song in question is entitled La Saint-Copain, composed by Jean-Max Rivière. It includes numerous allusions to a returning soldier.

19. It is important to note that this longing to forget about Algeria's recent past also appears to coexist with a desire to remember what Algeria was like before the conflict (see the point below about how the directors assemble a 'vision of Algeria as an Edenic, almost prehistoric idyll', alongside the symbolism of ancient ruins). Although

I have chosen to analyse *Au biseau des baisers* through theories associated with the (late-colonial) gaze, another way of approaching the narrative would therefore be through a conceptual framework associated with memory studies, and, in particular, the critical concept of colonial nostalgia, or 'nostalgérie' (nostalgeria). For more details on this phenomenon, and on the relationship between settler culture and representations of memory, see Hubbell (2011; 2015: 155–62). Gaël Lépingle has also talked about the recurring theme of memory in Gilles's oeuvre, particularly in relation to the work of Marcel Proust (2014b: 11, 15, 17, 23, 26, 30).

20. The reason for this revision is open to discussion. Perhaps the directors decided to include images of La Madrague (Algiers) in their film as a self-reflexive allusion to Gilles's childhood home? Or to dilate the scope of the late-colonial gaze as much as possible, by proposing two locations (Algiers and Tipaza), joined by images of motion, instead of the one that features in Camus's novella (Tipaza)?

21. A phenomenon ingrained within a long history of Western representations of the non-West, produced by poets, painters, writers and photographers, in relation to my argument, two aspects of Urry's 'tourist gaze' seem pertinent. First, that the tourist gaze 'is not directly experienced reality', but 'ideal representations of the view in question'; and second, that the 'tourist gaze' transforms the Western spectator into a kind of 'virtual tourist' (1990: 86). Reading *Au biseau des baisers* in relation to the 'tourist gaze' would also chime with the fact that the narrative is largely set in settler-tourist hotspots (La Pointe Pescade, La Madrague, Tipaza). For more information on images of 'tourist gazing' in settler cinema see Stadler and Mitchell (2010: 180–4).

22. I am thinking particularly of Meursault's description of the sun when he kills 'the Arab' as 'a long sparkling blade which struck my forehead' (Camus [1942] 1957: 94).

23. These ruins form the remains of a tripartite of famous churches, erected during the pre-Arab, Christian-Latin-Roman period in Algeria. They were also a popular tourist destination for settlers (Hubbell 2011). Although the ruins are not technically seen on-screen, their sheer proximity to the beach on which the couple stroll invests the scene with meaning, especially given that, as Philip Dine claims, 'a constantly recurring feature of the literature of the Algerian conflict is the appeal to the ancient history of the territory in an attempt to legitimise the contemporary colonial presence' (1994a: 157).

24. It is worth mentioning here that Algerian nationalism was largely initiated, organised and increasingly fought in mountainous/rural areas such as Mount Chenoua. See, for example, the long history of Berber-nationalist activity, orchestrated against Arab, Ottoman and French forces in Kabylia (including the Soummam Conference, held in 1956), alongside the violent spate of nationalist attacks that took place in the Aurès Mountains in 1954 (an event that, although chaotic, effectively catalysed the war). See Austin (2007a) and Sharpe (2013).

7. THE WAR AS SPOKEN BY ALGERIANS AND THE LEFT

In Chapter 5, we encountered two fictional films that have often been grouped under the rubric of 'parallel cinema': *Le Retour/The Return* (Goldenberg, 1959), and *Secteur postal 89098/Postal Sector 89098* (Durand, 1961), both of which, I argued, exemplified a process of 'guilt displacement'. In the final chapter of this book, I would like to return to the politics and ethics of 'parallel cinema', scrutinising two leftist documentaries that have been associated with this trend: *Octobre à Paris/October in Paris*, by Jacques Panijel (1962), and *J'ai 8 ans/I Am 8 Years Old* (1961), by Yann Le Masson, Olga Baïdar-Poliakoff, and René Vautier (henceforth attributed to Le Masson). Focusing on questions of speech and silence, in both documentaries, I will suggest, we can find a comparable tension: between a discourse of anti-colonial pacifism, orientated towards chronicling the victimhood of indigenous Algerians, and a discourse of leftist militancy, orientated towards redeeming the reputation of the metropolitan Left.

The Left: Complicity, Mythologisation and Redemption

The Left's relationship with decolonisation was an ambivalent one. From the 1920s to the early 1950s, the official Left, represented by the French Communist Party (the PCF), considered colonialism as a financially and politically beneficial ideology to be maintained, Algerian nationalism as a violent insurrection to be denounced, Algerian independence as a 'difficult idea to accept', and the war more generally as a transitory phrase that could be resolved, either through 'peace' or a 'wait and see attitude', all of which were criticised by thinkers such as Frantz Fanon and Jean-Paul Sartre as symptomatic of colonial paternalism or political quietism (House and MacMaster 2006: 195, 208). It was not until 1956 that the Left made its first foray into the politics of the war, when the French Communist Party pledged unanimous support to a radical law, predicated on granting special powers to the army in Algeria, and orchestrated by the Socialist Prime Minister, Guy Mollet.[1] It was a decision that quickly proved disastrous. Over the following months, the army proceeded not so much to capitalise on its newfound special powers as it did abuse them, carving the country up into regulated zones, some open to the public, others completely forbidden or circumscribed by curfews, and privileging excessive military tactics that increasingly bordered upon illegality, including indiscriminate racial discrimination, extrajudicial detention and institutionalised torture, as deployed notably during the Battle of Algiers in 1956–7 (see Introduction). Not only that, but during the 1950s, many members of the Left made what would turn out to be an equally controversial decision to support Stalin, even as the world recoiled in horror when faced with the knowledge of concentration camps and show trials erected in his name. So calamitous was this string of political policies that by the late 1950s and early 1960s certain leftist militants had begun to consider whether they had tumbled into a state of complicity with various perpetrators of atrocity.

Leftist militants dealt with this burden of complicity in several ways. Some, such as Yann Le Masson, decided to distance themselves from the party, tainting it with the sobriquet the respectful or submissive Left to emphasise their own, self-proclaimed irreverence, as the disrespectful, insurgent or oppositional left, or simply left the PCF altogether, leading to 'a mass exodus from it during the 1950s' (Péju 1960: 1512–20; Evans 1997: 137; Judt 1992: 215). Others, for example the sociologist and cultural analyst Edgar Morin, forced themselves to enter a quasi-masochistic period of intellectual 'self-criticism' and 'exculpation' known as *autocritique* (Margulies 2004: 179, 184). Contributing to the 1957 turn against silence, other leftist militants threw themselves into a campaign of anti-colonial militancy, writing for radically leftist journals such as *Les Temps modernes*, founded by Jean-Paul Sartre and Simone de Beauvoir in 1945; *Témoignages et Documents/Testimonies and Documents*, founded in 1957 by Maurice Pagat; or *Vérité-Liberté/Freedom-Truth*, co-founded by Jacques Panijel in 1960, which would gain a certain degree of notoriety in September 1960 with the publication of the Manifesto of the 121 (*Manifeste des 121*). This was an open letter to the government, signed by 121 high profile intellectuals, which justified acts of military disobedience. Still others went further, offering various forms of direct support to Algerian nationalists, including transporting money or arms for them. This was notably the case for those who joined the Jeanson Network (see Introduction), like Yann Le Masson.

Beyond this political activity, another way that the Left managed the perceived failures of the past was by concocting a range of myths that served to absolve it of guilt (Stora 2002). One such myth was voiced during the PCF Congress in 1961, when a party spokesperson speciously claimed that it had 'fought for the recognition of the right to [Algerian] independence since the first days of the Algerian War', even though a cursory examination of the history of the party would suggest otherwise (Joly 1991: 51). Another myth 'articulated the notion that Algerian nationalists were primarily Communists and that any nationalist or anticolonial politics were secondary to this global Communist project', with this myth being woven into Jean-Luc Godard's *Le Petit soldat/The Little Soldier* (1960/1963), a film in which militants of the FLN are depicted reading works by Mao Tse-tung and Lenin (Adams 2016: 116). Another myth – more orientated towards the ethics of suffering – framed the Left as an organisation composed of innocent victims of colonial atrocity rather than guilty abettors of colonial atrocity, with this vision being conveyed, albeit inadvertently, in Henri Alleg's anti-war treatise *La Question/The Question* (1958), in which Alleg – a Communist – shares stark details of the pain that he has experienced during torture sessions orchestrated by paratroopers in French Algeria. A similar emphasis on leftist suffering can be glimpsed in the principles of the Maurice Audin Committee, a political organisation set up to uncover the truth behind the death of a young Communist settler mathematician in French Algeria (Maurice Audin), or the ways in which the Left responded to a famous act of police brutality, committed against leftist militants at Charonne metro station on 8 February 1962, through an obsessive campaign of commemoration (see below for more details). In each case, the Left, alongside its members, affiliates, and militants, emerged as neither complicit in, nor culpable of, the perpetration of colonial crimes, including torture, rape, and widespread discrimination, but instead bathed in a redeeming aura of victimisation and exculpation.

Documentary Voices

Before we identify how both *Octobre à Paris* and *J'ai 8 ans* contributed to this discourse of mythologisation and redemption, it is important to point out that both films were released at a crucial juncture in the continuum of the documentary genre. Before the late 1950s, documentarians tended to rely on tactics of exposition fuelled by the 'Voice of God' style of narration, a mode of non-diegetic narration originally pioneered during the late 1920s and 1930s by filmmakers affiliated with the British Documentary Movement, including John Grierson, Harry Watt, Basil Wright and others (see *Night Mail* [Watt and Wright, 1936]), and regurgitated ad infinitum by a range of cineastes working in different contexts. Both John Hudson's *The Battle of San Pietro* (1945), and

The March of Time, an American newsreel series, screened from 1935 to 1951, were, for example, indebted to the Voice of God tradition, revelling in the authority of a 'detached male voice' (Youdelman 1982: 9) above any kind of engagement with, or commitment to, the largely mute subjects, seen on-screen. By the late-1950s, however, this aesthetic doxa had begun to fissure. No longer was the Voice of God style of narration perceived as an unequivocally unproblematic expository strategy, but as one that was rooted in what was seen as an increasingly archaic history of Eurocentrism, in the sense that it had often been used to provide quasi-anthropological information about racialised Others, as within *The Hunters* (Marshall and Gardner, 1957), and androcentrism, in that it was unequivocally masculine. According to Pascal Bonitzer, the Voice of God was 'a stolen power, a usurpation', which prevented questions about authorial identity from being posed (1975a: 26). Mary Ann Doane has defined the same technique as deriving its supremacy 'from the possession of knowledge and in the privileged, unquestioned activity of interpretation' (1980: 42).

Buoyed by technological innovations of the period – for example, the Nagra, a portable tape recorder geared towards recording synchronous speech, or the Caméflex, a shoulder-held 35mm camera used by Jacques Panijel, alongside many New Wave cineastes – from the late-1950s onwards, a generation of documentarians therefore repudiated the Voice of God tradition, in turn, engendering three 'modes' of filmmaking, all of which generated the impression of a shift, from 'an author-centered voice of authority to a witness-centered voice of testimony' (Nichols 1991: 48). One of these was the observational mode. Often aligned with American Direct Cinema, the observational mode was predicated upon an understanding of the director as a non-interventionist, invisible witness to the events that unfolded before them (see Chapter 6 for a discussion of how *Les Oliviers de la justice/The Olive Trees of Justice* [Pélégri and Blue, 1962] mirrors the observational mode). Another was the reflexive mode, a mode associated generally with *cinéma vérité*, and specifically with *Chronique d'un été*, in which the directors, Morin and Rouch, not only placed themselves within the cinematic frame – as embodied speaking subjects – but also deployed a provocative style of interviewing, according to which 'truth' was aligned with moments of psychological fragility, 'when the subject was on the verge of a mental breakdown' (Margulies 2004: 173). This brings us to a third mode of documentary that emerged in the 1950s and 1960s: the interactive mode. Like reflexive documentaries, interactive documentaries eschewed Voice of God narration in favour of dynamic interviews with a range of subjects. However, unlike the hermeneutics of the former, whose intention to uncover 'truths' repressed by the unconscious mind evoked Freudian psychoanalysis, with director-interviewers adopting the role of surrogate analysts, interviewees adopting the role of patients, and subsequent encounters approximating the dynamics of 'the talking cure'; the hermeneutics of the latter were generally more aligned with the parameters of the trial, with interviewers adopting the role of surrogate prosecutors, interviewees adopting the role of surrogate witnesses, and subsequent encounters assuming the conventions of 'the talking head' (see below for details on how this strategy is deployed in *Octobre à Paris*). Furthermore, interactive documentaries were, and remain, frequently anchored in an aesthetic doxa inherited from the judicial parameters of the courtroom: habeas corpus – a Latin phrase translated as 'you must have the body', and used to summon the body of the detainee to the courtroom in the interest of justice. Examining precisely this documentary imaginary of surrogate witnesses, 'talking heads' and habeas corpus, Bhaskar Sarkar and Janet Walker have suggested that

> in our latter twentieth and twenty-first century 'era of the witness', media testimonial initiatives – be they official, grassroots, guerrilla, transitory, insistent, or any combination thereof – participate in the creation of ethical communities by bringing testifiers and testimonial witnesses together at the audio-visual interface. (2009: 1)

Beyond the theorists cited above, one final thinker who has done much to advance theories about the politics and ethics of speech in the realm of documentary is Bill Nichols, whose work has formed a cornerstone for this chapter. In his article, 'The voice of documentary' (1983), for instance, Nichols explores a number of films that – like *J'ai 8 ans* and, to a certain extent, *Octobre à Paris* – repudiate the Voice of God tradition, choosing instead to foreground patterns of direct speech provided by interviewees, who appear, in turn, empowered as privileged vectors of testimony and truth. Yet, according to Nichols, this process of empowerment often functions to mask the fact that the messages and meanings conveyed in interviews are ultimately dictated by the frequently invisible and mute author-director, who does not just establish the conditions of possibility in the pro-filmic scene through a circumscribed series of questions, but also decides what is left in or left out of the film in post-production. 'We may think we hear history or reality speaking to us through a film' demurs Nichols, 'but what we actually hear is the voice of the text, even when that voice tries to efface itself' (1983: 20). A similar understanding of 'a textual voice that exists apart from that of the characters represented' (1983: 28) also informs many of the ideas elaborated in a more recent chapter by Nichols entitled 'What gives documentary films a voice of their own?' (2010), alongside his seminal monograph *Representing Reality* (1991: 128–9, 252–3). Both texts draw attention to how many interview-based documentaries – for example, *All my Babies* (Stoney, 1953), *Harvest of Shame* (Friendly, 1960), and *16 in Webster Groves* (Barron and Kuralt, 1966) – frame those interviewed as if constructing an oral history which is in reality constructed by the (silent) author-director. Writing in 1980, Mary Ann Doane similarly noted, the proliferation of new documentaries which reject the absolute of the voice-over and, instead, claim to establish a democratic system, 'letting the event speak for itself'. Yet, what this type of film actually promotes is the illusion that reality speaks and is not spoken, that the film is not a constructed discourse. In effecting an 'impression of knowledge', a knowledge which is given and not produced, the film conceals its own work and posits itself as a voice without a subject. (1980: 46)

Developing the questions raised in this introduction, this chapter is split into four parts. Part one is concerned with how Panijel weaponises the voices of the survivor-witnesses that feature in his documentary, chronicling the after-effects of a state-orchestrated massacre known as 'October 17', and assembling a poignant pacifist plea against colonial violence. Part two shifts focus, examining the many silences that linger just beneath the soundtrack of *Octobre à Paris*, before edging into various discussions about leftist suffering and 'the textual voice of the Left', to reformulate the vocabulary of Nichols. Part three edges the debate towards *J'ai 8 ans*, interrogating the dynamics of what I will call, following Michel Chion, 'acousmatic testimony', before the fourth part concludes with some conjectural thoughts about 'the textual voice' of Le Masson's documentary. Both documentaries, I will argue, function in an ideologically ambivalent manner, on the one hand, promoting peace in Algeria (and Paris) through the medium of audio-visual interviews, and, on the other hand, redeeming the political identity of the Left after it had been accused of complicity in the perpetration of colonial atrocities.

Octobre à Paris (1962)

On the evening of 17 October 1961, approximately 20–30,000 Algerians (technically considered French by the state until 1962) congregated in the central boulevards of Paris to demonstrate against discriminatory patterns of policing instigated by the Chief of Police, Maurice Papon, who is now equally known for his role in the deportation of Jews during his time as a prefect under Vichy (Silverman 2013: 15; see Chapter 4 for more details). What happened in the following hours – when the protesters came into contact with the approximately 7,000 police and special units of the French anti-riot police – is now well documented. As darkness fell, the police resorted to untempered violence to 'pacify' the protestors, strangling, shooting and indiscriminately beating them with long sticks known as *matraques* and *bidules*, jettisoning the bodies of many unconscious or fatally wounded demonstrators into the swell of the Seine, before incarcerating thousands of men in insalubrious makeshift detention centres located in the fringes of the city, including the *Palais des Sports*, the *Parc des Expositions*, the *Stade de Coubertin* and the *Beaujon* stadium. Due to the paucity of official archives, the precise number of Algerians killed during this night remains hotly contested (see Brunet 1999: 329; Einaudi 2001: 11; House and MacMaster 2008: 213).

One individual who witnessed the violence of 17 October first-hand was Jacques Panijel, a committed militant of the Left, who had already made a name for himself in the world of literature as the author of the politico-existentialist novel *La Rage/Rage* (1948); cinema, as the co-director of *La Peau et les Os/Skin and Bones* (Panijel and Sassy, 1961); science, as a successful immunologist at the National Centre for Scientific Research; and anti-colonial politics, as a co-founder of *Vérité-Liberté* and member of the Audin Committee. Carried out in the six months following 17 October 1961, with the financial support of *Vérité-Liberté*, the Audin Committee and Panijel's own mother, *Octobre à Paris* was conceived with the specific aim of documenting and historicising this event, largely through stark face-to-face interviews with Algerian men, women and children. Panijel himself has designated his documentary 'a tragedy in three acts' that unfolds in different times and spaces across Paris, in Sartrouville, Nanterre, Gennevilliers, Vitry and Ivry, and elsewhere (Saint-Saëns and Renouard [2000] 2014). In the first act, the spectator is faced with interviewees who talk candidly about the violence that occurred during the months leading up to the massacre – notably torture sessions, choreographed in zones such as the Goutte d'Or, by French police and the Harkis, a group of Algerian auxiliary units that helped the police to combat nationalism in the capital. In the second act, Panijel furnishes us with further information about the history of 17 October, first through footage of a group of Algerians who re-enact the lead up to the demonstration, and then through a montage of photographs, including several shots of assailed Algerians taken by Elie Kagan, a Jewish-Polish freelance journalist (see Chapter 4). The third act of the documentary then dilates the significance of this protest in relation to the plight of leftist French militants, with interviews again forming the crux of this drive towards historical analogy. It is also worth pointing out that the documentary is underpinned by a subtext of 'truth' that encourages us to tacitly accept what we see as indexical evidence of unmediated 'reality'. This subtext of truth can be heard in the soliloquies that feature on the soundtrack ('I have lived in Paris throughout the Algerian War, and all of this is true'; see below), linking the film to a wider 'discourse of "truth"' that was circulating in leftist militant circles at the time (Rothberg 2009: 194). Allusions to this wider discourse of truth could be found, for example in the titles of three clandestine journals, *Vérités anticolonialistes/Anticolonial Truths*, *La Vérité des travailleurs/The Truth of Workers* and, in particular, *Vérité-Liberté/Freedom-Truth*, co-founded by Panijel. Discussing the political significance of *Octobre à Paris*, Yann Le Masson and Olga Baïdar-Poliakoff meanwhile defined 'parallel cinema' as 'a cinema of truth [*un cinéma de vérité*]' (1962: 18).

In existing critical writing on *Octobre à Paris*, scholars and journalists have tended to favour questions of production, distribution and reception over questions of form or content. This approach is at once enlightening and restrictive: enlightening given the undeniable bravery and ingenuity of Panijel's clandestine modus operandi, especially considering the regime of censorship operating during the period; restrictive as much of this scholarship ends up by repeating a by now well-established genealogy concerning the gestation and subsequent occultation of Panijel's project, banned until 1973 by the state. Corroborating recent interventions on the subject by Maria Flood (2016; 2018) and Lia Brozgal (2019), this chapter thus aims to theorise rather than historicise *Octobre à Paris* in relation to the audio-visual techniques used by Panijel, alongside further questions related to visibility, testimony and disembodiment. Central to my analysis will be the ways in which Panijel initially banishes himself from both the diegetic and non-diegetic realm, as part of a cinematic idiom known as the masked interview, before harnessing the power of the human voice – *his* voice – to propel an argument that has not been articulated by any of his interviewees.

The voice of the survivor-witness

In their illuminating introduction to *The Image and the Witness*, Frances Guerin and Roger Hallas state that

> the testimony of the survivor-witness is dependent on her [sic] embodied presence at the moment of enunciation. No one can bear witness in her place. Thus, when acts of bearing witness to historical trauma are mediated through the material image, corporeal inscription of the witness often provides the foundation for both bringing the event into presence and establishing the inter-subjective relations between the survivor-witness and the listener/viewer-witness. (2007: 14)

Foregrounding the testimonies of precisely this type of 'survivor-witness', much of *Octobre à Paris* is composed of audio-visual fragments of face-to-face interviews with Algerian men, women and children, many of whom quite simply lament the extent to which they have been dehumanised by the French police (Figure 7.1). Depending on whether we focus on their form or content, these testimonies can be apprehended in different ways. In terms of form, for example, it is noticeable that their articulation frequently coincides with facial close-ups or frontal mid-shots, both of which enable the spectator to see the source of the speech being articulated – the mouth – and leading us to designate this speech as 'facialised' in the sense that the camera generally privileges the visible arena of the speaking face over other parts of the head: the crown,

Figure 7.1 Image of a survivor-witness being interviewed.

the ear, the neck (Chion 1994: 72; McNeill 2010: 88). Even more specifically, *Octobre à Paris* can be seen to uphold generic conventions according to which documentaries generally revolve around full-face close-ups, 'in which [the face in question] looks out of the image at the spectator' whereas fictional films generally revolve around three-quarter facial close-ups, notably to facilitate scopic and aural interactions with other characters (Coates 2012: 29). Where Panijel's non-fictional narrative *does* overlap with fictional ones is in terms of synchronisation: taking advantage of audio-visual innovations made available to directors working in the late 1950s, Panijel precisely stitches the voices of his interviewees to images of their speaking bodies, crafting, in turn, what Mary Ann Doane has called 'a fantasmatic body', demarcated by 'unity and presence-to-itself' (1980: 34), and Michel Chion has termed 'visualised speech' (1999: 18). 'The physical nature of film necessarily makes an incision or cut between the body and the voice', opines Chion, before directors generally attempt to 're-stitch the two together at the seam' (1999: 125). This may seem like a rather facile point, but it isn't: as we will see later in this chapter, an altogether different, *un-visualised* mode of registering voices is used by Le Masson in *J'ai 8 ans*.

In terms of content, meanwhile, undoubtedly the most damning element of the testimonies included in *Octobre à Paris* is that they provide ample if not irrefutable evidence that violence enacted against Algerians by the French state not only proliferated in the early 1960s, but was excessive, indiscriminate and institutional, and that 17 October should 'not be viewed as a one-off event [. . .] but rather as the apex of a long phase of brutal repression that was organised at the highest levels of the French State' (House and MacMaster 2006: 15). To adumbrate but a few notable examples, at one point we watch and listen as a man named Mohamed recounts his experience of being beaten by the police during 'the events'. 'They smashed my head in', he states soberly, before disconsolately reprimanding the officers in question for flinging him into the Seine with two other men, both presumably emptied of sentience. Other younger subject-witnesses recall seeing babies ripped from the arms of their mothers, before they too were thrown into the Seine. Still others invoke equally nightmarish scenes of trigger-happy police officers indiscriminately spraying machine-gun rounds into crowds of demonstrators, coupled with derogatory exclamations ('where do you think you're going, you bastards'). It is for this reason that Isabelle Saint-Saëns has spoken of *Octobre à Paris* as an 'archaeology of silence', intimating that Panijel figuratively unearths voices buried by the machinery of censorship ([2000] 2014).

Just as these interviews function in an evidentiary fashion, with 'talking heads' being instrumentalised in a similar way to witnesses in a trial, so too do other parts of the documentary provide further evidence of the criminal culpability of the state. One way that Panijel does this, for instance, is by assembling a multimedia recreation of the 'events', forming a counterpoint to the news 'blackout' that took place immediately after 17 October (Rancière 2008: 28). To this end, Panijel fuses oral testimony provided by Algerians with footage of some of the fifty photographs[2] of the 'events' that had been released, sometimes legally, sometimes clandestinely, into the public domain, imbuing them with an impression of movement using a high-speed varifocal zoom lens, known as a Pan Cinor, posed on a rostrum table, alongside archival footage of police attacking demonstrations in a nocturnal urban milieu. Only through sustained scholarly research would the spectator learn that this archival footage,[3] in particular, was not captured during the events of 17 October (as is the case with other clips in the documentary),[4] but rather a leftist demonstration organised by the National Union of Students of France on 27 October 1960, whose message was not the liberation of Algeria but peace in Algeria, with this motto of the Left notably reemerging in the soundtrack of *J'ai 8 ans* (see below). A further strategy of evidence-building can be found in the ways in which, through an aesthetics of habeas corpus, Panijel specifically spurs those present in the world of the living to bear witness for those now absent from it. Whenever subject-witnesses anguish over demonstrators being thrown, bloodied and beaten, into the Seine, what they are likely referring to is thus 'the ultimate witness – the one who has not survived' (Guerin and Hallas

2007: 13). In a eulogistic approximation of ventriloquism, the former speaks for the latter to prevent deaths like theirs from reoccurring.

What is perhaps less evident whilst listening to these testimonies is that they are often predicated upon a series of silences. One such silence emanates from the perpetrators of the violence in question – that is to say, the police and the Harkis – neither of whom are solicited through interviews in the film in the same way as Algerians. Clearly this decision was taken out of pragmatism, insofar as soliciting the state would have inevitably inculpated the directorial team in the 'crime' of producing a film outside the parameters of censorship. Yet, by restoring speech to Algerians and Algerians alone, Panijel nonetheless erects a narrative that is perforce one-sided, lacking the totality of testimonies that could have ensured an even more comprehensive oral history of 'the events'. This is in contrast to two later 'interactive' documentaries, *Le Chagrin et la pitié/The Sorrow and the Pity* (Ophüls, 1969), and *Shoah* (Lanzmann, 1985), both of which are punctuated with interviews with the victims *and* the perpetrators of historical violence (the Holocaust). Second, to the silence of state officials can be added the silence of subject-witnesses, some of whom display a melancholy inability or unwillingness to articulate their pain through speech. Panijel's interest in this voice of silence is particularly evident directly after the aforementioned multimedia recreation of the 'events', during which he bombards the spectator with nineteen shots of pained corporeality: silent faces, downturned into apperception, limbs marked by wounds, an eye socket fractured, a hand etched with scratches, indented skin pulled tightly over a spine, etcetera. Neither language nor narration is articulated here, erecting a prolonged pause, pregnant with pain, and instead infused with non-language and non-narration. The only sound that can be heard is a dull non-diegetic drone, an excerpt of the *musique concrète* woven into the soundtrack. Approximating the tonality of what Mladen Dolar has theorised as the 'aphonic' or 'mere voice', this drone is notably more aligned with the 'senseless' vocalisation of non-human communication – a low, reverberating groan – than the sense-making verbalisation of human language (Dolar 2006: 114). 'When a narrative is not sufficient, because the speaker cannot voice or the listener cannot hear, the physical marks left by violence can offer an alternative form of testimony', opines Maria Flood (2018: 168), whilst both Jonathan Kear and Edith Wyschogrod have vaunted the supremacy of silent witnessing. For Kear, images of witnesses who do not speak are, for example, often more poignant than images of those who do. 'Describing abstracts the event' he suggests, 'it distances us from it and replaces its reality with representation' (2007: 140). Wyschogrod is more insistent, explaining that 'by bringing forth the silences of the other rather than by forcing silence into speech, by devising strategies of encounter that simultaneously attest and preserve that silence, silence itself can become a speech-act' (1998: 32).

A final silence, embedded deep within the film, relates to Panijel's use of the masked interview, a formal technique through which the director erases – or masks – traces of their body and voice from the image-track and soundtrack, leaving them visible and unheard, whilst the bodies and voices of those interviewed are amplified on the image-track and soundtrack, leaving them, conversely, both visible and heard (Nichols 1981: 281–3; 1991: 51–5). Pioneered by Arthur Elton and Edgar Anstey in their 1935 documentary *Housing Problems*, masked interviews often provoke ambivalence amongst film scholars, being at once exalted for helping to grant a voice to marginalised communities and criticised for 'having nothing to say about the rules that construct interviews' (King 1981: 14). This latter view is one shared by several theorists, including Paula Rabinowitz (1993), who remains sceptical of the masked interview, and indeed interviews in general, as vectors for testimony and truth. According to Rabinowitz, 'without the film-maker's body present on screen, the camera's view is de-historicised, while the filmed bodies are simultaneously over-invested with meaning and deprived of agency' (1993: 125). Bill Nichols concurs, stating that 'rather than making the interview structure evident, the masked interview slides towards the oblique stylistics of the fiction film, and the work of a *metteur en scène*' (1991: 52).

As a documentary subtended on precisely such a notion of the director-interviewer as an absence, a void, a silence, who lurks just outside the fringes of the soundtrack and the image-track, *Octobre à Paris* could be accused of a similar propensity towards 'oblique stylistics' and 'de-historicisation'. To watch Panijel's documentary is thus to learn nothing about the unwieldy regime of state censorship that had already led to the imprisonment of two leftist militant filmmakers – René Vautier and Pierre Clément – and from which Panijel undoubtedly aimed to shield himself, precisely through the aesthetic shell, the carapace, the *mask*, of the masked interview. Nor are we told why this privilege has not been extended to Panijel's subject-witnesses, none of whom are anonymised, and thus all of whom 'expose themselves to enormous personal risk by being filmed' including the potential for retributive violence inflicted by the same police implicated in the 'events' of 17 October (Flood 2018: 157). Nor are we informed as to whether any of those interviewed in the documentary have been impelled to testify by the FLN; or, in a related point, what questions Panijel asked them, with their responses often approximating the contours of what Bill Nichols has discerned as 'pseudomonologues' (1991: 54), 'pseudo' in the sense that interviewees often seem to convulsively erupt into speech, into monologues, without having been prompted. Nor do we acquire any knowledge about the highly complex clandestine preliminaries that enabled the execution of the project (hideouts, surveillance, reconnaissance missions), alongside the undoubtedly more discordant fact that, in the final stages of the war, Algerian nationalists had begun to cast an increasingly jaundiced eye over leftist militants such as

Panijel, first for supporting the Special Powers Act in 1956, but also due to the 'French penchant for speaking *for* the Algerians' in a paternal and thus arguably neo-colonial fashion (D. Le Sueur 2001: 8 [emphasis in original]). Indeed, it was only recently that Panijel admitted that the film almost did not come to fruition due to his political affiliations, as a 'French republican militant removed from the memory of Algeria' rather than an unconditional and unequivocal partisan of the FLN (Saint-Saëns and Renouard [2000] 2014). And only through close textual analysis of *Octobre à Paris* do we realise that Panijel may grant Algerians a voice throughout the early stages of *Octobre à Paris*, but as the documentary comes to a close, another voice speaks.

The voice of the Left

For the majority of *Octobre à Paris*, Panijel chooses to silence himself in the soundtrack, consistently encouraging us to understand the documentary as one in which the voice of the colonised Other takes precedence over the voice of the colonial Self, and in which an oral history articulated *by* racialised Others takes precedence over an oral commentary *about* racialised Others. When oral commentary is used, it is provided by a man named Kader, whose disembodied voice can be heard in the prelude of the film,[5] and whose avowed Algerian identity clearly sets him apart from the traditionally Eurocentric narrator of expository documentaries.

Nonetheless, close inspection of the final stages of the documentary reveals that it does not just operate in this fashion. As images of an Algerian man shuffling towards an open door flash up on-screen, diegetic image and non-diegetic sound momentarily coalesce as Panijel himself suddenly barks,

> the door is closing on Algerians. But don't go! October 17 is continuing! The door is going to open again . . . and it's going to open on us. On us: who aren't Arabs [bicots], who weren't Jews [youpins][6] twenty years ago.[7]

To say that this non-diegetic monologue is a turning point in *Octobre à Paris* is not an exaggeration. Not only does it mark the first time that Panijel appropriates the authority of the 'Voice of God', wrestling back the vocal power he previously conferred upon Kader and his survivor-witnesses, and thus, in turn, enunciating an argument that nobody in the documentary has articulated. But it also the moment at which the documentary itself begins to perform a curious pivot in focus: from the victimhood of Algerians subjected to state violence on 17 October 1961 to the victimhood of French leftist militants – the implicit 'us' of the commentary – subjected to state violence on 8 February 1962, when eight leftist militants were killed by the police during an anti-fascist demonstration at Charonne metro station in Paris. In *May '68 and its Afterlives*, Kristin

Ross writes eloquently about the cultural history of these two events, deducing that they were often 'conflated' in the public domain, with the excessive memorialisation of Charonne causing 17 October to 'disappear' (2002: 48). Evoking the lexicon of Ross's thesis, Gilles Manceron has similarly suggested that 'the dominant memories of Charonne overshadowed those associated with the night of October', devoid, as the latter was, of a localised setting and identifiable victims (2011: 173), whilst Jim House and Neil MacMaster are even more insistent, stating that the key transitional period between October 1961 and February 1962 'eclipsed the visibility' of 17 October through an obsessive emphasis on commemorating the victims of Charonne (2006: 242). Underpinned by traces of this 'conflation', 'overshadowing' and 'eclipse', the following scene of *Octobre à Paris* thus shifts to archival footage of leftist demonstrators subjected to police violence at Charonne, before this footage is followed by images of a staged political meeting, one at which several of these demonstrators speak their suffering in the presence of other Algerians. One leftist militant bemoans how he witnessed police intent on killing the peaceful protesters present; another testifies to being forced, tumbling, face down, into the descending opening of Charonne metro station. Still another identifies being *matraqued* (beaten with police truncheons) as the most harrowing part of her ordeal. All of the testimonies proffered contribute to a vision of the Left as a community of innocent victims.

It is also during this political meeting that one of the most puzzling monologues voiced in Panijel's documentary transpires, when an Algerian man named Hamid addresses the throng of attendees (Figure 7.2).

> For the last seven years, Algerians have noticed how the French have awoken. When French mothers prevented trains from taking the guys to Algeria. When conscientious objectors, young people aged nineteen to twenty, became acutely aware, even more aware than certain politicians, preferring to go to prison rather than put on a uniform and fight Algerians. During the Manifesto of the 121 [see above], against torture . . . all of which bears witness to the honour of the French.[8]

Subtended by a high degree of historical precision, this soliloquy is clearly the result of a sustained period of reflection and preparation, despite the fact that, as with the majority of the 'pseudomonologues' that scaffold the film, it is presented as spontaneous and unsolicited. But what is even more telling than the verbal content of this soliloquy are the types of shot used to frame it, the associative patterns of editing deployed during it (a technique originally linked to 1920s Soviet Montage cinema; see below and Chapter 5), alongside the 'textual voice' – to requote Bill Nichols – that is spoken subtly through the visual images that accompany it. As Hamid slowly chronicles how 'the French have

Figure 7.2 Wide shot of Hamid (back to camera) addressing attendees of a political meeting.

awoken . . .', for instance, the camera cuts to close-ups of four leftist militants present at the meeting (Figure 7.3), subsequently immersing us in two illusions. One of these is formal: that these close-ups were captured as Hamid's soliloquy was being articulated, when, upon reflection, the only way that Panijel could possibly have filmed them is by dislodging the participants from where they are positioned during the establishing shot that precedes them. The other illusion articulated through these close-ups is ideological: that these leftist militants had been indirectly instrumental in the '[political] awakening' articulated in Hamid's speeech. It is a reading corroborated by the following few seconds of the documentary, when Panijel combines archival footage of leftist demonstrators marching uniformly at Charonne with another burst of disembodied commentary ('down with fascism, down with the war, say the French'), further bolstering our impression of the Left as both surreptitiously associated with a legacy of anti-colonial opposition from which it had been largely absent ('down with the war'), and implicitly aligned with the collective wishes of the French nation ('say the French'). As Jim House and Neil MacMaster suggest, 'the PCF retrospectively presented Charonne as a key "stage" in the conclusion

Figure 7.3 Close-up of a leftist militant.

of "Peace in Algeria" – as a belated vindication of its strategy to induce mass action to pressure de Gaulle in that direction' (2006: 256). Joseph Daniel sees the audio-visual strategies deployed in this scene through a similar lens, framing them 'as the logical culmination of a film that erases the silence of the Left' (1972: 345), with the 'silence' in question referring to the guilt experienced by many leftist militants as they tumbled into a state of complicity in the perpetration of colonial atrocities, notably after voting in favour of granting special powers to the army in 1956. To put it another way, in Panijel's documentary, the more the leftist militants recruited by the director are encouraged to speak their pain, the less the Algerian subject-witnesses are given space to do so; and the more the guilt of the Left is edged into the realm of silence, the more the leftist militants that feature therein are redeemed through speech.

J'AI 8 ANS (1961)

Like Panijel, Yann Le Masson was as committed to leftist militancy as he was to anti-colonial action. Le Masson was also an impassioned pacifist, with concrete plans to become a conscientious objector, until the French

Communist Party remarkably persuaded him to assume his military duties, suggesting that this would enable Le Masson to spread their ideological message amongst conscripts in Algeria. What was intended as a political expedition, however, quickly became a personal ordeal, as Le Masson was promoted to the status of paratrooper, spending twenty-seven unwilling months, from 1955 to 1958, stationed on the Algerian-Moroccan border, until he eventually resumed civilian life. Appalled by what he had witnessed during the war, and disillusioned by the Left's willingness to authorise the colonial atrocities in which he had personally become complicit, on his return to Paris, Le Masson threw himself into a campaign of political redemption, joining the French Leninist-Marxist Communist Party; consorting with the Jeanson Network; and contributing to the shooting of a number of late-colonial films, such as *La Récréation/Break Time* (Carpita, 1958), *Le Retour/The Return* (Goldenberg, 1959; see Chapter 5), *Le Joli Mai/The Lovely Month of May* (Marker, 1963), *Le Combat dans l'île/The Combat on the Island* (Cavalier, 1962), and, finally, *Octobre à Paris*, having filmed the aforementioned archival footage of leftist militants succumbing to police violence at Charonne. As for *J'ai 8 ans*, the project began in 1961 when Le Masson travelled to Dovar Chott in Tunisia to meet René Vautier and Frantz Fanon, who was working as a psychotherapist for a group of young Algerians living in a refugee camp.[9] It was these refugees that provided the drawings of war that feature on the image-track of *J'ai 8 ans* (Figure 7.4), alongside the testimonies that feature on the soundtrack.

Figure 7.4 An example of one of the drawings stitched into the image-track of *J'ai 8 ans*.

Since its clandestine release in 1961, its official release in 1974, and the seventeen times it was seized by authorities in the interim, *J'ai 8 ans* has unsurprisingly received relatively scant critical attention, certainly within the world of film studies. Early journalistic articles on *J'ai 8 ans* tend to see it simply as a politically radical paragon of parallel cinema (like *Octobre à Paris*), whose trenchant combination of oral and visual testimony 'amplified the voices' of those subjected to the racialised violence of colonialism, transforming the war into a 'psychodrama' saturated with 'horror' (Bory 1973: 163–4; Boudjedra 1971: 40). The few scholars who have written about it are generally associated with cultural studies, including: Guy Austin (2007b; 2009: 20), who explores the artwork woven into the film, focusing specifically upon how it can be seen as invaluable evidence of 'visual testimony and drawn trauma' (2007b); Nicholas Mirzoeff, who identifies *J'ai 8 ans* as an unusual blend of psychiatry and activist cinema (2011: 246–55), noting that the oral and visual testimonies embedded in the film were published as an edited collection by Giovanni Pirelli, entitled *Racconti di bambini d'Algeria/Tales of Children in Algeria* (1962); and Alexis Artaud de la Ferrière (2014), whose invaluable reading of *J'ai 8 ans* I will be returning to throughout this section. Extending the theories elaborated in the first section of this chapter, my central argument will be that *J'ai 8 ans* is propelled by two ideological objectives: one aligned with capturing the suffering of Algerians victimised by colonialism, the other with rehabilitating public opinion of the metropolitan Left, with the latter gradually overshadowing the former as the documentary develops.

Acousmatic testimony

Often bracketed together under the rubric of 'parallel cinema', *Octobre à Paris* and *J'ai 8 ans* share a number of similarities. Both documentaries required the directors in question to execute logistically and legally challenging clandestine journeys, from central spaces to peripheral ones (Paris *intramuros* to Paris *extramuros* in *Octobre à Paris*; France to Tunisia in *J'ai 8 ans*). Both were at least partly funded by the Audin Committee, enabling the directors to broach topics banned or curtailed under official censorship. Both films unambiguously contend that colonialism has led to an inexorable descent into French state violence, and that this violence must cease. And both films craft this pacifist argument by encouraging us to listen to, and therefore empathise with, a community of Algerians who speak to us directly about how they have suffered as a result of the colonial system, aligning both documentaries, in turn, with what Bill Nichols terms 'the interactive mode'. In *J'ai 8 ans*, instances of this spoken suffering abound. At one point, for example, we hear a young interlocutor talk about how French soldiers forced their way into his community, massacring three men before leaving 'to have lunch'. Another recounts seeing his own father seized by French army officials, with the latter subsequently plunging the former into hot and cold water, until he is likewise killed with machine guns. Still another boy recalls peering up at a military plane in the sky, until realising the mortal danger posed by this panoptic machine. 'I was scared', he laments. 'It was shooting at me.' Many of these testimonies pivot around a logic of 'cognitive dissonance' (de la Ferrière 2014: 116), with this 'dissonance' being implied, on the one hand, in the youthful innocence of the boys, who are, as the title insists, *only* eight years old, that is to say, too young to have experienced the voice break of puberty; and, on the other hand, a loss of innocence implied by the extensive military paraphernalia enumerated by them throughout. 'Their technical knowledge is staggering' wrote Raymond Borde, citing terms such as 'machine guns, rockets, shells, prison, helicopters, and raids' as an oblique symptom of how the war has corrupted the psychology of those interviewed, forcing them into adulthood (1962a: 17). For Guy Austin, meanwhile, these testimonies incarnate a need 'to speak the unspeakable' (2009: 20), with their shared emphasis on 'unspeakable' acts committed during the war both recalling and revising the turn against silence: recalling insofar as, like documents released in the turn against silence, *J'ai 8 ans* clearly alludes to the perpetration of military atrocities in French Algeria; revising insofar as *J'ai 8 ans* exposes us to oral testimonies of Algerians directly victimised by such atrocities, rather than written testimonies of soldiers indirectly complicit in them. In the case of Borde, the soundtrack of *J'ai 8 ans* proved so affective that the critic found himself gripped by reverent non-speech. 'There's nothing left to say', he stated soberly in a 1962 review of the film, published in *Positif*. 'That's it [c'est ça]' (1962a: 16).

Beyond the evidentiary content of these testimonies, notable too are the ways in which they were captured. In a fascinating article, Baptiste Vidal has charted the challenging production of *J'ai 8 ans*, noting in particular how the documentary was completed in a staggered and inconsistent fashion by four different militant cineastes (excluding Fanon's psychotherapeutic input), catalysing a high degree of antagonism between them, and leading Vidal to diagnose the film as one consumed by an authorial crisis (2019: 183–6). According to Vidal, production began in earnest in June 1961, when Vautier and Masson recorded a range of silent images of the children and their drawings in Tunisia, before Vautier returned to interview them alone using a voice-recorder. Judging from epistolary documents indexed by Vidal, Vautier's initial aspiration was to stitch no more than four or five testimonial 'phrases' into the soundtrack, harnessing the power of non-diegetic music over non-diegetic voice-overs, and thus, in turn, shielding the directors against any accusations that they had 'deformed the intentions of the children through commentary' (Vautier cited in Vidal 2019: 184). Upon receiving recordings of these 'phrases' by post, however, Le Masson deemed their quality insufficient and their quantity lacking, prompting him to ask his then partner, Olga Baïdar-Poliakoff, to return to the camp in late 1961 to re-record an archive of much more comprehensive oral testimonies from the refugees *in situ* (notably without corresponding with Vautier), before the film was finally edited together in France by Le Masson's acquaintance Jacqueline Meppiel, again without Vautier's input. Crucially, for reasons that were undoubtedly as aesthetic as they were logistic, at no point in the evolution of the project did any of the directors consider recording the testimonies of the refugees as embodied speech, using audio-visual equipment wielded by Panijel, for example, but instead chose to capture them as oral testimonies alone. As a result, nowhere in *J'ai 8 ans* do we see a child speak, and rather than visualised speech, what we uncover is a stream of entirely un-visualised speech, comparable to the species of disembodied narration proffered by Kader and Panijel in *Octobre à Paris*, and what might be categorised, following Michel Chion, as acousmatic speech, or more specifically, acousmatic testimony (Chion 1999: 17–29).

In *J'ai 8 ans*, this 'acousmatic testimony' operates on several levels. In the first instance, by depriving the boys of their visual identities, Le Masson subjects them to what might be called a process of de-personalisation or de-subjectification, stripping them of what would have immediately helped to identify them – their speaking faces – and, in turn, anticipating the type of formal techniques used by many participatory documentarians to preserve the anonymity of their subjects (Parr 2007: 122–3). At no point in the documentary do any of the boys introduce themselves, and it is unclear whether the silent embodied faces that we sporadically see (discussed below) belong to the disembodied voices that we hear. Coinciding with this shift from disclosure to non-disclosure is a further shift, from the individual to the collective. Thus, unlike *Octobre à Paris*, in which image-sound relations enable us to grasp the contours of a clearly demarcated carousel of different subject-witnesses – a man who talks about the lead up to 17 October, a woman who talks about its aftermath, etcetera – in *J'ai 8 ans*, ontological divisions between subject-witnesses are much fuzzier, evoking Chion's assertion that 'cinema has a frame, whose edges are visible, whereas [acousmatic media] do not allow us to perceive where things "cut", as sound itself has no frame' (1999: 22). How many boys speak in *J'ai 8 ans*? When does one boy stop speaking and another begin? Such are just some of the questions that crop up throughout *J'ai 8 ans*, exposed as we are to what often seems less like a series of monologues enunciated by a group of boys and more like a continuous monologue enunciated by a single boy, as encapsulated in the de-personalised and anonymous 'I', rather than 'we', of the film's title: *I Am 8 Years Old*. In fact, to examine the collective voice of *J'ai 8 ans* is to examine a film that arguably shares more parallels with radio broadcasting than with sound cinema, whilst the archive of still drawings inscribed in the image-track subverts the medium specificity of the film still further. Comparing *J'ai 8 ans* to radio

209

broadcasting also recalls Frantz Fanon's famous analysis of Algerian nationalist radio as the source of a 'phantom-like voice', enunciated by a similarly de-subjectified non-body. Fanon terms this 'The voice of fighting Algeria' ([1959] 1965: 69), stating that 'behind the crackling and modulation' of radio speech, Algerians listening to this voice 'would imagine not only words, but concrete battles' ([1959] 1965: 88).

Fanon's allusion to the 'imaginative' properties of acousmatic speech brings us to a final point regarding the sonic properties of Le Masson's documentary. In a chapter on Derek Jarman's 1993 *Blue* – a film with which *J'ai 8 ans* shares certain formal similarities, notably in the sense that the soundtrack is composed of various 'acousmatic witnesses' – Roger Hallas has suggested that Jarman 'stimulates the mind's eye to imagine images, rather than have the eye perceive them physically', with the 'images' in question pertaining to the director's own AIDS-attenuated body, which is notably absent from the image-track (2007: 41–3, 39). A similar argument could be made vis-à-vis Le Masson's film, with the acousmatic words of the boys gently compelling the spectator to imagine a community of bodies orally evoked yet visually absent from the image-track. Some of these bodies belong to the boys who bear witness. Others belong to the individuals of which the boys speak; bodies ravaged by artillery, bodies 'plunged into hot and cold water', several of whom find their avatars scrawled into the drawings that pulsate on-screen, yet many of whom are left entirely visually unrepresented. Less and less aligned with the largely embodied imaginary of *Octobre à Paris*, it is here that *J'ai 8 ans* begins to look, or rather, sound, a lot like Philippe Durand's modernist masterpiece *Secteur postal 89098/Postal Sector 89098* (1961), whose harrowing, quasi-acousmatic soundtrack is punctuated with a compendium of equally harrowing allusions to military atrocities (see Chapter 5). But is there anything, or anyone, that we don't hear in *J'ai 8 ans*, and if so, why?

Leftist militancy unspoken

In an article treating a range of childhood testimonies produced during the Algerian War of Independence, Alexis Artaud de la Ferrière has proposed a reading of *J'ai 8 ans* that has proved crucial to my own. Beginning with a general summary of the analytical and ethical stakes at play when dealing with testimonies such as these, de la Ferrière suggests that

> when we encounter a childhood testimony, what we find is a document which has been produced, filtered, perhaps modified or even forged, and distributed, by adults who have their own interests and motivations for bringing such material into the public sphere. In consequence, whatever special epistemic or moral status we attribute to such testimonies

by virtue of their childhood authorship is in part a product of (adult) editorial artifice. When we engage with these testimonies, we are in fact *not* engaging directly with child witnesses of war. And the discrepancy between the peculiar status of childhood testimonies of war and their actual conditions of production and distribution reveal the mechanism by which such testimonies are politically instrumentalised. (2014: 106 [emphasis in original])

One journalistic source that supports de la Ferrière's hypothesis regarding the 'filtering' of childhood testimonies in *J'ai 8 ans* is a 1962 article by Jean Carta, published in the radically leftist journal *Partisans*. Prefaced by a ringing endorsement of *J'ai 8 ans* as the work of 'a director who has redeemed our honour' – the 'our' presumably referring to the Left, considering the place of publication (1962: 111), and propelled by a reprint of Le Masson and Baïdar-Poliakoff's 'Manifesto for a parallel cinema', previously published in a June 1962 edition of *Positif* (18) – Carta's article is also illuminating in that it includes a collection of transcribed extracts provided by the boys during their interviews with Baïdar-Poliakoff, before they were carved up to be integrated into the soundtrack of *J'ai 8 ans*. Salah, Kherici, Kaddour: the inclusion of a child's name at the start of each extract is perhaps the most obvious sign of what was excised from Le Masson's documentary in the interim between production and post-production. But what these transcripts too reveal is the extent to which Le Masson purged the testimonies of what could persuasively be considered their most traumatic, affective moments.[10] This process of affective elimination is particularly evident in testimony provided by a boy named Merdaci, whose memories of colonial military violence, etched into the pages of Carta's article, prove nothing but chilling: 'They told me: here is my father, we are going to kill him. They killed with knives. They killed with machine guns. They said to my mother: are you happy or not? *My mother said: yes I am very happy*' (cited in Carta 1962: 114 [emphasis added by author]). Except that the crucial final line of this extract – the line that bears witness to the all-consuming, abject, crushing subjugation of the colonised by the coloniser – *my mother said: yes I am very happy* – is left out of the final version of *J'ai 8 ans*, yielding instead to both oral and visual testimony attesting of the benevolence of Algerian nationalist fighters, furnished with gently lilting stringed and percussive music. Severed too is the following troubling extract of testimony from a boy named Abdoulouahab, conspicuously present in Carta's article, yet conspicuously absent from the documentary. I have tried to preserve the fragmented orthography and syntax of the original extract in the translation.

J'ai (vis) avec mes familles et mon père il est mort et moi je vis avec maman et mon frère le petit et nous habitent dans une grande djebel et mon frère y pleure. Et moi je couche à près de maman – et un banc moi j'ai debout de coucher. Il m'a dit à maman: donne-moi du pain. Il m'a dit: y a pas du pain. Et maman elle m'a dit maintenant on va à le village de Tunisien. Mon frère il est pleure et moi je dis: ne pleure pas – et maman aussi li pleure – et moi je dis: ne pleure pas maman et maman elle m'a dit: laisse-moi . . . tranquille.

I have live with my families and my dad and he is dead and I live with mum and my dad and the baby and we living in a large hill [djebel] and my brother he cries there. And me I sleep next to mum – and a bench me I have stand sleep. He said to me to mum: give me some bread. He said to me: there isn't any bread. And mum she said to me now we go to the Tunisian village. My brother he is cry and I say: don't cry – and mum she also cries – and me I say: don't cry mum and mum she said to me: leave me alone [sic]. (Cited in Carta 1962: 117)

In many ways, Abdoulouahab's testimony forms the very antithesis of the testimonies that feature in *J'ai 8 ans*: where his syntax is disjointed and excessive, theirs is intelligible and contained; where his framing of time is fragmented, theirs remains linear; where his testimony at least leans towards the reflexes of paralinguistic affect (pauses, indicated through the use of spaced en dashes), theirs remain unaffected. Likewise, where the traumatic yet logical parameters of Mercadi's speech could be bent into shape to fit how Le Masson imagined and re-imagined the conflict, Abdoulouahab's words could not. Encroaching on the limits of illegibility, of incomprehensibility, of the abjection of the 'mere voice', as theorised by Mladen Dolar, his testimony proved to be at once too lacking in coherence and too pregnant with affect to be assimilated into the narrative. It had to be expelled.

There is another kind of unspoken voice that lingers, almost imperceptibly, within *J'ai 8 ans*. But it is not a voice that belongs to any of the subject-witnesses, but rather to Le Masson, whose voice, like Baïdar-Poliakoff's, Vautier's and Fanon's, is entirely eliminated from the soundtrack. Nor is Le Masson's unspoken voice, this 'textual voice', this authorial voice of authority, aligned with Algerian victimhood, but rather with the director's own leftist militancy. In a famous article on the various tactics of anti-colonial resistance adopted by different militants during the war, Pierre Vidal-Naquet (1986: 11) has located one of these tactics in 'the Bolshevik tradition', a 'tradition' with which, judging from interviews, Le Masson and his collaborators were very much aligned. As Pierre Vidal-Naquet states: Bolshevik anti-colonial militants 'wanted to be the heirs of the Bolshevik Revolution of October 1917 and its radical and betrayed hopes. For the most part, they hoped to reconnect with Lenin and revolutionary "purity"', namely by '"Marxizing" the Algerian

Revolution', that is to say, by understanding it as a replay of the Revolution of October 1917 (1986: 11). And, as Le Masson states,

> Communist society, as I had understood it in the works of Marx and Lenin, led from capitalism to Socialism to Communism – a society without classes – before finally generating the breakdown of the State, that is to say, to anarchism. That really suited me, a society without a State, which would allow those who had been adequately educated to govern their lives themselves, aided by real Soviets. (Cited in Charby 2004: 162)

In the interest of clarity, let me stress that Le Masson's ethos of anti-colonial Bolshevism is very much implicit within *J'ai 8 ans*, shorn as the documentary is of anything that even remotely approximates the type of expository 'Voice of God' narration that Panijel uses, for example, to edge his film away from 'the events' of 17 October and towards the events of Charonne. Instead, Le Masson performs this process of ideological re-framing by appropriating a visual language from directors aligned with 1920s Soviet Montage cinema, including Vsevolod Pudovkin, director of *Mat/Mother* (1926), Alexander Dovzhenko, director of *Zemlya/Earth* (1930), and Sergei Eisenstein, director of *Stachka/Strike* (1925), *Bronenosets Potyomkin/Battleship Potemkin* (1925), and *Oktyabr': Desyat' dney kotorye potryasli mir/October: Ten Days That Shook the World* (1927), all of whom were inspired by the ideology of Bolshevism as it was reaching its zenith. And so, the more we look, the more we unearth intertextual allusions to Soviet Montage scattered throughout *J'ai 8 ans*. They can be found, for example, in the patterns of rapid cutting (or what could be called metric montage) used in the film, a technique originally weaponised by Eisenstein to 'obtain the effect of mechanical acceleration and tension by shortening the [length of the shots]' (Eisenstein 1949: 72), and which Le Masson meanwhile weaponises to craft an impression of political agitation conspicuously lacking from the alternately therapeutic and contemplative archive of visual and oral testimonies upon which the project was originally founded. At one point in *J'ai 8 ans*, Le Masson thus pairs first-hand testimony from one of the boys ('and the battle started there'), with a propulsive cycle of rapidly edited together shots of drawings depicting nationalists clashing with the French army. It is a formal strategy through which the trauma and melancholia of the testimony is displaced by an emphasis on 'acceleration' and 'tension', insurgency and insubordination (see Chapter 5 for a discussion of how metric montage is used in *Secteur postal 89098*).

To this instance of excessive editing can be added a cycle of facial close-ups influenced by Soviet-style framing (Figure 7.5). Twelve close-ups feature in the film, each framing an infantile face contorted into an expression of resistance: brows knotted, muscles tightened, unyielding and unwieldy, silently addressing

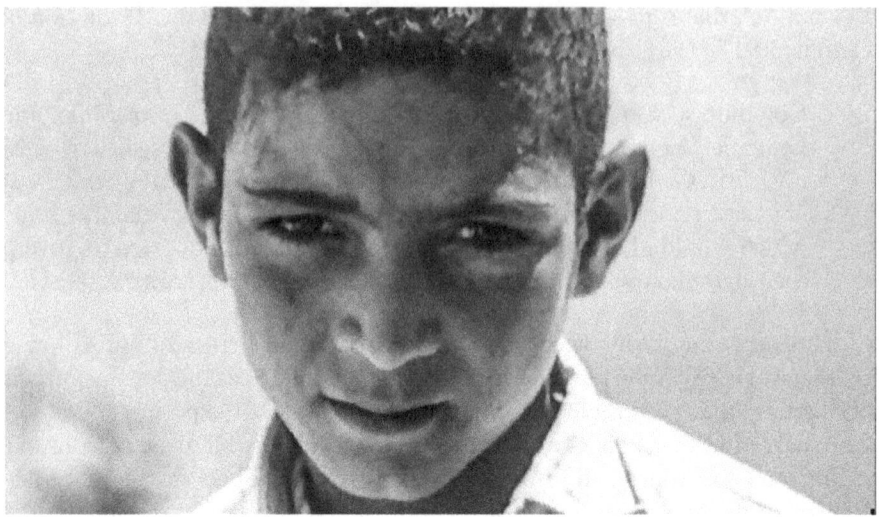

Figure 7.5 Close-up of one of the boys addressing the camera.

the camera in the kind of fourth wall break that we find in *Octobre à Paris*. These are faces positively imbued with the 'poster-like directness' and physiognomic micro-movements that trembled in the faces of Eisenstein's proletariat heroes in *Battleship Potemkin*, or those that punctuated Dovzhenko's *Earth* (Bordwell 2003: 368), spawning a certain degree of ontological and ideological confusion in *J'ai 8 ans*. Have these boys been instrumental in anti-colonial resistance, as these images, permeated with insubordination, seem to imply? Should we interpret these boys as victims, scarred by the war, or heroes of an unspecified insurrection? They are, after all, only eight years old. And – most importantly – is the revolution of which the film speaks inspired by Algerian nationalism, as some of the testimonial voices obliquely suggest, or the leftist Bolshevik tradition (to cite Vidal-Naquet), as the 'textual voice' of the film, woven into shots such as these, obliquely suggests, and as Le Masson himself elliptically intimated, notably by advertising *J'ai 8 ans* as 'an anti-colonial *agit-prop* film'? (cited in Charby 2004: 162 [emphasis added by author]). To these questions *J'ai 8 ans* may not propose an unequivocal answer, yet as the documentary edges towards its revolutionary climax, the spectator is nonetheless confronted with what is undeniably the most conspicuous evidence of the semi-submerged, quasi-subterranean 'textual voice' that reverberates deep within the narrative. As shots of idyllic landscapes drawn again by the boys flash up on the screen – a village, the sky, a town populated with people – the spectator is presented with a burst of acousmatic chanting, articulated by neither the boys nor the directors, but an un-visualised crowd: 'Peace in Al-ge-ria' (la paix en

Al-gé-rie).[11] This motto of the *metropolitan Left* is repeated eight times in the final few seconds of *J'ai 8 ans*, each time growing in amplitude, if not in clarity, until it resembles less a polyphonic assemblage of voices than a nebulous choral voice: a leftist alternative to Fanon's 'Voice of Algeria'. It also positions the documentary obliquely yet unmistakably in proximity to Gillo Pontecorvo's 1966 film, *La Bataille d'Alger/The Battle of Algiers*, which not only romanticises the war by projecting it through the ideological lens of Marxism-Leninism (Smith 2005), but also uses a similar sonic leitmotif of 'chorality' 'to construct a fantasmatic or imaginary social group rather than reflecting an existing one' (Alsop 2014: 27). Incidentally, Le Masson's 1972 documentary *Kashima Paradise* has been criticised in a similar fashion: for projecting Japanese class relations through a romantic-revolutionary Marxist-Leninist lens (Bonitzer 1975a: 25). In a 1975 interview with *Cahiers du cinéma*, Le Masson, for instance, claims that he had 'tried to analyse the things that were happening before [his] eyes [in Japan] from a Marxist point of view' (Kane et al. 1975: 47), even if, as Pascal Bonitzer wryly pointed out, 'the things that were happening' were not informed by Marxist ideology, but rather by the Giri, a culturally specific Japanese value roughly corresponding to 'duty' or 'obligation' (Bonitzer 1975b: 45). Like *Kashima Paradise*, *La Bataille d'Alger* and *Octobre à Paris*, *J'ai 8 ans* therefore concludes by usurping the testimony of the subjects ostensibly being granted a voice in the documentary, overpowering their voices with the all-consuming 'textual voice' of the (radical) Left. And only then do we realise that this choral voice, this textual voice, this voice of authority, is ultimately propelled by a desire to redeem the reputation of the Left, after the latter had been accused of complicity in precisely the type of colonial atrocities to which many Algerians in the documentary have been subjected.

Notes

1. The rationale behind this vote was complex. Jim House and Neil MacMaster point out that it was ratified partly in response to settler demonstrations that had taken place in February 1956, and partly in response to the perceived political impotence of the PCF (2006: 199).
2. Some of these photos were taken by freelance photojournalists present at the 'events', such as Raymond Darolle and Gérard Ménager, both working for Europress. Some of them were published in *France-Soir* and *Paris Match*, including the final photo of the sequence, in which protesters sit against the wall of the Rex Theatre. Many of the more harrowing shots in this sequence can be attributed to Elie Kagan, including one famous shot of a man named Abdelkader Bennehar, which featured in *France Observateur*. For more details see Hannah Feldman (2014: 159–99) and Chapter 4.
3. The footage can be consulted here: <https://fresques.ina.fr/independances/fiche-media/Indepe00012/la-manifestation-de-l-unef.html>. Incidentally, Robert Enrico

also uses excerpts from the same footage when Frédéric visits his lover, Christiane, in *La Belle vie/The Good Life* (1964) (see Chapter 1).
4. Likely shot by newsreel crews, two brief clips in particular display a cluster of police motorcycles and vans at the Place de la Défense; they are located at 43.54 and 44.58 in the DVD edition. As Brett Bowles (2022) points out, two other pieces of footage also exist from that night, although neither was included in Panijel's documentary. One of these depicts Kagan, alongside a handful of journalists, at the Place de la Défense, alongside a cluster of police motorcycles and vans. The other is more controversial, picturing a range of smashed store windows in the second *arrondissement*, before lingering on footage of police guiding bloodied Algerians into vans near the Arc de Triomphe. Both clips can be seen here: <www.gparchives.com>.
5. As Kader states: 'I would like to say something before the film starts: I am an Algerian. My name is Kader. I know what you are about to see and hear very well. I have lived in Paris throughout the Algerian War. And all of this is true. But it's also true that French people made this film; I know them very well, and I will never forget them.'
6. It should be noted that 'bicots' and 'youpins' are derogatory terms, used here ironically.
7. 'La porte se referme sur l'Algérien. Mais ne partez pas! Le dix-sept octobre continue. La porte va se rouvrir. Et c'est sur nous qu'elle se rouvre! Sur nous qui ne sommes pas des bicots, qui n'étions pas des youpins, il y a vingt ans . . .'.
8. 'Depuis sept ans, les Algériens ont tenu une espèce de comptabilité du réveil du peuple français. Quand les mères françaises ont empêché les trains de partir, d'emmener les gars en Algérie. Quand les objecteurs de conscience, des jeunes de dix-neuf, vingt ans, ont pris réellement conscience, et beaucoup plus que certains hommes politiques, ont préféré encore la prison que de prendre l'uniforme et de combattre les Algériens. Au Manifeste des 121 surtout, contre la torture . . . Justement, c'est là, l'honneur du peuple français.'
9. Fanon briefly alludes to this experience in his book *Les damnés de la terre/The Wretched of the Earth*, specifically in relation to the psychological damage that has been inflicted upon his young patients ([1961] 1963: 278–9).
10. This was an editorial approach likewise adopted in *Les enfants d'Algérie: Récits et dessins d'enfants réfugiés en Tunisie, en Libye et au Maroc/The Children of Algeria: Testimonies and Drawings of Refugee Children in Tunisia, Libya and Morocco*, a compilation of first-person accounts of the war, provided by a similar group of young Algerian refugees, and from which 'responses that did not sound like testimony', due to their perceived incoherence, 'were eliminated' (Anon. 1962b: 12).
11. The fact that the unseen demonstrators demand peace – rather than independence – casts doubt on Le Masson's claim that 'since my return from Algeria I had been distancing myself little by little from [the French Communist Party]. Its relation to Algeria was too ambiguous; for instance, they said "Peace in Algeria" and for me the rallying cry was rather "Victory for the Algerians"' (cited in Charby 2004: 163).

CONCLUSION

In his seminal book *Beyond the Subtitle*, Mark Betz ponders: 'what is a film on the Algerian question'? (2009: 103, 107). In this book, I have posed a similar question; however, it is one that is broader in scope and articulated differently: 'what is late-colonial French cinema'? By means of a conclusion, I would thus like to offer some provisional answers to this question, based on analysis conducted in previous chapters. As I suggested in the Introduction, late-colonial cinema should, in the first instance, be understood as a corpus of (mainly) French films that arose during, and commented on, the end of colonialism in French Algeria, as the region was engulfed by war in the late 1950s and early 1960s. This corpus did not respect generic boundaries, with a plethora of filmic influences and affiliations being laced into each of the case studies of my chapters, including film noir, the Second World War combat film, the so-called Right Bank of the New Wave, the so-called Left Bank of the New Wave, Soviet Montage cinema, Italian neorealism, as well as exercises in 'expository', 'interactive' and 'observational' documentary. In the second instance, this book has argued that late-colonial French films shared an important commonality insofar as they articulated two attendant messages. One of these was a pacifist understanding of the war as an ultimately futile endeavour that had yielded few concrete military results. The other was an ethical understanding of France as ultimately innocent of the atrocities committed during the war. Together, these messages coalesced to contribute to a discourse of 'redemptive pacifism'.

Propelled by a desire to show how this 'redemptive pacifism' manifested itself in various late-colonial films, each chapter of this book has come to a slightly different conclusion. In Chapter 1, for instance, I examined the domestically orientated iconographies of Jacques Rozier's *Adieu Philippine/Goodbye Philippine* (1963) and Robert Enrico's *La Belle vie/The Good Life* (1964), demonstrating how both films deploy the visual vocabulary of the privatised abode to temper the allusions to the war elaborated therein. In their framing of military identity, both films also introduce one of the recurring themes of late-colonial French cinema – absolution – with Dédé being depicted as ethically cleansed in the 'haven' of Michel's home, whilst a disengaged Frédéric redeems himself through a credo of domestic acquisition. Disengaged too is the former legionnaire, putschist and OAS affiliate Thomas, in *L'Insoumis/The Unvanquished* (Cavalier, 1964), the first of the two late-colonial films I analysed in the second chapter of this book. Harnessing Edgar's Morin's notion of 'neutralisation', alongside other concepts associated with star studies, Chapter 2 therefore began by showing how Cavalier both screens and sublimates the de-colonial debacle, notably by representing Thomas as violent yet victimised, cruel yet compassionate, guilty of a certain degree of complicity in an 'ugly' instance of pro-colonial terror, yet also physically flawless. Here, the aesthetic quality of attraction operates as a metonymy for the ethical quality of absolution: Thomas is innocent because he is beautiful and beautiful because he is innocent. Later in Chapter 2, I extended these theories to the shock and awe imagery of Mark Robson's barrelling *Les Centurions/Lost Command* (1966), demonstrating how the film represents the war in a similarly sublimated fashion, trading ethically abhorrent colonial atrocities for a cornucopia of visually pleasing spectacles, and re-imagining Marcel Bigeard as Raspéguy, an exemplar of paratrooper strength and virility. In both films, extra-filmic horror yields to filmic pleasure, as the French army is re-envisaged as something to be admired and adored.

Chapter 3 began by extending my analysis of paratroopers in *Les Centurions* to Jacques Dupont's *Les Distractions/Trapped by Fear* (1960), a film in which Jean-Paul Belmondo plays a supremely virile para-turned-Hussard named Paul. Less a political exposé than an attempt at rehabilitating the reputation of the French army, through the character of Paul, Dupont notably imagines paratroopers as pursuers of erotic encounters in metropolitan France, rather than as perpetrators of sexualised violence in French Algeria. But as I demonstrated towards the end of Chapter 3, even as Dupont invites us to marvel at the heady uber-masculinity of Paul, so too does he impel us to empathise with the maimed anti-masculinity of Laurent, who bears more than a semblance of similarity to Alain in Louis Malle's *Le Feu follet/The Fire Within* (1963). Both Laurent and Alain, for instance, are former soldiers. Both are held captive by the obscure signs of emasculation, with this predicament being affiliated, in both cases, with the castrating effects of military conflict and female desire. Both lastly hurl themselves out of the realm of the living into that of the dead with a resolve at once tragically vindicating and supremely self-victimising. Writes Claire Eldridge,

> with respect to the War of Independence, a conflict in which it is hard to find 'just' ends, certainly on the French side, the concept of victimhood has taken on particularly potent dimensions. Because no one emerged unsullied from this *sale guerre* [dirty war], the status of 'victim' was not definitively tied to any one group and has thus remained a prize to be fought over. In the absence of unambiguous glory, the next best thing is to be able to cast yourself as the innocent victim of events beyond your control. (2010: 125)

Suffering, victimisation, innocence: the qualities embodied by Laurent and Alain in *Les Distractions* and *Le Feu follet* are qualities also embodied by Michel in Jacques Doniol-Valcroze's *La Dénonciation/The Denunciation* (1962), the first of the two case studies of Chapter 4. At the start of Chapter 4, I thus mused about the ethical ambiguity of Michel's 'multidirectional' memories of torture, memories which curiously at once appear to allude to the victimisation of indigenous Algerians in French Algeria, whilst amplifying the pain of a bourgeois French Hussar. I also framed Michel's self-death as an ultimately exculpatory gesture; one that alleviates any guilt that accumulates in his political mutation: from French Resistant to disengaged dandy, from man of the moderate Left to abettor of the extreme Right. Even more atypical than Doniol-Valcroze's film, however, is Autant-Lara's *Tu ne tueras point/L'Objecteur/Thou Shalt Not Kill* (1963), which, like *La Dénonciation*, is orientated towards similar questions of amnesia and anamnesis, culpability and exculpation. As I showed towards the end of Chapter 3, Lara's narrative can be seen to turn around the corporeally, mentally and morally vigorous body of non-soldier Cordier, who figuratively immunises himself against the psycho-moral 'disease' infecting a generation of French soldiers during decolonisation through his act of conscientious objection. As the latter fell into a state of guilty complicity in the perpetration of colonial violence, the former soars above them, guiltless and transcendental. Ultimately, in neither *La Dénonciation* nor *Tu ne tueras point* are French citizens, be they ex-Resistants or conscientious objectors, depicted as anything other than absolved of culpability in the execution of military excesses; and in both films, images of amnesia prove key to this subtext of absolution.

Breaking away from the argumentative thrust of this book, Chapter 5 was less concerned with images of militarised masculine innocence than it was with images of civilian female guilt. At the start of this chapter, I thus demonstrated how Daniel Goldenberg's little-known short film *Le Retour/The Return* (1959) imputes two 'crimes' – emotional duplicity and sexual promiscuity – to its central female protagonist, whose perplexing behaviour, alternately cold and strange, is juxtaposed against that displayed by her returning soldier partner, himself an avatar of the trope of the innocent 'lost soldier', as seen within many films discussed in this book.[1] In both *Secteur postal 89098* and *Paris nous appartient/Paris Belongs to Us* (Rivette, 1961), meanwhile, we find an even more elaborate iteration of this 'guilt displacement', with female French citizens being obliquely aligned with brutal deeds performed by the French army in Algeria. In Durand's modernist masterpiece, this process is expedited through audio-visual strategies inspired by Soviet Montage (Eisenstein, in particular), with the Woman's face slowly transforming from an arena of innocence into a receptacle for Pierre's guilt-ridden epistolary monologues. The more Pierre bears witness to the 'crimes' he has seen during the war, the more his female partner, his inamorata, bears the burden for these 'crimes'. No less convoluted is Rivette's noir enigma *Paris nous appartient*, the second case study of Chapter 5, in which the rise of fascistic pro-colonial violence in French Algeria is obliquely attributed to the mysterious machinations of a femme fatale named Terry. Both films chime with Claire Eldridge's reading of late-colonial culture as 'littered with groups seeking to devolve responsibility onto an external party or force' (2010: 125), with the 'party' in this case being female civilian partners.

Glossing the politics of a spate of post-colonial narratives released in the late 1980s and early 1990s, for instance *Outremer/Overseas* (Roüan, 1990), and *Chocolat/Chocolate* (Denis, 1988), Marie Louis has opined: 'in films such as these, the failure of colonisation is attributed to the colonial system, or politico-economic factors, whilst the guilt of the settlers is mitigated' (2007: 2). As we saw in Chapter 6 of this book, a similar point could be made in relation to *Les Oliviers de la justice/The Olive Trees of Justice* (1962), by Jean Pélégri and James Blue, and *Au biseau des baisers/Slanted Kisses* (1962), by Guy Gilles and Marc Sator, both of which project the brutality ravaging French Algeria through a soft-focus lens composed of images of settler love and ethical purity. In *Les Oliviers de la justice*, Jean is thus the protagonist deemed responsible for dreaming up a 'just' future for the country, built upon an ideology of inter-ethnic reconciliation, and comprising a community of Algerian acquaintances (Fatima, Boralfa) whose gazes he takes as a token of allegiance. As for *Au biseau des baisers*, the directors go one step further, suturing the spectator into a god-like perspective from which they can contemplate, and vicariously possess, the landscape of colonial Algeria, through what I called patterns of late-colonial gazing. As demonstrated in Chapter 6, *Au biseau des baisers* is really less a narrative in the Hollywood tradition than it is a tapestry of quasi-pictorial visual spectacles; a cinematic postcard, whose compositional harmony often edges the diegesis into a half-Platonic, half-Cartesian world of abstract forms, upon which Alain and Madeleine look, with rapt fascination. And when the couple do not contemplate the landscape around them – conspicuously evacuated of anything or anyone that could rupture their beatific peregrinations across the region, in short, evacuated of indigenous Algerians or any zone associated with Algerians, for example shantytowns – they contemplate themselves, spinning a perfect circle of amorous glances that once again transmutes Algeria into a zone 'beyond time and beyond politics' (Gilles 2014: 51). As the two young lovers stare romantically into each other's eyes, the war is nothing but a distant drama on a love-struck horizon.

In Chapter 7, I discussed two 'parallel' documentaries, both of which were made by anti-colonial leftist militants, and both of which are ostensibly about the plight of Algerians oppressed by the French state. One of these was *Octobre à Paris/October in Paris*, by Jacques Panijel (1962), in which Algerians living in Paris bear witness to the 'events' of 17 October 1961 through often agonised embodied testimonies, captured through the audio-visual tactics of the 'masked interview'. Given the paucity of contemporaneous interventions surrounding this event, Panijel's documentary holds clear historical value, as a film that attempts to render visible what the state had attempted to invisibilise, grant a voice to those rendered voiceless, and proffer an image to those denied one. But as I suggested towards the end of Chapter 7, *Octobre à Paris* also does more than this, raising the question of whether the documentary is as concerned with the so-called colonial Other as it first might seem. By steering the latter act of his film towards the plight of leftist militants, brutalised by the police during the events of Charonne, Panijel could, for example, be accused of contributing to a more general tendency to conflate and confuse these two events – 17 October and Charonne – in the cultural imaginary of the Left. Likewise, just as many of the late-colonial films parsed in Part I of this book amplify the virtuous victimhood of French soldiers, so too does *Octobre à Paris* seemingly conclude by amplifying the virtuous victimhood of French militants, as the pain of Algerians once more recedes into the invisible folds of cinematic space. As Sarah Cooper suggests,

> It is perhaps inevitable that war and its aftermath bring out a form of universalism in documentary: people are encouraged, through the commentary, the images, or accompanying critical discourse, to recognise themselves and their history across geographical and temporal boundaries. Yet in such an act of self-recognition there is a risk that the distinctiveness of any one particular experience will be erased. (2006: 2)

The second film that I looked at in Chapter 7 was *J'ai 8 ans/I Am 8 Years Old* (1961), a deceptively simple, collaborative endeavor by Yann Le Masson, Olga Baïdar-Poliakoff, and René Vautier, with input from Frantz Fanon. Beginning with a discussion of the extremely unusual modus operandi adopted by the directorial team, I showed how the configurations of speech woven into *J'ai 8 ans* could be seen as an instance of 'acousmatic testimony', following Michel Chion. I also questioned the imaginative properties of this testimony, linking it to Fanon's notion of 'The voice of fighting Algeria', alongside the formal-visual language of Soviet Montage. Finally, I concluded Chapter 7 by connecting both *Octobre à Paris* and *J'ai 8 ans* to a more general attempt at 'rejuvenating' or rehabilitating the Left, notably after it had tumbled into a state of complicity with the perpetrators of colonial atrocity after the Special Powers Act of 1956 (D. Le Sueur 2001: 237). Deep within both documentaries thus lies a subtext of 'redemptive pacifism' that links them to the films glossed above.

As we come to the end of this brief foray into the ethics and politics of what I have been calling 'late-colonial French cinema', I should say that there is still more – much more – work to be done on the subject, primarily due to the myriad academic and logistical hurdles faced by researchers working on it. Many of the key scholarly texts on late-colonial cinema, for instance, have not been published in anything other than French, posing an immediate obstacle for non-francophone scholars (see Daniel 1972; Jeancolas 1979; and Stora 1998, 2004). So too for important late-colonial films such as *Octobre à Paris*, *Secteur postal 89098* and *Les Suspects* (see Chapter 4), none of which have been released with any kind of interlingual subtitles, whilst many are extremely difficult to access, rendering sustained textual analysis of them challenging if not impossible. As I mentioned in Chapter 5, the only way to watch Daniel Goldenberg's *Le Retour*, for example, is by consulting on-site archives at Le Forum des images in Paris; another valuable establishment is La Cinémathèque française, which houses many rare films and journalistic press releases. Other works, including Jean Herman's *Actua-tilt*, Paul Carpita's *Demain L'amour* and Philippe Durand's *Secteur postal 89098*, are currently available to watch for free online;[2] however, accessing them requires membership and academic status. Still other films, such as *Au biseau des baisers*, are currently consultable on YouTube, though, given the archival instability of the platform, clearly this is an imperfect solution to the problem at hand, and more must be done to improve the availability of this corpus.

In the Introduction to this book, I alluded to an important article by Marcel Martin (1963a: 60–4, 143–6), in which the critic lists no fewer than seventy late-colonial French films, all of which include more or less explicit references to the politics of the war. Undoubtably due to the factors elaborated above, only a fraction of these works have been analysed in any depth by scholars working in the field – in England, France, America or elsewhere – and, whilst I have done my best to sketch out the defining traits of this corpus, ultimately what I have come to uncover whilst writing this book is less a coherent cinematic archive than what Lia Brozgal has termed an 'anarchive', that is to say, a body of films often 'produced outside of the aegis of the State' before being placed under erasure through censorship (2014: 50). In the absence of an archive, uncertainty abounds, leading me personally to compile a list of films that I knew existed, but could not locate. They included: Raymond Lefèvre's *Les Désaccords d'Evian/The Evian Disagreements* (1966);[3] Louis Terme's *Fille de la route/The Girl of the Road* (1962);[4] and René Wheeler's *Vers l'extase/Towards Ecstasy* (1959),[5] amongst others. In which (un)official archive or private collection might we uncover these spectral films, and what other scholarly enquiries, and spectatorial pleasures, might watching them generate? Ultimately, it is on this conjectural note that I would therefore like to end this book, with neither an authoritative claim to knowledge, nor a definitive argumentative conclusion, but a series of questions – and an invitation to investigation.

NOTES

1. For example, *Adieu Philippine* (Dédé), *La Belle vie* (Frédéric), *L'Insoumis* (Thomas), *Les Distractions* (Laurent), *Le Feu follet* (Alain), *Le Retour* (the Soldier) and *Secteur postal 89098* (Pierre).
2. Each of these films can be seen here: <https://www.cimalpes.fr/>.
3. Lefèvre himself has written about the film, revealing that it includes a series of curiously inverted allusions to Alain Resnais's *Hiroshima mon amour* (1959): 'you saw everything at Evian' ... 'Oh yes, I saw everything ...' (see Lefèvre 1997: 44–5).
4. According to Joseph Daniel, Terme's film conveys a range of 'separation anxieties' that are probably linked to the absence of a conscript from the home front (1972: 342).
5. In *Vers l'extase*, a young woman marries a wealthy settler in North Africa, against the wishes of her relatives (Martin 1963a: 61).

BIBLIOGRAPHY

Adams, A. (2016), *Political Torture in Popular Culture: The Role of Representations in the Post-9/11 Torture Debate*, London: Routledge.

Alleg H. (1958), *La Question*, Paris: Les Éditions de Minuit.

Alsop, E. (2014), 'The imaginary crowd: neorealism and the uses of Coralità', *The Velvet Light Trap*, 74, pp. 27–41.

Amad, P. (2013), 'Visual riposte: looking back at the return of the gaze as postcolonial theory's gift to film studies', *Cinema Journal*, 52: 3, pp. 49–74.

Anon. (1957), *Des Rappelés témoignent*, Clichy: Comité Résistance Spirituelle.

Anon. (1959), *La Gangrène/The Gangrene*, Paris: Les Éditions de Minuit.

Anon. (1961), 'Notre Couverture', *Cahiers du cinéma*, 125: 25, inside cover.

Anon. (1962a), *Le Nouveau Candide*, 14 June.

Anon. (1962b), *Les enfants d'Algérie: Récits et dessins d'enfants réfugiés en Tunisie, en Libye et au Maroc*, Paris: Maspero.

Anon. (1966), 'Les Centurions', *Le Canard Enchaîné*, 12 October.

Arnault, H. (1970), 'Entretien avec Philippe Durand', *La Revue du cinéma: Image et son*, 239, pp. 32–5.

Arnault, H. and C. Cobast (1964), 'Entretien avec Robert Enrico', *Image et son*, 174, pp. 71–7.

Asibong, A. (2012), '*Nouveau désordre*: diabolical queerness in 1950s French cinema', in H. Bauer and M. Cook (eds), *Queer 1950s: Genders and Sexualities in History*, London: Palgrave Macmillan, pp. 29–40.

Atack, M. (2006), '*L'Armée des ombres* and *Le Chagrin et la pitié*: reconfigurations of law, legalities, and the state in post-1968 France', in H. Peitsch, C. Burdett and

C. Gorrara (eds), *European Memories of the Second World War*, New York and Oxford: Berghahn Books, pp. 160–74.
Aubriant, M. (1962), *Paris Presse*, 9 June.
Audé, F., J-P. Jeancolas and F. Ramasse (1981), 'Entretien avec Alain Cavalier', *Positif*, 240, pp. 4–17.
Austin, G. (1999), *Claude Chabrol*, Manchester and New York: Manchester University Press.
Austin, G. (2003), *Stars in Modern French Film*, London: Arnold.
Austin, G. (2007a), 'Representing the Algerian War in Algerian cinema: *Le Vent des Aurès*', *French Studies*, 2, pp. 182–95.
Austin, G. (2007b), 'Drawing trauma: visual testimony in *Caché* and *J'ai 8 ans*', *Screen*, 48: 4, 529–36.
Austin, G. (2008), *Contemporary French cinema*, Manchester: Manchester University Press.
Austin, G. (2009), 'Trauma, cinema and the Algerian War', *New Readings*, 10, pp. 18–25.
Austin, G. (2011), 'Spaces of the dispossessed in Algerian cinema', *Modern & Contemporary France*, 19:2, pp. 195–208.
Austin, G. (2012), *Algerian National Cinema*, Manchester: Manchester University Press.
Bachelard, G. (2014), *The Poetics of Space*, London: Penguin.
Badley, L. and R. B. Palmer (2006), 'Introduction', in L. Badley and R. B. Palmer (eds), *Traditions in World Cinema*, Edinburgh: Edinburgh University Press, pp. 1–12.
Barclay, F., C. Chopin, and M. Evans (2018), 'Introduction: settler colonialism and French Algeria', *Settler Colonial Studies*, 8: 2, pp. 115–30.
Barnouw, E. (1993), *Documentary: A History of the Non-fiction Film*, New York and Oxford: Oxford University Press.
Barthes, R. [1957] (1989a), 'Soap powders and detergents', in *Mythologies*, Paris: Seuil (Points), pp. 36–8.
Barthes, R. [1957] (1989b), 'Wine and milk', in *Mythologies*, Paris: Seuil (Points), pp. 69–72.
Barthes, R. [1957] (1989c), 'Myth today', in *Mythologies*, Paris: Seuil (Points), pp. 181–233.
Barthes, R. [1957] (1989d), 'The new Citroën', in *Mythologies*, Paris: Seuil (Points), pp. 140–2.
Basinger, J. (1986), *The World War II Combat Film: Anatomy of a Genre*, New York and Guildford: Columbia University Press.
Baudrillard, J. [1968] (2005), *The System of Objects*, London and New York: Verso.
Bazin, A. (1951), 'Le stylistique de Robert Bresson', *Cahiers du cinéma*, 3, June, 7–21.
Bazin, A. [1957] (1985), 'The death of Humphrey Bogart', in J. Hillier (ed.), *Cahiers du Cinéma: The 1950s*, Cambridge, MA: Harvard University Press, pp. 98–101.
Beattie, K. (1998), *The Scar That Binds: American Culture and the Vietnam War*, New York and London: New York University Press.
Bédjaoui, A. (2014), *Cinéma et guerre de libération: Algérie, des batailles d'images*. Algiers: Chihab.
Benayoun, R. (1962), 'Le roi est nu', *Positif*, 46 (June), pp. 1–14.

Benayoun, R. (1963), 'Les naufrages du hasard', *Positif*, 56, November, pp. 5–8.
Bénédict, S. (2001), 'Détruire disent-elles', in E. Burdeau (ed.), *Jacques Rozier: Le funambule*, Paris: *Cahiers du cinéma*, pp. 82–6.
Bertho, R. (2014), 'The grands ensembles', *Études photographiques*, 31, pp. 1–23.
Bertin-Maghit, J-P. (2015), *Lettres filmées d'Algérie: Des soldats à la caméra (1954–1962)*, Paris: Nouveau Monde éditions.
Bertin-Maghit, J-P. and A. Marty (2001), '*Tu ne tueras point* de Claude Autant-Lara (1961–1963): Des lectures de l'objection de conscience sous influence', in J-P. Bertin-Maghit and B. Fleury-Vilatte (eds), *Les institutions de l'image*, Paris: EHESS, pp. 137–45.
Betz, M. (2009), *Beyond the Subtitle: Remapping European Art Cinema*, Minneapolis: University of Minnesota Press.
Beugnet, M. and J. Sillars (2001), '*Beau travail*: time, space and myths of identity', *Studies in French Cinema*, 1: 3, pp. 166–73.
Blanchard, P., S. Lemaire, N. Bancel, D. Thomas and D. Richard (2014), *Colonial Culture in France Since the Revolution*, Bloomington: Indiana University Press.
Bleys, J-P. (2018), *Claude Autant-Lara*, Arles: Actes Sud.
Blondin, A. (1963), 'Nous sommes Alain', *L'Avant-scène du cinéma*, 30, March, p. 7.
Bonitzer, P. (1975a), 'Les silences de la voix', *Cahiers du cinéma*, 256, February–March, pp. 22–33.
Bonitzer, P. (1975b), '*Kashima Paradise*', *Cahiers du cinéma*, 254–5, pp. 44–5.
Bonnaud, R. (1957), 'La Paix des Nementchas', *Esprit*, 249: 4, pp. 580–92.
Borde, R. (1962a), 'le Cinéma marginal et la guerre d'Algérie', *Positif*, 46, pp. 15–17.
Borde, R. (1962b), 'San Sebastian: Les Nullités', *Positif* (October), p. 48.
Borde, R. and E. Chaumeton [1955] (2002), *A Panorama of American Film Noir: 1941–1953*, San Francisco: City Lights Books.
Bordwell, D. (2003), 'Monumental heroics: form and style in Eisenstein's silent films' in L. Grieveson and P. Krämer (eds), *The Silent Cinema Reader*, London: Routledge, pp. 368–88.
Bordwell, D. and K. Thompson (2017), *Film Art: An Introduction*, New York: McGraw-Hill Education.
Bory, J-L. (1973), *Questions au cinéma*, Paris: Stock.
Boudjedra, R. (1971), *Naissance du cinéma algérien*, Paris: François Maspero.
Bourdet, C. (1951), 'Is there an Algerian gestapo?', *L'Observateur*, 6 December.
Boutaghou, M. (ed.) (2019a), *Représentations de la guerre d'indépendance algérienne*, Paris: Classiques Garnier.
Boutaghou, M. (2019b), 'Introduction', in M. Boutaghou (ed.), *Représentations de la guerre d'indépendance algérienne*, Paris: Classiques Garnier, pp. 7–20.
Bowles, B. (2022, forthcoming), 'Fragmentary, censored, indispensable: the audiovisual archive of October 17, 1961', *French Historical Studies*, 46: 2 (pagination TBC).
Branche, R. (1997), '1963–1977, quinze ans et dix-sept films: douloureuses mémoires', in G. Hennebelle, M. Berrah and B. Stora (eds), *La guerre d'Algérie à l'écran*, Condé-sur-Noireau: Éditions Corlet, pp. 57–67.
Branche, R. (2001), *La torture et l'armée pendant la guerre d'Algérie, 1954–1962*, Paris: Gallimard.

Branche, R. (2003), 'La sexualité des appelés en Algérie', in J-C. Jauffret (ed.), *Des hommes et des femmes en guerre d'Algérie*, Paris: Autrement, pp. 402–15.

Branche, R. (2004), 'La masculinité à l'épreuve de la guerre sans nom', *Clio: Histoire, femmes et sociétés*, 20, pp. 111–22.

Branche, R. (2005), *La Guerre d'Algérie: une histoire apaisée?*, Paris: Éditions du Seuil.

Branche, R. (2010), *L'embuscade de Palestro: Algérie 1956*. Paris: Armand Colin.

Branche, R. (2020), *'Papa, qu'as-tu fait en Algérie?': Enquête sur un silence familial*, Paris: La Découverte.

Braudy, L. (1996),'"No body's perfect": Method acting and 50s culture', *Michigan Quarterly Review*, 35: 1, pp. 191–215.

Bremond, C., E. Sullerot and S. Berton (1961), 'Les héros des films dits de la Nouvelle Vague', *Communications*, 1, pp. 142–77.

Brenez, N. (2004), 'Forms 1960–2004', in M. Temple and M. Witt (eds), *The French Cinema Book*, London: British Film Institute, pp. 230–46.

Breton, E. (2016), '*Rivette, jeux d'enfant et inventions d'un défricheur*', *L'Humanité*, <http://www.humanite.fr/rivette-jeux-denfant-et-inventions-dun-defricheur-597615> (accessed 19 July 2017).

Britton, C. (1990), 'Broken images in Resnais's *Muriel*', *French Cultural Studies*, 1: 1, pp. 37–46.

Brown, J. (2004), '*"Sensing", "seeing", "saying" in Camus'* Noces: *A Meditative Essay*, Amsterdam: Editions Rodopi.

Brozgal, L. (2014), 'In the absence of the archive (Paris, October 17, 1961)', *South Central Review*, 31: 1, pp. 34–54.

Brozgal, L. (2019), 'Gros plan sur le 17 octobre 1961: violence coloniale, cinéma documentaire et le sujet algérien', in M. Boutaghou (ed.), *Fictions et représentations de la guerre algérienne*, Paris: Classiques Garnier, pp. 99–114.

Brun, C. and T. Shepard (eds) (2016a), *Guerre d'Algérie: le sexe outragé*, Paris: CNRS Éditions.

Brun, C. and T. Shepard (2016b), 'Introduction: guerre des sexes, politiques des genres' in C. Brun and T. Shepard (eds), *Guerre d'Algérie: le sexe outragé*, Paris: CNRS Éditions, pp. 11–28.

Brune, J. (1961), *Cette haine qui ressemble à l'amour*, Paris: La table ronde.

Brunet, C. (1999), *Police contre FLN: le drame d'octobre 1961*, Paris: Flammarion.

Cadé, M. (1997), 'Les films des années 60: d'abord les effets sur les français', in G. Hennebelle, M. Berrah and B. Stora (eds), *La guerre d'Algérie à l'écran*, Condé-sur-Noireau: Éditions Corlet, pp. 49–56.

Camus, A. [1937] (1959), *Noces: suivi de L'été*, Paris: Gallimard.

Camus, A. [1942] (1957), *L'Étranger*, Paris: Gallimard.

Camus, A. (1947), *La Peste*, Paris: Gallimard.

Capdenac, M. (1963), *Les Lettres françaises*, 12–18 June.

Carroll, D. (2007), *Albert Camus the Algerian: Colonialism, Terrorism, Justice*, New York and Chichester: Columbia University Press.

Carta, J. (1962), 'Un document: "*J'ai 8 ans*"', *Partisans*, 4, pp. 111–19.

Chambers, R. (2010), 'The long howl: serial torture', *Yale French Studies*, 118/119, pp. 39–51.

Chapeu, S. (2004), *Des chrétiens dans la guerre d'Algérie, L'action de la Mission de France*, Paris: Éditions de l'Atelier.
Chapier, H. (1961), '*Tu ne tueras point:* un premier prix de veulerie', *Combat*, 22 August.
Chapier, H. (1963), '*Tu ne tueras point:* une imposture morale', *Combat*, 6 June.
Chapman, J. (2008), *War and Film*, London: Reaktion Books.
Charby, J. (2004), *Les porteurs d'espoir. Les réseaux de soutien au FLN pendant la guerre d'Algérie: les acteurs parlent*, Paris: La Découverte.
Chevassu, F. (1962), 'Secteur postal 89098 (fiche filmographique)', *Image et son*, 149, pp. 23–31.
Chion, M. (1994), *Audio-Vision: Sound on Screen*, New York: Columbia University Press.
Chion, M. (1999), *The Voice in Cinema*, New York: Columbia University Press.
Chion, M. (2009), *Film, A Sound Art*, New York: Columbia University Press.
Cilento, F. (2018), *An Investigative Cinema Politics and Modernization in Italian, French, and American Film*, London: Palgrave.
Clover, C. (2015), *Men, Women, and Chainsaws: Gender in the Modern Horror Film*, Princeton: Princeton University Press.
Coates, P. (2012), *Screening the Face*, London: Palgrave Macmillan.
Cohen, S. (2011), *States of Denial: Knowing about Atrocities and Suffering*, Cambridge: Polity Press.
Collet, J. (1963), 'Entre le badinage et le chagrin', *L'Avant-scène du cinéma*, 31, p. 6.
Comité de Résistance Spirituelle (1957), *Des Rappelés témoignent*, Paris: Comité de Résistance Spirituelle.
Comolli, J-L. (1963), 'La Belle vie', *Cahiers du cinéma*, 148, p. 21.
Conesa, G. (1970), *Bab-El-Oued, notre paradis perdu*, Paris: Robert Laffont.
Cooper, S. (2001), 'Je sais bien, mais quand même . . .: fetishism, envy, and the queer pleasures of *Beau travail*', *Studies in French Cinema*, 1: 3, pp. 174–82.
Cooper, S. (2006), *Selfless Cinema? Ethics and French Documentary*, London: Legenda.
Coureau, D. (1996), 'L'Insoumis ou L'Abeille, le revolver, la serrure', *Etudes cinématographiques*, 61, pp. 45–56.
Cox, G. (2006), *Sartre: A Guide for the Perplexed*, London: Continuum.
Croombs, M. (2010), 'Algeria deferred: the logic of trauma in *Muriel* and *Caché*', *Scope: An Online Journal of Film and Television Studies*, 16, <https://www.nottingham.ac.uk/scope/documents/2010/february-2010/croombs.pdf> (last accessed 8 November 2020).
Croombs, M. (2013), 'An opposition in search of itself: modern French cinema and the Algerian War', unpublished doctoral thesis, Carleton University, Ottawa.
Croombs, M. (2014), 'French Algeria and the police: horror as political affect in three short documentaries by Alain Resnais', *Screen*, 55: 1, pp. 29–47.
Croombs, M. (2017), '*La jetée* in historical time: torture, visuality, displacement', *Cinema Journal*, 56: 2, pp. 25–45.
D. Le Sueur, J. (2001), *Uncivil War: Intellectuals and Identity Politics during the Decolonization of Algeria*, Philadelphia: University of Pennsylvania Press.
D'Hugues, P. (2006), 'Les hussards et le cinéma', in A. Ferrari (ed.), *Le Poing dans la vitre: scénaristes et dialoguistes du cinéma français*, Arles: Actes Sud, pp. 497–516.

Dambre, M. (1989), *Roger Nimier: Hussard d'un demi-siècle*, Paris: Flammarion.
Dambre, M. (2014), 'The Hussars: a young literary Right faced with Camus (1945–1962)' *South Central Review*, 31: 3, pp. 82–92.
Daniel, J. (1972), *Guerre et cinéma: grandes illusions et petits soldats, 1895–1971*, Paris: Colin.
Dawson, G. (1994), *Soldier Heroes: British Adventure, Empire and the Imagining of Masculinities*, London: Routledge.
De Baecque, A. (1998), *La nouvelle vague: portrait d'une jeunesse*, Paris: Flammarion.
De Baecque A. (2012), *Camera Historica: The Century in Cinema*, New York: Columbia University Press.
De Baroncelli, J. (1966), 'Les Centurions', *Le Monde*, 11 October.
De Beauvoir, S. (1960), 'Pour Djamila Boupacha', *Le Monde*, 2 June.
De Beauvoir, S. (1962), *Brigitte Bardot and the Lolita Syndrome*, London: Four Square.
De Beauvoir, S. [1963] (2014), *La Force des choses: II*, Paris: Éditions Gallimard.
De Beauvoir, S. (1966), *Les Belles Images*, Paris: Éditions Gallimard.
De La Ferrière, A. A. (2014), 'The voice of the innocent: propaganda and childhood testimonies of war', *History of Education*, 43: 1, pp. 105–23.
De la Rochelle, D. (1959), *Le Feu follet*, Paris: Gallimard.
Debord, G. (1967), *La société du spectacle*, Paris: Buchet/Chastel.
Deleuze, G. and F. Guattari (1987), *A Thousand Plateaus: Capitalism and Schizophrenia*, Minneapolis: University of Minnesota Press.
Denis, S. (2006), 'Métaphores cinématographiques en situation coloniale. Le cas de la censure française en Algérie (1945–1962)', *1895. Mille huit cent quatre-vingt-quinze*, 48, pp. 6–25.
Denis, S. (2009), *Le cinéma et la guerre d'Algérie*, Paris: Nouveau Monde.
Desbois, E. (1997), 'Les actualités françaises pendant le conflit: des images en quarantaine', in G. Hennebelle, M. Berrah and B. Stora (eds), *La guerre d'Algérie à l'écran*, Condé-sur-Noireau: Éditions Corlet, pp. 560–71.
Deshayes, F. and A. Pohn-Weidinger (2017), *L'Amour en guerre. Sur les traces d'une correspondance pendant la guerre d'Algérie*, Paris: Bayard.
Dine, P. (1994a), *Images of the Algerian War: French Fiction and Film, 1954–1992*, Oxford: Oxford University Press.
Dine, P. (1994b), 'Thinking the unthinkable: the generation of meaning in French literary and cinema images of the Algerian War', *Maghreb Review*, 19: 1/2, pp. 123–32.
Dine, P. (1995), 'The inescapable allusion: the Occupation and the Resistance in French fiction and films of the Algerian War', in H. R. Kedward and N. Wood (eds), *The Liberation of France: Image and Event*, Oxford: Berg, pp. 269–82.
Dine, P. (1997), 'Trois regards étrangers: "*Les oliviers de la justice*" de James Blue, "*La Bataille d'Alger*" de Gillo Pontecorvo, "*Les centurions*" de Mark Robson', in G. Hennebelle, M. Berrah and B. Stora (eds), *La guerre d'Algérie à l'écran*, Condé-sur-Noireau: Corlet, pp. 80–6.
Dine, P. (2016), 'Écrire le sexe (masculin) dans la littérature française de la guerre d'Algérie', in C. Brun and T. Shepard (eds), *Guerre d'Algérie Le sexe outragé*, Paris: CNRS, pp. 121–40.

Dittmar, L. and G. Michaud (1991), 'America's Vietnam War films: marching towards denial', in L. Dittmar and G. Michaud (eds), *From Hanoi to Hollywood: The Vietnam War in American Film*, New Brunswick, New Jersey: Rutgers University Press, pp. 1–15.

Dixon, W. W. (1997), *The Films of Jean-Luc Godard*, Albany: State University of New York Press.

Doane, M. A. (1980), 'The voice in the cinema: the articulation of body and space', *Yale French Studies: Cinema/Sound*, 60, pp. 33–50.

Doane, M. A. (1991), *Femmes Fatales: Feminism, Film Theory, Psychoanalysis*, New York and London: Routledge.

Dolar, M. (2006), *The Voice and Nothing More*, Cambridge and London: MIT Press.

Donadey, A. (2020), *The Algerian War in Film Fifty Years Later, 2004–2012*, Lanham, MD: Lexington Books.

Doty, A. (1993), *Making Things Perfectly Queer: Interpreting Mass Culture*, Durham, NC: Duke University Press.

Duchen, C. (1994), *Women's Rights and Women's Lives in France, 1944–1968*, London: Routledge.

Dupont, J. (2013), *Profession: cinéaste . . . politiquement incorrect!* France: Éditions Italiques.

Durand, P. (1961), '*Les Distractions*', *Image et son*, 61, December, p. 91.

Durand, P. (1988), *Moteur! Coupez!*, Paris: Edilig.

Duras, M. (1958), *Moderato Cantabile*, Paris: Éditions de Minuit.

Dyer, R. [1979] (1998), *Stars*, London: BFI.

Dyer, R. (1997), *White*, New York and London: Routledge.

Dyer, R. (2000), 'No place for homosexuality: Marcel Carné's *L'Air de Paris* (1954)', in S. Hayward and G. Vincendeau (eds), *French Film: Texts and Contexts*, London and New York: Routledge, pp. 127–41.

Eades, C. (2006), *Le Cinéma post-colonial français*, Paris: Collections 7eArt, Editions du Cerf.

Einaudi, J-L. (2001), *Octobre 1961: un massacre à Paris*, Paris: Fayard.

Eisenstein, S. (1949), *Film Form: Essays in Film Theory*, New York: Harcourt.

Eldridge, C. (2010), 'Blurring the boundaries between perpetrators and victims: *Pied-noir* memories and the *harki* community', *Memory Studies*, 3: 2, pp. 123–36.

Eldridge, C. (2016), *From Empire to Exile: History and Memory Within the Pied-noir and Harki Communities, 1962–2012*, Manchester: Manchester University Press.

Elsaesser, T. (2014), *German Cinema: Terror and Trauma, Cultural Memory Since 1945*, New York and London: Routledge.

Elsaesser, T. and M. Hagener (2015), *Film Theory: An Introduction Through the Senses*, New York: Routledge.

Eluard, P. [1946] (1960), *Le Dur désir de durer*, Paris: Seghers.

Eshun, K. and R. Gray (2011), 'The militant image: a ciné-geography; editors' introduction', *Third Text*, 25: 1, pp. 1–12.

Evans, M. (1989), 'A Story of Censorship and Forgetting: French Cinema and the Algerian War', *Modern and Contemporary France* 39, pp. 46–49.

Evans, M. (1997), *The Memory of Resistance: French Opposition to the Algerian War (1954–1962)*, Oxford: Berg.
Evans, M. (2012), *Algeria: France's Undeclared War*, Oxford: Oxford University Press.
Eveno, P. (2005), 'Paroles de soldats en guerre d'Algérie', *Le Temps des Médias*, 1: 4, pp. 127–36.
Ezra, E. (2000), *The Colonial Unconscious: Race and Culture in Interwar France*, Ithaca, NY: Cornell University Press.
Ezra E. (2010), 'Cléo's masks: regimes of objectification in the French New Wave', *Yale French Studies*, 118/119, pp. 177–90.
Ezra, E. (2018), *The Cinema of Things: Globalisation and the Posthuman Object*, New York and London: Bloomsbury.
Fabre, J. (1961), 'Entretien avec Jacques Doniol-Valcroze', *Libération*, 28 October.
Fanon, F. [1952] (2008), *Black Skin, White Masks*, London: Pluto Press.
Fanon, F. [1959] (1965), *A Dying Colonialism*, New York: Grove Press.
Fanon, F. [1961] (1963), *The Wretched of the Earth*, New York: Grove Press.
Fargier, J-P. (2014), 'Hors la vague?: sur quelques films français oubliés d'une déferlante fameuse', *Trafic*, 92, pp. 66–80.
Fathy, S. and J. Derrida (2000), *Tourner les mots: Au bord d'un film*, Paris: Galilée.
Feldman, H. (2014), *From a Nation Torn: Decolonizing Art and Representation in France, 1945–1962*, Durham and London: Duke University Press.
Ferro, M. (1988), *Cinema and History*, Detroit: Wayne State University Press.
Flitterman-Lewis, S. (1990), *To Desire Differently: Feminism and the French Cinema*, Urbana: University of Illinois Press.
Flood, M. (2016), 'Politics and the police: documenting the 17th October 1961 Massacre', *Contemporary French and Francophone Studies*, 20: 4–5, pp. 599–606.
Flood, M. (2017), *France, Algeria, and the Moving Image: Screening Histories of Violence, 1963–2010*, Cambridge: Legenda.
Flood, M. (2018), '(Un)Familiar fictions: the 17 October 1961 Massacre and Jacques Panijel's *Octobre à Paris* (1962)', *Forum for Modern Language Studies*, 54: 2, pp. 157–75.
Flood, M. (2019), 'Torture in word and image: inhuman acts in Resnais and Pontecorvo', *JCMS: Journal of Cinema and Media Studies*, 58: 3, pp. 26–4.
Flood, M. (2020), 'From colonial Casbah to Casbah-*Banlieue*: settlement and space in *Pépé le Moko* (1937) and *La Haine* (1996)', in J. Lahti and R. Weaver-Hightower (eds), *Cinematic Settlers: The Settler Colonial World in Film*, London: Routledge, pp. 177–89.
Foucault, M. [1975] (1995), *Discipline and Punish: The Birth of the Prison*, New York: Vintage Books.
Frank, B. (1952), 'Grognards et Hussards', *Les Temps modernes*, 86, pp. 1005–18.
Frey, H. (2004a), 'Pierre Drieu la Rochelle, Louis Malle and the ambiguous memory of French fascism', in W. Kidd and B. Murdoch (eds), *Memory and Memorials: The Commemorative Century*, London: Routledge, pp. 220–32.
Frey, H. (2004b), *Louis Malle*, Manchester: Manchester University Press.
Frey, H. (2014), *Nationalism and the Cinema in France: Political Mythologies and Film Events, 1945–1995*, New York: Berghahn Books.

Frodon, J-M. (1995), *L'âge moderne du cinéma français: de la Nouvelle Vague à nos jours*, Paris: Flammarion.
Frodon, J-M. (2004), 'Le regard du juste', *Cahiers du cinéma*, November, p. 24.
Fugler, R. (1964), *Les Dernières Nouvelles d'Alsace*, 15 January.
Gaffney, J. and D. Holmes (2007), 'Introduction', in J. Gaffney and D. Holmes (eds), *Stardom in Postwar France*, New York: Berghahn, pp. 1–6.
Gallien, C. (2020), 'A decolonial turn in the humanities', *Alif: Journal of Comparative Poetics*, 40, pp. 28–58.
Garson, C. (2009), 'Dossier *Adieu Philippine*', <www.cnc.fr> (last accessed 15 June 2015).
Gaston-Mathé, C. (1997), 'Le règne de la censure', in G. Hennebelle, M. Berrah and B. Stora (eds), *La guerre d'Algérie à l'écran*, Condé-sur-Noireau: Corlet, pp. 33–9.
Gauch, S. (2001), '*Muriel*, or the disappearing text of the Algerian War', *L'Esprit Créateur*, 41: 4, pp. 47–57.
Gilles, G. (2014), 'Montage d'entretiens avec Guy Gilles', in G. Lépingle and M. Uzal (eds), *Guy Gilles: Un cinéaste au fil du temps*, Crisnée: Éditions Yellow, pp. 41–66.
Gilroy, P. (2005), *Postcolonial Melancholia*, New York: Columbia University Press.
Giroud, F. (1957), *L'Express*, 16 August.
Giroud, F. (1961), *L'Express*, 30 November.
Gozlan, G. (1962), 'Eloge d'André Bazin', *Positif*, 46 (June), pp. 39–69 and 47 (July), pp. 16–60.
Grant, N. (2018), *The Luger*, Oxford: Osprey.
Greene, N. (1999), *Landscapes of Loss: The National Past in Postwar French Cinema*, Princeton, NJ: Princeton University Press.
Greene, N. (2007), *The French New Wave: A New Look*, London: Wallflower.
Guerin, F. and R. Hallas (2007), 'Introduction', in F. Guerin and R. Hallas (eds), *The Image and the Witness: Trauma, Memory and Visual Culture*, London: Wallflower Press, pp. 1–20.
Guibbert, P. (1992), 'La guerre d'Algérie sur les écrans français', in G. Laurent, J. P. Rioux and B. Stora (eds), *La France en guerre d'Algérie, novembre 1954–juillet 1962*, Paris: Bibliothèque de documentation internationale contemporaine, pp. 247–55.
Haggith, T. (2002), 'D-Day filming: for real. A comparison of "truth" and "reality" in "*Saving Private Ryan*" and combat film by the British Army's Film and Photographic Unit', *Film History*, 14: 3/4, pp. 332–53.
Hallas, R. (2007), 'Sound, image, and the corporeal implication of witnessing in Derek Jarman's *Blue*', in F. Guerin and R. Hallas (eds), *The Image and the Witness: Trauma, Memory and Visual Culture*, London: Wallflower Press, pp. 37–51.
Harrison, N. (2007), 'Pontecorvo's "documentary" aesthetics', *Interventions*, 9: 3, pp. 389-404.
Hayes, G. (2004), 'Framing the wolf: the spectacular masculinity of Alain Delon', in P. Powrie, A. Davies and B. Babington (eds), *The Trouble with Men: Masculinities in European and Hollywood Cinema*, London and New York: Wallflower Press, pp. 42–53.
Hayward, S. (1993), *French National Cinema*, London: Routledge.

Hayward, S. (2001), 'Claire Denis' films and the post-colonial body, with special reference to *Beau travail* (1999)', *Studies in French Cinema*, 1: 3, pp. 159–65.
Hayward, S. (2005), 'Framing national cinema', in M. Hjort and S. Mackenzie (eds), *Cinema & Nation*, London and New York: Routledge, pp. 81–93.
Hennebelle, G., M. Berrah and B. Stora (1997), *La guerre d'Algérie à l'écran*, Condé-sur-Noireau: Corlet.
Herman, J. (1963), 'Interview de deux jeunes délinquants: Jean-Claude et Colette', *Cinéma 63*, pp. 47–9.
Heter, S. (2006), *Sartre's Ethics of Engagement: Authenticity and Civic Virtue*, London: Continuum.
Hewitt, N. (1995), 'The literature of the Right and the liberation: the case of the "Hussards"', in H. R. Kedward and N. Wood (eds), *The Liberation of France: Image and Event*, Oxford: Berg Publishers, pp. 285–96.
Higgins L. (1996), *New Novel, New Wave, New Politics: Fiction and the Representation of History in Postwar France*, Nebraska: Nebraska University Press.
Higonnet, M. (1987), 'Introduction', M. Higonnet (ed.), *Behind the Lines: Gender and the Two World Wars*, New Haven and London: Yale University Press, pp. 1–17.
Hill, R. (2008), 'The New Wave meets the tradition of quality: Jacques Demy's "The Umbrellas of Cherbourg"', *Cinema Journal*, 48: 1, pp. 27–50.
Hillier, J. (1985), 'Introduction', in J. Hillier (ed.), *Cahiers du Cinéma: The 1950s*, Cambridge: Harvard University Press, pp. 1–17.
Hipkins, D. and G. Plain (2007), 'Introduction', in D. Hipkins and G. Plain (eds), *War-Torn Tales: Literature, Film and Gender in the Aftermath of World War II*, Oxford: Peter Lang, pp. 9–22.
Hoffmann, S. (1991), 'Foreword', in H. Rousso, *The Vichy Syndrome: History and Memory in France since 1944*, Cambridge, MA, and London: Harvard University Press, pp. vii–x.
Horne, A. (2006), *A Savage War of Peace: Algeria, 1954–1962*, New York: New York Review Books.
House, J. and N. MacMaster (2006), *Paris 1961: Algerians, State Terror, and Memory*, Oxford: Oxford University Press.
House, J. and N. MacMaster (2008), 'Time to move on: a reply to Jean-Paul Brunet', *Historical Journal*, 51, pp. 205–14.
Hubbell, A. (2011), '(Re)turning to ruins: Pied-Noir visual returns to Algeria', *Modern & Contemporary France*, 19: 2, pp. 147–61.
Hubbell, A. (2015), *Remembering French Algeria: Pieds-Noirs, Identity, and Exile*, Lincoln and London: University of Nebraska Press.
Hughes, A. and J. Williams (2001), 'Introduction', in A. Hughes and J. Williams (eds), *Gender and French Cinema*, Oxford and New York: Berg, pp. 1–19.
Ingman, N. (1995), 'Pacifism and the Liberation', in H. R. Kedward and N. Wood (eds), *The Liberation of France: Image and Event*, Oxford: Berg, pp. 209–24.
Inrep, J. (2011), 'Le Problème, ce n'est pas de raconter, c'est d'être entendu', *Alternatives non-violentes*, 161, pp. 43–7.
Jaspers, K. (2000), *The Question of German Guilt*, New York: Fordham University Press.

Jauneau, E. (2012), 'Les "mortes pour la France" et les "anciennes combattantes": l'autre contingent de l'armée française en guerre (1940–1962)', *Histoire@Politique*, 3: 18, pp. 1–17.
Jeancolas, J-P. (1979), *Le Cinéma des Français, la Vème République*, Paris: Stock.
Jeancolas, J-P. (2005), 'Colonisation and engagement (ou défaut d'engagement) du cinéma français, 1945–1965', in G. Hayes and M. O'Shaughnessy (eds), *Cinéma et engagement*, Paris: L'Harmattan, pp. 27–47.
Joly, D. (1991), *The French Communist Party and the Algerian War*, New York: St Martin's Press.
Judt, T. (1992), *Past Imperfect: French Intellectuals 1944–1956*, Berkeley: University of California Press.
Kane, P., J. Narboni and S. Toubiana (1975), 'Entretien avec Yann Le Masson and Bénie Deswarte', *Cahiers du cinéma*, 254–5, pp. 46–55.
Kaplan, E. A. (1998), 'Introduction to new edition', in E. A. Kaplan (ed.), *Women in Film Noir*, London: Palgrave Macmillan, pp. 1–14.
Kear, J. (2007), 'A game that must be lost: Chris Marker Replays Alain Resnais's *Hiroshima mon amour*', in F. Guerin and R. Hallas (eds), *The Image and the Witness: Trauma, Memory and Visual Culture*, London: Wallflower Press, pp. 129–42.
Khanna, R. (2008), *Algeria Cuts: Women and Representation, 1830 to the Present*, Stanford, CA: Stanford University Press.
King, N. (1981), 'Recent "political" documentary: notes on "*Union Maids*" and "*Harlan County USA*"', *Screen*, 22: 2, pp. 7–18.
Koide, E. (2019), 'Le fantôme de la guerre d'Algérie à Paris dans *Le Joli mai* (1962) de Chris Marker', in M. Boutaghou (ed.), *Représentations de la guerre d'indépendance algérienne*, Paris: Garnier, pp. 115–35.
Kristeva, J. (1989), *Black Sun: Depression and Melancholia*, New York and Oxford: Columbia University Press.
Kuby, E. (2013), 'From the torture chamber to the bedchamber: French soldiers, antiwar activists, and the discourse of sexual deviancy in the Algerian War (1954–1962)', *Contemporary French Civilization*, 38: 2, pp. 131–53.
Kunkle, R. (2013), '"We must shout the truth to the rooftops:" Gisèle Halimi, Djamila Boupacha, and sexual politics in the Algerian War of Independence', *Iowa Historical Review*, 4: 1, pp. 5–24.
Lack, R-F. (2010), '*Paris nous appartient*: reading without a map', *Australian Journal of French Studies*, 47: 2, pp. 133–45.
Lanta, A. (1999), *Algérie, ma mémoire*, Paris: Éditions Bouchène.
Laubier, C. (ed.) (2005), *The Condition of Women in France: 1945 to the Present*, London and New York: Routledge.
Laurent, J. (1947), *Caroline Chérie*, Paris: Jean Froissart.
Lazreg, M. (2008), *Torture and the Twilight of Empire*, Princeton, NJ: Princeton University Press.
Le Carvennec, A. (1983), *La Mémoire chacale*, Paris: La Hachette.
Le Masson, Y. and O. Poliakoff (1962), 'Manifeste pour un cinéma parallèle', *Positif*, 46, p. 18.

Leahy, S. (2003), 'The matter of myth: Brigitte Bardot, stardom and sex', *Studies in French Cinema*, 3: 2, pp. 71–81.
Leahy, S. (2007), 'Gender panic: the "*garce*" and the "Good Girl" in postwar French cinema', in D. Hipkins and G. Plain (eds), *War-Torn Tales: Literature, Film and Gender in the Aftermath of World War II*, Oxford: Peter Lang, pp. 105–22.
Leahy, S. and S. Hayward (2000), 'The tainted woman: Simone Signoret, site of pathology or agent of retribution?', in U. Sieglohr (ed.), *Heroines Without Heroes: Reconstructing Female and National Identities in European Cinema, 1945–51*, London and New York: Cassell, pp. 77–88.
Lebeau, V. (2001), *Psychoanalysis and cinema: the play of shadows*, London: Wallflower.
Lebeau, V. (2008), *Childhood and Cinema*, London: Reaktion Books.
Leenhardt, J. (1973), *Lecture politique du roman: la Jalousie d'Alain Robbe-Grillet*, Paris: Éditions de Minuit.
Lefebvre, H. [1961] (2008), *Critique de la vie quotidienne II: Fondements d'une sociologie de la quotidienneté*, Paris: L'Arche.
Lefebvre, H. (1966), 'Preface', in H. Raymond, M. G. Raymond, N. Haumont and M. Coornaert (eds), *L'Habitat pavillonnaire*, Paris: CRU, pp. 3–23.
Lefeuvre, D., N. Jungerman and J. Segura (eds) (2004), *Lettres d'Algérie: André Segura, la guerre d'un appelé*, Paris: Éditions Nicolas Philippe.
Lefèvre, R. (1997), 'Une censure à képi étoilé', in G. Hennebelle, M. Berrah and B. Stora (eds), *La guerre d'Algérie à l'écran*, Condé-sur-Noireau: Corlet, pp. 40–5.
Lemalet, M. (1992), *Lettres d'Algérie*, Paris: JC Lattès.
Lépingle, G. (2014a), 'Les Modèles', in G. Lépingle and M. Uzal (eds), *Guy Gilles: Un cinéaste au fil du temps*, Crisnée: Éditions Yellow, pp. 227–34.
Lépingle, G. (2014b), 'Une filmographie', in G. Lépingle and M. Uzal (eds), *Guy Gilles: Un cinéaste au fil du temps*, Crisnée: Éditions Yellow, pp. 9–40.
Lequeret, E. (2004), 'Rencontre avec Marc Sator', *Cahiers du cinéma*, November, p. 25.
Lindeperg, S. (2014), *Les écrans de l'ombre: la seconde Guerre mondiale dans le cinéma français, 1944–1969*, Paris: Edition Points.
Livak, L. (2000), 'The place of suicide in the French avant-garde of the inter-war period', *Romanic Review*, 91: 3, pp. 245–62.
Louis, M. (2007), 'Caroline Eades, *Le cinéma post-colonial français*', *Questions de communication*, 12, pp. 1–3.
Lowenstein, A. (1998), 'Films without a face: shock horror in the cinema of Georges Franju', *Cinema Journal*, 37: 4, pp. 37–58.
Lowenstein, A. (2005), *Shocking Representation: Historical Trauma, National Cinema and the Modern Horror Film*, New York: Columbia University Press.
Lunenfeld, P. (1994), '"There are people in the streets who've never had a chance to speak": James Blue and the complex documentary', *Journal of Film and Video*, 46: 1, pp. 21–33.
MacCabe, C. and L. Mulvey (1989), 'Images of women, images of sexuality: some films by J. L. Godard', in L. Mulvey (ed.), *Visual and Other Pleasures*, Houndsmill and New York: Palgrave, pp. 49–62.

McDonnell, H. (2020), 'Complicity and memory in soldiers' testimonies of the Algerian war of decolonisation in *Esprit* and *Les Temps modernes*', *Memory Studies*, 13: 6, pp. 952–68.

McDougall, J. (2017), *A History of Algeria*, Cambridge: Cambridge University Press.

Macheret, M. (2008), 'Guy Gilles: *L'Amour à la mer/Au pan coupé/Le clair de terre*', *Critikat*, 9 December, <https://www.critikat.com/dvd-livres/dvd/coffret-guy-gilles/> (last accessed 25 February 2020).

MacMaster, N. (2009), *Burning the Veil: The Algerian War and the 'Emancipation' of Muslim Women, 1954–62*, Manchester: Manchester University Press.

McNeill, I. (2010), *Memory and the Moving Image: French Film in the Digital Era*, Edinburgh: Edinburgh University Press.

Manceron, G. (2011), 'La Triple occultation d'un massacre', in M. Péju and P. Péju (eds), *Le 17 octobre 1961 des Algériens*, Paris: La Découverte, pp. 111–85.

Marchand, B. (1993), *Paris : Histoire d'une ville*, Paris: Éditions du Seuil.

Margulies, I. (2004), '*Chronicle of a Summer* (1960) as *Autocritique* (1959): a transition in the French Left', *Quarterly Review of Film and Video*, 21: 3, pp. 173–85.

Marie, M. (2003), *The French New Wave: An Artistic School*, Oxford: Blackwell.

Marie, M. and F. Vanoye (1983), 'Comment parler la bouche pleine?', *Communications*, 38, pp. 51–77.

Marker, C. (2001), 'Self-censorship and Chris Marker's *Le Joli Mai*', *French Cultural Studies*, 12: 34, pp. 23–41.

Martin, C. (2013), 'Skin deep: bodies without limits in "Hiroshima mon amour"', *French Forum*, 38: 1/2, pp. 267–82.

Martin, M. (1962), *Les Lettres françaises*, 26 July.

Martin, M. (1963a), 'Un problème: la Guerre d'Algérie au cinéma', *Cinéma 63*, 72, pp. 58–64, 143–49.

Martin, M. (1963b), 'Entretien avec Louis Malle', *Les Lettres françaises*, 10–16 October.

Martini, L. (1997), *Racines de papier: essai sur l'expression littéraire de l'identité pieds-noirs*, Paris: Publisud.

Mattei, G-M. (1958), 'La Génération algérienne', *Esprit*, May, pp. 818–24.

Mauriac, C. (1963), *Le Figaro littéraire*, 17 October.

Memmi, A. (2003), *The Colonizer and the Colonized*, New York: Routledge.

Metz, C. [1974] (1991), *Film Language; A Semiotics of the Cinema*, New York: Oxford University Press.

Meur, J. L. (1959), 'Histoire d'un acte responsable, le cas Jean Le Meur', *Esprit* 27: 279, pp. 675–707.

Meurice, J-M. (1962), 'Le réel et le fictif (*Les Oliviers de la justice*)', *Cahiers du cinéma*, 134, August, pp. 56–60.

Mignolo, W. D. (2007). 'Delinking: the rhetoric of modernity, the logic of coloniality and the grammar of de-coloniality', *Cultural Studies*, 21: 2–3, 449–514.

Mignolo, W. D. and C. Walsh (2018), *On Decoloniality: Concepts, Analytics, Praxis*, Durham, NC: Duke University Press.

Mirzoeff, N. (2011), *The Right to Look: A Counterhistory of Visuality*, Durham and London: Duke University Press.

Monjo, A. (1960), *L'Humanité*, 9 November.

Morag, R. (2012), 'Perpetrator trauma and current Israeli documentary cinema', *Camera Obscura*, 80, 27: 2, pp. 93–132.
Morag, R. (2013), *Waltzing with Bashir: Perpetrator Trauma and Cinema*, London: I. B. Tauris.
Morin, E. [1957] (1984), *Les Stars*, Paris: Editions Galilée.
Morrey, D. and A. Smith (2015), *Jacques Rivette*, Manchester: Manchester University Press.
Muller, J. (1957), *De La pacification à la répression*, Paris: Cahiers du Témoignage Chrétien.
Multeau, N. (2006), 'Quand la guerre est un spectacle', in H. Coutau-Bégarie and P. d'Hugues (eds), *Le cinéma et la guerre*, Paris: CFHM, pp. 147–55.
Mulvey, L. (1996), *Fetishism and Curiosity*, Bloomington and Indianapolis: Indiana University Press.
Murphet, J. (1998), 'Film noir and the racial unconscious', *Screen*, 39: 1, pp. 22–35.
N'Guyen, L. (2006), 'Jean-Luc Godard, René Vautier: "Au nom des larmes dans le noir"', in N. Brenez (ed.), *Jean-Luc Godard: documents*, Paris: Éditions du Centre Pompidou, pp. 398–405.
Naficy, H. (2001), *An Accented Cinema: Exilic and Diasporic Filmmaking*, Princeton, NJ: Princeton University Press.
Narboni, J. (1965), 'Entre deux chaises', *Cahiers du cinéma*, pp. 161–2.
Narboni, J. (2004), 'Une malédiction historique', *Cahiers du cinéma*, November, p. 26.
Naremore, J. (1998), *Acting in the Cinema*, Berkeley and Los Angeles: University of California Press.
Neale, S. (1983), 'Masculinity as spectacle: reflections on men and mainstream cinema', *Screen*, 24: 6, pp. 2–17.
Neupert, R. (2011), '*Adieu Philippine* and Rozier's alternative sound practice', *Studies in French Cinema*, 11: 1, pp. 31–41.
Nichols, B. (1981), *Ideology and the Image: Social Representation in the Cinema and Other Media*, Bloomington: Indiana University Press.
Nichols, B. (1983), 'The voice of documentary', *Film Quarterly*, 36: 3, pp. 17–30.
Nichols, B. (1991), *Representing Reality*, Bloomington: Indiana University Press.
Nichols, B. (2010), 'What gives documentary films a voice of their own?', in *Introduction to Documentary*, Bloomington: Indiana University Press, pp. 67–93.
Nimier, R. (1950), *Le Hussard bleu*, Paris: Gallimard.
Nimier, R. (1953), *Histoire d'un amour*, Paris: Gallimard.
Nora, P. [1961] (2012), *Les Français d'Algérie*, Paris: Christian Bourgois.
O'Brien, A (2000), 'Manipulating visual pleasure in *Muriel*', *Quarterly Review of Film and Video*, 17: 1, 49–61.
O'Leary, A. (2019), *The Battle of Algiers*, Milan: Mimesis International.
O'Riley, M. (2010), *Cinema in an Age of Terror: North Africa, Victimization, and Colonial History*, Lincoln and London: University of Nebraska Press.
Orpen V. (2007), *Cléo de 5 à 7*, London: I. B. Tauris.
Orr, J. (1993), *Cinema and Modernity*, Cambridge: Polity Press.
Ory, P. (1985), *L'anarchisme de droite*, Paris: Grasset.
Osteen, M. (2013), *Nightmare Alley: Film Noir and the American Dream*, Baltimore and London: Johns Hopkins University Press.

Panijel, J. (1948), *La Rage*, Paris: Les Éditions de Minuit.
Parr, H. (2007), 'Collaborative film-making as process, method and text in mental health research', *Cultural Geographies*, 14, pp. 114–38.
Péju, M. (1960), 'Une gauche respectueuse', *Les Temps modernes*, 169–70, pp. 1512–20.
Pelko, S. (1992), 'Punctum caecum, or, of insight and blindness', in S. Žižek (ed.), *Everything You Always Wanted to Know About Lacan: But Were Afraid to Ask Hitchcock*, London and New York: Verso, pp. 106–21.
Père, O. (2017), 'Rencontre avec Alain Cavalier', <http://cinema.arte.tv/fr/article/linsoumis-rencontre-avec-alain-cavalier-lundi-20-mars-22h15> (last accessed 22 March 2018).
Perrault, G. (1961), *Les Parachutistes*, Paris: Éditions du Seuil.
Philippe, C-J. (1966), *Télérama*, 9 January.
Pirelli, G. (ed.) (1962), *Racconti di bambini d'Algeria*, Torino: Einaudi.
Place, J. (1989), 'Women in film noir', in A. Kaplan (ed.), *Women in Film Noir*, London: British Film Institute, pp. 35–67.
Planchais, J. (1958), *Le Malaise de l'armée*, Paris: Plon.
Planche, J-L. (2006), *Sétif 1945: Histoire d'un massacre annoncé*, Paris: Perrin.
Poppi, F. and Eduardo Urios-Aparisi (2018), '*De Corporibus Humanis*: metaphor and ideology in the representation of the human body in cinema', *Metaphor and Symbol*, 33: 4, pp. 295–314.
Portuges, C. (1996), '*Le Colonial Féminin*: women directors interrogate French cinema', in D. Sherzer (ed.), *Cinema, Colonialism, Postcolonialism: Perspectives from the French and Francophone World*, Austin: University of Texas Press, pp. 80–102.
Pozner, V. (1959), *Le lieu du supplice*. Paris, Julliard.
Quemeneur, T. (2011), 'Refuser l'autorité ? Étude des désobéissances de soldats français pendant la guerre d'Algérie (1954–1962)', *Outre-mers*, 98: 370–1, pp. 57–66.
Rabinowitz, P. (1993), 'Wreckage upon wreckage: history, documentary and the ruins of memory', *History and Theory*, 32: 2, pp. 119–37.
Ranchal, M. (1963), 'Tu ne tueras point', *Tribune socialiste*, 18 June.
Rancière, J. (2008), 'The cause of the other', *Parallax*, 4: 2, pp. 25–33.
Rascaroli, L. (2017), *How the Essay Film Thinks*, New York: Oxford University Press.
Rebérioux, M. (1964), 'La gauche socialiste française: "La Guerre sociale" et "Le Mouvement socialiste" face au problème colonial', *Le Mouvement social*, 46, pp. 91–103.
Rees-Roberts, N. and D. Waldron (2015), 'Introduction: Alain Delon, *Then* and *Now*' in N. Rees-Roberts and D. Waldron (eds), *Alain Delon: Style, Stardom, and Masculinity*, New York and London: Bloomsbury, pp. 1–12.
Rejali, D. (2007), *Torture and Democracy*, Princeton and Oxford: Princeton University Press.
Renard, P. (2010), 'La littérature et le cinéma à la hussarde', *Roman 20–50*, 49, pp. 147–56.
Ricoeur, P. (2004), *Memory, History, Forgetting*, Chicago and London: University of Chicago Press.
Robbe-Grillet, A. (1955), *Le Voyeur*, Paris: Les Éditions de Minuit.
Robbe-Grillet, A. (1957), *La Jalousie*, Paris: Les Éditions de Minuit.

Roche, A. (1990), 'La Perte et la parole: témoignages oraux de pied-noirs', in J-P. Rioux (ed.), *La Guerre d'Algérie et les Français*, Paris: Fayard, pp. 526–37.
Ross, K. (1995), *Fast Cars, Clean Bodies: Decolonization and the Reordering of French Culture*, Massachusetts: MIT Press.
Ross, K. (2002), *May '68 and its afterlives*, Chicago: University of Chicago Press.
Rothberg, M. (2009), *Multidirectional Memory: Remembering the Holocaust in the Age of Decolonization*, California: Stanford University Press.
Rousso, H. (1987), *Le Syndrome de Vichy (de 1944 à nos jours)*, Paris: Seuil.
Rousso, H. and E. Conan (1992), *Vichy, un passé qui ne passe pas*, Paris: Fayard.
Ruscio, A. (2012), 'Deux ou trois choses que nous savons du général Bigeard', <http://journals.openedition.org/chrhc/2647> (last accessed 29 March 2018).
Saddington, J. (2010), 'The Representation of Suicide in the Cinema', unpublished doctoral thesis, University of York.
Sadoul, G. (1962a), *Les Lettres françaises*, 24 January.
Sadoul, G. (1962b), *Les Lettres françaises*, 14 June.
Saint-Saëns, I. [2000] (2014), '17 octobre 1961: archéologie d'un silence: avant-propos', *Vacarme*, <http://www.vacarme.org/article44.html> (last accessed 28 August 2015).
Saint-Saëns, I. and J-P. Renouard [2000] (2014), 'Festivals d'un film maudit: entretien avec Jacques Panijel', *Vacarme*, <http://www.vacarme.org/article221.html> (last accessed 28 August 2015).
Sanaker, J. K. (2015), 'Voir avec qui? La guerre d'Algérie à l'écran et la question de la focalisation', in D. Dumontet, V. Porra, K. Kloster and T. Schüller (eds), *Les lieux d'oubli de la Francophonie*, Hildesheim, Zürich and New York: Olms, pp. 123–44.
Sanyal, D. (2010), 'Crabwalk history: torture, allegory, and memory in Sartre', *Yale French Studies*, 118/119, pp. 52–71.
Sanyal, D. (2015), *Memory and complicity: migrations of Holocaust remembrance*, New York: Fordham University Press.
Sarkar, B. and J. Walker (2009), 'Introduction: moving testimonies', in B. Sarkar and J. Walker (eds), *Documentary Testimonies: Global Archives of Suffering*, New York and London: Routledge, pp. 1–34.
Sartelle, J. (1996), 'Dreams and nightmares in the Hollywood blockbuster', in G. Nowell-Smith (ed.), *The Oxford History of World Cinema*, Oxford: Oxford University Press, pp. 516–26.
Sartre, J-P. (1943), *L'Être et le néant*, Paris: Gallimard.
Sartre, J-P. (1948), *Qu'est-ce que la littérature?*, Paris: Gallimard.
Sartre, J-P. [1948] (1964/1965), 'Black Orpheus', *Massachusetts Review*, 6: 1, pp. 13–52.
Sartre, J-P. [1957] (2001), 'You are wonderful', in A. Haddour, S. Brewer and T. McWilliams (trans.), *Colonialism and Neocolonialism*, New York: Routledge, pp. 24–8.
Sartre, J-P. [1958] (2001), 'A victory', in A. Haddour, S. Brewer and T. McWilliams (trans.), *Colonialism and Neocolonialism*, New York: Routledge, pp. 31–8.
Sartre, J-P. [1958] (2001), 'We are all murderers', in A. Haddour, S. Brewer and T. McWilliams (trans.), *Colonialism and Neocolonialism*, New York: Routledge, pp. 29–30.
Sartre, J-P. (1960), *Les Séquestrés d'Altona/The Condemned of Altona*, Paris: Gallimard.
Sartre, J-P. [1962] (2001), 'The sleepwalkers', in A. Haddour, S. Brewer and T. McWilliams (trans.), *Colonialism and Neocolonialism*, New York: Routledge, pp. 72–4.

Scharold, I. (ed.) (2016a), *La guerre d'indépendance algérienne à l'écran*, Würzburg: Königshausen and Neumann.
Scharold, I. (2016b), 'Introduction: La guerre d'indépendance algérienne à l'écran', in I. Scharold (ed.), *La guerre d'indépendance algérienne à l'écran*, Würzburg: Königshausen and Neumann, pp. 7–33.
Scharold, I. (2016c), 'Guerre et torture face à la censure: *Le petit soldat* (1960/63) de Jean-Luc Godard', in I. Scharold (ed.), *La guerre d'indépendance algérienne à l'écran*. Würzburg: Königshausen and Neumann, pp. 67–103.
Schatz, T. (1981), *Hollywood Genres: Formulas, Filmmaking, and the Studio System*, Boston, MA: McGraw Hill.
Schrader, P. (2018), *Transcendental Style in Film: Ozu, Bresson, Dreyer*, Berkeley and Los Angeles: University of California Press.
Sellier, G. (2000), 'Masculinity and politics in New Wave cinema', *Sites: The Journal of Twentieth-Century/Contemporary French Studies*, 4: 2, pp. 471–87.
Sellier, G. (2008), *Masculine Singular: French New Wave Cinema*, Durham, NC: Duke University Press.
Sellier, G. (2010), 'French New Wave cinema and the legacy of male libertinage', *Cinema Journal*, 49: 4, pp. 152–58.
Sellier, G. and N. Burch (2000), 'Evil women in post-war French cinema', in U. Sieglohr (ed.), *Heroines Without Heroes: Reconstructing Female and National Identities in European Cinema, 1945–51*, London and New York: Cassell, pp. 47–62.
Sellier, G. and N. Burch (2014), *The Battle of the Sexes in French Cinema, 1930–1956*, Durham, NC, and London: Duke University Press.
Servan-Schreiber, J-J. (1957), *Lieutenant en Algérie*, Paris: Julliard.
Sessions, J. (2011), *By Sword and Plow: France and the Conquest of Algeria*, Ithaca, NY: Cornell University Press.
Sharpe, M. (2013), 'Representations of space in Assia Djebar's *La nouba des femmes du Mont Chenoua*', *Studies in French Cinema*, 13: 3, pp. 215–25.
Sharpe, M. (2015), 'Representing masculinity in postcolonial Algerian cinema', *Journal of North African Studies*, 20: 3, pp. 450–65.
Sharpe. M. (2017), 'Screening decolonisation through privatisation in two New Wave films: *Adieu Philippine* and *La Belle Vie*', *Studies in French Cinema*, 17: 2, pp. 129–43.
Sharpe, M. (2019a), 'Star faces and star bodies in an age of atrocity: Alain Cavalier's *L'Insoumis* and Mark Robson's *Les Centurions*', *French Studies*, 74: 1, pp. 55–70.
Sharpe, M. (2019b), 'Tracing the shadows of Occupation: memory as "screen" in *La Dénonciation* (1962) and *Tu ne tueras point* (1961/1963)', *Modern and Contemporary France*, 28: 1, pp. 1–17.
Shepard, T. (2017), *Sex, France, and Arab Men: 1962–1979*, Chicago and London: University of Chicago Press.
Sherzer, D. (1996), 'Introduction', in D. Sherzer (ed.), *Cinema, Colonialism, Postcolonialism: Perspectives from the French and Francophone World*, Austin: University of Texas Press, pp. 1–19.
Shohat, E. (1991), 'Imaging terra incognita: the disciplinary gaze of empire', *Public Culture*, 3: 2, pp. 41–70.

Shohat, E. and R. Stam (1994), *Unthinking Eurocentrism: Multiculturalism and the Media*, New York: Routledge.
Shohat, E. and R. Stam (2014), 'Afterword: history, empire, resistance', in R. Weaver-Hightower and P. Hulme (eds), *Postcolonial Film: History, Empire, Resistance*, London and New York: Routledge, pp. 282–300.
Sigg, B. (1989), *Le Silence et la honte*, Paris: Messidor/Éditions sociales.
Silverman, M. (1999), *Facing Postmodernity: Contemporary French Thought on Culture and Society*, London and New York: Routledge.
Silverman, M. (2013), *Palimpsestic Memory: The Holocaust and Colonialism in French and Francophone Fiction and Film*, New York and Oxford: Berghahn.
Silverman, M. (2015), 'Introduction: Lazarus and the modern world', in M. Silverman and G. Pollock (eds), *Concentrationary Art: Jean Cayrol, the Lazarean and the Everyday in Post-war Film, Literature, Music and the Visual Arts*, New York and Oxford: Berghahn, pp. 1–28.
Simon, P-H. (1957), *Contre la torture*, Paris: Editions du Seuil.
Simonet, T. and Enrico, R. (1974), 'Filming inner life: the works of Robert Enrico', *Cinema Journal*, 14: 1, pp. 51–9.
Smith, M. (2005), '*The Battle of Algiers*: colonial struggle and collective allegiance', in D. Slocum (ed.), *Terrorism, Media, Liberation*, New Brunswick, New Jersey and London: Rutgers University Press, pp. 94–110.
Sobchack, V. (1984), 'Inscribing ethical space: ten propositions on death, representation, and documentary', *Quarterly Review of Film Studies*, 9: 4, pp. 283–300.
Solanas F. and Getino, O. (1970–1), 'Towards a third cinema', *Cinéaste*, 4: 3, pp. 1–10.
Sontag, S. (2009), *Against Interpretation*, London: Penguin.
Southern, N. and J. Weissgerber (2006), *The Films of Louis Malle: A Critical Analysis*, Jefferson: McFarland.
Stadler, J. and P. Mitchell (2010), 'Never-Never Land: affective landscapes, the touristic gaze and heterotopic space in Australia', *Studies in Australasian Cinema*, 4: 2, pp. 173–87.
Stam, R. (2004), *Film Theory: An Introduction*, Oxford: Blackwell.
Stam R. and L. Spence (1983), 'Colonialism, racism, and representation: an introduction', *Screen*, 24: 2, pp. 2–20.
Steimatsky, N. (2017), *The Face on Film*, Oxford: Oxford University Press.
Steinlein, A. (2007), *Une esthétique de l'authentique: les films de la nouvelle vague*, Paris: L'Harmattan.
Stil, A. (1957), *Nous nous aimerons demain*, Paris: Les éditeurs français réunis.
Stora B. (1998), *La Gangrène et l'oubli: la mémoire de la guerre d'Algérie*, Paris: La Découverte.
Stora, B. (2001), *Algeria, 1830–2000: A Short History*, Ithaca, NY: Cornell University Press.
Stora, B. (2002), '*La mémoire retrouvée de la guerre d'Algérie*', *Histoire coloniale et postcoloniale*, <https://histoirecoloniale.net/Benjamin-Stora-la-memoire.html> (last accessed 5 July 2021).
Stora, B. (2004), *Imaginaires de guerre: Algérie, Viêt-Nam, en France et aux États-Unis*, Paris: La Découverte.

Stora, B. (2014), 'The Algerian War: memory through cinema', *Black Camera*, 6: 1, pp. 96–107.
Surkis, J. (2010), 'Ethics and violence, Simone de Beauvoir, Djamila Boupacha, and the Algerian War', *French Politics, Culture and Society*, 28: 2, pp. 38–55.
Talbott, J. (1976), 'The myth and reality of the paratrooper', *Armed Forces and Society*, 3: 1, pp. 69–86.
Talbott, J. (1981), *The War Without a Name: France in Algeria, 1954–1962*, London: Faber and Faber.
Tasker, Y. (1993), *Spectacular Bodies: Gender, Genre, and the Action Cinema*, London and New York: Routledge.
Temple, M. and M. Witt (2004), 'Introduction: 1960–2004, a New World', in M. Temple and M. Witt (eds), *The French Cinema Book*, London: British Film Institute, pp. 183–93.
Thénault, S. (2008), 'L'OAS à Alger en 1962. Histoire d'une violence terroriste et de ses agents', *Annales. Histoire, Sciences Sociales*, 63: 5, pp. 977–1001.
Thénault, S. (2012), *Histoire de la guerre d'indépendance algérienne*, Paris: Flammarion.
Thiher, A. (1973), 'The drug addict as a tragic hero', *PMLA*, 1: 88, pp. 34–40.
Thirard, P. L. (1961), 'L'affaire "Tu ne tueras pas"', *Les Lettres françaises*, 18 October.
Thomas, M. (2000), *The French North African Crisis: Colonial Breakdown and Anglo-French Relations 1945–1962*, London: Palgrave Macmillan.
Todorov, T. (1992), *Les abus de la mémoire*, Paris: Arléa.
Tomlinson, E. (2001), 'Torture, fiction and the repetition of horror: ghost-writing the past in Algeria and Argentina', unpublished doctoral thesis, University of Cambridge.
Tomlinson, E. (2004), 'Rebirth in sorrow: *La Bataille d'Alger*', *French Studies*, 58: 3, pp. 357–70.
Torok, J.-P. (1964), 'La Gangrène', *Positif*, 60, pp. 82–5.
Truffaut, F. (1954), 'Une certaine tendance du cinéma français', *Cahiers du cinéma*, 6: 31, p. 15.
Turim, M. (1989), *Flashbacks in Film: Memory and History*, London and New York: Routledge.
Urry, J. (1990), *The Tourist Gaze: Leisure and Travel in Contemporary Societies*, London: Sage.
Uzal, M. (2014), 'Un film à la mer', in G. Lépingle and M. Uzal (eds), *Guy Gilles: Un cinéaste au fil du temps*, Crisnée: Éditions Yellow, pp. 67–70.
Vergès, F. (2010), 'Wandering souls and returning ghosts: writing the history of the dispossessed', *Yale French Studies*, 118/119, pp. 136–54.
Vidal, B. (2019), 'De dessins d'enfants au film d'agit-prop : la genèse du film *J'ai huit ans*', *Genesis*, 49, pp. 179–85.
Vidal-Naquet, P. (1963), *Torture: Cancer of Democracy: France and Algeria 1954–62*, London: Penguin.
Vidal-Naquet, P. (1972), *La Torture dans La République*, Paris: Les Éditions de Minuit.
Vidal-Naquet, P. (1986), 'Une fidélité têtue', *Vingtième Siècle, revue d'histoire*, 10, 1986, pp. 3–18.
Vidal-Naquet, P. (2001), *Les crimes de l'armée française, Algérie 1954–1962*, Paris: La Découverte.

Vince, N. (2015), *Our Fighting Sisters: Nation, Memory and Gender in Algeria, 1954–2012*, Manchester: Manchester University Press.
Vince, N. (2020), *The Algerian War, The Algerian Revolution*, Switzerland: Palgrave.
Vincendeau, G. (2000), *Stars and Stardom in French Cinema*, London and New York: Continuum.
Vincendeau, G. and C. Gauteur (2006), *Jean Gabin: Anatomie d'un mythe*, Paris: Nouveau Monde.
Virilio, P. (1999), *War and Cinema, The Logistics of Perception*, London and New York: Verso.
Virtue, N. (2013), Jacques Demy's *Les Parapluies de Cherbourg*: a national allegory of the French-Algerian war', *Studies in French Cinema*, 13: 2, pp. 127–40.
Wallenbrock, N. B. (2020), *The Franco-Algerian War through a Twenty-First Century Lens*, London: Bloomsbury.
Weaver-Hightower, R. and J. Lahti (2020), 'Reel settler colonialism: gazing, reception, and production of global settler cinemas', in R. Weaver-Hightower and J. Lahti (eds), *Cinematic Settlers: The Settler Colonial World in Film*, New York: Routledge, pp. 1–10.
Weiner, S. (2001), *Enfants terribles: youth and femininity in the mass media in France, 1945–1968*, Baltimore and London: Johns Hopkins University Press.
Wetta, F. (1992), *Celluloid Wars: A Guide to Film and the American Experience of War*, New York: Greenwood Press.
Wiles, M. (2012), *Jacques Rivette*, Illinois: Illinois University Press.
Williams, T. (2018), 'Escape from an oppressive present: the French occupation films of Claude Autant-Lara', *FilmInt.*, 16: 2, pp. 121–5.
Wilson, E. (2006), *Alain Resnais*, Manchester: Manchester University Press.
Wyschogrod, E. (1998), *An Ethics of Remembering: History, Heterology, and the Nameless Others*, Chicago and London: University of Chicago Press.
Xavier, I. (2004), 'Historical allegory', in T. Miller and R. Stam (eds), *A Companion to Film Theory*, Oxford: Blackwell Publishing, pp. 333–62.
Yampolsky, M. and L. Joseph (1994), 'Mask face and machine face', *TDR*, 38: 3, pp. 60–74.
Youdelman, J. (1982), 'Narration, invention and history: a documentary dilemma', *Cinéaste*, 12: 2, pp. 8–15.
Zand, N. (1963), 'Le Dossier philippine', *Cahiers du cinéma*, 148: 25, pp. 32–9.
Zand, N. (1964), 'Entretien avec Alain Cavalier', *Le Monde*, 28 September.
Zarobell, J. (2009), *Empire of Landscape: Space and Ideology in French Colonial Algeria*, Pennsylvania: Penn State University Press.
Zimmerman, D. (1961), *80 exercices en zone interdite*, Paris: Éditions Robert Morel.
Zimmerman, D. (1989), 'Préface', in B. Sigg (ed.), *Le Silence et la honte*, Paris: Messidor/Éditions sociales, pp. 8–10.

FILMOGRAPHY

Akerman, Chantal, 1968: *Blow Up My Town (Saute ma ville)*
Allégret, Marc, 1949: *Merry-Go-Round (Manèges)*
Autant-Lara, Claude, 1946: *The Devil in the Flesh (Le Diable au corps)*
Autant-Lara, Claude, 1956: *The Trip Across Paris (La Traversée de Paris)*
Autant-Lara, Claude, 1958: *Love Is My Profession (En cas de malheur)*
Autant-Lara, Claude, 1963: *Thou Shalt Not Kill (Tu ne tueras point/L'Objecteur)*
Baratier, Jacques, 1962: *The Doll (La Poupée)*
Bardem, Juan Antonio, 1955: *Death of a Cyclist*
Beauvois, Xavier, 2010: *Of Gods and Men (Des hommes et des dieux)*
Bernard-Aubert, Claude, 1960: *My Baby is Black! (Les lâches vivent d'espoir)*
Blasetti, Alessandro, 1959: *European Nights (Nuits d'Europe)*
Blier, Bertrand, 1974: *Going Places (Les Valseuses)*
Blue, James, 1960: *Amal*
Blue, James, 1978: *Who Killed the Fourth Ward?*
Blue, James, 1979: *The Invisible City*
Bresson, Robert, 1951: *Diary of a Country Priest (Journal d'un curé de campagne)*
Bresson, Robert, 1956: *A Man Escaped (Un condamné à mort s'est échappé)*
Bresson, Robert, 1959: *Pickpocket*
Broca, Philippe de, 1960: *The Love Game (Les jeux de l'amour)*
Broderie, Bernard, 1959: *Sergeant X. (Sergent X.)*
Carné, Marcel, 1958: *Young Sinners (Les Tricheurs)*
Carpita, Paul, 1958: *Break Time (La Récréation)*
Carpita, Paul, 1961: *Marseille Without Sun (Marseille sans soleil)*
Carpita, Paul, 1962: *Love, Tomorrow (Demain L'amour)*

Cavalier, Alain, 1962: *The Combat on the Island* (*Le Combat dans l'île*)
Cavalier, Alain, 1964: *The Unvanquished* (*L'Insoumis*)
Cayatte, André, 1954: *Before the Deluge* (*Avant le déluge*)
Cedar, Joseph, 2007: *Beaufort*
Chabrol, Claude, 1958: *The Cousins* (*Les Cousins*)
Chabrol, Claude, 1958: *Handsome Serge* (*Le Beau Serge*)
Chabrol, Claude, 1969: *The Butcher* (*Le Boucher*)
Chalon, Guy, 1959: *58 2/B*
Charef, Mehdi, 2007: *Summer of '62* (*Cartouches Gauloises*)
Cimino, Michael, 1978: *The Deer Hunter*
Clément, Pierre, 1958: *Algerian Refugees* (*Réfugiés algériens*)
Clément, Pierre, 1958: *Sakiet sidi Youssef*
Clément, René, 1946: *The Battle of the Rails* (*La Bataille du rail*)
Clément, René, 1960: *Purple Noon* (*Plein Soleil*)
Clouzot, Henri-Georges, 1947: *Quay of the Goldsmiths* (*Quai des Orfèvres*)
Colpi, Henri, 1961: *A Very Long Absence* (*Une aussi longue absence*)
Cosmatos, Georges P., 1985: *Rambo: First Blood Part II*
Cuau, Bernard, 1962: *Nanterre One Day* (*Nanterre un jour*)
Cziffra, Geza von, 1955: *Bandits of the Autobahn* (*Banditen der Autobahn*)
Daquin, Louis, 1946: *Homeland* (*Patrie*)
Decoin, Henri, 1959: *The Cat* (*La Chatte*)
Demy, Jacques, 1964: *The Umbrellas of Cherbourg* (*Les Parapluies de Cherbourg*)
Denis, Claire, 1988: *Chocolate* (*Chocolat*)
Denis, Claire, 1999: *Good Work* (*Beau travail*)
Djebar, Assia, 1979: *The Nouba of the Women of Mount Chenoua* (*La Nouba des femmes du Mont Chenoua*)
Dmytryk, Edward, 1944: *Murder My Sweet*
Doniol-Valcroze, Jacques, 1962: *The Denunciation* (*La Dénonciation*)
Dovzhenko, Alexander, 1930: *Earth* (*Zemlya*)
Dréville, Jean, 1957: *The Suspects* (*Les Suspects*)
Drew, Robert, 1960: *Primary*
Dupont, Jacques, 1950: *Savage Africa* (*Congolaise*)
Dupont, Jacques, 1954: *Truckers in the Desert* (*Les Routiers du désert*)
Dupont, Jacques, 1955: *Heartbreak Ridge* (*Crèvecoeur*)
Dupont, Jacques, 1960: *Trapped by Fear* (*Les Distractions*)
Durand, Philippe, 1961: *Postal Sector 89098* (*Secteur postal 89098*)
Duvivier, Julian, 1935: *La Bandera*
Duvivier, Julian, 1937: *Pépé le Moko*
Duvivier, Julian, 1946: *Panic* (*Panique*)
Duvivier, Julian, 1959: *The Devil is a Woman* (*La Femme et le Pantin*)
Dwan, Allan, 1949: *Sands of Iwo Jima*
Elton, Arthur and Edgar Anstey, 1935: *Housing Problems*
Eisenstein, Sergei, 1925: *Battleship Potemkin* (*Bronenosets Potyomkin*)
Eisenstein, Sergei, 1925: *Strike* (*Stachka*)
Eisenstein, Sergei, 1927: *October: Ten Days That Shook the World* (*Oktyabr': Desyat' dney kotorye potryasli mir*)

Enrico, Robert, 1964: *The Good Life (La Belle vie)*
Feuillade, Louis, 1915-1916: *The Vampires (Les Vampires)*
Feyder, Jacques, 1934: *Le Grand jeu*
Franju, Georges, 1960: *Eyes Without a Face (Les Yeux sans visage)*
Freund, Karl, 1932: *The Mummy*
Garnett, Tay, 1943: *Bataan*
Gentilomo, Giacomo and Sergio Corbucci, 1961: *Maciste Against the Ghost (Maciste contre le fantôme)*
Gilles, Guy, 1958: *Setting Sun (Soleil éteint)*
Gilles, Guy and Marc Sator, 1962: *Slanted Kisses (Au biseau des baisers)*
Godard, Jean-Luc, 1960: *Breathless (À bout de souffle)*
Godard, Jean-Luc, 1960/1963: *The Little Soldier (Le Petit soldat)*
Godard, Jean-Luc, 1961: *A Woman is a Woman (Une Femme est une femme)*
Godard, Jean-Luc, 1962: *To Live Her Life (Vivre sa vie)*
Godard, Jean-Luc, 1963: *Contempt (Le Mépris)*
Godard, Jean-Luc, 1989–1999: *Histories of Cinema (Histoire(s) du cinéma)*
Goldenberg, Daniel, 1959: *The Return (Le Retour)*
Hädrich, Rolf, 1962: *The Sleep of the Righteous (Der schlaf der gerechten)*
Hawks, Howard, 1953: *Gentlemen Prefer Blondes*
Herman, Jean, 1961: *Actua-tilt*
Herman, Jean, 1962: *The Wrong Path (Le Chemin de la mauvaise route)*
Herman, Jean, 1963: *On-Leave (La Quille)*
Hitchcock, Alfred, 1954: *Rear Window*
Hitchcock, Alfred, 1958: *Vertigo*
Hitchcock, Alfred, 1959: *North by Northwest*
Hudson, John, 1945: *The Battle of San Pietro*
Hudson, John, 1950: *The Asphalt Jungle*
Jarman, Derek, 1993: *Blue*
Kelly, Gene and Stanley Donen, 1952: *Singin' in the Rain*
Kubrick, Stanley, 1987: *Full Metal Jacket*
Kyrou, Ado, 1959: *Sometimes on Sunday (Parfois le Dimanche)*
Lang, Fritz, 1959: *The Indian Tomb (Le Tombeau hindou)*
Lanzmann, Claude, 1985: *Shoah*
Lean, David, 1962: *Lawrence of Arabia*
Lefèvre, Raymond, 1966: *The Evian Disagreements (Les désaccords d'Évian)*
Le Masson, Yann, Olga Baïdar-Poliakoff and René Vautier, 1961: *I Am 8 Years Old (J'ai 8 ans)*
Luntz, Édouard, 1959: *Draft Children (Les Enfants des courants d'air)*
Malle, Louis, 1958: *Elevator to the Gallows (Ascenseur pour l'échafaud)*
Malle, Louis, 1963: *The Fire Within (Le Feu follet)*
Malle, Louis, 1987: *Goodbye, Children (Au revoir les enfants)*
Maoz, Samuel, 2009: *Lebanon*
Marker, Chris, 1957: *Letter from Siberia (Lettre de Siberie)*
Marker, Chris, 1962: *The Jetty (La Jetée)*
Marker, Chris, 1996: *Level Five*

Marker, Chris and Pierre Lhomme, 1963: *The Lovely Month of May* (*Le Joli Mai*)
Marshall, John and Robert Gardner, 1957: *The Hunters*
Maudet, Christian, aka Christian-Jaque, 1959: *Babette Goes to War* (*Babette s'en va-t-en guerre*)
Melford, Georges, 1921: *The Sheik*
Melville, Jean-Pierre, 1949: *The Silence of the Sea* (*Le silence de la mer*)
Melville, Jean-Pierre, 1961: *Léon Morin, Priest* (*Léon Morin, prêtre*)
Melville, Jean-Pierre, 1967: *The Samurai* (*Le Samouraï*)
Mograbi, Avi, 2008: *Z32*
Morin, Edgar and Jean Rouch, 1961: *Chronicle of a Summer* (*Chronique d'un été*)
Ophüls, Marcel, 1969: *The Sorrow and the Pity* (*Le Chagrin et la pitié*)
Panijel, Jacques, 1962: *October in Paris* (*Octobre à Paris*)
Panijel, Jacques and Jean-Paul Sassy, 1961: *Skin and Bones* (*La Peau et les Os*)
Pélégri, Jean and James Blue, 1962: *The Olive Trees of Justice* (*Les Oliviers de la justice*)
Pialat, Maurice, 1961: *Love Exists* (*L'Amour existe*)
Pontecorvo, Gillo, 1966: *The Battle of Algiers* (*La Bataille d'Alger*)
Powell, Michael and Emeric Pressburger, 1947: *Black Narcissus*
Pudovkin, Vsevolod, 1926: *Mother* (*Mat*)
Ray, Nicholas, 1948: *They Live by Night*
Renoir, Jean, 1937: *The Grand Illusion* (*La Grande Illusion*)
Renoir, Jean, 1939: *The Rules of the Game* (*La Règle du jeu*)
Resnais, Alain, 1956: *Night and Fog* (*Nuit et brouillard*)
Resnais, Alain, 1959: *Hiroshima, My Love* (*Hiroshima mon amour*)
Resnais, Alain, 1961: *Last Year in Marienbad* (*L'Année dernière à Marienbad*)
Resnais, Alain, 1963: *Muriel or the Time of a Return* (*Muriel ou le temps d'un retour*)
Rivette, Jacques, 1961: *Paris Belongs to Us* (*Paris nous appartient*)
Rivette, Jacques, 1966: *The Nun* (*La Religieuse*)
Robson, Mark, 1949: *Home of the Brave*
Robson, Mark, 1954: *The Bridges at Toko-Ri*
Robson, Mark, 1966: *Lost Command* (*Les Centurions*)
Rossellini, Roberto, 1948: *Germany, Year Zero* (*Germania anno zero*)
Roüan, Brigitte, 1990: *Overseas* (*Outremer*)
Rozier, Jacques, 1963: *Goodbye Philippine* (*Adieu Philippine*)
Saslavsky, Luis, 1959: *Way of the Wicked* (*Ce corps tant désiré*)
Sator, Marc, 1964: *The Algerian Summer* (*L'Été algérien*)
Sautet, Claude, 1960: *Consider All Risks* (*Classe tous risques*)
Schoendoerffer, Pierre, 1977: *The Drummer Crab* (*Le Crabe-tambour*)
Sica, Vittorio De, 1948: *Bicycle Thieves* (*Ladri di biciclette*)
Siri, Florent-Emilio, 2007: *The Intimate Enemy* (*L'Ennemi intime*)
Terme, Louis, 1962: *The Girl of the Road* (*Fille de la route*)
Thiele, Rolf, 1959: *Eva* (*Die Halbzarte*)
Thompson, Lee, 1961: *The Guns of Navarone*
Truffaut, François, 1957: *The Mischief Makers* (*Les Mistons*)
Truffaut, François, 1962: *Jules and Jim* (*Jules et Jim*)
Truffaut, François, 1981: *The Last Metro* (*Le Dernier métro*)

Vadim, Roger, 1956: *And God Created Woman (Et Dieu . . . créa la femme)*
Vadim, Roger 1962: *Love on a Pillow (Le Repôs du guerrier)*
Valère, Jean, 1961: *Time Out for Love (Les Grandes personnes)*
Varda, Agnès, 1962: *Cléo from 5 to 7 (Cléo de 5 à 7)*
Vaudoux, Philippe, 1960: *Bitter Aftertaste (La Bouche amère)*
Vautier, René, 1950: *Africa 50 (Afrique 50)*
Vautier, René, 1958: *Algeria is Burning (Algérie en flammes)*
Verneuil, Henri, 1962: *A Monkey in Winter (Un singe en hiver)*
Vertov, Dziga, 1929: *Man with a Movie Camera (Chelovek s kino-apparatom)*
Vidor, King, 1932: *Bird of Paradise*
Villiers, François, 1959: *Green Harvest (La Verte moisson)*
Wagner, Jean, 1960: *This Dull World (Ce monde banal)*
Walsh, Raoul, 1947: *The Man I Love*
Watt, Harry and Basil Wright, 1936: *Night Mail*
Welles, Orson, 1941: *Citizen Kane*
Welles, Orson, 1947: *The Lady from Shanghai*
Wheeler, René, 1959: *Towards Ecstasy (Vers l'extase)*
Wilder, Billy, 1944: *Double Indemnity*

INDEX

Page numbers in *italics* refer to images; 'n' to chapter note number.

Abbas, Ferhat, 3
abjection, 69, 82, 83, *83*, 211, 212
absence
   of Algerians, 108, 116, 117, 131n6, 181, 182, 188n15
   of soldiers, 135, 139, 147–9, 152, 154, 158n8, 158n11
absolution, 2, 9, 10, 23, 66, 119, 130, 162, 175, 177, 218, 219
acousmatic, the, 209, 214
acousmatic testimony, 195, 207–10, 222
acquisition, 50, 51, 52, 53, 76, 86, 218
Actualités françaises, Les, 45–6
Adams, Alex, 6, 69, 107–8, 115
adolescence *see* youth
Akerman, Chantal, *Saute ma ville/Blow Up My Town* (1968), 54n2
alcoholism, 77, 92, 93, 94, 97
Algerian National Liberation Front (*Front de libération nationale*, FLN), 4, 5, 8, 9, 19, 71n7, 115, 131n3, 162, 165, 171, 172, 178, 183, 192, 201, 202; *see also* National Liberation Army (*Armée de libération nationale*, ALN)
Algerian War of Independence, 3–7, 19, 26n3, 27n10, 38, 80, 100n7, 105, 107, 114, 119, 131n9, 133, 134, 135, 138, 141, 143, 192, 196, 210, 217
Algerians, absence of, 108, 116, 117, 131n6, 181, 182, 188n15
Algiers, 3, 4, 9, 61, 71n2, 79, 161, 162, 165–6, 169–72, *172*, 175, 176, 179, *179*, 181–5, 187n8, 187n10, 189n20
   Battle of, 6, 66, 70, 113, 171, 191
   Madrague, La, 176, 188n15, 189nn20–1
Alleg, Henri, 6, 7, 26n5, 75, 192
allegory, 6, 23, 29n26, 108, 113, 114–15, 126, 128–9, 130n2, 131n4, 138, 143–4, 165, 166, 170, 186
Allégret, Marc, *Manèges/Merry-Go-Round* (1949), 136

249

Alsop, Elizabeth, 178
amnesia *see* forgetting
anamnesis *see* remembering
Anstey, Edgar *see* Elton, Arthur, and
anti-colonialism, 1, 14, 16, 27n14, 49, 76–7, 108, 163, 183, 187n9, 190, 191, 196, 204, 205, 212–13, 214, 221
anti-Semitism, 77, 92, 126, 131n8
anxiety, 16–17, 41, 63–4, 95–6, 138–9, 156, 162, 170, 176, 223n4
aphonic voice, 200
archival footage, 26n1, 38, 45, 49, 106, 199, 203, 204, 206
    newsreels, 45–6, 47, 193, 216n4
archive, 20, 22, 50, 51, 139, 196, 209, 213
    anarchive, 222–3
art cinema, 97
    European, 170–1
    modernist, 158n12, 210, 220
associative montage, 203
atrocity, 1, 2–3, 5, 7–8, 10–11, 12, 13, 24, 25, 27n10, 27n14, 35, 38, 43, 44, 54, 60, 61, 64, 65, 66, 67, 70, 71, 79, 84, 89, 106, 108, 109, 115, 126, 127, 129, 136, 141, 152–6, 162, 165, 175, 176, 191, 192, 195, 205, 206, 208, 210, 215, 217, 218, 222
Audin, Maurice/Maurice Audin Committee, 192, 196, 207
Aurenche, Jean, 119
Austin, Guy, 13, 59–60, 64, 131n6, 149, 164–5, 181, 207, 208
Autant-Lara, Claude, 119–20, 131n8
    En cas de malheur/*Love Is My Profession* (1958), 119
    La Traversée de Paris/*The Trip Across Paris* (1956), 59, 119
    Le Diable au corps/*The Devil in the Flesh* (1946), 11
    Tu ne tueras point/*L'Objecteur*/*Thou Shalt Not Kill* (1963), 18, 20, 25, 105, 109, 110, 117, 119–30, *121*, *130*, 130n1, 131nn9–10, 219

auteur film, 15, 16, 18, 21, 24, 174
automobiles *see* cars
avance sur recettes, l' (advance against earnings), 18, 45
Avant-scène du cinéma, L', 37

Bachelard, Gaston, 124
bad faith, 10, 112, 113, 118
Badley, Linda, 14
Baecque, Antoine de, 19, 29n26, 37, 77, 96, 109
Baïdar-Poliakoff, Olga, 21, 209, 211; *see also* Le Masson, Yann, and
Balzac, Honoré de, 145
Baratier, Jacques, *La Poupée*/*The Doll* (1962), 34
barbouzes, les, 117
Bardem, Juan Antonio, *Death of a Cyclist* (1955), 159n20
Bardot, Brigitte, 39, 58, 60, 67, 100n2, 149, 176, 188n15
Baroncelli, Jean de, 19
Barsky, Georges, 139
Barthes, Roland, 42, 56, 64, 87
Baudrillard, Jean, 35, 40, 87
Bazin, André, 15, 62, 145
Beattie, Keith, 12
Beauregard, George de, 36
beauty, 60–6, 69, 76, 80, 147, 156, 159n20, 180, 182, 218
Beauvoir, Simone de, 39, 54n2, 75, 157n3, 191
Beauvois, Xavier, *Des hommes et des dieux*/*Of Gods and Men* (2010), 23, 181
Belmondo, Jeal-Paul, 80, *81*, 84, 85–6, 88, 90–1, 218
Benayoun, Robert, 94, 99
Bénédict, Sébastian, 43
Bennehar, Abdelkader, 116
Bernard-Aubert, Claude, *Les lâches vivent d'espoir*/*My Baby is Black!* (1960), 93
Bertin-Maghit, Jean-Pierre, 74, 91, 129–30

betrayal, 9, 63, 68, 93, 136, 149, 155, 159n15, 212
Betz, Mark, 14, 23, 138, 170, 187n7, 217
Bigeard, Marcel, 68, 69, 70–1, 171, 218
blame, 8, 10, 11, 143
Blasetti, Alessandro, *Nuits d'Europe/ European Nights* (1959), 150
Bleys, Jean-Pierre, 120
Blier, Bertrand, *Les Valseuses/Going Places* (1974), 60
blindness, 122, 181
Blondin, Antoine, 76, 77, 79, 85, 97
Blue, James, 170, 175, 187n10
  Amal (1960), 168
  The Invisible City (1979), 187n8
  Who Killed the Fourth Ward? (1978), 187n8
  see also Pélégri, Jean and
body, 1, 2, 6–7, 28, 58, 61, 63, 64, 65, 66, 68, 91, 94, 99, 121, 124, 125, 126, 129, 156, 158n14, 194, 198, 201, 210, 219
  female, 23, 39, 60, 82, 113, 149, 150
  see also faces
Bolshevism, 212–14
Bonitzer, Pascal, 193, 215
Borde, Raymond, 118, 147, 157n6, 208
Bordwell, David, 153
Bost, Pierre, 119
Boulevard de l'Impératrice, 170–1
Boupacha, Djamila, 8, 26n6, 75
Boutaghou, Maya, 11, 24
Bowles, Brett, 216n4
Branche, Raphaëlle, 7, 44, 71n5, 73, 114
Brando, Marlon, 63
Brasseur, Claude, 79, *81*, *83*, 88
Braudy, Leo, 63
Braunberger, Pierre, 131n8
Bresson, Robert, 174, 175, 187n10
  Journal d'un curé campagne/Diary of a Country Priest (1951), 174, 187n11
  Pickpocket (1959), 174
  Un condamné à mort d'est échappé/A Man Escaped (1956), 174

Breton, Émile, 143
Broca, Philippe de, *Les jeux de l'amour/ The Love Game* (1960), 55n6
Broderie, Bernard, *Sergent X./Sergeant X.* (1959), 59
Brown, James, 182
Brozgal, Lia, 20, 197, 222
Brun, Catherine, 75–6
Brune, Jean, 180
Burch, Noël, 136, 137

Cadé, Michel, 16
Cahiers du cinéma, 15, 21, 22, 36, 109, 187n10, 215
Camera Obscura, 22
Camus, Albert, 108, 180, 182, 184, 185, 189n22
cancer (figurative), 5–6, 114
Capdenac, Michel, 129
Carné, Marcel, *Les Tricheurs/Young Sinners* (1958), 96, 100n2, 132n10
Carpita, Paul, 17
  Demain L'amour/Love, Tomorrow (1962), 17, 28n21, 222
  La Récréation/Break Time (1958), 17, 28n19, 206
  Marseille sans soleil/Marseille Without Sun (1961), 17, 28n20
Carrefour, 79
Carroll, David, 181
cars, 38, 41, 49, 62, 76, 77, 84, 85–8, 88, 90, 100n3, 138, 171, 186
Carta, Jean, 211–12
cartography, 183
castration, 7, 25, 71n4, 72–6, 78, 80–4, 85, 90, 91, 92, 94, 96–8, 99, 101n9, 119, 219
Catholicism/Catholic Church, 29n24, 120, 122, 123, 127
Cavalier, Alain
  Le Combat dans l'île/The Combat on the Island (1962), 65, 77, 78, 206
  L'Insoumis/The Unvanquished (1964), 24, 51, 58, 60–6, *61*, 71, 71n2, 113, 156n1, 218

Cayatte, André, 21
  Avant le déluge/Before the Deluge (1954), 137
Cedar, Joseph, *Beaufort* (2007), 12
censorship, 1, 17–21, 24, 26n5, 28n17, 29nn24–5, 45, 65, 108, 114, 145, 146, 154, 197, 199, 200, 201, 207, 223
  'Anastasia's Scissors', 17, 20
  pre-censorship, 18, 20
  self-censorship, 18, 20, 44, 56
Centre national du cinéma et de l'image animée, Le see National Centre for Cinema and the Moving Image
Chabrol, Claude, 15, 20
  Le Beau Serge/Handsome Serge (1958), 96
  Le Boucher/The Butcher (1969), 83
  Les Cousins/The Cousins (1958), 77, 85
Chalon, Guy, *58 2/B* (1959), 148, 158n9
Champs Élysées, Les, 51, 87, 100n4
Chapier, Henry, 20, 128
Chapman, James, 68
Charef, Mehdi, *Cartouches Gauloises/Summer of '62* (2007), 23
Charonne (massacre), 106, 192, 202–4, 206, 213, 221
Chenoua, Mount, 186, 189n24
Chevassu, François, 157n6, 159n21
child witnesses, 175, 196, 197, 208–11
childhood, 39, 82, 166, 168, 174, 175, 208, 209, 210–11; *see also* youth/adolescence
Chion, Michel, 147, 155, 159n20, 198, 209, 222
choral voice, 215
Christianity, 52, 154, 189n23; *see also* Catholicism/Catholic Church
Cimino, Michael, *The Deer Hunter* (1978), 12
cinéma vérité, 20, 193
Clair, René, 20
Clément, Pierre, 16, 27n14, 201

Réfugiés algériens/Algerian Refugees (1958), 27n14
Sakiet sidi Youssef (1958), 27n14
Clément, René
  La Bataille du rail/The Battle of the Rails (1946), 112
  Plein Soleil/Purple Noon (1960), 63
close-ups, 55n9, 64, 87, 88, 139, 147, 149, 150, 151, 152, 153, 155, 156, 158n12, 159n15, 159n20, 172, 174, 175, 197, 198, 204, 205, 213–14, 214
Clouzot, Henri-Georges, *Quai des Orfèvres/Quay of the Goldsmiths* (1947), 137
CNC *see* National Centre for Cinema and the Moving Image
Cohen, Stanley, 10–11
collaboration, 11–12, 59, 76, 98, 108, 110, 112, 114, 122, 124, 126, 127, 131nn8–9, 134, 139, 165, 212, 221
Collet, Jean, 37
colonial cinema, 164, 169, 170, 187n9
  late-, 17, 20, 21, 22, 23, 24, 25, 28n16, 34, 106, 133, 137–8, 139, 146, 148, 158n8, 161, 181, 206, 217, 218, 221, 222
  post-, 13, 22, 23, 220
colonialism/colonisation, 1, 3, 9, 13, 15, 38, 66, 72, 73, 79, 108, 134, 165, 169, 190, 207, 217, 220; *see also* anti-colonialism; de-colonial; de-colonisation; neo-colonialism
Colpi, Henri, *Une aussi longue absence/A Very Long Absence* (1961), 106
Combat (newspaper), 20, 128
communism, 9, 190, 191, 192, 206, 213; *see also* French Communist Party
Comolli, Jean-Luc, 54
complicity, 2, 23, 25, 26n2, 40, 61, 64, 66, 75, 79, 84, 108, 118–19, 141, 144, 155, 175, 190–2, 195, 205, 215, 218, 219, 222
Conesa, Gabriel, 168

conscientious objection, 25, 109, 120, 126–9, 133, 205, 219
conscription, 5, 8, 20, 34, 37, 38, 44, 45, 49, 50, 69, 73, 75, 93, 106, 133, 135, 140, 153–4, 158n10, 206, 223n4
consent, 89, 187n8
conspiracy, 61, 142, 144, 145, 152, 156
consumerism, 35, 36, 38, *51*, 51–4, 86, 100n4
Cooper, Sarah, 221
copains (male friends), 90
copines (female friends), 39
Corbucci, Sergio *see* Gentilomo, Giacomo and
Cornu, Richard, 84, 91
corpus, 11, 13–14, 17, 23, 74, 114, 170, 180, 217, 222
corvée de bois, la (wood duty), 125
Cosmatos, Georges P., *Rambo: First Blood Part II* (1985), 12
courtrooms, 130, *130*, 194
cover-girls, 51, 85, 87, 89, 150
Cox, Gary, 10
Croombs, Matthew, 19, 22, 35
Cuau, Bernard, *Nanterre un jour/Nanterre One Day* (1962), 34
culpability, 2, 10, 58, 108, 123, 136, 175, 188n17, 192, 199, 219
Cziffra, Geza von, *Banditen der Autobahn/Bandits of the Autobahn* (1955), 11

Dadaism, 98, 99
Dambre, Marc, 77
dandy, 25, 77, 85, 96, 97, 98, 100, 108, 118, 219
Daniel, Joseph, 21–2, 79, 120–1, 149, 157n6, 205, 223n4
Daquin, Louis, *Patrie/Homeland* (1946), 112
darkness, 62, 145, 165, 184–6, 195
daydreams, 46, 47, *48*
De Gaulle, Charles, 4, 9, 10, 71n2, 112
Dean, James, 63

death, 2, 7, 37, 38, 46, 66, 69, 109, 116, 119, 125, 134, 135, 143, 144, 145, 155, 159n21, 192, 200; *see also* suicide
Debord, Guy, 87
Decoin, Henri, *La Chatte/The Cat* (1959), 121
de-colonial, 10, 13–14, 27n11, 56, 218
decolonisation, 7, 13–14, 17, 21–4, 26n2, 36, 37, 39, 45, 49, 50, 59, 60, 65, 69, 71, 72, 73, 96, 107, 109, 114, 126, 131n6, 134, 154, 162–3, 164, 186, 188n17, 190–1, 219
Deleuze, Gilles, 24, 160n22
Delon, Alain, 60–6, *61*, 67, 69, 71
demonstration, 55n10, 106, 114, 162, 196, 199, 202, 215n1
Demy, Jacques, *Les Parapluies de Cherbourg/The Umbrellas of Cherbourg* (1964), 29n26, 38, 60, 149, 158n11, 181
Deneuve, Catherine, 60
denial, 9, 10–11, 105, 112, 130n2
Denis, Claire
  Beau travail/Good Work (1999), 91
  Chocolat/Chocolate (1988), 13, 220
denunciation, 112–13
Depardieu, Gérard, 60
depoliticisation, 21, 22, 37–9, 41, 44, 52, 108, 116, 134
depression, 92, 93, 98
depth, 67, 124, 128, 180
Derocles, Georges, 165
Derrida, Jacques, 184
Deshayes, Fabien, 135, 157n4
desire, 13, 50, 60, 65, 91, 94, 96, 97, 99, 101n9, 118, 142, 144, 151, 161, 174, 176, 182, 219
Dien bien Phu, Battle of, 68
Dine, Philip, 8, 14, 22, 75, 76, 100n5, 106, 107, 130n2, 180, 187n9, 189n23
direct cinema, 193
disciplinary gaze of empire, the, 164, 166, 182

disclosure, 105, 107, 113, 130n2, 209
disease (figurative), 126, 128, 219; see also cancer (figurative); gangrene (figurative); hygiene; sickness (figurative)
disembodiment, 28n16, 106, 140, 159nn20–1, 164, 165, 166, 168, 171, 183, 184, 197, 202, 204, 209
Dittmar, Linda, 12
Djebar, Assia, *La Nouba des femmes du Mont Chenoua/The Nouba of the Women of Mount Chenoua* (1979), 23
Dmytryk, Edward, *Murder My Sweet* (1944), 144–5
Doane, Mary Ann, 193, 194–5, 198
documentary, 16, 20, 25, 27nn13–14, 28n17, 34, 46, 79, 108, 137, 150, 171, 190–215, 221–2
  poetic, 170–1; see also archival footage; non-fiction
Dolar, Mladen, 200, 212
domesticity, 22, 33–6, 38, 40, 41–50, 54n2, 80, 81, 91, 111, 119, 164, 218; see also home-as-haven; interior design
Donadey, Anne, 24, 29n30
Donen, Stanley see Kelly, Gene and
Doniol-Valcroze, Jacques, 15, 20, 109, 112, 128
  La Dénonciation/The Denunciation (1962), 15, 25, 105, 108–19, *110*, *111*, *116*, *117*, 131n8, 131nn5–6, 219
Doty, Alexander, 91
Dovzhenko, Alexander, *Zemlya/Earth* (1930), 213, 214
Dréville, Jean, *Les Suspects/The Suspects* (1957), 110, 131n3, 222
Drew, Robert, *Primary* (1960), 171
Duchen, Claire, 34, 134
duplicity, 136, 138, 141, 151–2, 155, 159n20, 220
Dupont, Jacques, 2, 16, 77–8, 79, 86
  Congolaise/Savage Africa (1950), 79

Crèvecoeur/Heartbreak Ridge (1955), 79
Les Distractions/Trapped by Fear (1960), 25, 51, 72, 75, 76, 77–8, 79–92, *81*, *83*, *88*, 100nn3–4, 218–19
Les Routiers du désert/Truckers in the Desert (1954), 79
Durand, Philippe, 2, 150, 157n6, 158n8
  Secteur postal 89098/Postal Sector 89098 (1961), 16, 19, 25, 51, 133, 136, 139, 146–56, *148*, *156*, 157n7, 158n12, 158n14, 159n21, 159nn17–19, 210, 220, 222
Duras, Marguerite, 176–8
Duvivier, Julian
  La Bandera/Escape from Yesterday (1935), 13, 59
  La Femme et le Pantin/The Devil is a Woman (1959), 149
  Panique/Panic (1946), 11, 137
  Pépé le Moko (1937), 13, 164, 172
Dwan, Allan, *Sands of Iwo Jima* (1949), 68
Dyer, Richard, 58–9, 61, 101n8

Eades, Caroline, 131n6
Echo d'Alger, L', 175
editing, 15, 28n16, 150, 203, 213
Éditions de Minuit, Les, 6
Eisenstein, Sergei
  Bronenosets Potyomkin/Battleship Potemkin (1925), 150, 213, 214
  Oktyabr': Desyat' dney kotorye potryasli mir/October: Ten Days That Shook the World (1927), 150, 213
  Stachka/Strike (1925), 150, 213
Eldridge, Claire, 9, 163, 173, 219, 220
Elsaesser, Thomas, 11, 24, 27n8
Elton, Arthur, and Edgar Anstey, *Housing Problems* (1935), 201
Eluard, Paul, 105
emasculation, 13, 71, 82, 88, 91, 93, 98, 99, 218–19

embodiment, 49, 58–9, 64, 67, 81, 85, 94, 98, 99, 100n3, 122, 123, 127, 130, 148, 154, 159nn20–1, 162, 164, 165, 166, 168, 171, 183, 184, 193, 209, 210, 219, 221; *see also* disembodiment
Enrico, Robert, 44–5, 47
  La Belle vie/The Good Life (1964), 15, 18, 24, 36, 44–54, *48*, *51*, *53*, 55nn6–10, 86, 100n4, 106, 215n3, 218
epistles *see* letters
epistolary, 135–6, 153, 155, 208, 220
Eshun, Kodwo, 16
Esprit (journal), 5, 7, 8, 128
ethics, 2, 8, 10, 11, 12, 23, 24, 25, 36, 40, 44, 52, 56, 58, 60, 63–5, 72, 74, 85, 94, 99, 107–9, 115, 117, 119, 120, 122, 125, 127–8, 130, 133, 134, 174, 186, 188n12, 190, 192, 194, 210, 217–20, 222
Eurocentrism, 13, 79, 115, 172, 193, 202
European art cinema, 170–1
Evans, Martin, 117, 153–4, 157n3, 171
Evian Accords (1962), 4, 10, 18
evidence, 63, 68, 114, 128, 174, 196, 199, 207
expiation, 10, 13, 44, 126–30
Express, L', 5, 20, 60, 75
Ezra, Elizabeth, 136

faces, 24, 34, 39, 42, 51, 53, 60–4, 69, 71, 81, 99, 110, 119, 121–4, 138, 139, 141, 144, 146–56, *156*, 158n13, 159n15, 160n22, 172, 174, 175, 197, 198, 200, 209, 213, 214, 220
  mask-like, 64, 123, 141, 146, 152, 159n15
faciality, 64, 160n22, 197
Fanon, Frantz, 106, 161, 163, 206, 208, 210, 215, 216n9, 221
Fargier, Jean-Paul, 45

fascism, 49, 74, 77, 89, 106, 109, 111, 113, 115, 139, 142–4, 145, 146, 155, 220
  anti-, 118, 119, 202
Fathy, Safaa, 184
Feldman, Hannah, 83, 170
female body, 23, 39, 60, 82, 113, 149, 150
femme fatale, 88, 113, 137, 138–9, 142, 144, 146, 155, 159n20, 220
Ferrière, Alexis Artaud de la, 207, 210–11
Ferro, Marc, 113
Feuillade, Louis, *Les Vampires/The Vampires* (1915–1916), 136
Feyder, Jacques, *Le Grand jeu* (1934), 13
fiction, 25, 38, 46, 47, 54, 187n5, 190, 198, 201; *see also* non-fiction
Figaro, Le, 79
Film français, 20
film noir, 58, 62–6, 87, 110, 115–16, 137, 144, 151, 217, 220
Flament, Marc, 74
flânerie, 165, 171
flâneur, le, 170, 181
flâneuse, la, 138, 170, 187n7
flashback, 28n21, 108–12, 114–15, 119, 123, 125, 127, 128, 148, 152, 157n7, 166, 168, 178, 184
FLN *see* Algerian National Liberation Front
Flood, Maria, 23, 24, 73, 181, 197, 200
forgetting/amnesia, 25, 105, 107, 109, 117–20, 126–30, 180, 219
Foucault, Michel, 24, 182
France Observateur, 112
France-Soir, 10, 215n2
Franju, Georges, *Les Yeux sans visage/Eyes Without a Face* (1960), 138, 155
Frank, Bernard, 76, 77
French Communist Party (*Parti Communiste Français*, PCF), 9, 190, 191, 192, 204, 215n1, 216n11
French New Wave *see* New Wave
Freund, Karl, *The Mummy* (1932), 164

255

Frey, Hugo, 96, 131n8
Front de libération nationale (FLN) *see* Algerian National Liberation Front
Fugler, René, 94

Gabin, Jean, 59
Gaffney, John, 59, 71
gangrene (figurative), 5–6, 49, 53, 113, 114
Gangrène, La/The Gangrene (Anon 1959), 6
Gardner, Robert *see* Marshall, John and
Garnett, Tay, *Bataan* (1943), 68
Gauteur, Claude, 59
gaze/looking/the look, 25, 42, 43, 56, 80, 86, 95, 97, 124, 141, 149, 155, 157n5, 159n16, 163–84, 172, 173, 187n9, 187n11, 188n19, 189nn20–1, 220
  the disciplinary gaze of empire, 164, 166, 182
  imperial visuality, 165, 166, 168, 169, 169, 182
  panoramic gazing, 165, 181–4, 185
  return of the gaze, 187n9
  the tourist gaze, 182, 189n21
  the white gaze, 164, 166, 182, 183
gender, 58, 60, 72–6, 87–8, 90, 96, 97, 99, 134–9, 142, 144–6, 152, 158n14
genre, 24, 91, 192
Gentilomo, Giacomo, and Sergio Corbucci, *Maciste contre le fantôme/Maciste Against the Ghost* (1961), 176
Germanophobia, 121–2
Germany, 76, 120, 122, 136; *see also* National Socialism; Nazism
Gestapo, 106, 120–1, 131n5; *see also* SS
Getino, Octavio, 15
Gilles, Guy, 175, 176, 178, 188n14, 188n19
  and Marc Sator, *Au biseau des baisers/ Slanted Kisses* (1962), 16–17, 25, 156n1, 161, 175–86, 177, 179, 188–9nn15–21, 189n23, 220–1
  Soleil éteint/Setting Sun (1958), 186

Gilroy, Paul, 11, 27n9
Giroud, Françoise, 75
Godard, Jean-Luc, 15, 19
  À bout de souffle/Breathless (1960), 16, 36, 84, 86, 96, 196
  Histoire(s) du cinéma/Histories of Cinema (1989–99), 160n22
  Le Mépris/Contempt (1963), 54n2
  Le Petit soldat/The Little Soldier (1960/1963), 17, 19, 77, 78, 99, 107–8, 115, 118, 152, 159n15, 192
  Une Femme est une femme/A Woman is a Woman (1961), 55n6
  Vivre sa vie/To Live Her Life (1962), 49–50, 138
Goethe, Johann Wolfgang von, 98
Goldenberg, Daniel, *Le Retour/The Return* (1959), 16, 18–19, 25, 133, 136, 138–41, 140, 144, 146, 148, 155, 206, 219–20
Gray, Ros, 16
Greene, Naomi, 9, 13, 22, 112, 163
Guattari, Félix, 24, 160n22
Guerin, Frances, 197
guilt, 2, 8, 9, 10, 11–12, 21, 23, 24, 25, 26n6, 27nn8–9, 40, 42, 44, 54, 61, 65, 71, 83, 84, 99, 105, 109, 112, 113, 115, 118–26, 128, 129, 162–3, 176, 184, 186, 192, 205, 218–20
  displacement, 25, 112, 126, 133, 136–9, 141, 144–6, 149, 151–2, 155, 156, 158n12, 159n20, 190, 220

habeas corpus, 194, 199
Hadj, Messali, 162
Hädrich, Rolf, *Der schlaf der gerechten/ The Sleep of the Righteous* (1962), 11
Haggith, Toby, 68
Halimi, Gisèle, 26n6
Hallas, Roger, 197, 210
Harvey, David, 23–4

hate, 116, 188n12
Hawks, Howard, *Gentlemen Prefer Blondes* (1953), 91
Hayward, Susan, 112, 136
height, 165, 183
Herman, Jean, 2
　Actua-tilt (1961), 17, 28n16, 49, 222
　La Quille/On-Leave (1963), 17, 28n18
　Le Chemin de la mauvaise route/The Wrong Path (1962), 17, 28n17
Heter, Storm, 10
Higgins, Lynn, 11–12, 125–6
Higonnet, Margaret, 135
Hill, Rodney, 158n11
Hillier, Jim, 21
Hitchcock, Alfred
　North by Northwest (1959), 159n20
　Rear Window (1954), 82
　Vertigo (1958), 82
Hollywood, 15, 39, 58–9, 63, 68, 69, 81, 87, 91, 164, 174, 220; see also Western, the
Holmes, Diana, 59, 71
home-as-haven, 24, 37–40, 53
homosexuality see queerness
homosociality, 74, 90, 91–2
Horne, Alistair, 134
horror, 37, 63, 65, 83, 138, 144, 154, 156, 178, 207, 218
House, Jim, 203, 204, 215n1
housing, 33–4, 52–3, 187n8, 201
　les grands ensembles, 52
　pavillons, 42
　see also domesticity; privatisation
Hudson, John
　The Asphalt Jungle (1950), 62
　The Battle of San Pietro (1945), 192
　The March of Time (1935–51), 193
Hughes, Alex, 72
Hussards/Hussars, 19, 25, 76–9, 85–90, 96–8, 100, 100n2, 108, 109, 118, 119, 132n10, 218, 219
Hutin, Stanislav, 154
hygiene, 35, 36, 37, 39, 42; see also disease (figurative)

imperial visuality, 165, 166, 168, 169, *169*, 182
implication, 2, 7–8, 10–11, 44, 54, 64, 67, 70, 71, 98, 109, 154, 169, 186, 201
impotence, 25, 41–2, 63, 75–6, 79, 82, 93–6, 98, 99, 215n1
Indochina War (Indochina), 5, 143
infidelity, 92, 149, 159n20
innocence, 2, 8, 9, 10, 11, 12, 23, 24, 25, 36, 37, 39, 40, 44, 54, 58, 60, 65, 66, 71, 83, 84, 85, 100, 109, 115, 122–3, 129, 130, 144, 149, 152, 162–3, 165, 166, 169, 176, 184, 186, 192, 203, 208, 217, 218–20
interactive mode see documentary
interior design, 34, 42, 49, 53, 175
intertextuality, 40, 83–4, 144, 166, 180, 182, 213
interviews, 20, 34, 45, 131n5, 186, 187n10, 193–201, *198*, 208, 211, 212, 215, 221
　masked, 197, 201, 221
　see also testimony
Italian neorealism, 170, 217

Jarman, Derek, *Blue* (1993), 210
Jaspers, Karl, 123
Jauneau, Élodie, 157n2
Jeancolas, Jean-Pierre, 16, 21–2
Jeanson Network, 9, 117, 157n3, 191, 206
Jews, 106, 107, 108, 126, 131n8, 195, 196, 200, 202
　anti-Semitism, 77, 92, 126, 131n8

Kagan, Elie, *117*, 196, 215n2, 216n4
Kaplan, Ann, 137
Kast, Pierre, 20
Kear, Jonathan, 200
Kelly, Gene, and Stanley Donen, *Singin' in the Rain* (1952), 91
Kubrick, Stanley, *Full Metal Jacket* (1987), 12

Kuby, Emma, 8, 75
Kuleshov, Lev, 151, 158n13
Kuleshov effect, 151
Kyrou, Ado, *Parfois le Dimanche/ Sometimes on Sunday* (1959), 148, 158n10

Lack, Roland-François, 51, 145
Lahti, Janne, 16, 181
landscape, 19, 23, 38, 62, 71n6, 77, 106, 110, 116, 123, 149, 159n17, 164, 166–9, *167*, *169*, 172, 174, 176, 178, 181–2, 184, 214, 220–1
Lang, Fritz, *Le Tombeau hindou/The Indian Tomb* (1959), 186
Langois, Jean-Charles, 183–4
Lanzmann, Claude, *Shoah* (1985), 200
Lartéguy, Jean, 68
late-colonial cinema, 13–17, 20, 21, 22, 23, 24, 25, 28n16, 34, 106, 133, 137–8, 139, 146, 148, 158n8, 161, 181, 206, 217–18, 221, 222
Latin Quarter, 47–8, 53
Laubier, Claire, 134
Laurent, Jacques, 76, 79, 85, 96
Law of the Seven Monuments, The, 33, 82–3
Lazreg, Marnia, 8, 70
Le Carvennec, Alain, 75
Le Masson, Yann, 2, 17, 21, 139, 191, 206, 211, 212–13
  Kashima Paradise (1972), 215
  and Olga Baïdar-Poliakoff and René Vautier, *I Am 8 Years Old/J'ai 8 ans* (1961), 16, 19, 25, 190/192, 205–15, *206*, *214*, 216nn9–11, 221–2
Le Meur, Jean, 128
Le Sueur, James D., 5
Leahy, Sarah, 59, 60, 136–7
Lean, David, *Lawrence of Arabia* (1962), 69
Léaud, Jean-Pierre, 97
Lebeau, Vicky, 46
Lecoin, Louis, 128
Leenhardt, Jacques, 164, 168, 184

Lefebvre, Henri, 34, 35, 42, 47
Lefèvre, Raymond, 157n6
  Les Désaccords d'Evian/The Evian Disagreements (1966), 223, 223n3
Left, the, 9, 10, 13, 14, 21, 24, 25, 49, 78, 131n9, 190–2, 195, 196, 199, 202–7, *204*, 219, 221, 222; *see also* French Communist Party
Left Bank, 15, 21, 22–3, 35, 107, 217
leftists, 7, 8, 19, 20, 27n13, 61, 65, 76, 109, 117, 118, 131n9, 175, 190–2, 195, 196, 199, 201–6, *205*, 210–15, 221
Legion, the, 7, 59, 62, 73
Leninism, 206, 215
Lépingle, Gaël, 188n14, 188n19
letters, 5, 60, 79, 109, 118, 125, 135, 152–9, 191
Lhomme, Pierre *see* Marker, Chris and
Libération, 131n5
light, 42, 62, 165, 170, 176, 178, 180, 184–6; *see also* sun, the
Lindeperg, Sylvie, 131n8
Livak, Leonid, 98
Lolita syndrome, 39
look, the *see* gaze
loss, 12, 13, 52, 53, 80, 93, 98, 152, 170, 208
lost soldier, the, 78, 80–4, 91, 220
Louis, Marie, 220
love, 9, 25, 89, 99, 135–6, 139, 152, 165, 175–6, 178, 180–1, 185, 186, 188n12, 220
Lownstein, Adam, 137–8
Luntz, Édouard, *Les Enfants des courants d'air/Draft Children* (1959), 34
lust, 37, 67, 151, 152, 176, 179

McDonnell, Hugh, 8
McDougall, James, 3–4
Macheret, Mathieu, 185
MacMaster, Neil, 203, 204, 215n1
McNeill, Isabelle, 160n22
Madrague, La, 176, 188n15, 189nn20–1

Malle, Louis, 15–16, 77, 93, 99
  Ascenseur pour l'échafaud/Elevator to the Gallows (1958), 77, 78, 86, 96, 138
  Au revoir les enfants/Goodbye, Children (1987), 11–12
  Le Feu follet/The Fire Within (1963), 15, 25, 72, 76, 77, 78–9, 81, 82, 85, 92, 92–100, 218–19
Malraux, André, 18, 33, 71n3, 82
Manceron, Gilles, 203
Manifesto of the 121 (*Manifeste des 121*), 109, 128, 191
Maoz, Samuel, *Lebanon* (2009), 12
Marchand, Bernard, 33–4
marginal cinema *see* parallel cinema
Margulies, Ivone, 20
Marie, Michel, 36, 41, 143
Marker, Chris, 15, 107
  La Jetée/The Jetty (1962), 15, 35, 115
  Lettre de Sibérie/Letter from Siberia (1957), 153
  Level Five (1996), 160n22
  and Pierre Lhomme, *Le Joli Mai/The Lovely Month of May* (1963), 34, 206
Marshall, John, and Robert Gardner, *The Hunters* (1957), 193
Martin, Marcel, 119, 222
Martini, Lucienne, 180
Marty, Alain, 129–30
Marxism, 21, 22, 206, 212–13, 215
masculinity, 23, 25, 52, 58, 59, 60, 64, 72, 77–8, 88, 91, 133, 136, 138, 193, 218–19
  in crisis, 76, 93
  hypermasculinity, 74, 90, 218
masked interviews, 197, 201, 221
masks, 138, 149, 174
  mask-like faces, 64, 123, 141, 146, 152, 159n15
masochism, 81, 89, 98, 99, 191
Massu, Jacques, 7, 68, 75
Mastroianni, Marcello, 97
Mattéi, Georges-Mathieu, 7

Maudet, Christian (Christian-Jaque), *Babette s'en va-t-en guerre/Babette Goes to War* (1959), 112
Mauriac, Claude, 94
Melford, Georges, *The Sheik* (1921), 164
Melville, Jean-Pierre
  Le Samouraï/The Samurai (1967), 64
  Le silence de la mer/The Silence of the Sea (1949), 131n7
  Léon Morin, prêtre/Léon Morin, Priest (1961), 121
Memmi, Albert, 106, 175
memory, 22, 25, 26n2, 39, 44, 50, 55n8, 78, 105–15, 117, 120–7, 155, 188n19, 211
  multidirectional, 106–9, 114, 125, 219
  palimpsestic, 107–9
  studies, 22, 25, 105, 108, 188n19
  see also forgetting; remembering
men, 7, 33, 44, 47, 67, 73–4, 81–2, 88, 90, 126–7, 128, 136, 175, 197; *see also* castration; *copains* (male friends); emasculation; gender; impotence; masculinity; masochism; misogyny; soldiers
mere voice, the, 200, 212
metric montage, 213
Metz, Christian, 54n3
Meurice, Jean-Michel, 187n5
Michaud, Gene, 12
Ministries of Defence and Information, 17
Ministry for Cultural Affairs, 18, 33
Mirzoeff, Nicholas, 165, 169, 171, 182, 207
misogyny, 38, 60, 78, 89, 90, 98, 99, 116, 149, 159n20
modernisation, 11, 14, 28n16, 33, 37, 78, 87, 100n3; *see also* consumerism; privatisation
modernism, 2, 15, 45, 52, 91, 146, 147, 150, 153
modernist art cinema, 158n12, 210, 220
Mograbi, Avi, *Z32* (2008), 137
Mollet, Guy, 4, 9, 191, 215n1
Monde, Le, 19, 75, 79

Monjo, Armand, 80
Monroe, Marilyn, 58
Morag, Raya, 12, 43, 137
morbid geometrism, 164, 168, 184
Morin, Edgar, 58, 59, 62, 63, 64, 191, 218
  and Jean Rouch, *Chronique d'un été/Chronicle of a Summer* (1961), 20, 106, 193
Muller, Jean, 154
multidirectional memory, 106–9, 114, 125, 219
Murphet, Julian, 115–16
music/score/soundtrack, 3, 37, 84, 91, 110, 147, 153, 154, 155, 180, 188n15, 195, 196, 199, 200, 201, 202, 206, 208, 210, 211, 212
mystery, 144–6
myth, 22, 42, 52, 168, 175, 192
mythologisation, 12, 112, 190–2

Narboni, Jean, 64, 165
National Centre for Cinema and the Moving Image (*Le Centre national du cinéma et de l'image animée*, CNC), 17
National Liberation Army (*Armée de libération nationale*, ALN), 4
National Socialism, 106, 121
Nazism, 7, 59, 92, 98, 106, 108, 114, 115, 126, 131nn7–8, 134, 178; see also Gestapo; SS
Neale, Steve, 64
neo-colonialism, 15, 164, 181, 202
Neupert, Richard, 38
New Left Review, 22
New Wave (*Nouvelle Vague*), 14–16, 21, 23, 24, 29n26, 36, 37, 50, 77–8, 87, 116, 120, 125, 138, 170, 176, 188n14, 193, 217
Nichols, Bill, 194, 201, 207
Nimier, Roger, 77, 78, 79, 85, 86
  Histoire d'un amour/Love Story, 86
  Le Hussard bleu/The Blue Hussar, 76, 96

non-fiction, 116, 137, 171, 175, 187n5, 187n9, 198
Nora, Pierre, 162, 181
nostalgeria (*nostalgérie*), 188n19
nostalgia, 9, 13, 91, 97, 126, 127, 156, 188n19
Nourissier, François, 67, 71n4

OAS *see* Secret Armed Organisation
observational mode *see* documentary
October 17, 1961 (massacre), 49, 55n10, 114, 116, *117*, 195–6, 199, 201, 202–3, 209, 213, 221
O'Leary, Alan, 14
Ophüls, Marcel, *Le Chagrin et la pitié/The Sorrow and the Pity* (1969), 200
Organisation armée secrète see Secret Armed Organisation
O'Riley, Michael, 115, 116
Orpen, Valerie, 40
Orr, John, 12, 86
Osteen, Mark, 115
Other, the, 115–17, 121, 193, 202, 221
Otherness, 40, 122

pacifism, 1, 2, 3, 5, 13, 24, 37, 63, 74, 127–30, 131n9, 190, 195, 205, 207, 217
  redemptive, 3, 7–13, 24, 25, 108, 129–30, 162, 217–18, 222
Pagat, Maurice, 191
pain, 9, 11, 63, 64–5, 114–15, 192, 200, 205, 219, 221
palimpsestic memory, 107–9
Palmer, R. Barton, 14
Panijel, Jacques, 191, 193, 196, 201–2
  and Jean-Paul Sassy, *La Peau et les Os/Skin and Bones* (1961), 196
  Octobre à Paris/October in Paris (1962), 16, 19, 25, 34, 106, 131n6, 190, 192, 195–205, *198*, 204, 205, 215–16nn2–6, 221, 222
panorama, 168, 183–4

panoramic, 87, 165, 168, 169
  gazing, 165, 181–4, 185
  perception, 182–3
Papon, Maurice, 114, 116, 126, 195
parallel cinema, 16, 17, 18, 20, 21, 27nn13–14, 146, 157n6, 190, 196, 207, 221
paratroopers (paras), 4, 5, 6, 7, 25, 26n5, 45, 46, 49, 61, 66, 67–70, 71n7, 73–5, 77, 78, 79–80, 82, 83, 84, 85–90, 91, 100n5, 109, 113, 133, 138, 139, 164, 171, 192, 206, 218
Paris, 6, 15, 33–4, 37, 40, 45, 46–54, *48*, *51*, 55nn8–9, 79–80, 82, 86–9, 90, 93, 100n4, 106, 116, 120, 123, 131n6, 143, 145, 146, 147, 149, 159n21, 178
  Champs Élysées, Les, 51, 87, 100n4
  Latin Quarter, 47–8, 53
Paris Match, 56, 57, 66, 71n1, 215n2
Paris-presse, 67
Partisans (journal), 211–12
PCF *see* French Communist Party
peace, 2, 9, 60, 105, 162, 173, 191, 195, 199
  "Peace in Algeria" slogan, 131n9, 205, 214–15, 216n11
Pélégri, Jean, 165–6, 174
  and James Blue, *Les Oliviers de la justice/The Olive Trees of Justice* (1962), 16–17, 25, 161, 165–75, *167*, *169*, *172*, *173*, 186n1, 187nn3–5, 187nn8–9, 188nn12–13, 220
perpetration, 12, 23, 27n10, 35, 43, 71, 115, 154–5, 188n17, 192, 195, 205, 208, 219
Perrault, Gilles, 8
perspective, 13, 14, 23, 26n3, 26n6, 45, 78, 85, 87, 141, 166, 172, 183, 220
Philippe, Claude-Jean, 145
Philippeville Massacre, 162
photographs/photography, 38, 50–1, *51*, 52, 74, 80, 85, 86, 116, 149–50, 159n15, 171, 196, 199, 215n2

Pialat, Maurice, *L'amour existe/Love Exists* (1961), 34
Pirelli, Giovanni, 207
poetic documentary, 170–1
Pohn-Weidinger, Axel, 135, 157n4
Poiré, Alain, 20–1
police, 4, 5, 45, 49, 79–80, 82, 84, 91, 101n8, 110, 114, 143, 174, 195–6, 199–203, 216n4; *see also* Charonne (massacre); October 17, 1961 (massacre)
politique des auteurs, la, 15
Pontecorvo, Gillo, *La Bataille d'Alger/The Battle of Algiers* (1966), 17, 134, 164–5, 171–2, 187n8, 215
Poppi, Fabio, 66
porteurs de valises, 9
Positif, 21, 22, 45, 157n6, 208, 211
post-colonial cinema, 13, 22, 23, 220
post-traumatic stress, 93, 100n7
Poujadism, 78
Powell, Michael, and Emeric Pressburger, *Black Narcissus* (1947), 14
Pozner, Vladimir, 8
Prassinos, Gisèle, 139
pre-censorship, 18, 20
Pressburger, Emeric *see* Powell, Michael and
privatisation, 24, 34–6, 39, 40, 41, 42, 46, 47, 50, 52–3, 60, 218
promiscuity, 139, 144, 220
prostitution, 73, 74, 88, 89, 138
protesters, 114, 165, 186n2, 195, 196, 203, 215n2
Pudovkin, Vsevolod, *Mat/Mother* (1926), 213
Putsch, 71n2, 79, 143, 218

queerness, 25, 74, 90–2, 95–6, 98, 101n8, 188n14
Quemeneur, Tramor, 129
Quinn, Anthony, 66, 67, 69–70, 71

Rabinowitz, Paula, 201
radio, 10, 42, 83, 84, 100n3, 209–10

Ranchal, Marcel, 119–20
Rancière, Jacques, 24
rape, 6, 8, 10, 65, 73, 75, 90, 192
Ray, Nicholas, *They Live by Night* (1948), 87
reality, 43, 45, 52, 58, 65, 100nn3–4, 163, 194–6
reconciliation, 9, 13, 25, 162, 165, 173–5, 180, 220
redemption, 2, 9, 10, 11, 13, 24, 41–4, 52, 75, 109, 130, 174, 190–2, 195, 206
redemptive pacifism, 3, 7–13, 24, 25, 108, 129–30, 162, 217–18, 222
re-enactment, 196
Rees-Roberts, Nick, 63
reflexive mode *see* documentary
refugees, 162, 206, 209, 216n10
Rejali, Darius, 7
religion, 29n24, 42, 123, 124; *see also* Christianity; Catholicism/Catholic Church
remembering/anamnesis, 105, 110–13, 124, 219
Renoir, Jean, 169
  La Grande Illusion/The Grand Illusion (1937), 166
  La Règle du jeu/The Rules of the Game (1939), 166
repression, 9, 13, 29n30, 49, 50, 71, 91, 109–10, 113, 114, 141, 193, 199
  return of the repressed, 29n30, 110
Resistance, the, 25, 109, 111, 112, 117–18, 119, 120, 122, 123–4, 126, 127, 219
Resnais, Alain, 15, 107, 124, 130n2
  Hiroshima mon amour/Hiroshima, My Love (1959), 121, 153
  L'Année dernière à Marienbad/Last Year in Marienbad (1961), 176
  Muriel ou le temps d'un retour/Muriel or the Time of a Return (1963), 1–2, 11, 15, 17, 26n1, 35, 38, 106
  Nuit et brouillard/Night and Fog (1956), 108

responsibility, 2, 8, 10, 36, 99, 118, 123, 220
return of the gaze, 187n9
return of the repressed, 29n30, 110
Richou, François, 44
Ricoeur, Paul, 27n8, 122, 129
Rigaut, Jacques, 98–9
Right, the, 14, 21, 49, 96, 115, 118, 219
Right Bank, 15, 19, 21, 22–3, 217
right-wing anarchism, 70, 77, 79, 106, 108, 109, 118; *see also* Secret Armed Organisation
Rivette, Jacques, 15
  La Religieuse/The Nun (1966), 29n24
  Paris nous appartient/Paris Belongs to Us (1961), 15, 25, 113, 133, 137, 139, 141–6, *142*, 155, 220
Rivière, Jean-Max, 188n15, 188n18
Robbe-Grillet, Alain, 163–4, 169, 176, 186
Robson, Mark
  The Bridges at Toko-Ri (1954), 66
  Home of the Brave (1949), 68
  Les Centurions/Lost Command (1966), 16, 24–5, 58, 61, 66–71, *67*, 100n5, 156n1, 218
Roche, Anne, 8–9
Rochelle, Drieu de la, 77, 92, 95, 97, 98, 101n9
Rogers, Will, 58
Rohmer, Eric, 15
Romanticism, 78, 98, 99, 119
Ronet, Maurice, 66, 69, 78, 92, 109, 118
Ross, Kristin, 22, 35–6, 42, 47, 60, 86, 182–3, 202–3
Rossellini, Roberto, *Germania anno zero/Germany, Year Zero* (1948), 178
Rothberg, Michael, 11, 106, 107, 108, 114
Roüan, Brigitte, *Outremer/Overseas* (1990), 13, 163, 220
Rouch, Jean *see* Morin, Edgar and
Rousso, Henri, 162

Rozier, Jacques, *Adieu Philippine/ Goodbye Philippine* (1963), 15, 18, 24, 36–44, *40*, *41*, *43*, 50, 51, 54nn3–4, 84, 148, 218
ruins, Roman, 185, 189n23
Ruscio, Alain, 70

Saddington, John, 99
Sadoul, Georges, 129
Sagan, Françoise/Saganism, 100n2
Saint-Saëns, Isabelle, 199
Sanyal, Debarati, 26n2, 108, 115, 131n4
Sarkar, Bhaskar, 194
Sartelle, J., 12
Sartre, Jean-Paul, 9–10, 27n8, 75, 77, 106, 130n2, 154, 163, 182, 183, 191
Saslavsky, Luis, *Ce corps tant désiré/Way of the Wicked* (1959), 150
Sassy, Jean-Paul *see* Panijel, Jacques and
Sator, Marc, 165, 175, 186, 187n10, 188n13
  L'Été algérien/The Algerian Summer (1964), 188n13
  see also Gilles, Guy and
Sautet, Claude, *Classe tous risques/ Consider All Risks* (1960), 91
scapegoats, 137, 139
Scharold, Irmgard, 24, 29n28
Schatz, Thomas, 60
Schoendoerffer, Pierre, *Le Crabe-tambour/ The Drummer Crab* (1977), 13
score *see* music
Screen, 22
Second Cinema, 15
Second Intifada, the, 12
Secret Armed Organisation (*Organisation armée secrète*, OAS), 8, 19, 26n7, 49, 77, 79, 86, 93, 95, 96, 97, 106, 109, 113, 114, 116, 118, 119, 138, 162, 165, 183, 186n1, 218
Segura, André, 154
self-censorship, 44, 56

Sellier, Geneviève, 19, 22–3, 24, 38, 55n6, 78, *96*, 99, 119, 136, 137
settler cinema, 16, 168, 181, 184
settlers (*pieds-noirs*), 3, 4, 6, 8–9, 10, 13, 16–17, 24, 25, 26n7, 33, 134, 156n1, 161–86, 188n17, 189n23, 220; *see also Toussaint Rouge* (Red All-Saints Day)
17 October *see* October 17
sex, 29n24, 40, 50, 64, 67, 73, 74–6, 80, 82, 89, 90, 93–7, 144, 159n17, 220; *see also* prostitution
sexual guilt, 136, 137, 138–9, 143, 144, 146, 151–2, 158n12
sexual intercourse, 76, 82, 87, 93–4
Shepard, Todd, 72, 75–6
Shohat, Ella, 164, 169, 182
Sica, Vittorio De, *Ladri di biciclette/ Bicycle Thieves* (1948), 170
sickness (figurative), 5–6, 7, 10; *see also* disease (figurative)
Sigg, Bernard, 44
silence, 20, 43–4, 63, 66, 113, 118, 124, 139, 174, 190, 195, 199, 200–1, 202, 205
  turn against, 5, 6, 7, 8, 58, 67, 69, 75, 191, 208
Silverman, Max, 106–7, 108
Siri, Florent-Emilio, *L'Ennemi intime/ The Intimate Enemy* (2007), 23
Solanas, Fernando, 15
soldiers, 1, 2, 4, 5, 6, 7–9, 10, 12, 13, 16, 24, 26n1, 28n16, 28n18, 28n21, 36, 38, 39, 43–4, 47, 49, 68–9, 71nn5–6, 73–6, 93, 113–14, 121, 125, 126, 129, 170, 186, 187n5, 187n7, 188n18, 207, 208, 218–19, 221
  absence of, 135, 139, 147–9, 152, 154, 158n8, 158n11
  female friends/lovers of, 25, 135–41, *140*, 146–9, 154–6, *156*, 157n5, 159n18, 220
  the lost soldier, 78–84, 91, 220
  see also conscientious objection; conscription; paratroopers (paras)

263

soundtrack *see* music
Souther, Nathan, 94
Soviet Montage cinema, 150, 151, 203, 213–14, 217, 220, 222
special powers, 8, 191, 205
Special Powers Act (1956), 5, 9, 202, 222
spectacle, 51, 61, 64, 66, 68, 71, 87, 176, 184, 218, 220
speech, 7, 20, 36, 80, 81, 139, 147, 153, 155, 159n20, 174, 190, 193, 194, 197, 200, 201, 205, 208, 209, 212, 222
   un-visualised, 1, 198, 209
   visualised, 198, 209
   see also voice
SS (Schutzstaffel), 106, 111, *111*, 114, 120, 131n5; *see also* Gestapo
Stalin, Josef, 191
Stam, Robert, 164
stardom, 16, 24–5, 39, 56–71, 90, 94, 149–51, 218
state, the, 1, 18, 19, 20, 24, 25, 26n4, 49, 52, 54, 65, 84, 85, 107, 108–9, 112, 114, 173, 195, 197, 199–202, 207, 221, 222; *see also* censorship; police
Steimatsky, Noa, 64, 174
Steinlein, Almut, 145, 146
Stewart, Alexandra, 85
Stora, Benjamin, 6, 10, 19, 22, 27n10, 107, 115, 129, 131n6, 134, 162
suffering, 6, 69, 88, 90, 108, 115, 117, 192, 195, 203, 207, 219
suicide/self-death, 80, 81, 84, 89, 92, 93, 98–100, 142, 144, 145, 219
sun, the, 157n7, 176, 184–6, 189n22
Surrealism, 98, 99, 139, 158n10
survivor-witnesses, 195, 197–202, *198*

tabula rasa, 181
talking cure, 193–4
talking heads, 87, 194, 199
Témoignages et Documents (journal), 191
Temple, Shirley, 58, 59

temporality, 14, 15, 28n21, 47, 55n8, 105–6, 107, 123, 147, 152, 157n7, 158n12, 163
Temps modernes, Les, 8, 10, 76, 191
Terme, Louis, *Fille de la route/The Girl of the Road* (1962), 223, 223n4
terra nullius, 181
Terrenoire, Louis, 17–18
Terzieff, Laurent, 128, 132n10
testimony, 5–6, 8, 43, 44, 45, 125, 146, 154, 156, 193, 194, 197, 198–201, 203, 206, 207–12, 213, 214, 215, 216n10, 221, 222
   acousmatic testimony, 195, 207–10, 222
   see also interviews; witness; witnessing
textual voice, the, 194, 195, 203, 212, 214, 215
Thiele, Rolf, *Die Halbzarte/Eva* (1959), 150
Thiher, Allen, 101n9
Thirard, Paul-Louis, 119–20
Third Cinema, 16
Thompson, Kristin, 153
Thompson, Lee, *The Guns of Navarone* (1961), 69
Tipasa/Tipaza, 176, *179*, 182–3, 184, 185, 189nn20–1
Todorov, Tzvetan, 115
Tomlinson, Emily, 115, 117
Torok, Jean Paul, 47
torture, 1, 2, 6–8, 10, 26n5, 29n27, 60, 65, 70–1, 74–6, 90, 93, 106, 111, 112, 113–17, 128, 131n5, 138, 143, 154–5, 191, 192, 196, 219
tourist gaze, the, 182, 189n21
Toussaint Rouge (Red All-Saints Day), 4, 56
trauma, 43, 45, 56, 115, 128, 135, 147, 162, 178, 180, 207, 211, 212, 213
   post-traumatic stress, 93, 100n7
trial, 8, 26n6, 112, 119, 130, 191, 194
Truffaut, François, 15, 20, 119
   Jules et Jim/Jules and Jim (1962), 95

Le Dernier métro/The Last Metro (1981), 11–12, 125
Les Mistons/The Mischief Makers (1957), 178
truth, 29n26, 70, 73, 107, 109, 112, 113, 114, 117, 118, 128, 142, 152, 193, 194, 196, 201
Turim, Maureen, 110

un-visualised speech, 1, 198, 209
Urios-Aparisi, Eduardo, 66
Urry, John, 182, 189n21

Vadim, Roger
   Et Dieu . . . créa la femme/And God Created Woman (1956), 100n2, 138
   Le Repôs du guerrier/Love on a Pillow (1962), 137
Valère, Jean, *Les Grandes personnes/ Time Out for Love* (1961), 86
Vanoye, Francis, 41
Varda, Agnès, 15
   Cléo de 5 à 7/Cléo from 5 to 7 (1962), 6, 15, 17, 35, 40, 138, 157n5, 170
Vaudoux, Philippe, *La Bouche amère/ Bitter Aftertaste* (1960), 69, 71n6
Vautier, René, 16, 19, 29n25, 201, 206, 208
   Afrique 50/Africa 50 (1950), 27n14
   Algéri en flammes/Algeria is Burning (1958), 27n14, 29n25, 134
   see also Le Masson, Yann
Vergès, Françoise, 11
Vérité-Liberté (journal), 191, 196
Verneuil, Henri, *Un singe en hiver/A Monkey in Winter* (1962), 91
verticality, 124, 129
Vertov, Dziga, *Chelovek s kino-apparatom/ Man with a Movie Camera* (1929), 171
victimhood, 12, 23, 43, 108, 113–17, 143, 190, 202, 212, 221
victimisation, 9, 13, 25, 73, 78–9, 100, 114, 115, 117, 119, 134, 192, 207, 208, 218, 219

Vidal, Baptiste, 208
Vidal-Naquet, Pierre, 70, 212
Vidor, King, *Bird of Paradise* (1932), 164
Vietnam War, 12, 27n10
Villiers, François, *La Verte moisson/ Green Harvest* (1959), 112
Vincendeau, Ginette, 59, 64, 90
violence, 4, 5, 6, 7, 9, 33, 37, 45–7, 49–50, 61–71, 71n1, 71n3, 85, 89–90, 93, 95, 105, 108, 111, 113, 114–15, 125, 134, 136, 138, 144, 147, 156, 162, 178, 186, 189n24, 190, 195–6, 199–203, 206, 207, 211, 218, 219, 220
Virilio, Paul, 171
virility, 25, 59, 67, 68, 71, 72–6, 84, 88–90, 93, 94, 95, 97, 98, 99, 100n5, 218
Virtue, Nancy, 29n26
visibility, 68, 107, 108, 141, 151, 166, 174, 197, 203
vision, 42, 60, 87, 105, 108, 173–5, 181–5, 188n17, 188n19, 203
visualised speech, 198, 209
voice
   aphonic, 200
   choral, 215
   the mere, 200, 212
   the textual voice, 194, 195, 203, 212, 214, 215
   the voice of the text, 194
   see also speech
Voice-of-God narration, 16, 168, 192–4, 202, 213

Wagner, Jean, *Ce monde banal/This Dull World* (1960), 70, 71n7
Waldron, Darren, 63
Walker, Janet, 194
Wallenbrock, Nicole Beth, 23
Walsh, Raoul, *The Man I Love* (1947), 115
Watt, Harry, and Basil Wright, *Night Mail* (1936), 192
Wayne, John, 58, 69–70

Weaver-Hightower, Rebecca, 16, 181
Wehrmacht, the, 106, 120, 123
Weiner, Susan, 40, 100nn2–3, 128, 132n10, 136, 137
Weissgerber, Jacques, 94
Welles, Orson
  Citizen Kane (1941), 110
  The Lady from Shanghai (1947), 87
Western, the, 24, 58, 66, 69, 168, 169–70
Wetta, Frank, 13
Wheeler, René, *Vers l'extase/Towards Ecstasy* (1959), 223, 223n5
white gaze, the, 164, 166, 182, 183
whiteness, 12, 39–40, 44, 46, 60, 115–16, 163, 185
Wilder, Billy, *Double Indemnity* (1944), 110, 144
Wiles, Mary, 142–4
Williams, James S., 72
Wilson, Emma, 2
witnesses, 178, 194, 199–201, 205, 209, 210
  child, 175, 196, 197, 208–9, 210–11
  survivor-, 195, 197–202, *198*
witnessing, 127, 175, 193, 199, 200, 210, 211, 220, 221; *see also* testimony

women, 1, 25, 28n21, 33, 37–9, 44, 50–1, 55n6, 73, 87–90, 94, 97, 99, 134–56, 157nn2–3, 170, 173, 196, 197; *see also copines* (female friends); cover-girls; female body; femme fatale; gender; soldiers: female friends/lovers of
World War Two, 11, 12, 76, 106, 108, 114, 119, 122, 123, 126–7, 131n9, 134, 136, 137
  combat films, 16, 66, 68, 69, 217
  see also National Socialism; Nazism; Resistance, the
Wright, Basil *see under* Watt, Harry
Wyschogrod, Edith, 200

Xavier, Ismail, 128–9

Young Turks, 15, 19, 21, 23, 29n26, 109
youth/adolescence, 36, 37, 39, 41, 64, 81, 96, 168, 176–80, *177*, 186, 188n17, 208; *see also* childhood

Zarobell, John, 183
Zimmerman, Daniel, 44, 75

EU representative:
Easy Access System Europe
Mustamäe tee 50, 10621 Tallinn, Estonia
Gpsr.requests@easproject.com

www.ingramcontent.com/pod-product-compliance
Lightning Source LLC
Chambersburg PA
CBHW050843230426
43667CB00012B/2119